The Great War

The Great War

William R. Griffiths

Thomas E. Griess
Series Editor

DEPARTMENT OF HISTORY
UNITED STATES MILITARY ACADEMY
WEST POINT, NEW YORK

Series Editor: Thomas E. Griess
Cover Designer: Phaedra Mastrocola
In-House Editor: Joanne Abrams

Square One Publishers
Garden City Park, NY 11040
(516) 535-2010
www.squareonepublishers.com

Illustration Credits
The publisher would like to thank Dr. George Lankevich
for the use of his historical library collection, which was
the source of much illustrative material.

All original artwork was produced by Edward J. Krasnoborski.

Library of Congress Cataloging-in-Publication Data

Griffiths, William R.
 The Great War / William R. Griffiths.
  p. cm.—(The West Point military history series)
 Originally published: Wayne, N.J. : Avery Pub. Group, 1986.
 Includes bibliographical references and index.
 ISBN 0-7570-0158-0
1. World War, 1914–1918—Campaigns. I. Title. II. Series.

 D521. G76 2003
 940.4–dc21

                                   2003045484

ISBN 0-7570-0158-0

10 9 8 7 6 5 4 3 2 1

Printed in the United States of America

Contents

To those who confronted the problems of the Great War
with courage and diligence. Their sacrifices transformed
the world. May their example inspire soldiers to study
their profession and prepare for Armageddon.

Illustrations

Acknowledgements

This work was originally designed to support the instruction of cadets enrolled in the course entitled History of the Military Art at the United States Military Academy. The text is a synthesis of the vast amount of material now available on the First World War. Attention has been focused upon some of the critical issues raised by the war, especially those that made this period a seminal one in the evolution of warfare.

Brigadier General Thomas E. Griess, editor of the series, continued to be the source of inspiration and support for the entire project, as he was throughout the development of the first edition. My original collaborators, C. Reid Franks and the late James B. Agnew, provided expert research and helpful insights for the chapters on peripheral operations and the Eastern Front, respectively.

My colleagues in the Department of History at the Military Academy provided critical advice. In particular, John Hixson, Dr. Jay Luvaas, and Dr. Frank Vandiver shared their insight on content and continuity. Mr. Edward Krasnoborski, the Department of History's experienced cartographer, produced the superb maps that do so much to clarify the military operations. Mrs. Sally French produced the initial manuscript, while Mrs. Diana Wattenburger provided expert support in the revision of the current edition; my heartfelt thanks go to both of these fine ladies.

Despite this generous assistance, I am sure that lapses of continuity and balance remain; for this, I beg the reader's indulgence. If the importance of the Great War in the evolution of warfare, as well as the horror that modern war brought to the twentieth century, are conveyed in this work, my purpose will have been served.

William R. Griffiths
St. Petersburg, Florida

Foreword

Cadets at the United States Military Academy have studied military campaigns and institutions for almost a century in a course entitled History of the Military Art. Beginning in 1938, that study of history was supported by texts and maps that were prepared by departmental faculty under the direction of T. Dodson Stamps, who was then Head of the Department of Military Art and Engineering. The first integrated treatment of the First World War under this program was introduced in 1950 with the publication of *A Short Military History of World War I*, a text that was jointly edited by Stamps and Vincent J. Esposito. That work, with an accompanying atlas that depicted the military operations described in the text, served cadets until 1959, when Esposito adopted the commercially published *The West Point Atlas of American Wars*. Departmentally prepared and edited by Esposito, *The West Point Atlas of American Wars* included coverage of World War I.

In 1967, the course in the History of the Military Art was restructured around themes that broadened its coverage to accommodate new events and the need to teach more than purely operational military history. Shortly thereafter, work commenced on the first edition of the present text, which offered a different perspective on World War I than had previous departmental texts.

Although the participants could not anticipate it at the beginning, World War I was a cataclysmic experience for nations and individuals alike. Expected to be a short, almost surgically neat war, it did not so turn out. Nor was it the desperately hoped for "war to end wars." Taken in the context of the times, it truly was the Great War. This text surveys predominantly the military aspects of that war rather than the political or social aspects that became so important to the world of nations after 1918. As such, it examines how the art of war stagnated under the incorrectly interpreted impact of technology.

The revolution in war wrought by Napoleon and the Industrial Revolution came together with full force during World War I. Nationalism provided popular support and masses of men for the conflict that military doctrine organized, trained, and brought to the battlefield. Technology created marvelously lethal weapons that industry could supply in large quantities. Thus, the mass armies could kill one another's soldiers with awful efficiency. The result was a protracted, bloody war that changed the path of history. However, the war's technological promises, such as tanks and planes, also meant that the stalemate would not be repeated in 1939. Perhaps just as important as the stalemate in the West was the mobile war in the East which led to revolution in Russia and the development of an all-encompassing, siren-like ideology that has affected nations ever since.

The first edition of *The Great War*, which was printed at West Point in 1977, was the product of three faculty members of the Department of History. C. Reid Franks prepared a chapter on peripheral operations, and James B. Agnew wrote the chapters on the Battle of the Marne and the Eastern Front. William R. Griffiths authored the remaining chapters and the supporting end matter; he also developed the organizational framework for the text. All three officers designed supporting maps. A number of West Point graduates and the Department of History are indebted to them for their efforts, which were made under the pressure of time and with minimal resources.

When Square One Publishers decided to publish The West Point Military History Series, as general editor, I elected to ask the principal author, Colonel Griffiths, to revise the original text, rewriting parts of it and condensing the coverage of some campaigns. The present edition is the result of his revisionary endeavor. As editor, I have attempted to clarify certain passages for the general reader, amplify purely military terminology, and improve the evenness of the narrative. The editor is grateful for the advice and suggestions that were tendered by Rudy Shur and Joanne Abrams of Square One Publishers. Their assistance was timely and helpful. Ms. Abrams immeasurably improved the narrative through her painstaking editing, corrections of lapses in syntax, and penetrating questions related to clarity of expression.

Thomas E. Griess
Series Editor

Introduction

To many observers, August 1914 marked the end of the nineteenth century. With the outbreak of general war on the European Continent, life throughout the world would change—imperceptibly at first, perhaps, but irreversibly. War came because the European nations had been unwilling to deal with the many international crises that could have been easily resolved if approached singly. In fact, the direct cause of the conflict was one of the most trivial of these international issues. The assassination of the pretender to the Austro-Hungarian throne was not construed as being serious enough to alter the summer holidays of the leaders of Europe. The Dual Monarchy's precipitate reaction to the event, however, laid bare the numerous conflicts and deep-seated antagonisms that had plagued Europe since 1870. While the rigid structure of military and naval policies did not cause the war, it did hasten its arrival once the ministers had set the wheels in motion.

There can be no more tragic example of the failure of military theory to prepare soldiers and sailors for the next war than that in vogue prior to the Great War of 1914–1918. Most military leaders optimistically believed that an offensive tactical doctrine and an efficient mobilization plan would bring about a quick and decisive victory. In fact, the offensive spirit and rapid mobilization plunged Europe into four years of bloody attrition that ended in an unstable and inconclusive peace. The Great War was fought on such an unprecedented scale that both political and military leaders were incapable of directing its course. Both the war itself and the monstrous battle engagements of which it was composed assumed a life and will of their own. The war became a juggernaut that had to be fueled but could not be stopped.

Contrary to the popular view of how military theory and doctrine developed during the war, they evolved with renewed vigor and flexibility as the war progressed. The integration of new weapons into the arsenal was rapid and, for the most part, effective. Because entire societies were affected by the war, military institutions were closely examined by civilian authorities. The military and naval leadership was forced to accommodate to change wrought by conscription, the organization of the national economies, and the systematic support of the scientific community. Unfortunately, these same leaders tried to return to their former methods following the war, wishing to cleanse themselves of the new experiences rather than to learn from them.

The Great War, as it was known before people had need to keep such events in chronological order, brought with it the greatest tests that mankind had experienced to that date. Monarchy, imperialism, and societies structured on the basis of birth were, for the most part, found defective and either destroyed or dealt mortal blows. Politically, the war brought with it radical change. New ideologies based upon the dream of utopian democracy or Marx' Communist philosophy replaced the old verities. On the international level, unfamiliar boundaries and sovereignties appeared. Internally, all nations experienced the awakening of powerful groups that demanded recognition.

From both military and economic standpoints, the First World War ended an era of national self-sufficiency. The countries that emerged from the caldron of conflict were interconnected as much by military treaties as by the flow of goods and services. The League of Nations, which was a feeble expression of this interdependence, was the immediate offspring of the war.

The great upheaval that accompanied and followed the First World War has obscured the men who inhabited the world of the nineteenth century from the view of those of us who live in the last quarter of the twentieth. However, we can empathize with those who fought and suffered during the First World War. We can also trace much of our world's cynicism and instability to this war that ended a period of relative tranquility.

"This, the Greatest of All Wars, Is Not Just Another War—It Is the Last War!"* 1

. . . the generation of 1914–1918 was [not] unequal to or incapable of tragedy. . . . From every standpoint the generation that fought in the Great War was a generation made for suffering and heroism in a "war against war." That they were an unsuspicious generation with a passion for idealism and justice and freedom; that they were responsive to "cause" and "principle" and "duty"; that they were as proud and self-confident as they were romantic and naïve; that they were a generation that believed in creative reason, in progress, in civilization, and hence in man's destiny are qualities that the men of 1914 reveal without conscious effort. But if this generation was worthy of heroic attitudes and gestures that still looked back to early times, they were not ready for the changes that affected tragic experience in the modern world.

George A. Panichas, *Promise of Greatness*

The First World War—called in its own time the Great War—had an almost cataclysmic effect upon the history of mankind. It has been aptly compared to an impenetrable veil that sharply separated a former, more tranquil way of life from our own confused and frenetic existence.[1] Certainly the military and political institutions that emerged from this great conflict are much more understandable to modern man than they were to those nineteenth century human beings who helped to bring it about. Aside from its unprecedented scale and the toll that it levied on the world's resources, the Great War is significant because of the changes that occurred during its course. This is not to say that the war caused anything in and of itself. But wars—especially large destructive ones—must at least be

*HG Wells, *The War That Will End War*.

credited with accelerating changes already in progress and with initiating programs that inevitably and irreversibly change societies and the perception of mankind. Despite the sense of revulsion that caused many to condemn military leaders as butchers, these changes were particularly notable in the area of military science.

Ironically, Europe stumbled unexpectedly into war in the summer of 1914. The reasons for the expansion of the war, once it erupted, are understandable. Long recognized as the leaders of the world's affairs, the principal European nations had greatly increased their imperial domains during the latter half of nineteenth century. This fact alone dictated that the scope of the war would be global. (*See Atlas Map No. 1.*) However, the reasons for the outbreak of general war in August 1914 still remain vague and subjects of violent disagreement. Even after the presentation of innumerable studies and the publication of most of the original documents relating to the war's outbreak, this remains so. Perhaps, as A.J.P. Taylor has commented:

> Men are reluctant to believe that great events have small causes. Therefore once the Great War started, they were convinced that it must be the outcome of profound forces. It is hard to discover these when we examine the details. Nowhere was there a conscious determination to provoke a war.[2]

Conversely, there is no dearth of evidence that war was far from a remote possibility in 1914. Although the one hundred years following the downfall of Napoleon now seems to have been a relatively tranquil period, in fact, numerous disputes and wars punctuated the era.[3] These affairs, however, were either internal, such as the American Civil War, or sharply limited in their impact on the world, such as the Crimean War. The first fact that must be emphasized in the study of the First World War is that it effectively ended a long period of national military self-sufficiency. It was fought by two military coalitions of sovereign states that sprang naturally from the peacetime alliances that were characteristic of the period from 1871 to 1914.*

The Political and Diplomatic Landscape

In order to understand the long-range problems that confronted Europe in 1914, it is necessary to retrace the path of history from the Treaty of Frankfort, which ended the Franco-Prussian War of 1870–1871. (*See Atlas Map No. 2.*) With the unification of Germany under Prussia, the Second Reich became the most powerful and influential continental state; its potential for growth seemed great.[4] Concurrently, the humiliating terms imposed upon France (a five-billion-franc indemnity and the loss of the provinces of Alsace and Lorraine) brought not only the re-establishment of a French Republic but also proved the temporary impotence of France.[5] Under the strict control of the German Chancellor, Otto von Bismarck, this situation continued until he was asked to step down in 1890 by the new Kaiser, Wilhelm II. Before then, however, Bismarck wrought a revolution in diplomacy.[6]

The End of an Empire: German Chancellor Otto von Bismarck Escorts Napoleon III into Captivity

Bismarck's Entangling Alliances

In contrast to the manner in which he had brought about the unification of Imperial Germany, Bismarck's program for the development of her national power required peace. To achieve this condition, he carefully controlled Germany's territorial and colonial ambitions and made every effort to insure that France remained weak and isolated. Immediately after the war with France, he set about forming alliances with the Austro-Hungarian Empire, which Prussia had humbled in war in 1866, and with Russia. The "Iron Chancellor" realized that the five great powers (France, Germany, Great Britain, Austria-Hungary, and Russia) and one power that aspired to greatness (Italy) would determine the course of European relations. Therefore, peace and prosperity for his nation lay in maintaining collective superiority.[7] In 1873, the German statesman performed the diplomatic miracle of uniting the competing powers of Russia and Austria-Hungary with Germany in an alliance known as the League of the Three Emperors. While, for the

*Hereinafter, these military coalitions will be referred to by their commonly accepted titles. The coalition of Germany, Austria, and later Turkey and Bulgaria, was known as the Central Powers because of geographical position. The Entente Powers (Great Britain, France, and Russia), along with the 29 other nations that joined their cause, came to be known as the Allies.

time being, this move erased the threat of a two-front war against Germany, it only papered over Russia and Austria-Hungary's conflicting interests in the Balkans.[8]

The Balkan area, which would later prove to be the "Powderkeg of Europe," was particularly vulnerable during the years prior to the outbreak of the First World War. The Ottoman Empire, which had once controlled the lands from Persia to Hungary and from the Crimea to North Africa, was at the end of a serious decline in both power and prestige. It was beset by nationalist revolts within the borders of its European holdings and overt encroachment from other states. Behind many of these troubles lay czarist Russia, which—often without reasonable caution—continued to pursue her desire to control the Dardanelles passage to her Black Sea ports. Under a vague and unofficial program of Pan-Slavism, Russia also encouraged and patronized the nationalist feelings of the Slavic peoples in the Balkan provinces.[9]

In 1875, following a local rebellion in the Turkish provinces of Bosnia and Herzegovina, the issue of Pan-Slavism surfaced. Serbia and Montenegro actively supported their ethnic brothers in Bosnia. In 1877, Bulgaria, and finally Russia, joined in the hostilities. The inefficient Turkish forces quickly succumbed, and the war was concluded by the Treaty of San Stefano in March 1878.[10] Under the terms of this treaty, European Turkey was virtually elimi-nated. Bulgaria became a large, autonomous principality that was to be occupied by Russian troops for two years. Rumania, Serbia, and Montenegro were declared independ-ent, thus formalizing their status. Bosnia and Herzegovina were to become autonomous—a condition that would even-tually lead to their becoming a direct threat to Austria-Hun-gary's internal stability. Russia received substantial territorial compensation and a huge indemnity, as well as practical control over the entire area of southeast Europe. This victor's peace reflected the extent of military superior-ity, but its blatant terms were too much for the other great powers, all of whom had definite interests in the division of Turkey's crumbling empire.[11]

The two powers most offended by Russia's crude power play were Austria-Hungary and Great Britain. The Dual Monarchy had been in decline for many years, and her own multi-racial composition, which included large numbers of discontented Slavs, made the outcome of the Russo-Turk-ish War most disquieting. Although the British had more subtle reasons for dissatisfaction, the initial reaction of the imperialist-minded Prime Minister, Benjamin Disraeli, was to dispatch units of the Royal Navy to Constantinople in order to insure that Russia did not achieve its goal of con-trolling the Dardanelles. England made it very clear that she would go to war to preserve the delicate balance of world power.

This crisis brought Bismarck into action. Although his nation was not directly involved, his two allies were at each other's throats, and war appeared likely. In order to restore political calm, Bismarck convened the Berlin Congress in the summer of 1878. The agreements reached there by the assembled powers stripped Russia of some of her win-nings.[12] Although she retained most territorial gains, and Serbia and Montenegro were confirmed as independent states, the other powers decided to further dismantle the Ot-toman Empire to their own advantage. Great Britain an-nexed Cyprus, France was granted the right to seize Algeria and Tunisia, and Austria-Hungary received the right to "oc-cupy and administer" the provinces of Bosnia and Herze-govina—the cause of the war in the first place. Russia felt betrayed and humiliated by the return of some territory to Turkey, but her true irritation resulted from an apparent inability to assist her "little brothers" in the Balkans. Thus the war and the Congress had settled little and had left all parties, especially Russia and the Balkan states, irreconcil-ably opposed to the final settlement. Not surprisingly, the League of the Three Emperors lapsed in 1879 to be re-placed by a Dual Alliance between Austria and Germany. This treaty was a defensive one, obligating the two states to come to each other's aid if Russia should attack either.[13]

In spite of these diplomatic maneuverings, Bismarck's

The "Iron Chancellor," Otto von Bismarck

program of keeping the other great powers, especially France, disunited was preserved. In 1880, Russia was too ideologically different and geographically separated to per-mit an effective liaison with either France or Great Britain. Within months, Russia requested a renegotiation of the Russo-German treaty system. Bismarck deftly insisted that Austria-Hungary be included once more. Thus, the Three Emperors' League was renewed in 1881, after Russia had overcome her rebuff in the Balkans. The new treaty called for the neutrality of the other two parties if the third found itself at war with a fourth nation. This achieved Germany's main objective of a neutral Russia in the event of a war with France. The specter of a two-front war against Germany had once again been avoided.[14] For her part, Russia was as-sured that while she could not control the straits into the Black Sea, they would be closed to all warships; this effec-tively protected her from an attack in the south. Austria's right to annex the provinces of Bosnia and Herzegovina was reaffirmed, as long as she consulted with Russia.[15]

In 1882, Germany became allied with the recently uni-fied state of Italy. Despite the fact that Italy and Austria were old enemies, Italy decided to join with the powerful Germans and the Austrians to form the Triple Alliance. Italy took this step in hopes of gaining support for her dream of acquiring a colonial empire. This, too, was a de-fensive treaty in that each party pledged to support the others only in the event of an attack by France.[16] Now Germany was formally allied with three powers: Russia, Austria-Hungary, and Italy. In addition, she maintained friendly economic and diplomatic relations with Great Britain. France remained diplomatically isolated, and her hopes to gain revenge for the defeat of 1871 receded perceptibly.

In 1885, the unrest in the Balkans once again erupted into conflict that would lead to the final destruction of Bismarck's artificial alliance with Austria and Russia.[17] In that year, Bulgaria, which had been severely reduced in size by the Berlin Congress, grasped at an opportunity to regain autonomous East Rumelia from Turkey. As in the past, rebellion within the largely Bulgar population spurred the war. Serbia, however, chose to oppose Bulgaria's expansion and also to seize Macedonia. Bulgaria easily routed the Serbian forces, and only Austria's alliance with the latter saved her from complete occupation. But now Russia, which up to this point had disassociated herself from the Bulgarian crisis, decided to take up Serbia's cause, thus threatening to crush Bulgaria. Once Russia intervened, Austria felt it necessary to shift her protection to Bulgaria. Neither Austria nor England could abide a Russian-dominated Balkans. Therefore, as had happened in 1878, both states resorted to brinksmanship in order to thwart Russia's hopes. As a direct result, the furious Russians refused to renew the League of the Three Emperors in 1887.[18]

The crafty Bismarck, however, did not let this setback affect his diplomatic program, which required peace in Europe and called for Germany to be part of a strong alliance system. In place of the old three-way league, a bilateral agreement, known as the Reinsurance Treaty, was signed between Germany and Russia in 1887.[19] This provided for the benevolent neutrality of either partner if the other should find herself at war. The only exceptions were that if Russia attacked Austria or Germany attacked France, the treaty partner was free to consult her own interests.

This labyrinth of diplomatic and military alliances was the monument that Bismarck had built for Germany. Certainly no other diplomat could have so skillfully controlled the power rivalries of the six sovereign states that dominated Europe. Not surprisingly, the very complexity of the program, which was often Byzantine in its deviousness and subtlety, served to focus attention on its originator. Bismarck had achieved his aims: first, the delimitation of Germany's territorial demands, especially in the imperialist race for colonies; second, general peace in Europe.[20] His major problem in achieving the latter goal had been the unending squabbling in the Balkans. This situation was caused by nationalist aspirations in the area and the conflicting interests of the great powers.

With Bismarck's retirement in 1890, the diplomatic community feared that those who would follow him would be

**"Dropping the Pilot": English View of the
Departure of Bismarck from Power**

less adept at balancing the passions and rivalries of Europe. Kaiser Wilhelm II, who had asked Bismarck to leave, was a vainglorious and unstable man.[21] Unfortunately, he was the true center of power in the Reich when he chose to exercise his prerogatives. If one man's act can be seen as beginning Europe's downhill tumble into war in 1914, it was Wilhelm's relief of Bismarck and his assumption of real power.

Shortly after Bismarck's dismissal, the Kaiser decided to allow the Reinsurance Treaty with Russia to lapse.[22] Despite pleas from Czar Alexander III of Russia, Wilhelm blandly allowed Germany's eastern and western borders to become insecure, a situation that Bismarck had toiled endlessly to avoid. At the same time, he turned his attention briefly to England and made a series of friendly gestures aimed at convincing that country to join the Triple Alliance. In this he failed. Despite the interest of some of her statesmen, Great Britain remained aloof from continental ties.

Competing Alliances

In the meantime, Russia, set adrift, was anxiously seeking friends elsewhere. France now saw an opportunity to break out of diplomatic isolation. Swallowing her republican pride, she began a program of reconciliation with and financial assistance to autocratic Russia that culminated in a series of bilateral agreements. The most important of these was the secret Franco-Russian Military Convention signed in 1894.[23] This bound both parties to mobilize for war in the event that any member of the Triple Alliance did so. If war were to break out and Germany attacked France or Austria and Germany attacked Russia, the other partner would fight on the side of the attacked party. This agreement, in conjunction with the Austro-German alliance, provided the longstanding framework within which the world would go to war in August 1914. For the time being, however, Europeans turned their interests to other international matters.

During the ensuing years, much of Europe's attention was focused upon the glittering collection of colonies that the great powers already had or were then collecting. The Germans and Italians were latecomers to the race for colonial possessions, and often collided with the interests of the more established French and British. During this period, however, it was the competition between France and England that generated the most friction.[24] Therefore, it may be concluded that the conflicts which took place outside of Europe, while serious and often producing bellicose threats, were never important enough to produce a world conflict. Instead, a firm case can be presented to show that the competition for colonies was merely a symptom of continental rivalry and only served to exacerbate existing problems.

Here again, Kaiser Wilhelm's bluster magnified a problem far beyond its true significance. Continually voicing Germany's dissatisfaction with the status quo in the colonial empires, he provoked numerous confrontations in North Africa and the Pacific Ocean over spheres of influence that were claimed by others or that involved compensation to Germany.[25] In an almost petulant manner, Wilhelm reversed Bismarck's policy of shunning overseas possessions, and succumbed to the desire of German business interests to gain sources of raw materials and markets for the country's burgeoning industry.[26] With the resultant need to protect and expand colonial holdings, as well as the Kaiser's claim that the country's future now lay on the world's oceans, the creation of a strong navy became an integral part of Germany's policy.

This policy could do nothing but irritate and worry Great Britain. Long dominant on the high seas, the British recognized the naval competition from Germany as a threat to their existence. To them this was yet another example of the arrogant German movement toward European and world domination. The naval arms race between these two powers would continue until the eve of war. Both sides continually increased their expenditures, sought technological advance-

Kaiser Wilhelm II of Germany

ments (such as the dreadnought class of battleships), and increased the number of capital ships in their navies.[27] By 1914, Germany had a navy second only to England's. This second-class ranking and the geographic position of Germany would combine to assure the impotence of the German surface fleet during the war.*

A more subtle threat to England's security appeared during her inglorious war against the Boer farmers in South Africa from 1899 to 1902.[28] During this conflict, the vulnerability of the British Empire, which was due in part to its lack of allies, became evident to her statesmen. She had no friends, but many envious rivals. The inconclusiveness of

---

*One aspect of the naval arms race between England and Germany that is often overlooked is that in 1914 the two countries voluntarily agreed to limit the construction of new battleships to a ratio of 16:10 in England's favor. This lessened the importance of the naval race as a direct cause of the war. However, the effect of the arms race upon public opinion magnified its importance in political considerations, despite the fact that technical naval considerations could be controlled.

the British military victory also indicated that England needed the support of a continental land power. Here, again, skillful French statesmen stepped in to further the French break from isolation. In 1904, an understanding (the *Entente Cordiale*) was reached between England and France, resolving many of their outstanding colonial disputes. While not a formal alliance, this entente led to secret military and naval discussions that would eventually bind the British Empire to France's cause in the event of war.[29] The agreement also led to a resolution of Russo-British problems in the Near East in 1907. Having been humiliated in the Russo-Japanese War, Russia was willing to accept England as a friend in exchange for her vague promise to support Russia aspirations for control of the Dardanelles.

By 1908, French diplomacy, amply assisted by German bungling, had triumphed in completely altering the weak and isolated condition in which France had found herself in 1871. There now existed two competing alliance systems among the great powers of Europe: the Triple Alliance (Germany, Austria-Hungary, and Italy) and the Triple Entente (France, Russia, and England).* This is not to say that Europe found itself divided into armed camps, awaiting the signal for war; on the contrary, from a military standpoint these agreements were purely defensive in nature. The atmosphere created by these alliances, however, made the agreements more powerful than any of their specific commitments and, in this case, was to lead to actions never envisioned by the leaders who had made them. This would be especially true during the times of crisis that were to follow.

In October of 1908, such a crisis did arise, once again in the Balkans. Austria decided in that month to exercise her prerogatives and annex the provinces of Bosnia and Herzegovina. While she had been granted this option by previous bilateral agreements with Russia, the Dual Monarchy chose this moment to act in order to demonstrate her ability to respond decisively as well as to clarify the status of the area after a coup had forced a change in the Turkish Government.[30] However, the abruptness of the annexation and Austria's failure to consult Russia in the matter led Europe to the brink of war. Russia denounced the action because she had understood that Austria would not move until a new settlement on the Dardanelles had been confirmed. France and Great Britain supported their ally's position, but not to the extent of risking general war. Germany, influenced by the public agitation in Serbia, assured Austria of her support. Still recovering from her ill-starred clash with Japan, Russia realized that she was far too weak to act unilaterally. Eventually, the crisis passed without conflict. But the Russians were chagrined by the fact that they had been outmaneuvered in the Balkans once again and distressed by the knowledge that their Slavic brothers had been disappointed by their lack of firm action. The Triple Entente had not proven strong enough to provide Russia with the support she felt she needed.[31] As it turned out, this crisis was a precursor of the situation that would bring the world to war in six short years.[†] Then Russian and Austrian interests would again clash in the Balkans, but Russia would be militarily prepared and confident of her allies' firm support.

The European Military Powers of 1914

Conditions Affecting the Military Potential of the Nations

Perhaps the most important influence upon European military and naval institutions of the early twentieth century was the largess bestowed upon European societies by the Industrial Revolution. Mechanization and factory production during the last half of the nineteenth century brought about a wealth of goods, rising productivity, and material well-being.[33] In varying degrees, this situation allowed the great powers to expend more money on their military and naval forces and to maintain relatively large standing armed forces.

This period of economic growth also gave rise to social pressures for more responsive, democratic political institutions and a more equitable distribution of material wealth. With each right of citizenship and each social or economic benefit, however, the citizen was expected to shoulder a concomitant responsibility to the nation. Of particular importance was the responsibility to perform military service in the reserve military forces when required. The greater availability of education for the lower classes was another factor that affected the outlook of the citizenry as a whole. Better and more widespread educational opportunities enabled citizens to comprehend more readily the political and military affairs of the state. This, in turn, encouraged nationalistic feelings that tended to inflame the rivalries on the international scene. Another result of the general increase in the educational levels of the peoples of Western Europe was the increased competence of soldiers. The men who were called to the colors were

---

*While these alliances may appear to have been firm, such a view is misleading. Italy's commitment to her allies was weak, and, in fact, she had other agreements with France. Similarly, England was only in the broadest sense of the word allied with France and Russia. Moreover, she had a naval alliance with Russia's enemy, Japan, that dated from 1902.

†Prophetically, when he was resigning from the office of foreign secretary in 1909, Count Bülow advised Kaiser Wilhelm: "Do not repeat the Bosnian affair."[32]

French Mobilization Posters

now capable of learning the intricate details required to manipulate the modern tools of war.[34]

The table below provides some indicators of the relative strengths of the armies that opposed each other in 1914. It should also allow an appreciation of the growing strength of all of Europe's military powers.

The military forces that would be called upon to execute the war plans of the belligerent powers were greatly changed from those that had taken to the field in 1870, during the last major conflict. Transformed by the technological advances of the intervening years, these land and naval forces were the beneficiaries of their governments' mounting fiscal expenditures on armaments and the maintenance of standing forces. However, they were also increasingly susceptible to the problems of technological obsolescence,

since with each new development came the problems of producing, procuring, and paying for replacement weapons. Once an army was equipped with new weapons, its military leadership had the tasks of distributing them, maintaining duplicate stocks of ammunition and spare parts during the transition, and training commanders and troops in the use of the weapons. All of these problems seemed to be solvable, and the vigorous economies of Europe were able to meet the challenges of rapid improvement. The single problem with which the military leaders seemed utterly unable to cope was the integration of improved weapons into their tactical doctrine. They consistently refused to foresee the need for changing their methods of employing weapons.[36] Military men also failed to discern the impact that the increased range, rapidity of fire, and lethality of the new weapons would have upon modern war.*

Many lessons of the American Civil War and the Wars of German Unification had been absorbed by the military institutions of Europe. First among these was the strategic importance of railroads in transporting and concentrating large bodies of troops for battle.[37] Mass armies could now be quickly moved and adequately supplied. Second, and perhaps more important, these armies were now readily available to the military commands. Aside from England, all of the European nations had adopted the principle of universal military service to provide a larger reservoir of trained manpower with which to supplement the standing regular forces in times of war.[38] Unfortunately, the greatest lesson of the more recent conflicts, such as the Boer War and the Russo-Japanese War, had gone unheeded. This was that the increase in the lethality of modern weapons had given a very great advantage to the defensive forms of

---

*This criticism is made with the knowledge that it is based upon retrospective wisdom. Solving contemporary problems—or even recognizing that problems exist—is always much easier for those who have the advantage of hindsight. Therefore, these comments are not offered as a denunciation of the military leaders of 1914, but as an introduction to the problems that would become all too apparent during the first few months of the war.

Nation	Population (in millions)		Per Capita Defense spending (in 1967 dollars)		Mobilized Army Strength (in millions)	
	1870	1914	1870	1914	1870	1914
Austria-Hungary	35.8	49.9	$1.08	$3.10	—	2.3
France	36.0	39.6	2.92	7.07	.40	4.5
Germany	41.0	65.0	1.28	8.19	.43	5.7
Great Britain	31.0	46.4	3.54	8.23	—	0.7
Italy	26.0	36.0	1.38	3.16	—	—
Russia	77.0	167.0	1.28	3.44	—	5.3
Turkey	37.0	21.4	unknown	unknown	—	0.4

Comparison of Strengths of European Powers[35]

**A German Battery Commander Adjusts
the Fire of his Artillery Pieces**

warfare. A relatively few men, protected by permanent fortifications or earthen field works and armed with automatic weapons, were now able to defeat hundreds, if not thousands, of attackers. In another area of tactics, the magazine rifle, the machinegun, and the quick-firing artillery piece had effectively ended the days of horse-mounted cavalry charges and tightly packed infantry formations. Moreover, sheer firepower had superseded individual bravery on the battlefield. Unfortunately, the military leaders generally were enthralled by romantic visions of the glorious battles of the past. Wedded to outmoded methods, they were unable to admit the need for changes in tactical doctrine.

The command and control facilities available to all of the military leaders had been significantly improved since Europe's last war. In one significant aspect, however, the organization of the forces was faulty. Control of the forces in the field ran directly from the Commander-in-Chief's general headquarters to the field armies. Russia alone provided for the intermediate headquarters of the army group. This shortcoming in the chain of command would have serious consequences during the first few weeks of the war, and would necessarily lead to various improvisations. Communications from the higher command centers had been improved by the introduction of the telephone and expanded telegraphic systems, and while wireless radio communication was in its infancy, it was used from the outset. Semaphore signaling, runners carrying written messages, and

liaison officers, however, remained the most reliable methods of communication.[39]

The organizations of the principal military formations initially employed by the belligerents were very similar.[40] The field armies were composed of from two to seven corps.[41] A corps was a tactical headquarters that controlled two or more divisions. The heart of all armies was the infantry division, which ranged in strength from 15,000 to 18,000 men with about 4,500 horses. Below the division level there were two brigade headquarters that controlled two regiments of three battalions each. The British organization called for three brigades to control four infantry battalions directly, and did not contain a regimental headquarters.

Combat support and service units were provided at both division and corps levels. Cavalry, light and medium artillery, engineer, and logistical units were provided at the divisional level. In this regard, the Germans furnished their formations with a greater amount and higher quality of support than did the other powers.[42] Exploiting the machinegun, an item of equipment that would very quickly make its importance felt, all of the principal armies called for each infantry division to be supported by 24 of these weapons.* Each of the armies had also integrated the capabilities of the airplane into its organization. Generally, these machines were formed into squadrons of 12 each. These were assigned under corps control for reconnaissance. This mission was the only one envisioned for aircraft at the outbreak of hostilities.[43]

France

Of all the states, France was perhaps the most sensitive to military defeat. After her humiliation in the Franco-Prussian War, her army quickly adopted the German method of organizing reserve units to support the standing army. In numbers, however, France was at a disadvantage when compared with Germany. The Second Reich had not only an overwhelming economic advantage but also a population base that was rapidly expanding, while that of France had leveled off. Thus, although France maintained a large standing army and increased her military expenditures each year, in numbers of young men she could no longer compete with Germany. As a short-range solution, the term of service in the French Regular Army was increased from two to three years and the maximum age for service was

---

*The doctrine for the employment of the machinegun was in a state of flux. Some armies envisioned the direct support of infantry battalions with a team of two guns, while others held control of the guns at a higher level. However, Germany alone had organized machinegun companies outside of the divisional structure. These served as a basis for the rapid expansion of machinegun use and gave the Germans a decided advantage during the initial stages of the war.

**Automatic Weapons Such as the Machinegun
Would Extract a Huge Toll of Lives**

The French Army, especially, was imbued with the romantic notion that brave and gallant soldiers would be irresistible in the attack. Thus, French military doctrine and training emphasized only offensive maneuvers.[48] The élan and spirit of the French infantryman were counted as all-important in a clash of arms that would be decided by superior will, and not by firepower, terrain, or even maneuver. Therefore, the direct fire support required by the French formations had to be mobile and accurate but not particularly heavy in caliber since it would be employed against enemy formations in the open. Similarly, the cavalry, which armed with saber or lance, would be used on the flanks of the massed infantry charges against all enemy formations.

Germany

Following her victories in the Wars of Unification, Germany maintained an active army somewhat smaller than that of France. Because of her large mobilization base, which was twice the size of France's, Germany's young men had only to serve for two years on active duty and then be on call in the reserves for a period of 23 years. Of the eligible young men in each class or year group, only one-half were called to active duty for training.[49]

During peacetime, the German Army, also, was based upon a corps organization. For purposes of better training and more rapid concentration during mobilization, each of the corps areas corresponded to a territorial region. There were 25 German corps, each of which consisted of two 17,500-man divisions. A major advantage that Germany possessed over all other nations was her efficient reserve organization. While others copied the structure of this Ger-

raised. While this gave Frenchmen a lengthy military obligation of 28 years, it did allow the active duty forces of nearly 800,000 men to draw upon a mobilization base of 4.5 million trained reservists.[44]

The French Army consisted of corps that were stationed throughout the country in peacetime so as to facilitate their rapid wartime expansion by the addition of reserves. There were 20 of these corps, each of which was composed of two 15,000-man divisions, a cavalry regiment, and 12 batteries of 6 artillery pieces each. The Franco-German border was patrolled by 10 separate cavalry divisions.† French war plans also took into account and relied upon regular units from France's colonial empire, especially North Africa.[45]

The pride of the French Army was its light artillery piece, the 75-mm gun. Because of its hydropneumatic recoil system and unitized rounds, the *soixante-quinze* could fire at a rate of 16 rounds per minute without having to be relaid on target. The Army had 700 batteries of these light, mobile, and accurate guns. The French General Staff, however, failed to pay sufficient attention to the need for supplementary medium and heavy artillery.[46] In large part, this was due to the tactical concepts of the military leaders.

As mentioned above, the lethality of modern weapons had been grossly underestimated during the prewar years.

**The Airplane Would Be Transformed from a Vehicle
for Sport to a Vital Weapon of War**

†Upon mobilization, these were to form a separate Cavalry Corps of three divisions, with the remaining seven divisions being assigned to the command of the five armies.[47]

man reserve system, they did not place sufficient confidence in the reservists' fighting ability or speed of mobilization to include them in their firstline fighting strength. In Germany, however, each corps, upon mobilization, was to be reinforced with a reserve infantry division. In addition, each active duty corps provided close supervision and training of the reserve units so that they were of much higher quality than the reserve organizations of France and England. This system afforded the Germans with the ability to expand their peacetime strength of 760,000 to a total of nearly 1,700,000 within two weeks.

Behind the active and reserve units, which would share the initial brunt of the fighting, was a force of nearly two million *Landwehr,* or national guard troops, who had completed their term of service with the reserves. Behind this force was the *Landsturm,* a force composed of the oldest classes of men and of younger men who had not been previously called to the colors for training. It was from this last group that *Ersatz,* or substitute units, were formed. These *Ersatz* corps were expected to carry out supporting missions in order to free the frontline forces for combat.[50] Thus, Germany was truly a nation in arms, with all segments of society providing soldiers for military duty throughout an extended period of their lives.

The German Army benefited from the traditions of excellent organization and superior staff training inherited from the Prussian system. In general, its leaders were extremely competent and were supported by a brilliant group of officers on the General Staff. While, like the French, the basic philosophy of the German tactical method was offensively oriented, there were significant differences. The main cause of the German deviation from a purely offensive tactical doctrine was the existence of certain defensive missions in the Army's strategic master plan. On the border common with France and in East Prussia, at least some units were expected to conduct defensive or retrograde operations. Also, in the German strategic plan, the offensive right wing would have to prepare for the methodical reduction of the fortifications along the Belgian and French borders. This requirement compelled military planners to develop excellent medium and heavy artillery pieces, as well as many of the accouterments of position warfare.* German units were therefore trained in maneuvers other than offensive ones and were more realistically equipped for the battles that they would soon have to fight.[51]

The German Navy, which has often been cited as one of the causes of the war itself, was a high quality force, but only a distant second to England's Royal Navy in size.

German Troops wearing the Old *Pickelhaube* Helmet Carry Machinegun Ammunition Forward

After Kaiser Wilhelm decided to reconstitute his navy, Admiral Alfred von Tirpitz conducted an efficient and highly successful program of construction and technological improvement. Tirpitz was a strong believer in Alfred Thayer Mahan's theories on the importance to any great power of the fleet-in-being.[52] He therefore tended to ignore the commerce-raiding capabilities of the submarine and concentrate his attention on building capital ships. The German Navy's goal was to construct a High Seas fleet that would be capable of threatening British supremacy on the seas.

In analyzing the naval situation, Tirpitz advanced what was known as the "risk theory." Tirpitz believed that even if the Royal Navy were to defeat that of Imperial Germany, England would never have a large enough military force to invade Germany or to defeat the powerful German land forces. On the other hand, if the Germans could inflict a defeat upon the British Navy, Germany could starve England into submission or invade her at will. It had always been British policy to maintain a fleet that was superior to the combination of the next two largest foreign fleets. Tirpitz reasoned that Germany did not have to build a fleet as large as that of the British; she had only to build a fleet that could inflict such damage upon the Royal Navy that England would be vulnerable to the combination of the French and Russian fleets. Of course, the major flaw in this theory was its assumption that England would

---

*Position warfare is a form of warfare in which the mobility of a force is severely restricted in and around those positions that are in the immediate proximity of an opposing force. Normally, position warfare implies that the opposing forces are entrenched.

**Admiral Alfred von Tirpitz, Father of
the Modern German Navy**

very large number of predreadnought ships, she had a vested interest in vessels that were inferior in speed and armament. The Germans, however, could conceivably begin a new building program and within a short rime be equal or even superior to the British. On the other hand, although the prewar naval arms race was extremely expensive for both sides, it hurt Germany more. It took funds away from the German land forces which needed them for expansion in order to conform to the requirements of the grand design of the Schlieffen Plan. Another irony was that the emphasis on the building of capital ships by the Germans diverted their attention and resources from the design and construction of submarines, or U-boats, which would prove to be the most potent weapon in their naval arsenal when war came. The chart below gives an overview of comparative naval strengths in 1914.

remain in an antagonistic position to Russia and France and would refuse to ally herself with any continental powers. As events unfolded, England was allied with both France and Russia in 1914, a situation that effectively negated Tirpitz' theory.

In any event, the Kaiser and his admirals continued to pour large amounts of money into a naval building program, thereby prompting the British to do the same. In 1906, a revolutionary type of battleship, the *H.M.S. Dreadnought,* was launched by the Royal Navy. This ship, which mounted ten 12-inch guns and possessed more speed and armor than any of her predecessors, made all older classes of battleships obsolete; all navies now began basing their strengths upon the number of dreadnought-style vessels in their fleets.[53] This apparent advantage, however, created several difficulties for England. Since she already had a

England

England was first and foremost a naval power. Although her supremacy at sea was challenged by the Germans, she remained preeminent in 1914. With her informal alliances with France and Russia and her 1902 agreement with Japan, there was little the Central Powers could do to challenge Allied naval power seriously at the outbreak of the war.[55]

In the event of war, England's naval plan called for the concentration of the Grand Fleet in the North Sea to bottle up the German fleet, while the French Navy assumed responsibility for the Mediterranean Sea and the Japanese controlled the Pacific Ocean. The most significant aspect of this plan was that it bound the British Empire to the French, since it promised that if Germany attacked France, England would protect the French coast from German action.[56] This could not be done unless England was at war with Germany.

Ship Type	England	Germany	France	Russia	USA	Austria-Hungary	Japan
Dreadnought Battleships	24	13	14	4	10	3	4
Battle Cruisers	10	6	0	1	0	0	2
Predreadnoughts	38	30	15	7	26	12	2
Cruisers	47	14	19	8	21	3	9
Light Cruisers	61	35	6	5	11	4	15
Destroyers	225	152	81	106	50	14	56
Submarines	76	30	76	36	39	14	15

Comparison of Naval Strengths[54]

As was discussed previously, it was the institution of informal and secret Franco-British military conversations in 1906 that eventually committed the British to send ground troops to France in the event of war. While there were no formal treaties to this effect, the British General Staff had only one plan of action if Germany attacked: the immediate dispatch of the small British Expeditionary Force (BEF) to the Continent in order to cooperate with the French Army on its left flank.[57] This plan was a distinct departure from the British tradition of providing naval forces and financial support, but only a few ground troops, to continental allies.

In the period between the Boer War and 1914, the English thoroughly reorganized their staff and training systems. Under the enlightened reform measures of Lord Reginald B. Esher and Richard Haldane, the Secretary of State for War, the BEF was organized, trained, and kept ready for action. It consisted of approximately 160,000 troops organized into six infantry and one cavalry division. Behind this tiny force, however, there was very little else. The Territorial Army was a home defense force that could not be involuntarily sent out of the home islands. Moreover, it was poorly trained and equipped. Additionally, once the Regular Army had been dispatched, there would be precious few officers and non commissioned officers remaining to train and cadre any new organizations. There was, however, still a large but uncertain source of military strength in Britain's far flung empire. The dispatch of Dominion troops, however, would take time, and their usefulness—especially that of the Indian Army—would be doubtful in a large land war in Europe. It appears that the tradition of naval supremacy in England forced military strategy to be misjudged. In any event, all of the prewar military planners expected the war to be an extremely short one, so there seemed little reason to plan for a long-range program of reinforcement for the BEF.

Russia

In direct contrast to the small but superb force that the British could field, the Russian contribution was to be a mass of poorly trained and poorly equipped peasants. Although Russia had extensively reorganized her army following the Russo-Japanese War, the task was so great that there was never any pretense that the Russian Army could be the qualitative equal of other European armies.[58] Russia's lack of industrial facilities was partially offset by materials from her French ally. Aside from her seemingly inexhaustible supply of hardy and untrained troops, Russia's greatest advantage lay in the very vastness of her territories. Her military situation almost dictated that she should initially adopt a defensive strategy. The only offensive operation that could conceivably be in her national interest would be one directed against her traditional competitors in southeastern Europe, Austria-Hungary and Turkey. Instead, her alliance with France and her dependent status in that alliance would force her to engage in an initial two-front offensive against both Austria and Germany. This strategy was far too ambitious and would ultimately lead to military and political disaster.

Upon mobilization, the Russian plan called for the disposition of 1,300,000 troops divided into two army groups (fronts) of three armies each. Behind these forces were 4,000,000 reserves, which were the least trained of any in Europe. As might be expected, the artillery and logistical support for this sprawling force was of extremely poor quality. Only in the cavalry arm (the famed mounted Cossacks) did Russia possess a force anywhere equal in quality to those of her opponents. The leadership of the Army was corrupt and inefficient. It was only because of her loyalty to the alliance and the devotion of her illiterate and stalwart soldiers that Russia had considerable influence during the opening months of the war. Her stoic acceptance of huge casualties and her insistence upon seizing the initiative before she was fully prepared would swing the balance of combat power just enough to prevent an early victory by the Central Powers.

Austria-Hungary

The Army of the Austro-Hungarian Empire mirrored all of the weaknesses from which the Empire's social and political structures suffered. Nevertheless, the Army may well have been the most cohesive and efficient institution in the crumbling Hapsburg Empire. It was composed of a polyglot force that represented the 12 ethnic groups living within the national borders.[59] The officer corps was predominantly of Germanic-Austrian stock, and German was the language of command in the Army. More than 75 percent of the troops, however, were from the other races of the Empire. This caused the formations of the various units to have unique characteristics, and made any uniform military organization virtually impossible. Another serious problem that resulted from this ethnic diversity was that some units could not be employed against certain enemies. For example, a regiment of Slavs could not be expected to fight well, if at all, against their brothers from Serbia or Russia. At the same time, units composed of troops with an Italian heritage would certainly desert if asked to man the defenses on Italy's Isonzo front. Meanwhile, the leaders could never fully trust the loyalties of the Hungarian contingents, which had little interest in the war and thought only of Hungarian interests within the Dual Monarchy.

The Austrian Army was patterned after the military organization of its German ally. However, it could never come close to an effective emulation of the spirit and efficiency found in the German system. The reserve of 1,000,000 trained forces was relatively poor, while the Austrian *Landwehr* and the Hungarian *Honveds* were known to be unreliable and poorly led. Although the Austro-Hungarian Army could boast of its efficient and balanced artillery support,[60] this advantage could not compensate for the poor quality of its non commissioned officers, its diverse racial makeup, and the overly ambitious plans of its leader, Field Marshal Franz Conrad von Hötzendorf.

Thus supplied with the fruits of scientific and industrial progress, each great power felt confident of its ability to equip its huge army. The materials for a great conflict were at hand. The armies had only to be given definite missions and the order to march.

War Plans

The Army had been the instrument of German unification, and it remained in a position of central importance throughout the period of the Second Reich. Supported by the personal interest and influence of Kaiser Wilhelm II, the Army maintained its prestige and power without external political criticism. With characteristic thoroughness, the Prussian General Staff integrated the military forces of the other Germanic states into the Prussian system.

In 1891, Count Alfred von Schlieffen assumed the duties of Chief of the German General Staff. Schlieffen was a serious student of both military history and the theoretical basis of war.[61] After the 1893 military alliance between France and Russia, Schlieffen became convinced that Germany would eventually have to face a war on two fronts. He therefore began a series of studies and plans that dealt militarily with this difficult situation. At the heart of his final judgment was the decision to concentrate a superior German force against the more dangerous threat from France and rapidly defeat her army, while assuming a strategic defensive in East Prussia against the slow moving Russian enemy.[62] Once the French Army had been decisively beaten, the efficient and militarily oriented railroad system within Germany would transport her armies to the East to deal with the Russians. In contrast to his predecessor, Field Marshal Helmuth von Moltke, who had believed that a military planner could only foresee the concentration and the first clash of battle, Schlieffen prepared a detailed plan for the entire war. (*See Atlas Map No. 3.*)

Because of his abhorrence of frontal assaults, Schlieffen planned a wide turning movement of the French forces through the Flanders Plain with an overwhelmingly superior right wing of five armies. To achieve the essential combat superiority of this offensive group, Schlieffen employed economy of force on the defensive left wing, where he positioned just two armies. Furthermore, in East Prussia he provided for only territorial and fortress troops to guard against the Russians. The enveloping right wing would have to violate the neutrality of Luxembourg, the Netherlands, and Belgium in its wide-arcing maneuver, but the military planner cared only for his own problems and discounted the ramifications of these acts.[63]

The Germans fully expected the French to act offensively along the common border with Germany, in the broken terrain of Alsace and Lorraine. Therefore, Schlieffen rejected the idea of converting his plan into a double envelopment on the model of Hannibal's victory at Cannae. Instead, he assigned his left wing the mission of opposing the anticipated French attack without becoming decisively engaged. The two armies there were to retreat, if necessary—both to gain time for the completion of the right wing's enveloping maneuver and to induce the further commitment of French forces. Once the offensive group had completed its movement and had placed superior forces west of the Meuse River on the relatively undefended Franco-Belgian border, the defensive wing would halt its retirement. Then, as the heavily weighted right wing moved west of Paris, pivoting on the Merz-Thionville area, it would attack the flanks and rear of the French Army and destroy it against the combination of rough terrain and the defenses of the left wing. (*See Annex C, Appendix 2.*)

Bold and imaginative, the Schlieffen plan was based upon military requirements. It achieved its purpose by maneuvering concentrated military forces at a decisive point. Superior combat power was attained by employing economy of force in less critical sectors. In its simplicity and maintenance of the offensive, the plan was a model of military theory. It attained its objective of destroying the French Army first and then turning on the Russians by using interior lines and by seizing and retaining the initiative. The final draft of the plan was completed in 1905 and passed on to Schlieffen's successor, General Helmuth von Moltke, the nephew of the hero of the Franco-Prussian War.

In the years between 1906 and 1914, Moltke continued to base his strategic plans on his inheritance from Schlieffen. Those years, however, brought pressures and considerations that the originator had ignored, forcing Moltke to modify the plan. First, Moltke determined to preserve the neutrality of Holland. He hoped that this concession might keep England out of the war and allow Germany a neutral outlet to the world's commerce.[64] Therefore, the movement of Schlieffen's right wing was restricted to the fortified Belgian frontier in its initial deployment. However, detailed plans were prepared for the reduction of the fortresses of Liège and Namur.

An even more serious modification of the original concept of the Schlieffen Plan was the continual erosion of the combat power allotted to the offensive right wing. One of the principal reasons for this modification was that by 1914 the provinces of Alsace and Lorraine had become important sources of coal and iron for German industry. Moltke could not allow his left wing to retire voluntarily from these areas, as Schlieffen had envisioned. He therefore changed the mission of the left wing from one of delay to one of solid defense. This change required the reinforcement of the two armies of the left wing with an additional three and a half army corps and six *Ersatz* divisions that had originally been assigned to the right wing.

The situation on Germany's eastern frontier had also changed dramatically during Moltke's tenure in office. While Schlieffen had to protect East Prussia against a Russian Army that had proven itself unwieldy and inefficient during the Russo-Japanese War, Moltke had to face a revitalized enemy. The Russians had reorganized their forces, and with considerable French assistance and prodding had prepared to move much more rapidly in the event of war. Therefore, Moltke organized the Eighth Army for the defense of East Prussia and provided it with four and a half corps drawn from the West.

Finally, the fact remained that, due to social and economic constraints, neither Schlieffen nor Moltke had ever been able to amass the number of troops required to implement the great plan.

The end result of these modifications was that, between the inception of the plan in 1905 and its execution in 1914, the striking or offensive arm of the German war plan was reduced from 35.5 corps to 27.5 corps.[65] Also, the provisions for the left wing to reinforce the right and for the deployment of six *Ersatz* corps to follow it in a support echelon were eliminated.

The Schlieffen Plan of 1905 and its subsequent modifications by Moltke have long been the subject of heated debate. Some critics see the plan as the embodiment of military wisdom, while Moltke's adjustments are viewed as the cause of its ultimate failure. Others argue that the changes were made in reaction to substantial alterations in the strategic situation and were the result of social, economic, and diplomatic factors that had been ignored by Schlieffen. In any event, there is serious doubt that the plan would have succeeded even if it had been executed in the manner foreseen by Schlieffen.[66] This speculation is based upon the difficulty of supporting the huge right wing logistically and on the advantage given to defensive tactics by the technological development of the machinegun and rapid-fire artillery. That it came so near to achieving its initial goal of destroying the enemy armies, can, in large measure, be attributed to the nature of French planning.

Virtually all war planning in the early twentieth century

was based on the valid judgment that decisive results could only be achieved through the employment of offensive tactics and strategy. The French Army carried this precept to absurd lengths in its strategic plan. Known by its numerical designation, Plan XVII was the ultimate in offensive doctrine. *(See Annex C, Appendix 1.)* In keeping with Moltke the Elder's dictum that battle can only be anticipated as far as the first encounter, the French General Staff evolved a plan that called for an immediate concentration and attack into the sacred lost provinces of Alsace and Lorraine.[67] *(See Atlas Map No. 3.)* The offensive was to be carried out by four armies advancing on both sides of the Metz-Thionville fortresses, with one army, the Fourth, in reserve. French planners discounted the likelihood of a German attack through the Low Countries, but a last-minute alternative called for the deployment of the Fourth and Fifth Armies to the north to cut off any German pincer. One of many flaws in this concept was that, in spite of adequate warnings, it seriously underestimated the initial strength of the German enemy.*

The French professional officer corps did not trust the quality of its reserve forces or their ability to mobilize rapidly. Therefore, the French plan envisioned only the use of the firstline troops during the critical first days of combat. The planners assumed that the same situation would exist on the other side of the Franco-German border. In the final analysis, they were entranced with the élan of their troops and felt that the actions of the enemy were of little account. They fervently believed that French offensive actions would disrupt any German war plans and hurl the enemy troops back in confusion. Additionally, they expected some assistance from a relatively small expeditionary force sent from Great Britain.

To their credit, the French had stimulated reforms and modernization in the Russian Army. Moreover, through financial and diplomatic pressure, they had induced the Russians to accelerate their mobilization and planned movement into East Prussia.[68] This, it was hoped, would further weaken any German offensive thrust in the West.

While the Central Powers were better prepared for the land war, their conceptions of naval operations were faulty. Germany's Army held primacy in preparation for the coming war; despite the money and attention that had been lavished on the High Seas Fleet, the planners had failed to create any real mission for the Navy. On the other side, the Entente Powers had provided definite and coordinated naval missions. Along with their military agreements, which were never binding, the English had promised that in the event of a war between Germany and France, the Royal Navy would protect the French Channel coast. This was designed to allow

---

*The French knew of the high state of readiness of the German reserves. In 1904, a German officer-turned-informer gave the French intelligence service an accurate estimate of German troop strengths and stated that Germany intended to attack through Belgium.

the French Navy to concentrate its power in the Mediterranean Sea and to support the transfer of regular troops from Africa to Europe. With little realism and even less coordination, the British Army and the Royal Navy had morally obligated the political leaders of Great Britain to war without their consent and with only the vaguest knowledge of the nature of England's detailed naval and military plans.[69] While the major powers concentrated their thoughts on the area that would become the Western Front, Russian and Austrian planners considered potential operations in the East.

The plans for the employment of the sizable Russian forces were necessarily tied both to the much longer period required to assemble these armies and to their comparatively unsophisticated means of logistical support and armament. *(See Atlas Map No. 4.)* Russian Poland formed a salient that was surrounded on three sides by Germany and Austria. Communications within the Polish Salient had been extremely primitive for many years. In addition, the Pripet Marshes to the east provided a great defensive barrier. Therefore, the Central Powers held a decided edge in the ability to concentrate forces for war. However, the conscious decision of the German staff to assume an initial defensive posture in the East, as well as the lack of Austro-German coordination, left the Russian Army time to set its ponderous war machine in motion.

Russia had two plans of concentration and campaign. The first (Plan G) assumed that Germany would commit the bulk of its forces against Russia, and was therefore defensive in nature. This plan called for the Fourth Army to be deployed on the northern flank. After the Germans had begun their move to the east, both the Northwest and Southwest Army Groups would begin a deliberate withdrawal into the interior of Russia. Whenever sufficient combat power could be marshaled, a counteroffensive would be launched all along the front. Under the insistent urging of their French allies, the Russian *Stavka,* or General Staff, prepared an alternate plan (Plan A), which was predicated upon Germany's main effort being directed against France. This was an offensive plan that envisioned simultaneous advances into East Prussia and Galicia.[70] Once the vulnerable flanks of the Polish Salient had been cleared, the Russian troops would continue their march into Silesia. In this plan, the Fourth Army was to concentrate in southern Poland.

The military plans of the Austro-Hungarian Army, which would ignite the war, also were flexible enough to allow for two differing sets of conditions in the event of war. *(See Atlas Map No. 4.)* The first plan (Plan B), which was the one eventually set in motion, assumed that war would be with Serbia alone. This supposition called for the mobilization of six armies, three being used to attack across the vulnerable Serbian frontier. The remaining forces would keep watch over the potential threat from Russia.

Under the ambitious direction of their Chief of the General Staff, General Franz Conrad von Hötzendorf, the Austrians had another plan (Plan R), which committed them to a two-front war in the event that Russia actively supported Serbia. Under this plan, the Serbian invasion would be conducted by only two armies, while four armies commenced an immediate drive into the Polish Salient from the south. This plan, which was agreed to by Conrad and Moltke, called for a simultaneous German attack from the north. This course of action promised to seriously disjoint the actions of the Russian Army. However, as we have already seen, the Germans could not provide sufficient forces to carry out their part of the plan.[71]

At a distance of more than half a century, it is tempting to make a critical evaluation of the military conceptions of the planners. While it would be presumptuous to recommend alternatives, a few observations are valid. The first and foremost of these is that all of the war plans failed in execution. Second, all of them, with the exception of Russia's Plan G, called for the immediate seizure of the initiative by offensive action. Third, all were based upon the rapid concentration of forces on the respective borders and the simultaneous mobilization of vast numbers of trained reserve troops. Of course, there were marked differences in the timetables by which each plan was to be implemented. But the speed and mass of the various offensives were expected to bring about a violent clash of arms and rapid decisive victory. Ironically, it was only the two least sophisticated powers, Russia and Austria-Hungary, that had the foresight to plan for more than one contingency. Finally, all of the plans were designed to be executed within a framework of coalition warfare. This situation sprang naturally from the intricate alliance systems that had developed during the preceding half century. Unfortunately, the military planners did not accurately foresee the conditions on the battlefields of 1914. Their plans would shatter against the tactical realities of the strength of defensive tactics. In turn, this would lead to a prolonged war that required close military cooperation between coalition partners. The resulting war would also demand the complete organization of society to support its requirements.

The End of an Era

The event that actually precipitated war in 1914 was a political assassination. On the morning of June 28, 1914, a young Bosnian nationalist named Gavrilo Princip fired two pistol shots and murdered the heir to the Hapsburg throne of the Austro-Hungarian Empire, Archduke Francis Ferdinand, and his wife. The degree of exact involvement of members of the Serbian Government remains unclear, but

None Knew and Few Foresaw What Modern War Would Entail

it was generally assumed at the time that it had condoned the act.[72] Moreover, it is apparent that the murderer was a member of a group sent to Sarajevo, Bosnia with the intention of disrupting Austro-Hungarian and Slavic relations. The group was armed and assisted by a revolutionary Pan-Slavic society called the Black Hand.

The Austro-Hungarian Empire had been steadily diminishing in prestige and power for many years. Because of its internal problems, it was particularly sensitive to nationalist aspirations within its own borders, and felt compelled to react strongly to this supreme insult by the bothersome Serbs who continued to call for a greater Slav state.[73] Characteristically, the Austrians hesitated in reacting until the complicity of Serbia could be verified. This was never established.

Count Leopold von Berchtold, the Austrian Foreign Minister, took charge of the situation. He consulted with Conrad, and was told that a punitive military expedition against Serbia was required, but that it could not be mounted unless the Army was placed upon a war footing. Berchtold also sent a message to his Triple Alliance partner, Germany, whereupon the Austrian Ambassador met with Kaiser Wilhelm II at Potsdam. The Kaiser reacted violently against the murder of his friend and agreed that Austria-Hungary had to move against Serbia. He also impulsively promised German support if Russia attempted to intervene on behalf of Serbia.[74]

The Austrian statesmen and soldiers were now satisfied that their plan for resolute action would dispel the belief that theirs was a feeble and declining power. Austria would punish Serbia in a local war, provide a stern example for her own Slavic population, and force the Russians to back down once again in a Balkan crisis. Without adequately assessing the full import of their actions, the Austrians initiated a chain of political and military events that would end in war.

Her army exhausted and disorganized by the Balkan Wars, Serbia awaited the demands from Vienna. She had to wait until July 23, when the Austrians finally presented the infamous ultimatum that called not only for the suppression of all revolutionary activities but also for the participation in internal Serbian affairs by Austrian officials. The Serbian response, which turned out to be most conciliatory, was really unimportant—Austria had already decided to mobilize and go to war.[75]

The Russians became aware of the ultimatum and began the preliminary steps necessary for mobilization. The Russian Army's great size and the extremely poor transportation facilities available to it required much more time and a more deliberate series of actions than those of other armies in preparing for military contingencies. The Russian Foreign Minister, Sergei Sazonov, thought that he could ask the Army to mobilize only those units on the border with

Archduke Francis Ferdinand and His Family

The Official Announcement of the Mobilization of French Forces

Bosnian Nationalist Gavrilo Princip is Taken into Custody Following the Assassination of Archduke Francis Ferdinand

Austria-Hungary, as a veiled warning that Russia was prepared to stand with its brother Slavs. But the Chief of the Russian General Staff, Nicholas Janushkevich, informed him that there could only be a general mobilization; there were no plans for partial mobilization. This meant that the entire Army would be deployed against both Germany and Austria-Hungary.

On July 28, Serbia and Austria both ordered mobilization and were theoretically at war.* But the scene of action now shifted away from the Balkans and to the powerful friends and allies of the two belligerents. The key decisions would be made in Berlin. Austria required proof of Russian neutrality by August 1 if she were to implement her Plan B for a localized war with Serbia. If Conrad did not have this guarantee, he would have to order the execution of Plan R for a two-front war against Russia and Serbia.

He called upon Germany to fulfill her promises and insure that Russia would be neutralized by the German threat of retaliation.

The Russians, however, were determined not to repeat their weak showing in the Bosnian Crisis of 1908. They would not only support the Serbs diplomatically, but would also negotiate with a show of military force. After complex discussions, Czar Nicholas II finally agreed to the general mobilization order on July 30.

When knowledge of the Russian mobilization reached Moltke, the Chief of the German General Staff, he telephoned Conrad: "Mobilize at once against Russia."[77] This required a shift from Austria's Plan B, which was in motion, to Plan R. But, as with Russian mobilization, that of the Austro-Hungarian Army was not yet a decision for general war. The German leaders, however, were trapped with only one plan for war—the Schlieffen Plan—which committed their nation to war with France and Russia in the event of mobilization. They assumed that this was true for the other powers as well. With this misconception weighing heavily upon them, General Moltke and the German Chancellor, Theobald von Bethmann-Hollweg, prodded each other into war. The Germans, therefore, sent an ultimatum to Russia, demanding that she cease mobilization. From France, Germany demanded a promise not to mobilize at all. The Russians answered negatively, while the French stated that they would "consult their own interests." Knowing that their demands would be rejected, the Germans had already decided to order general mobilization and the execution of the Schlieffen Plan on August 1. The next day, Germany demanded free passage through Belgium. By the time this demand was refused, German divisions were already beginning their march through Flanders. The Great War had begun.

---

*Ironically, the Austrians knew that they could not even begin military operations until August 12, at the earliest. In fact, no serious military operations took place between the two initial belligerents until the autumn.[76]

Notes

[1]Barrie Pitt, "Writers and the Great War," *Journal of Royal United Services Institution,* 109 (August, 1964), pp. 246–248; Barbara W. Tuchman, *The Proud Tower* (New York, 1966), p. xiii.

[2]A.J.P. Taylor, *The First World War* (New York, 1972), p. 16.

[3]Rene Albrecht-Carrie, *The Meaning of the First World War* (Englewood Cliffs, N.J., 1965), p. 1: Sidney B. Fay, *The Origins of the World War* (New York, 1966 [1928]), p. v.

[4]Immanuel Geiss, *July 1914* (New York, 1967), pp. 17–25; Koppel S. Pinson, *Modern Germany, Its History and Civilization* (New York, 1966), pp. 219–229.

[5]Charles D. Hazen, *Europe Since 1815* (New York, 1910), pp. 300–301.

[6]Fritz Fischer, *Germany's Aims in the First World War* (New York, 1967), pp. 3–8.

[7]Raymond I. Sontag, *European Diplomatic History, 1871–1932* (New York, 1933), p. 7; Erich Eyck, *Bismarck and the German Empire* (New York, 1950), pp. 187–188.

[8]A.J.P. Taylor, *The Struggle for Mastery in Europe, 1848–1918* (Oxford, 1957), pp. 219–220.

[9]Barbara Jelavich, *A Century of Russian Foreign Policy* (Philadelphia, 1964), pp. 173–175, 194.

[10]Joachim Remak, *The Origins of World War I, 1871–1914* (New York, 1967), pp. 9–13.

[11]Charles Seymour, *The Diplomatic Background of the War, 1870–1914* (New Haven, 1916), pp. 194–202.

[12]William L. Langer, *European Alliances and Alignments, 1871–1890* (New York, 1931), pp. 203–208.

[13]Remak, *Origins of World War I,* pp. 13–14.

[14]Laurence Lafore, *The Long Fuse: An Interpretation of the Origins of World War I* (Philadelphia, 1965), p. 99.

[15]Langer, *European Alliances and Alignments,* pp. 206–210; A.F. Pribram (ed.), *The Secret Treaties of Austria-Hungary. 1879–1914* (Cambridge, Mass., 1937), p. 43.

[16]Carlton J.H. Hayes, *A Generation of Materialism, 1871–1900* (New York, 1941), pp. 39–41.

[17]R.W. Seton-Watson, *The Rise of Nationality in the Balkans* (New York, 1918), pp. 119–120.

[18]Raymond Poincare, *The Origins of the War* (London, 1922), pp. 46–48.

[19]Fay, *Origins of the World War,* pp. 77–80.

[20]Eyck, *Bismarck,* pp. 272–273.

[21]Laurence Wilson, *The Incredible Kaiser: A Portrait of William II* (New York, 1963), pp. 9, 37–40.

[22]Remak, *Origins of World War I,* pp. 24–25.

[23]Lafore, *Long Fuse,* pp. 102–104.

[24]Remak, *Origins of World War I,* pp. 28–29.

[25]Taylor, *Struggle for Mastery in Europe,* pp. 372–373.

[26]Fischer, *Germany's Aims,* pp. 11–20; Taylor, *Struggle for Mastery in Europe,* pp. xxix-xxx.

[27]Arthur J. Marder, *From Dreadnought to Scapa Flow* (5 vols.; London, 1961), I, 43–45.

[28]Fay, *Origins of the World War,* pp. 136–139.

[29]Michael D. Krause, "Anglo-French Military Planning, 1905–1914" (unpublished dissertation. Georgetown University, 1968), pp. 126–127; Pribram, *Secret Treaties of Austria-Hungary,* p. 43.

[30]Lafore, *Long Fuse,* p. 151.

[31]Telegram, Isvolsky to Russian Minister at Belgrade, February 14, 1909, in George A. Schreiner (ed.), *Entente Diplomacy and the World* (New York, 1921), pp. 235–236.

[32]Taylor, *Struggle for Mastery in Europe,* p. 456.

[33]F.H. Hinsley, "Reflections on the History of International Relations," in Martin Gilbert (ed.), *A Century of Conflict, 1850–1950* (New York, 1967), pp. 24–31.

[34]Hazen, *Europe,* pp. 352, 381, 513–515; Llewellyn Woodward, *Prelude to Modern Europe, 1815–1914* (London, 1972), pp. 3–5.

[35]Data in table are drawn from: Remak, *Origins of World War I,* p. 87; Taylor, *Struggle for Mastery in Europe,* pp. xxv-xxxi; Peter Young (ed.), *History of the First World War* (8 vols.; London, 1969), I, 94–95.

[36]J.F.C. Fuller, *War and Western Civilization, 1832–1932* (London, 1932), pp. 150–164.

[37]Theodore Ropp, *War in the Modern World* (Durham, N.C., 1959), pp. 182–183.

[38]Basil H. Liddell Hart, *The Real War, 1914–1918* (Boston, 1930), pp. 38–39.

[39]David L. Woods, *A History of Tactical Communications Techniques* (Orlando, Fla., 1965), pp. 54–55, 194–197, 224–230.

[40]James E. Edmonds (ed.), *History of the Great War: Military Operations, France and Belgium, 1914* (2 vols.; London. 1925), I, 471–498, hereinafter cited as *BOH, 1914.*

[41]Edward Spears, *Liaison, 1914* (New York, 1968), Appendices I-IV, pp. 473–491.

[42]T. Dodson Stamps and Vincent I. Esposito (eds.), *A Short Military History of World War I* (West Point, N.Y., 1950), pp. 5–6.

[43]James E. Edmonds, *A Short History of World War I* (New York, 1951), p. 11.

[44]Stamps and Esposito, *World War I,* pp. 6–8.

[45]Sewell Tyng, *The Campaign of the Marne, 1914* (New York, 1935), p. 17.

[46]*Ibid.,* pp. 29–31.

[47]Edmonds, *BOH, 1914,* I, 488–489.

[48]P.M.H. Lucas, *The Evolution of Tactical Ideas In France and Germany During the War of 1914–1918,* trans. by P.V. Kieffer, Army War College (Paris, 1925), p. 6; B.H. Liddell Hart, "French Military Ideas Before the First World War," in Gilbert, *Century of Conflicts,* pp. 133–148.

[49]Stamps and Esposito, *World War I,* pp. 3–4.

[50]Tyng, *Campaign of the Marne,* p. 26.

[51]Lucas, *Evolution of Tactical Ideas,* pp. 12–20, 25–28; Gordon A. Craig, *The Politics of the Prussian Army, 1640–1945* (New York, 1956), pp. 173–198; Tyng, *Campaign of the Marne, 1914,* p. 28.

[52]Reinhardt Scheer, *Germany's High Seas Fleet in the World War* (London, 1920), pp. x–xiv, 3–9.

[53]Thomas G. Frothingham, *The Naval History of the World War* (3 vols.; Cambridge, 1925), I, 24–25.

[54]Young, *History of the First World War,* I, 178–179.

[55]Marder, *Dreadnought to Scapa Flow,* I, 233–239.

[56]Krause, "Anglo-French Military Planning," p. 282–284.

[57]Edmonds, *Short History of World War I,* pp. 17–18.

[58]Alfred Knox, *With the Russian Army, 1914–1917* (2 vols.; New York, 1921), I, xxv-xxxii.

[59]Remak, *Origins of World War I,* pp. 10–11.

[60]C.R.M.F. Cruttwell, *A History of the Great War, 1914–1918* 2nd ed. (Oxford, 1936), p. 48.

[61]Hajo Holborn. "Moltke and Schlieffen: The Prussian-German School," in Edward M. Earle (ed.), *Makers of Modern Strategy* (Princeton, 1943), pp. 172–205; Hugo F.P.J. Freytag-Loringhaven, *Generalfeldmarschall Graf von Schlieffen* (Leipzig, 1920); Hugo Rochs, *Schlieffen* (Berlin, 1921).

[62]Tyng, *Campaign of the Marne,* p. 5.

[63]Gerhard Ritter, *The Sword and the Scepter,* trans. by Heinz Norden (4 vols.; Coral Gables, Fla., 1970), II, 123.

[64]Helmuth von Moltke, "General Observation on the Schlieffen Plan, 1911," in Jere C. King (ed.), *The First World War* (New York, 1972), pp. 20–21.

[65]Tyng, *Campaign of the Marne,* Appendix I, pp. 353–354.

[66]Gerhard Ritter, *The Schlieffen Plan: Critique of a Myth* (New York, 1958), p. 66.

[67]Tyng, *Campaign of the Marne,* pp. 11–22.

[68]Nikolai N. Golovin, *The Russian Campaign of 1914* (Fort Leavenworth, Kansas, 1933), p. 49.

[69]Gordon A. Craig, *Europe Since 1815* (New York, 1971), pp. 442–443; C.L. Mowat (ed.), *The New Cambridge Modern History* (14 vols.; Cambridge, 1968), XII, 142–143.

[70]Golovin, *Russian Campaign,* pp. 45–47.

[71]Alan Clark, Suicide of the Empires: The Battles on the Eastern Front, 1914–1918 (New York, 1971), pp. 50–53.

[72]Taylor, *Struggle for Mastery in Europe,* p. 520 fn.

[73]Pierre Renouvin, "Background of the War" in *Histoire des relations internationales: VI Le Siècle; 2e Partie: De 1871 à 1914,* trans. by Dwight E. Lee (Paris, 1955), pp. 377–384.

[74]King, *The First World War,* pp. xxvi-xxvii.

[75]Remak, *Origins of World War I,* pp. 114–115.

[76]Great Britain, Ministry of Information, *Chronology of the War* (3 vols.; London, 1918), I, 12–20.

[77]Fischer, *Germany's Aims,* p. 85 fn.

The Great Wheel   2

It must come to a fight. Only make the right wing strong.

Count Alfred von Schlieffen
(Apocryphal Dying Words)

Your country's survival waits upon the outcome of this battle. Every nerve must be strained to attack and hurl back the enemy...Retreat would be unforgivable.

General Joseph Joffre
September 6, 1914

At 5:00 p.m. on August 1, 1914, Kaiser Wilhelm II signed the decree for general mobilization of the German Army. Because the decree set in train the tactical and logistical moves that would send German armies into Luxembourg and Belgium, the Kaiser's act, by violating Belgium's neutrality, was tantamount to a declaration of war on both France and Great Britain. The execution of the Schlieffen Plan was the culmination of 18 years of study and planning by the German General Staff. While some would applaud this application of the Clausewitzean linkage of political and military action, in fact, the military planners, beginning with Count Alfred von Schlieffen, had foreclosed political flexibility in time of crisis.[1] The timetables, mobilization plans, and training of the forces were geared solely to initiating a two-front war against France and crushing her armies in the field. (*See Atlas Map No. 3.*) Once this was accomplished, the German forces would be rapidly shifted by railroad to the Eastern Front to confront the slower mobilizing Russian Army. Thus, the plan envisioned defeating each enemy in turn. The key point is that the German military leaders had no alternate plans to accommodate situations requiring a response short of a general European war.

Literally at the eleventh hour, political and diplomatic considerations were surfaced in an attempt to avoid committing Germany to a world war. Prince Karl Maxmillian Lichnowsky, the German Ambassador to Great Britain, had sent a dispatch to Foreign Minister Gottlieb von Jagow, stating that England would remain neutral and attempt to restrain France from declaring war against Germany. This was contingent upon Germany taking no aggressive action against France or the Low Countries. Although he had conferred personally with Moltke, the Chief of the General Staff, twice that day, Kaiser Wilhelm did not understand Germany's lack of planning options. During the second meeting, he directed Moltke to halt the attacking columns and "march the whole army to the east." When Moltke attempted to explain the overpowering momentum of the plans then being executed and the disruption that would result from a modification, the Kaiser was unmoved. Nor were Bethmann-Hollweg or Jagow sympathetic to the entreaties of the Chief of Staff. A shaken Moltke returned to his headquarters to attempt to stem the implementation of the plan.[2] Already, an infantry company had crossed the Luxembourg border near Ulflingen.

At 11 p.m., Moltke was summoned once again by the Kaiser. By this time, another cable had been received from Prince Lichnowsky, stating that his earlier report had been wrong, having been based upon a misreading of British Foreign Secretary Edward Grey's diplomatic remarks.[3] Since England could not now be expected to restrain France, the Kaiser's previous orders were revoked. He told his military commander, "Now you can do what you like." Thus, the last chance to limit the chain of events begun at Sarajevo on June 28 was lost. Moltke returned to his office and, by unleashing the German armies on their march through Belgium, commenced the conflagration that would engulf Europe and the world.[4]

Kaiser Wilhelm II

Battle of the Frontiers, August 2 to 26, 1914

Since 1839, Belgium had retained its neutrality as guaranteed by international agreement. Nevertheless, King Albert and his Government had been placed on the horns of a dilemma by the periodic war alarms and shifting alliances prior to 1914. At different times, each of Belgium's strong neighbors, France and Germany, had been viewed as a threat to the independence and neutrality of the Low Countries. In the twentieth century, however, the Belgians had determined that the most probable threat was posed by Germany. Despite this judgment, Belgium scrupulously avoided coordinated military planning with either France or Great Britain.[5]

In another ironic twist, General Augustin F. Michel, the prewar French Army Commander-designate, had been dismissed. In part, this dismissal was a result of Michel's suggestion that, in the event of war with Germany, France's vulnerability in the north should be offset by shifting forces from the Franco-German border to the Belgian frontier for the purpose of either defending or making a preemptory attack into Belgium.[6] France insisted on avoiding any sign of

threatening Belgium; as a result, her northern border, protected only by the tiny Belgian Army (100,000 men in six divisions), lay open to the planned onslaught of the German right wing. There were, however, two strong barriers to a German advance: a series of rivers that had to be crossed and a strong fortress system. (*See Atlas Map No. 6a.*)

The Liège Bottleneck

To fend off invading armies, Belgium had prepared a highly regarded fortress system, particularly the works at Liège and Namur. The system had been completed in 1892 by General Henri Brialmont. Adopting German principles of fortification, Brialmont had made Liège into a citadel city, ringed by six pentagonal main forts. Supplemented by six triangular secondary forts, the main forts were linked by underground tunnels and contained ammunition magazines, quarters for crews, and ventilation systems. However, the planned rifle trenches, which would have protected the intervals between the forts, had not been prepared. Also, the guns in the forts were of obsolete design and, ironically, were under contract to be replaced by new ones ordered from the German Krupp Arms Works. German planners were well aware of these shortcomings in the Liège defensive system.[7]

The Liège fortress was positioned to cover the Meuse River between the Maastricht Appendix of the Netherlands and the Ardennes Forest. (*See Atlas Map No. 6a.*) Because

The Liège Fortification System

Moltke had modified the Schlieffen Plan to avoid violating Dutch neutrality, the German First and Second Armies were forced to traverse the area dominated by Liège. Recognizing this problem, German staff planners had devised a detailed solution. A special task force of six infantry brigades and three cavalry divisions under General Otto von Emmich was organized and maintained in a high state of readiness. The specific mission of Emmich's force was that of assaulting and reducing the Liège obstruction.[8]

On July 31, Germany had issued an ultimatum to Russia demanding that it demobilize its army within 12 hours; this expired at noon on August 1 without a Russian reply. The Germans thereupon instructed their ambassador in St. Petersburg to deliver a declaration of war by 5:00 p.m., at which time the Kaiser would decree a general mobilization. On August 2, German troops invaded the Grand Duchy of Luxembourg and secured the vital railheads into France and Belgium.

At 7:00 p.m. on August 2, the German minister in Brussels delivered an ultimatum to the Belgian Government.[9] The ultimatum, which had been written by Moltke a week earlier, alluded to a fictitious French advance into Belgium, and demanded passage for the German Army to "anticipate any such hostile attack." If Belgium opposed German passage, she would be regarded as an enemy at war with Germany. A direct reply was demanded within 12 hours (by 7:00 a.m., August 3). Despite an early morning attempt by the Germans to convince the Belgians to acquiesce, Albert's government delivered its reply at exactly 7:00 a.m.: if Belgian neutrality were violated, the Belgian Army would resist. King Albert assumed supreme command and ordered the destruction of rail lines and bridges at the Luxembourg frontier.

At 6:00 a.m. on August 4, the German Ambassador made his final visit to the Belgian Foreign Office. He delivered a *de facto* declaration of war, which stated that Germany was obliged to defend herself by force of arms in Belgium. Two hours later, the cavalry elements of Task Force Emmich stormed across the Belgian frontier at Gemmerich, brushing aside the Belgian *gendarmes*.

King Albert had personally appointed the commander of the Liège system of fortifications, General Gerard M. Leman. Despite interference from the Belgian General Staff, Leman carried out his orders from the King to hold the Liège fortress system until the end. As Emmich's task force converged on the city from north, south, and east, its units found that the bridges over the Meuse River into Liège had been destroyed. When the German infantry attempted to cross the river on pontoons, they were fired upon by the Belgian infantry. The war had begun in earnest.

While the German cavalry cordoned off the Liège area from reinforcement, the infantry attempted to infiltrate between the forts. The Belgian 3rd Division, which had been assigned to Leman's defensive forces, repulsed the German frontal attacks. The Belgian infantry, although outnumbered 5 to 1, took a heavy toll of the attackers from behind hastily constructed fortifications.

A Belgian Artillery Battery in Action

The Chief of Staff of the German Second Army, Major General Erich Ludendorff, accompanied Emmich's Army of the Meuse as an observer. As a prewar general staff officer, he had worked on the plans for capturing Liège. Ludendorff was accompanying the 14th Brigade in the center of the attack on the night of August 5 when its commander was killed by machinegun fire.[10] Ludendorff assumed command of the brigade and rallied the troops, who had suffered heavy casualties. Using skillful infiltration tactics, the 14th Brigade advanced between two of the forts; by the afternoon of August 6, its units were on the heights overlooking the citadel of the Liège fortification system.

Despite the fact that the remainder of the German brigades had halted, General Leman, seeking to prevent the capture of his infantry division, ordered it rearward to join the main army. This decision was in keeping with King Albert's plan to maintain an independent Belgian Army on Belgian soil. Leman personally chose to fight on from the now isolated forts. Shortly, the 14th Brigade began shelling the citadel with its field guns with little effect. Then a German Zeppelin dropped bombs in the city of Liège, killing nine civilians. Having met little resistance since the withdrawal of the Belgian division, Ludendorff ordered his brigade across two bridges to the gates of the citadel. Upon his arrival, the lack of fighting led Ludendorff to assume that the citadel had surrendered to his advance guard. Finding that there were no German soldiers in the citadel, how-

A German Siege Howitzer

ever, he banged on the gates himself and accepted its surrender on August 7. This completed the first step of the assault. Nevertheless, the isolated Belgian forts still commanded the area.

Having failed to reduce the entire fortress system by infiltration and surprise, the Germans implemented a previously prepared plan to reduce the forts by using siege artillery. The very heavy guns manufactured by the Krupp foundry had been developed specifically for this mission. Germany, unlike any other European nation, had understood the lessons of the Russo-Japanese War, and foresaw the possibility of static defenses and modern firepower halting offensive maneuver.[11] The Krupp 420-mm howitzer, soon to become famous as the "Big Bertha," as well as the 305-mm Skoda guns that had been borrowed from the Austrian Army, were ordered forward by rail and road to crush the forts ringing Liège.

On August 12, these guns began firing huge, delay-fuzed projectiles. The shells, fired at a high angle, landed on the forts perpendicularly from above and penetrated the targets before exploding. The Belgian garrison troops, suffering physically and mentally from the unprecedented bombardment, began surrendering the next day. The last fort capitulated on August 16.[12]

The remainder of the Belgian Army fell back upon Antwerp. (*See Atlas Map No. 6b.*) Initially, from its position in the great port of Antwerp, Albert's Army served as a threat to the right-wing German armies sweeping into

France. As the Germans advanced, they had to detach regular forces to defend against this threat and to invest Antwerp. These actions drained away troops needed on the fighting front for the success of the Schlieffen Plan. As the campaign neared its end, the Belgian Army broke out of Antwerp and joined the left flank of the Franco-British line, where it remained intact for the duration of the war.

The Belgian defense at Liège had been gallant and had managed to upset the German timetable for the approach march into France by at least two days.[13] It had also given the Allies two important advantages. First, it had forced Great Britain into the war as a guarantor of Belgian neutrality. Second, it had alerted the world and the French Army to the main attack of the German armies. To serve its purpose, however, this alert had to be believed by the headquarters receiving it.

General Joseph J.C. Joffre, located in his *Grande Quartiers Général* (GQG), remained adamant in his insistence on executing French Plan XVII. (*See Atlas Map No. 3.*) He and his staff continued to dismiss the seige of Liège and the reports of large German forces concentrating in Belgium as a feint.[14] The lack of interest in reported enemy actions on the part of France's *Deuxième Bureau* (Intelligence) during the opening phase of the war remains a classic example of how an army's preconceptions can cloud its eyes to reality. The French General Staff, committed to its offensive plans in Alsace and Lorraine, merely wanted the Belgians to hold fast until they could be joined by the BEF and the French Fifth Army.[15]

Nevertheless, the reports of German concentrations in Belgium caused the French to dispatch cavalry for confirmation. Crossing into Belgium on August 6, and reconnoitering the Ardennes and the Meuse River almost as far as Liège, the French horsemen failed to observe any substantial German forces west of the Meuse. However, this reconnaissance mission was conducted too early, for the Germans were then concentrating on the eastern bank of the river.[16] The German Uhlan cavalry, supported by bicycle-mounted infantry and machinegun fire, effectively screened the concentration from French observation.

Movement of the British Expeditionary Force to France

Germany's violation of Belgium's neutrality unified British public and political opinion behind England's August 4 declaration of war. Unlike the continental powers, England did not maintain a large standing army; however, it had committed its Regular Army of 160,000 troops to crossing the English Channel and linking up with the left flank of the French Army. Unofficial military conversations that had commenced between the two Army staffs in 1911 had laid the tactical and logistical plans for movement, which only required governmental approval when the time came.*

The plan called for the BEF to arrive in France four days after war was declared by England on Germany. Due to the unfounded fear that Germany would invade the home islands, however, the British War Council, including the newly appointed Secretary of State for War, Field Marshal Lord Herbert H. Kitchener, questioned the wisdom of honoring England's military commitment to France. Moreover, the British, particularly Kitchener, perceived the development of the Schlieffen Plan's giant turning movement through Belgium much more clearly than the French. As a result, the BEF commander, Field Marshal Sir John D.P. French, proposed scrapping the planned deployment of his army to northwest France. Instead, he suggested moving to Antwerp and cooperating with the Belgians on the flank of the German armies.†

As normally occurs in times of crisis, prepared plans had the advantage of thoroughness and the force of momentum. The British Government voted to move the BEF to France, but ordered only four of its six infantry divisions and one of its cavalry divisions to execute the plans agreed upon. Embarkation commenced on August 9. Under the protection of the Royal Navy, the transports landed at Rouen, Boulogne, and Le Havre. The troops, horses, and equipment then entrained for a concentration area near Le Cateau. (*See Atlas Map No. 6b.*) The movement was conducted flawlessly and without detection by German intelligence.[19] On August 14, amid the enthusiastic welcome of the French people, the BEF began its march forward toward Mons.

Although the French had achieved their goal of engaging the British Army as an active ally,‡ the principle of unity of command between the two armies had been ignored. French's written instructions†† from the British Cabinet stated that the BEF was to be considered "entirely independent" and "in no case [would] come . . . under the orders of any Allied General." These instructions foreshadowed

great problems for Allied cooperation during the coming campaign—indeed, throughout the war.

The Execution of the Schlieffen Plan

With the fall of Liège and the withdrawal of the Belgian Army, the German right wing, paced by the First Army (General Alexander von Kluck) and the Second Army (General Karl von Bülow), passed through the country. (*See Atlas Map No. 6a.*) In order to coordinate the movements of the two forces, the General Staff placed the First Army "under the orders" of Bülow's Second Army.[20] This unusual arrangement was intended to keep the advance aligned and to prevent gaps from developing between the armies. In practice, the friction created by command prerogatives and professional jealousy between the commanders made this control measure a less than ideal solution. The reason for the arrangement was the location of the German Army's supreme headquarters (*Oberste Heeresleitung,* or OHL). Situated in Coblenz, more than 200 miles away from the advancing armies, OHL could not effectively direct Kluck's and Bülow's movements.

The distance between OHL and the front existed for a number of reasons. First, Moltke and his staff at OHL had made a conscious effort to follow the methods of Moltke the Elder, which called for higher headquarters to issue only mission-type orders.[21] Under this method of control, subordinates were expected to exercise wide latitude in executing operations within the framework of the commander's plan. As a result, OHL was located too far to the rear to direct operations closely during the campaign. Second, the Kaiser insisted on being located near OHL and

---

*These unofficial talks had a substantial influence both on French planners and on the action of the British Government in 1914. The dangers inherent in such unofficial or unsanctioned action by the military services in a democratic society should be obvious to those who might depend upon them (e.g., France) and those who might be inexorably forced to approve them (e.g., Great Britain).[17]

†The BEF commander was expressing a view popular with both the Royal Navy and those political leaders who were unfamiliar with the obligations made in the British-French military conversations.[18]

‡When asked in 1910 to estimate the size of the smallest British military force needed in case of war, Marshal Foch replied: "A single British soldier—and we shall see to it that he is killed. Then we will know we have the entire nation in arms."

††See Annex B, Appendix 6.

Field Marshal Helmuth Graf von Moltke

being advised daily on operations; since Moltke did not want to endanger the Kaiser or his court, he located OHL well to the rear. The third reason for the remoteness of OHL was that, unlike Joffre's GQG, it was in command of operations on the Eastern Front and therefore had to remain centrally located.

The problem of distance from the front might have been solved in one of two ways. The first solution would have been to form army groups in order to more easily control and coordinate the army headquarters. The second would have been to improve the system of electrical communications (radio, telegraph, and telephone), which was inadequate to the pressing and ever-changing requirements of command and control.

The German troops were pushed forward relentlessly in order to meet the ambitious schedule of the Schlieffen Plan. The vast columns of field gray uniforms tramped through Belgium, screened by the cavalry. A pattern of advance soon developed in which the Allies would throw up strongpoints or, if time permitted, a defensive line. Concurrently, the advancing German armies would deploy their artillery from column of march to support the hasty attack of the infantry, while the cavalry screened the flanks. The Allied defenders would then deploy in ranks and fight the attackers to a standstill. Thus encouraged, the Allies would follow their offensive doctrine by mounting a counterattack to seize the initiative. However, the Germans, having been better trained in defensive techniques, would dig in and seek cover. When the bravely attacking Allies advanced, they would be decimated at close range by accurate and devastating rifle and machinegun fire. Forced to retreat, the Allies would be pursued by the Germans, who continued to extract a toll of casualties and prevent a consolidation of the defense. This tactical pattern was repeated time and again, as Allied defenders were pushed back and victories were recorded at German headquarters. (*See Atlas Map No. 6b.*) Louvain fell on August 19; Brussels surrendered the next day. On August 23, Namur, the other supposedly impregnable Belgian fortress, was captured, after being pounded into submission by German heavy artillery. The flow of German victories seemed irreversible as the Allies continued to withdraw toward France.

Throughout their advance, German commanders and soldiers alike were confronted by the resistance of the Belgian nation and people. A policy of intimidation and reprisals against the Belgian population was instituted, despite the prohibition of such action by the Geneva Convention.[22] The justification for this policy was the elimination of Belgian interference in order to keep the offensive on schedule and reduce troop requirements for securing the lines of communication. The Belgian people displayed their hatred for their Germanic conquerors by sniping, laying ambushes, and de-

Allied Propaganda Cartoon Depicting German "Huns"

stroying bridges, rail lines, and communication facilities. Individual snipers (*francs-tireur*) were summarily executed.[23] When attacks or acts of sabotage could not be blamed on individuals, hostages, taken from the local populace, were imprisoned or executed at the discretion of the commander on the ground. In such an atmosphere, the individual soldiers felt no need to treat the conquered people with respect. Soon, vandalism, rape, and arson were being reported by the Belgian Government and the neutral press corps that was covering the operations.[24] This harsh treatment, coupled with the violation of the neutral nation's sovereignty, gave rise to an Allied propaganda campaign against German brutality. Playing on the people's natural sympathy for innocent victims of the war, this campaign was refined and repeated throughout Allied and neutral nations for the remainder of the war.

The Battles of the Sambre and Mons

In accordance with Plan XVII, the French Fifth Army, under the command of General Charles L.M. Lanrezac, was deployed on the left flank of the French line. (*See Atlas Map No. 3.*) Because of its vulnerable position, it was the only French unit that was aware of the German main attack through Belgium. As early as August 7, Lanrezac had warned GQG that the Germans were moving into Belgium in great strength. Although Joffre's plan called for the Fifth Army to attack into the Ardennes Forest in conjunction with the Third and Fourth Armies, Lanrezac constantly badgered GQG with reports of major German movements. Joffre and his staff initially dismissed these reports, either viewing them as exaggerations or reasoning that if more enemy troops were deployed west of the Meuse it would benefit the French, because the center of the German line would thus be weakened and vulnerable to the maneuvers of Plan XVII.[25] This analysis failed to admit to the possibility of the Germans using reservists in the frontlines, thereby increasing the total enemy strength. The French, once again prisoners of their own preconceptions, failed to grasp reality. Their intelligence assessment also failed to take into account the easily defended terrain in the Ardennes Forest.

This first test between the German right wing and the French Army was preceded by imprecise orders and poor communication between the French commanders, Joffre and Lanrezac. Having refused to give credence to intelligence reports of German strength, Joffre and the GQG staff, committed to the attack in the Ardennes, rejected what Lanrezac and his staff saw as the only correct defensive moves. When Lanrezac explained his fears in person, Joffre, who underestimated the total enemy strength by a half million troops, dismissed his arguments. Joffre also arranged for

A British Battery in Action at the Battle of Mons, August 1914

the British and Belgian forces at Namur to join with Lanrezac in the battle. Insisting that the Fifth Army's move north was only precautionary, he still tied its principal mission to support of the attack in the Ardennes.[26]

On August 9, Joffre reluctantly authorized Lanrezac to send reconnaissance elements north into Belgium. The results of this mission further convinced Lanrezac that he would be trapped in the Ardennes if he proceeded with the planned attack. By August 15, Joffre and his staff could no longer ignore the German strength, and so issued instructions for the Fifth Army to move north toward Namur into the salient formed by the Sambre and Meuse Rivers.[27] (*See Atlas Map No. 6b.*) It was there that Lanrezac's army collided with Bülow's Second Army on August 21.

Deeply frustrated by the Commander-in-Chief's indifference to danger, Lanrezac seems to have withdrawn into himself. At the same time, he decided to defend rather than attack, thereby discarding Joffre's instructions. Moreover, during the ensuing operation he failed to provide timely or clear guidance to his corps commanders. (*See map on page 28.*) For example, he did not state whether the defense of the river line was to be on the north or south side of the Sambre River. Without instructions, the French corps commanders established weak bridgeheads over seven of the eight bridge areas.[28] By the time Lanrezac decided to defend the south bank, it was too late; the lead elements of the French and German armies were already engaged. Lanrezac's troops were thrown back across the river, and the German advance guards secured the south bank. Bloody and disconnected, the battle of August 21 continued for the rest of the day and night.

Without firm guidance, the French corps commanders directed counterattacks the next day. Meanwhile, Bülow had ordered his forces to hold their position until the German Third Army, under the command of General Frieherr Max von Hausen, arrived to conduct a coordinated attack over

General Joffre Confers with General Foch, August 1914

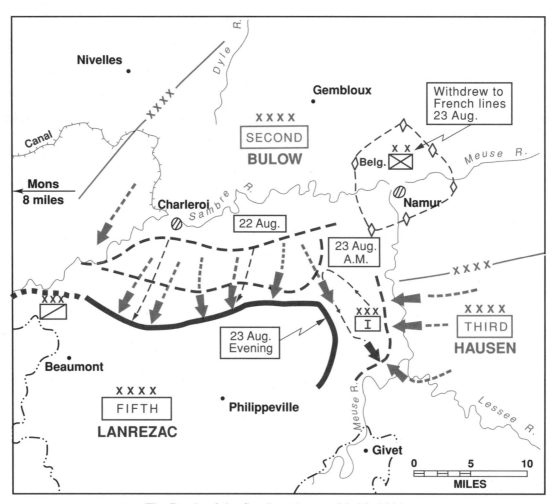

The Battle of the Sambre, August 21–23, 1914

the Meuse River. On August 22, the French attacks were repulsed with heavy losses. Bülow then decided that he had sufficient strength to counterattack without Hausen's support. By nightfall, this attack had driven the French line back several miles. Lanrezac then planned to attack Bülow's left flank with his I Corps, which had been guarding the Meuse River flank. On the morning of August 23, as General Louis Franchet d'Esperey's I Corps was preparing to attack Bülow's flank, Hausen's Third Army forced a crossing of the Meuse to the French rear. In response, d'Esperey canceled his attack and turned his corps around to meet the Germans. On the same day, the Belgian division at Namur, having lost the fortress there, withdrew behind the French lines.

The British Expeditionary Force, now in position at Mons although screening to the east with cavalry, was not in contact with the decisively engaged French Fifth Army. Lanrezac, ignoring the BEF and concerned only with his own plight, decided to withdraw on the night of the twenty-third; however, he failed to coordinate this move-

ment with that of the British. When Bülow and Hausen resumed their converging attacks the next morning, they struck thin air.[29]

Meanwhile, Kluck's First Army, under the operational control of Bülow, had been instructed to change the direction of advance from the southwest to the south in order to support the Second Army's attack on Lanrezac's left flank.[30] This brought on Kluck's unexpected encounter with the BEF at Mons. (*See Atlas Map No. 6b.*) The southward shift of the German First Army, which moved it farther away from the wide arc of the Schlieffen Plan, was an unnoticed but major change in execution, and would greatly affect the success of the campaign.

British and German Cavalry patrols collided at Mons on August 22. Thus alerted, the BEF moved into position at Mons that evening and began digging in along the east-west canal line.[31] The defensive positions took advantage of those fields of fire and cover that would best exploit the excellent marksmanship of the British regular infantryman. The British rifleman was trained to fire 15 aimed rounds per minute at 600 yards. This made the British battalion a formidable force in the defense.

The next day, Kluck launched a full-scale attack on the BEF's II Corps positions. First, the German artillery used a preparatory fire in an attempt to disrupt the British line. Then, at about 9:30 a.m., the German assault forces formed into compact columns and began advancing. Under the heavy and accurate rifle fire of the British defenders, the German lines soon broke. The attackers then moved forward in rushes, stopping to regroup in dead spaces. The fire was so heavy that the Germans assumed that it came from machineguns. As dead and wounded piled up at the canal line, the German attackers pulled back, planning to reorganize that night. The BEF, having blunted the German attack, prepared to continue defensive operations on August 24. Fortunately, late that night, the British liaison officer to the French Fifth Army arrived to inform Field Marshal French that Lanrezac was withdrawing. The British commander then decided to withdraw in conformance with Lanrezac's movement. However, Kluck's troops pursued the BEF relentlessly, inflicting a serious defeat on the British rear guard at the Battle of Le Cateau on August 26. The BEF then joined the French Fifth and Fourth Armies in retreat.

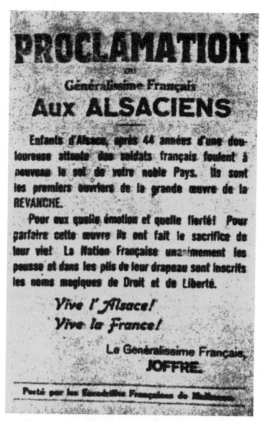

French Appeal to the Alsatians, 1914

Alsace and Lorraine, August 3 to 26

While Joffre was attempting to ignore operations in Belgium and northern France, he proceeded with the execution of the ambitious Plan XVII. (*See Atlas Map No. 3.*) The underlying premise of the plan was that by seizing the initiative, the French could regain the provinces of Alsace and Lorraine, which had been seized by Germany in 1871. The plan was politically acceptable in France because it was designed to counter a German attack without involving neutral states. France's political sensitivity was evidenced by the fact that she held her troops back 10 kilometers along the entire border in order to preclude being accused of hostile intentions. In addition, Plan XVII was the strategic embodiment of the tactical doctrine of *offensive à l'outrance* (attack to the utmost), which had been ingrained in the French Army during the previous three decades.

On August 3, GQG ordered the VII Corps at Besancon to move on Mulhouse[32] in southern Alsace. (*See Atlas Map No. 6c.*) Expecting a rapid advance, Joffre considered the movement of the corps far too slow in covering only 15 miles on August 7 and 8. Claiming that his troops were fatigued by their advance over rough terrain, the commander managed to occupy Altkirch on August 7 and to secure Mulhouse on the next night. The German forces, following their orders, had withdrawn to the east. The French occupa-

tion was to prove all too brief, for on August 10, the Germans counterattacked and pushed the French corps back across the border. Infuriated by what he considered a lack of offensive spirit, Joffre relieved the corps commander and several subordinates. This was the first of what would prove to be an extensive French series of replacements for failure to succeed.*

Despite this preliminary setback, Joffre remained determined to implement Plan XVII. On August 8, Joffre had issued General Instruction No. 1. This ordered an August 14 implementation of the plan's head-on offensive. Two armies were to advance into Lorraine while three armies moved into the Ardennes Forest. Avoiding the fortified zones of Metz and Thionville, the French planned to strike what they perceived to be the center of the enemy forces and to destroy them by offensive action. Beyond these general actions, the offensive had no specific objectives.

On August 14, the French First Army, under General August Y.E. Dubail, and Second Army, under General Edouard de Currières de Castelnau, set out in the direction of Sarrebourg and Morhange, respectively. (*See Atlas Map No. 6c.*) In keeping with the Schlieffen Plan, the German Sixth and Seventh Armies fell back carefully. As they with-

---

*The term used for such relief was "to be Limogé," or sent to the city of Limoges where officers relieved for cause were reassigned. Joffre relieved 40 general officers during the campaign.[33]

drew, the German forces made the advancing French columns pay dearly by employing artillery and machineguns at close range. The French advance continued until August 19, when German resistance stiffened. During the French advance, Joffre had stripped one corps from the Second Army to move it toward Belgium. At the same time, his counterpart, Moltke, found himself dealing with a very real situation in which enemy troops were seizing German territory, rather than a theoretical withdrawal in a plan. He therefore ordered the transfer of six *Ersatz* (replacement) divisions to strengthen Crown Prince Rupprecht's Sixth Army.* The French, encouraged to believe that their offensive actions were succeeding, continued to pay heavily for small gains.

Prior to the war, Moltke had modified Schlieffen's concept; in order to limit the French penetration of German territory, Germany would conduct an early counterattack.† In accordance with this modification, Rupprecht's Chief of Staff, General Krafft von Dellmensingen, directed an end to the withdrawal and ordered a counterattack by the left wing. On August 20, the German counterattack caught the French by surprise and in a greatly weakened state. Having no prepared defenses, and being inferior in artillery and machineguns, the French relied on their quick-firing 75-mm field guns to answer the attack. That night, the French, pursued by the Germans, began to retrace their attack route. The First French Army retreated in an orderly manner, but the Second Army almost disintegrated under the onslaught of the German advance. By August 22, the French forces had been pushed back to their starting positions in the area of Nancy and Epinal.

Ironically, the success of the German counteroffensive in Lorraine helped to further unravel Moltke's version of the Schlieffen Plan. Having tasted success, Crown Prince Rupprecht, the commander of the left wing,‡ wanted to share the glory of victory with the right wing and to continue his offensive into France. His aggressive chief of staff, Dellmensingen, ably reinforced his argument. Moltke and his staff, isolated in their headquarters in Coblenz, lacked the will or foresight to refuse Rupprecht's request, and reinforced the left wing with forces earmarked by Schlieffen for the main attack.[34] Thus, the master plan drifted inexorably from a strategic single envelopment into what was now envisioned as a mammoth double envelopment of the Allied armies—a colossal Battle of Cannae.

*In the original plan, these divisions were to be used as a reinforcement of the right wing.

†Schlieffen would have allowed the French advance to continue, giving up more German territory while steadily sapping the strength of Joffre's armies.

‡Moltke had given Rupprecht, commander of the Sixth Army, control of the Seventh Army as well.

A French Observation Post in Lorraine

Once the French troops were forced back to their own territory, they too discovered the advantage of entrenched defensive positions. They dug in on the Grande Couronne ridge, overlooking the Meurth River. On August 24, the Bavarian troops of Rupprecht's Sixth Army commenced their attack, but soon disintegrated in the face of French defensive positions. The French First and Second Armies, having recovered from their defeat, counterattacked and held their positions. After a week's lull, another series of German attacks was directed at Nancy. These attacks continued until September 10, when Moltke finally accepted what Schlieffen had foreseen: this area was not suitable for offensive operations. By prematurely abandoning their role in the Schlieffen Plan—withdrawing in order to entice the enemy away from the main attack—the German left-wing armies had raised unrealistic hopes of a double envelopment. In addition, Rupprecht not only failed to cripple the French southern armies, but also proved incapable of pinning down the enemy and preventing Joffre from shifting forces to the north. Thus, the French continued to strip forces from their right to defend against the advance of the German right wing.

The Ardennes, August 20 to 26

The second French offensive, northeast of Metz, was directed into the broken terrain of the Ardennes Forest. As previously discussed, Joffre had wanted Lanrezac's Fifth Army to join the Third and Fourth Armies in a headlong charge into the Ardennes that was expected to split the center of the German forces. Although he had sent Lanrezac north to the Sambre River, Joffre proceeded with the Ardennes attack. In view of the disastrous results of the French offensive in Alsace and Lorraine, now just ending, and the growing realization that a strong German offensive was swinging through Belgium against unprepared French and British forces in the north, it would have been logical for the French commander to reconsider his plan. Joffre, however, steadfastly refused to change his orders.

On August 21, the French Third and Fourth Armies advanced northeastward toward Virton and Neufchâteau, respectively. (*See Atlas Map No. 6c.*) Almost immediately, the terrain channelized the attacking armies into isolated columns. The German defenders had been greatly underestimated by French intelligence analysts. Moltke's Fourth and Fifth Armies, regulating their march by the progress of the right wing, were preparing to advance; but, pending movement, they were entrenched and supported by medium and heavy artillery. They also had a numerical advantage of 20,000 troops. As might be expected, the French offensive was thrown back with very heavy losses. On the twenty-second, General Langle de Cary's report from the Fourth Army stated: "All corps engaged today. The whole result hardly satisfactory."[35] Following a futile attempt to resuscitate the attack the next day, Joffre permitted the defeated forces to return to their defensive positions behind the Meuse River.

Allied Retreat, August 27 to September 4

The French Army and the small BEF had suffered an unrelieved string of defeats. In three weeks, commanders and soldiers alike were taught painful lessons of the reality of twentieth century warfare. The benefits of technologically advanced weapons (such as the machinegun and heavy artillery) became obvious. The relative advantage of the defensive over the offensive form of warfare was illustrated by the opening battles on the Western Front, despite the prewar belief that offensive élan would always succeed. The Battle of the Frontiers—the collective name of the battles in Lorraine, the Ardennes, the Sambre, and Mons—was fought in only four days, but the casualties were appalling. The French alone lost more than 300,000 of their best soldiers and young officers.

The German armies had amassed a string of impressive tactical victories during the Battle of the Frontiers. As they rolled forward into France, their rate of advance varied from nearly 30 miles a day in the First Army on the right wing to virtually no movement on the left. (*See Atlas Map No. 7.*) The defeated Allied armies withdrew, creating obstacles as they tried to establish a defensive line to check the enemy's advance. Despite the outward impression that all was progressing well on the German side, obvious prob-

A German Field Telegraph Station

lems confronted the right-wing armies. Food and forage became scarce as the means of tactical resupply failed to keep pace with the advance of the fighting elements. Fatigue took its toll on the infantrymen, and discipline slipped. Combat losses were not replaced, and the sick and wounded were not treated and returned to duty.

Also, as the string of German victories lengthened, problems associated with command and control became evident. Tactical radio communication, although newly developed, had been integrated into all command systems. However, the limited range of the radio, coupled with its vulnerability to jamming and its lack of reliability, required that commanders rely upon telephone, messengers, and an extensive system of liaison officers. Believing that OHL could operate far to the rear, Moltke found himself unable to control and coordinate separate armies.[36] His unwise solution had been to subordinate one army headquarters to another.

As the long lines of communication stretched farther into enemy territory, the German transportation system began to break down. Accustomed to fine internal rail lines in their homeland, once in enemy territory the Germans were forced to rely upon marching and horse-drawn transport. Trucks, while available, were of limited use and dependent on the quality or existence of roadways. As the Allies withdrew, however, they came upon excellent and secure lines of communication. This provided them with interior lines that allowed them to transfer their waning combat power to threatened zones.

Meanwhile, Joffre, although thoroughly disillusioned by the failure of his plans and the seemingly unstoppable German advance, conveyed an aura of calmness and composure. Contrary to the situation prior to the war, the political leadership of France was unable to exert any influence on military operations. In fact, the only information that the

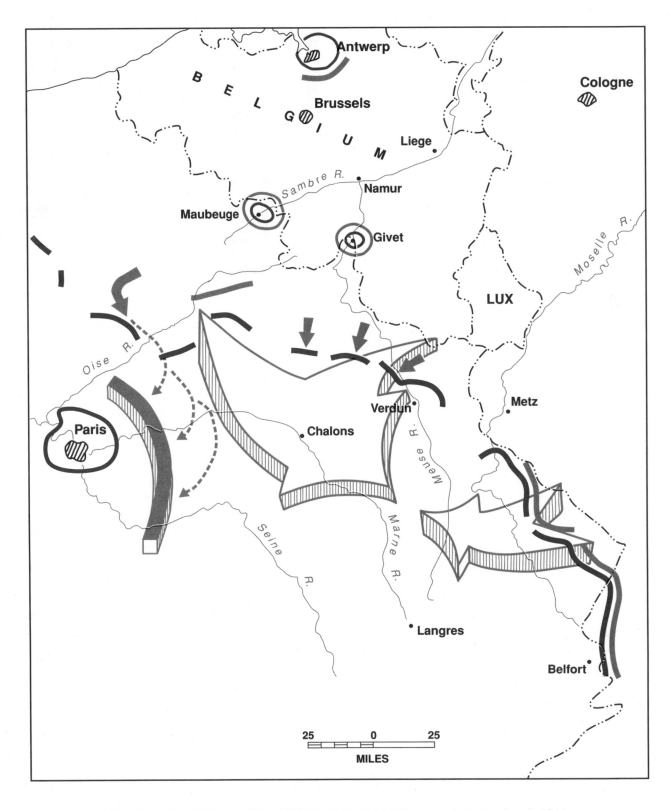

The Situation of August 30 and Moltke's Strategic Concept of September 2, 1914

Premier and his Government received was censored and approved by GQG. A Zone of the Armies had been established, and Joffre ruled it autocratically.* Now he began a historic restructuring of his forces and their method of operation, which he set forth in General Instructions No. 2, issued on August 25.†

Joffre's new instructions reoriented the French strategy to one essentially of defense, with priority being given to the armies in the north. GQG hoped that the BEF and the Fourth and Fifth Armies could maintain a cohesive front while falling back slowly to a line that was roughly an extension of the Sambre River. (*See Atlas Map No. 7.*) At the same time, Joffre would move troops from the right to the left and form a force near Amiens that would spearhead a counterattack against the German right wing. The next day, he designated the newly forming force the Sixth Army and placed it under the command of General Michel-Joseph Maunoury. At about the same time, Joffre formed the Foch Detachment—which would soon be redesignated Ninth Army—from left-wing elements of the oversized and unwieldy Fourth Army. The Detachment was placed between the Fourth and Fifth Armies.[38]

In the meantime, French Minister of War Adolphe Messimy had become extremely concerned about the defense of Paris. He realized that Joffre had not worried about the defenses of the city because it lay in the Zone of the Rear, outside of Joffre's jurisdiction. More critically, perhaps, Joffre had made it clear that he could not spare troops from the ongoing battles, and that the fate of Paris, in any event, would depend upon the success of the French field armies. Seeking inspired leadership, Messimy brought out of retirement the distinguished veteran of colonial wars, General Joseph S. Gallieni, and placed him in command of the Fortified Camp of Paris. Gallieni, who would prove to be a bulwark of strength in Paris, soon had the Sixth Army assigned to his command.

The Marne Campaign

By the third week of the German offensive, the hardships of war and the diminishing power of the attacker as he advanced had begun to take hold. While the Allies retreated in an orderly fashion back to a readily defensible line, the German High Command, under the unsure hand of Moltke, continued to make changes in the offensive that would snatch victory from the hands of the hard-marching soldiers of Germany's right wing.

*Joffre's power was greatly increased when the Government withdrew from Paris. The commander of the Fortified Camp of Paris reported directly to Joffre.[37]

†See Annex B, Appendix 4.

General Joseph S. Gallieni: Defender of Paris, 1914

As the offensive proceeded, sizable detachments were taken from the right-wing armies to garrison the line of communication at Brussels, provide security against Belgian forces in Antwerp, and invest the fortresses at Maubeuge and Givet. In addition, two corps were withdrawn from the First and Second Armies—the critical offensive force—and transferred to East Prussia in order to counter the unexpectedly rapid advance of Russian forces. Thus, the plan that had counted on 75 divisions available for operations on the right could now muster only 67 at a time, while the enemy's strength was growing daily.[39] As mentioned earlier, Crown Prince Rupprecht's operations against the French in Lorraine were continued and supported by six divisions in an attempt to achieve a double envelopment. This further weakened the overextended right wing without any benefit to the overall campaign.

Although Joffre remained in charge of the Allied withdrawal, personal disputes between the BEF Commander, Sir John French, and Lanrezac had strained relations. Following the bloody delaying battles at Moos and Le Cateau, French felt that his troops were bearing a disproportionate share of battle without support or cooperation from the French Army. Sir John, realizing that his small BEF was the sole force available to England until Lord Kitchener could mobilize new armies, had decided on unilateral retirement out of the line. He also recalled his written orders, which had made his command independent and warned him not to expose it to undue loss. As a result of this impasse, at Joffre's request, Lord Kitchener came to France to visit with French, and ordered him to cooperate fully with Joffre.[40] Before this high-level meeting occurred, however, Joffre, in consideration of the BEF's defeat at Le Cateau, realized that he must do something to relieve the pressure on the British forces. In addition to the need to lessen the pressure on the BEF, Joffre also had to gain time to move troops from his right wing to his left. In order to do this he had to maintain a cohesive, yet elastic, front. Thus, on August 27, he ordered Lanrezac to attack westward against the flank of the German First Army. With his own army withdrawing and being followed closely by Bülow's Second Army, Lanrezac was badly shaken by the implications of Joffre's order: he would have to turn the entire army 90 degrees to the west and then attack with his right flank exposed to Bülow's divisions. Unwillingly, he complied with the order, but on August 29, just as Lanrezac was about to advance to the west, Bülow's troops came down on his right flank. The resulting Battle of Guise involved hard fighting and culminated in a French counterattack late in the day that forced the Germans on to the defensive. Joffre then allowed Lanrezac to withdraw, while Bülow remained in position for another day and a half. In spite of the success his army had enjoyed at Guise, Lanrezac continued to be pessimistic, and his stormy relationship with GQG came to a head. On September 3, Joffre furthered the spirit of cooperation with the British by relieving Lanrezac of his command.

The Battle of Guise had an impact of a more negative nature on German plans and operations. On August 27, Moltke had instructed Kluck to resume his original route of march, which would take his army west of Paris; Moltke also released him from Bülow's operational control. Kluck drove his troops hard for the next three days, fighting a series of small actions against the BEF, the Group D'Amade, and elements of the newly forming French Sixth Army. (*See Atlas Map No. 7.*) Optimistic about the situation, Kluck was contemplating finding the French flank and driving it eastward when he received a message from Bülow on August 30, announcing a "victory" at Guise. Bülow wanted him to voluntarily turn east and advance on the line La Fère-Laon, thereby supporting Bülow's attack against Lanrezac's army and hopefully making it a decisive action. Kluck was in a quandary. He realized that, because of his atrocious wireless communications with OHL, there was not sufficient time for him to ask Moltke for instructions and release from the OHL orders of August 27. Forced to choose his own course, Kluck elected to support Bülow and made the fateful decision to turn in a direction away from Paris; on August 31, he moved his army to the southeast, toward Compiègne and Noyon. (*See Atlas Map No. 7.*) A day earlier, Moltke had issued instructions directing

German Cavalry Advances Near Rheims, 1914

Kluck and Bülow to close in on and follow the Third Army. (Later he approved Kluck's change of direction.) Even Kluck's change of direction, however, could not further Moltke's plan and mend the gaps that had opened between the right-wing armies. These gaps of 15 to 20 miles were the result of continuous marches, irregularly spaced battles, Bülow's delay in position after the Battle of Guise, and lack of firm direction from OHL.

As Kluck shifted his army to a direction of advance that would carry it east of Paris, General Gallieni, in charge of the fortified capital, watched. Using ground and, for the first time, effective aerial reconnaissance, he assessed the opportunity that had been presented. Joffre sensed that his final defense would have to be mounted farther to the south than he had originally hoped. As a result, on August 30 he placed the Sixth Army under Gallieni. With this rapidly forming army, Gallieni could now threaten the German flank army as it passed to the southeast of Paris.

Kluck proceeded to push his army in the new direction, but as a result of Bülow's delay, the First Army was a full day's march ahead of the Second Army on September 2. (*See Atlas Map No. 8.*) Basing his conclusion on reports received from his army commanders, Moltke had deduced that the French and British forces had been defeated. Thinking the Germans were now pursuing a disorganized and discouraged enemy, he issued orders early in the evening of September 2. The dispatched message implementing this order directed those five armies on the extreme right to change direction from southwest to south. In effect, Moltke had ordered them to close in on and follow the center (Third Army). Kluck's First Army was to act as a flank guard, remaining to the right of and echeloned behind Bülow's Second Army. (*See map on page 32.*) In this position, Kluck could defend against a French attack from Paris. In that city, as Moltke knew, Joffre was building up strength. However, the German Chief of Staff did not yet appreciate the extent of this buildup.

After receiving Moltke's message late on the night of September 2, Kluck made another fateful decision. Barred from direct communication with Moltke, he made his own estimate of the situation and decided to pursue the French in a southeasterly direction from Paris. One principle of command in the German Army was that the general intent of higher headquarters would be followed and applied by the local commander as the battle unfolded. Using this logic, Kluck, who had not been informed of the sizable French buildup near Paris, decided to ignore the flank guard order and continue southeast in pursuit of the French.[41] He so notified Moltke by wireless, and also berated OHL for its failure to provide him with adequate information about the movements of the German field armies. Soon a gaping hole would develop between the right flank of Kluck's advancing army and a weak Reserve Corps that he ordered to follow his right rear and to screen the right flank. *(See Atlas Map No. 8.)*

On September 4, there was an air of apprehension at OHL. Too many questions remained unanswered. Had Kluck taken the action specified in Moltke's September 2 wireless? Had Bülow managed to narrow the gap between his army and Kluck's? Moltke was aware of the large-scale French troop movements from east to west that Joffre could no longer conceal. Had the forces around Paris grown strong enough to launch a major attack on Kluck's army? The picture became clearer when Kluck's petulant message, arriving at 5:30 p.m., 28 hours after it had been dispatched, informed Moltke that Kluck had not obeyed the order to follow Bülow in echelon. The full extent of the gap between their two armies was now apparent to Moltke. Depressed and tired, the German Chief of Staff decided that he must arrest Kluck's drive across the Marne River. The action he took signaled the final destruction of the Schlieffen Plan: the First and Second Armies would face west and oppose any Allied attack from the Paris area; the Third Army would attack southward; the Fourth and Fifth Armies would drive limited French forces southeast into the arms of the Sixth and Seventh Armies, which would attack westward to complete a small double envelopment. Moltke's directive was dispatched to the field armies by wireless at about 8:00 p.m.

Shocked and uncomprehending. Kluck received Moltke's message 11 hours later, on September 5. Unaware of the sizable French force near Paris and unacquainted with the situations confronting the other German armies, the First Army commander concluded that, although the Schlieffen Plan had apparently failed, he would allow the advance to continue, at least for the rest of the day. Not until late in the

**General Alexander von Kluck,
Germany's Iron-Willed First Army Commander**

day, when Lieutenant Colonel Richard Hentsch, chief of OHL's Intelligence Section, visited him with a copy of the order and fully explained the true situation, did Kluck realize the precariousness of the position into which he had led the First Army. Even so, he and Hentsch seem to have agreed that Kluck could take several days to move his troops in an orderly fashion back to the northwest.[42] The orders Joffre had issued the day before, however, would make this leisurely schedule decidedly unrealistic.

This same day (September 5), Maunoury was shifting his army east to its designated line of departure along the Ourcq River. This movement was preparatory to the army's participation in the Allied counteroffensive, which Joffre had directed should commence on September 6.[43] Kluck's IV Reserve Corps commander, General Hans von Gronau, was given the mission of guarding the right flank of the First Army; at that time, he was moving his troops across the path of Maunoury's army. In the morning, Gronau received reports of movements to the west and ordered an attack to develop the situation. This attack, which surprised the leading French troops as they prepared their noonday meal, prematurely triggered the Battle of the Marne. Although he initially enjoyed success in pushing back the French, as soon as the combat action became intense, Gronau realized that he had engaged a formidable force. Wisely pulling back to establish a defensive position, he informed Kluck late that evening of the strength of the French to the west. Grudgingly, the First Army commander moved to reinforce Gronau with the corps that Kluck had earlier directed to begin a leisurely march north the next morning. In spite of the ominous information he had received from Hentsch and Gronau during the past few hours, Kluck still harbored hopes of returning to his original plan of advance.

On September 6, the Allied armies launched Joffre's counteroffensive. Kluck's army, now split, with units facing south on the Marne River and west on the Ourcq, held off Maunoury's attack. Reinforced with a third corps from Kluck's force, they continued to hold their own against Maunoury's troops on the seventh; but that night, the senior corps commander on the Ourcq asked Kluck for additional help. Earlier that day, Kluck had finally become convinced that Maunoury was launching a major attack when Moltke advised all army commanders that a copy of Joffre's order directing the counteroffensive had been found on the battlefield on September 6. At last, Kluck ordered the rest of his army north to the Ourcq River without delay.[44] This action would inevitably lead to a widening of the gap between Kluck and Bülow. *(See Atlas Map No. 9.)* By September 9, Kluck's operations against Maunoury were succeeding, as he was reinforced by his own troops moving from the south as well as by forces released from security missions on the line of communication.

Kluck had knowingly moved the remainder of his army away from Bülow's flank and risked a wide gap for two reasons. First, he felt that he could defeat Maunoury and eliminate this threat entirely. Second, he believed that the British Expeditionary Force, which was opposite his forces on the Marne, would not take advantage of the gap because its commander had lost the will to fight. Joffre, however, had assured himself of the British fighting spirit in a personal visit, during which Sir John French had promised to cooperate in the counteroffensive.

Meanwhile, near the center of the French line, Foch, who had been ordered to defend the St. Gond Marshes, ignored these orders and instead listened to Joffre's call back to the offensive on September 6. On that day, Foch's Ninth Army attacked Bülow and Hausen north of the St. Gond Marshes. There, Hausen succeeded in launching a coordinated night counterattack that threw Foch's army back three miles. Reinforcements sent by the Fifth Army, now under General d'Esperey, allowed Foch to hold his position there. D'Esperey also attacked on September 8. The net result of these actions was to tie Bülow down, peel back the German line, and further enlarge the gap between Kluck's army and that of Bülow.

If there was a "miracle of the Marne," it was the concomitant development of the 40 to 50 mile gap between the two German armies and the execution of Joffre's instructions to attack north. The BEF and the French Fifth Army moved north through the gap, which was manned only by reconnaissance troops. *(See Atlas Map No. 9.)* Without battle, they would succeed in causing a general German withdrawal, even though elsewhere on the battlefield the German situation was not unfavorable. Despite the desperate efforts of Gallieni to reinforce Maunoury's Sixth Army with all available reserves—during this time, 600 Paris taxi cabs transported the 3rd Division to the front—Kluck appeared capable of defeating the French and occupying Paris. Bülow's Second Army retained its tactical integrity, and the remainder of the German line appeared prepared to continue operations to wear down and defeat the Allied forces. However, the fact that neither Kluck nor Bülow were taking action to close the gap between their armies would have an overriding strategic implication. There was nothing to stop the continuous advance of the BEF and the French Fifth Army. The friction of war and the unsatisfactory responsiveness of the German command and control system now dictated the outcome of the campaign and the ultimate failure of Schlieffen's grand design in the West.

Moltke was extremely anxious over the vulnerable position of his First and Second Armies. Once again, he turned

The French Use Buses and Taxis to Transport Troops to the Western Front, September 1914

to chief intelligence officer Hentsch, this time instructing him to visit the headquarters of all field armies west of Verdun. Hentsch was to determine the situation on the ground for a more realistic analysis of the available options that could enable OHL to reassert its control over the campaign. The actual authority conferred upon Hentsch to act in Moltke's name remains unclear. However, a general staff officer was traditionally invested with the freedom to modify instructions in the field.

During the course of his staff visit, Hentsch received glowing reports from the armies on the German left. Similarly, the Third Army reported its situation as being "wholly favorable." When he reached Bülow's headquarters on the night of September 8, however, Hentsch received a pessimistic appraisal of the situation confronting the Second Army. Bülow was justifiably concerned about the sparsely manned gap between his army and Kluck's, and the fact that Kluck's attention was directed to the west and his fight with the French Sixth Army. Hentsch maintained his perspective, however, and wired OHL that the situation was "serious but not desperate."

The next morning, Hentsch departed from Bülow's headquarters with the impression that the Second Army was preparing to pull back and close the gap. At noon, he arrived at Kluck's headquarters at Mareuil-sur-Ourcq, where he met with Kluck's Chief of Staff, General Hermann von Kuhl. Within an hour, First Army received a message confirming Second Army's intention to retire to the Aisne River. This message appears to have convinced Hentsch that a general

withdrawal of the two right-wing armies was necessary and should be ordered despite Kluck's local success.* Postwar testimony provides contradictory evidence as to whether he ordered the withdrawal or merely indicated the route that a withdrawal should follow. The key point is that one hour later—at 2:00 p.m., on September 9—the First Army directed all its units to commence a withdrawal to the northeast and to re-establish contact with the Second Army.

The retreat of the First and Second German Armies ended the opening campaign of the war. It also marked a new low in despondency for Chief of Staff Moltke. Sick and dispirited, he would relinquish the direction of German operations within a week.

To their credit, the German General Staff and field commanders conducted a professional and orderly withdrawal—a very difficult operation after having come so close to victory. Even more, the withdrawal was a tribute to the capacity of the German soldier, who had marched so far, fought so hard, and persevered in spite of all the difficulties. The Allied armies were astounded that the withdrawal could be effected without a significant battle. Cavalry and aerial reconnaissance elements soon observed the columns of gray-clad soldiers moving back. The cry went up that the Germans were gone! It is easy to see how soldiers and civilians alike came to believe that divine intervention had created the "miracle of the Marne."

The Allied forces continued their cautious and uninspired pursuit. Rearguard fighting was sporadic and uneventful. It appears that the French and British commanders did not realize the great opportunity presented to them, especially after a string of disastrous battles. Consequently, they allowed the Germans to pull their right and center back into a continuous defensive line along the Aisne River. (*See Atlas Map No. 10.*) On September 11, Joffre informed the French Government of the Allied victory at "the Battle of the Marne."

The Opening Battles in Retrospect

With the failure of the Schlieffen Plan to provide Germany with a decisive victory in the West, a long war of attrition, which few prewar analysts had believed possible, became inevitable. Military professionals on both sides were confounded by their failure to foresee the lethality of technologically superior weapons that subjected both infantry and

French and British Soldiers Celebrate the Victory on the Marne

*Correlli Barnett disputes the contention that Hentsch had been given extraordinary powers. However, because of his training and close contact with the Supreme Commander, it is reasonable to assume that Hentsch's analysis and recommendations were respected by Kluck. In *Campaign of the Marne*, Sewell Tyng discusses the dominant roles of relatively junior officers, especially Hentsch and Lieutenant Colonel von Tappen, Chief of the Operations Section in Moltke's headquarters.[45]

cavalry to unacceptable loss. In addition, technological limitations in the area of transportation prevented rapid tactical movement, dealing the German timetable a severe blow. Rail lines could provide rapid strategic mobility, but the era of the gasoline engine and tactical mobility lay further in the future. The defense had regained ascendancy over the offensive form of warfare.

Lessons in tactics, strategy, generalship, and the application of technology abound in these opening battles. However, these are much clearer to the historian in the cloistered study than they were to the hard-pressed commanders and staffs who played out the war's first act. Many of these lessons had to be relearned repeatedly in the coming years.

The opening campaign proved that an imperfect plan—even an irrational one such as Plan XVII—that is modified properly in execution is superior to an excellent plan that is executed with ambivalence. The modifications of Schlieffen's plan before and during its execution insured its failure—if, in fact, it ever could have achieved its difficult goals. Perhaps the greatest lesson to be learned from an analysis of the Schlieffen Plan, however, is that the proper role of military planners is to provide political leaders with an array of options to be applied as the situation dictates.

As trench lines were gouged into the fields of France and Belgium, the realities of modern war were only beginning to be accepted by the participants. The tremendous consumption of supplies by the large field armies dwarfed prewar estimates. The horsed cavalry proved virtually useless in its traditional role of security and shock action; it would be replaced by the airplane. The air arm would become a full-fledged component of combat as the war progressed. Both sides integrated the valuable tool of radio communications into their command and control systems. However, procedures to make this new tool a reliable and secure method of supplementing other means of communication lay in the future.

The major result of the opening campaign in the West, however, was that the seemingly invincible German Army had been halted. France was saved for the moment, and had been joined by the powerful British Empire. Slowly, the power of the Allies would grow to overwhelming superiority. The seas were under the control of the Allies. The outside world was closed to the Central Powers, confirming Germany's prewar paranoia of being surrounded by hostile powers.*

To the individual soldier, hopes for a quick and glorious victory faded as the reality of brutal trench life began to impose itself.

A French Airplane Undergoes Repair

---

*At the outbreak of war, Kaiser Wilhelm wrote a minute that accused England, France, and Russia of conspiring "to fight together for [Germany's] annihilation . . . the notorious encirclement of Germany is at last an accomplished fact . . ."[46]

Notes

[1] Joachim Remak, *The Origins of World War I, 1871–1914* (New York, 1967), pp. 127–129.

[2] *Moltke's Memoirs* (Paris, 1933), pp. 19–23; Walter Gorlitz, *The Kaiser and His Court* (New York, 1959), p. 11.

[3] "Lichnowsky to the Foreign Office," 1st August 1914 in Prince Lichnowsky, *Heading for the Abyss, Reminiscences* (London, 1928), pp. 413–414.

[4] Barbara W. Tuchman, *The Guns of August* (New York, 1962), pp. 78–81. Quotation appears on p. 81.

[5] *Ibid.*, pp. 104–105.

[6] James L. Stokesbury, *A Short History of World War I* (New York, 1981), pp. 30–31; Vincent J. Esposito (ed.), *A Concise History of World War I* (New York, 1964), pp. 23–24.

[7] G.H. Perris, *The Campaign of 1914 in France and Belgium* (London, 1915), pp. 7–12.

[8] Basil H. Liddell Hart, *The Real War, 1914–1918* (Boston, 1930), pp. 54–55.

[9] "The German Request for Free Passage Through Belgium, August 2, 1914," in Louis L. Snyder (ed.), *Historic Documents of World War I* (Princeton, 1958), p. 89.

[10] Erich Ludendorff, *Ludendorff's Own Story* (2 vols.; New York, 1919), I, 38–43.

[11] Liddell Hart, *Real War,* p. 38.

[12] Frank H. Simonds, *History of the World War* (2 vols.; Garden City, 1919), I, 86–87.

[13] Esposito, *Concise History,* p. 52; Tuchman, *Guns of August,* p. 193.

[14] John Keegan, *Opening Moves: August 1914* (New York, 1971), pp. 92–98.

[15] "General Instructions No. 1," August 8, reproduced in Sewell Tyng, *The Campaign of the Marne, 1914* (New York, 1955), Appendix IV, pp. 362–364.

[16] Stokesbury, *History of World War I,* p. 56.

[17] Frederick Maurice. *Lessons of Allied Cooperation* (London, 1942), pp. 1–4.

[18] Paul Gwinn, *British Strategy and Politics, 1914–1918* (Oxford, 1965), pp. 17–19.

[19] Winston S. Churchill, *The World Crisis* (New York, 1949), p. 147.

[20] Alexander von Kluck, *The March on Paris 1914 and The Battle of the Marne* (London, 1923), pp. 21–22.

[21] Henri Isselin, *The Battle of the Marne,* trans. by Charles Connell (Garden City, N.Y., 1966), pp. 89–90.

[22] Leon Van Der Essen, *The Invasion and the War in Belgium* (London, 1917), pp. 132–134.

[23] J.E. Valluy, *La Premiere Guerre Mondiale* (Paris, 1925), pp. 40–50.

[24] Phillip Knightley, *The First Casualty* (New York, 1975), pp. 82–84.

[25] Edward Spears, *Liaison, 1914* (New York, 1968), p. 92.

[26] Joseph J.C. Joffre, *The Personal Memoirs of Joffre,* trans. by T. Bentley Mott (New York, 1932), p. 148.

[27] "Instructions Particuliere No. 10," Spears, *Liaison,* Appendix 10.

[28] Vincent J. Esposito (ed.), *The West Point Atlas of American Wars* (2 vols.; New York, 1959), II, Section 1, 6.

[29] Tuchman. *Guns of August,* p. 253.

[30] Kluck, *March on Paris,* p. 45.

[31] Arthur Conan Doyle, *The British Campaign in France and Flanders, 1914* (London, 1916), pp. 57–58.

[32] John Keegan, "Battle of the Frontiers," *History of the First World War* (London, 1971), Vol. I, No. 6, p. 146.

[33] Isselin, *Battle of the Marne,* p. 78.

[34] Tyng, *Campaign of the Marne,* pp. 67–68.

[35] Joffre, *Memoirs,* p. 78.

[36] Georges S. Blond, *The Marne* (Harrisburg, 1965), pp. 84–85.

[37] Blond, *Marne,* pp. 43–50.

[38] Robert B. Asprey, *The First Battle of the Marne* (Philadelphia, 1962), pp. 60–62; Tyng, *Campaign of the Marne,* pp. 130–131, 188–189; T. Dodson Stamps and Vincent J. Esposito (eds.), *A Short Military History of World War I* (West Point, N.Y., 1954), p. 41.

[39] Esposito, *Concise History,* p. 59. The three right-wing armies, which had entered Belguim with 16 corps, had only 11 corps in line on August 26.

[40] Tuchman, *Guns of August,* p. 393.

[41] Tyng, *Campaign of the Marne,* p. 172.

[42] *Ibid.*, pp. 204–209.

[43] Asprey, *First Battle of the Marne,* pp. 82–83.

[44] Keegan, *Opening Moves,* p. 151.

[45] Corelli Barnett, *The Swordbearers* (New York, 1964), pp. 82–92; Tyng, *Campaign of the Marne,* p. 36.

[46] C.R.M.F. Cruttwell, *A History of the Great War, 1914–1918* (Oxford, 1934), p. 66.

War in the East, 1914–1915   3

If for a space we obliterate from our minds the fighting in France and Flanders, the struggle upon the Eastern Front [was] incomparably the greatest war in history. . . . Nothing was gained by any.

Winston Churchill, *The Unknown War*

Karl Marx, the social philosopher who wished to establish Communist societies in the industrialized nations of the world, had a clear vision of the impact of modern war. He compared total war to fresh air let into a tomb. Those societies and institutions that were healthy and functional would survive and even thrive during a total war; those that were decayed from within and no longer served a useful purpose would be transformed into dust.* Although Marx predicated his vision of a new economic order on the industrialized states of Western Europe, it was in Eastern Europe, particularly in the least developed industrial states of Russia and Austria-Hungary, that his characterization of the effects of modern war would prove brutally and literally correct. The inefficient monarchies of Eastern Europe would be swept away by the winds of total war, while in Russia, an entirely new social and economic order would emerge. With the coming of peace, the maps of Eastern Europe would be redrawn along nationalistic lines, a process that would create a melange of new states.

Like the political leaders who committed their nations to war in 1914 without foreseeing the revolutionary potential of total war, military planners were unrealistic. They based their calculations on a quick, decisive clash in the West, expecting that the war in the East would play a secondary role. Even on the eve of war in July 1914, no major military power anticipated the titanic struggle that would be joined by the Russian Empire on one side and the German and Austro-Hungarian Empires on the other. The Eastern Front would match armies and situations far different from those in the West, dramatically affecting the outcome of the war and causing a reordering of world power. (*See Atlas Map No. 24a.*)

The Opposing Plans

Each of the nations had its own conception of how the war would proceed when it came. In Berlin, the German General Staff concentrated all effort and attention on the West, where they expected Count von Schlieffen's plan to decide the issue within six weeks. Despite superficial improvements in the Russian Army, the Germans were confident that the Czar's forces would be unable to mobilize, concentrate, and march into East Prussia before the French could be crushed. If it proved necessary, the German plan did call for the transfer of armies to the East on the superb German rail system to finish off the Russians in time to preclude any serious incursion of East Prussia.

In the Russian court at St. Petersburg, a new national spirit and pride in the military had largely erased the memories of its disastrous defeat in the Russo-Japanese War. An unrealistic optimism pervaded the leadership. Due, in part, to the military and economic alliance with France and the growing troubles of the ineffective Austro-Hungarian Empire, Russian military reforms and reorganization following the defeat by Japan in 1905 and the abortive revolution of that same year were, in fact, superficial. Corruption, inefficiency, and regionalism remained the chron-

---

*Marx' collaborator, Friedrich Engels, was even more prescient. In a letter to Friedrich Sorge in January 1888 he stated: "A war, on the other hand, would throw us back for years. Chauvinism would swamp everything, for it would be a fight for existence. Germany would put about five million armed men into the field. . . . there would be ten to fifteen million combatants. I should like to see how they would be fed; there would be devastation like that in the Thirty Year's War. And nothing could be settled quickly, despite the colossal fighting forces. . . . But once the first shot is fired, control ceases, the horse may bolt."[1]

**Czar Nicholas II and the Russian Commander-in-Chief,
the Grand Duke Nicholas**

ic problems of Russia. The two military advantages she had always had—a mammoth mobilization base of millions of sturdy and malleable troops* and the vastness of her territory—stood as obstacles in the path of any opponent.[2] French and Russian military planners created a self-serving myth of a "Russian steam roller" of hastily mobilized troops that by sheer momentum could sweep over any military adversary in central Europe.[3] The German General Staff had a new-found respect for Russia's Army, but still planned for only a single field army to conduct a delaying defense against any Russian incursion. They trusted that the undeveloped roads and railways in Poland[†] would retard or even stall the Russian advance until the main enemy, France, could be defeated.

Austria-Hungary, although alarmed by the improving industrial and military capacity of Russia, feared her chiefly as the source of support for Pan-Slavism. Because she encouraged the resistance of the Slavic minorities in Austria-Hungary, Russia was rightly viewed by the Hapsburgs as a direct threat to the fragile hegemony they maintained over the disparate factions of their empire.

Austria-Hungary and Russia had contingency plans[‡] for operations ranging from the Niemen River in the north to the Carpathian Mountains in the south. (*See Atlas Map No. 24b.*) The Austrian staff was dismayed by the German General Staff's fascination with Schlieffen's planned knockout blow in the West. The German concentration of forces there required economy of force and a defensive posture in the East. Schlieffen and his successors designated that the relatively weak Eighth Army (General Max von Prittwitz) and fortress troops would delay any Russian thrust into the German homeland. As the Kaiser's forces achieved success in the West, the General Staff expected to free army corps and move them by railroad into positions opposite the Polish Salient.[5] Having failed to convince the Germans to strengthen their forces in the East, Austria was torn between her commitment to oppose Russia and her need to settle once and for all the festering problem of Serbia, which had caused the war in the first place. While the Serbian front had first been situated on Austrian territory, the Austrian commander, Field Marshal Franz Conrad von Hötzendorf, also positioned four armies along the southern edge of the Polish Salient and eastern Galicia. These would conduct an offensive against the Russians, who were expected to be disposed from Brest-Litovsk southeastward to the Dniester River (Austrian Plan "R").[6] The Russian strategy, conceived under considerable French pressure, was to place the bulk of Russian forces (four armies) under a Southwest Army Group.[††] There, the armies would counter the Austrians in Galicia (Russian Plan "A"), absorbing whatever blows their opponents could deliver. Following the completion of mobilization, the Northwest Army Group (General Yakov G. Jilinsky), which consisted of the First and Second Armies, was to mount an offensive into East Prussia.[7]

During prewar combined planning conferences with the French, the Russian *Stavka* had declared that an offensive could not be mounted until at least the twentieth day after mobilization (M + 20). The French General Staff, which was advising and subsidizing the Russian Army's modern-

---

*Russia's mobilization base included a standing army of 1.3 million backed by 5 million reserves.

†In order to create a defensive barrier, the Russians had intentionally retarded the development of the transportation network in the Polish Salient. In 1914, however, they required such facilities for their own offensive intentions.[4]

‡Ironically, Austria-Hungary and Russia, the less sophisticated antagonists, had relatively flexible and realistic plans to cover contingencies. The purported leaders in military thought, Germany and France, were prisoners of single plans, regardless of the circumstances that led to war.

††Russia, the most backward of the belligerents, was nevertheless the only one to employ army groups as a command and control measure to coordinate operations.

izization, insisted that Russia be able to move with 900,000 men by M + 14. In 1913, the two allies arrived at a compromise whereby Russia agreed to move as soon after M + 15 as possible. This agreement was fraught with risk for the unsophisticated Russians. When war came, Joffre reacted to the intense pressure placed on his troops in the West by pleading with Russia to move against East Prussia even earlier than the agreed target date, Ever loyal to their ally, the Russian staff acquiesced; General Jilinsky's Northwest Army Group lurched uncertainly westward on August 13, 1914, less than two weeks after the order to mobilize and seven days prior to the more realistic prewar estimate of readiness.[8] The Russian leaders made this decision with full knowledge that while their infantry and cavalry units were nearing full strength—outnumbering the Germans almost 3 to 1—the supporting units were not yet assembled.[9] This was particularly critical since the lines of communication were in wretched condition and could not support the offensive. The opposing German and Austrian armies, while smaller, had their mobilized support base largely in place.

On August 17, the First Russian Army (General Paul V. Rennenkampf) crossed the international border into Germany. Jilinsky's orders prescribed that the Second Army (General Alexander V. Samsonov) was to keep pace with Rennenkampf's advance toward Königsberg. (*See Atlas Map No. 25.*) Samsonov was to cross the frontier in the vicinity of Soldau and pivot northwest to envelop the German Eighth Army; the entire army group was then expected to continue its march toward Berlin. The realities of geography, Russia's military ineptitude, and Germany's superior generalship would combine to foil this plan and prove the vulnerability of the Russian "steam roller."

Cossacks in Transit to East Prussia

The Tannenberg Campaign: German Superiority Is Established

Control of the Polish Salient had changed hands many times over the centuries. (*See Atlas Map No. 24b.*) German planners viewed the salient as a wedge separating and inhibiting lateral movement between East Prussia and Galicia. To the Russians, the salient was initially viewed as a vulnerable area that could not be easily defended. In the event of major German and Austrian drives from the northwest and southeast (respectively, the vicinities of Thorn and Cracow), the entire salient could easily be pinched off, thereby severing Russia's communications with the industrial centers of Warsaw, Lodz, and Ivangorod.[10] Reflecting this defensive attitude, the Russians intentionally retarded the development of the salient, hoping that any German invasion would be slowed or stalled by the poor roads, a railroad network of different gauge and limited reach, and the paucity of food and forage. This attitude prevailed prior to Russia's agreement to support French offensive plans. Consequently, when war came, the underdeveloped salient favored a Russian defense, but greatly hindered the offensive campaign that Russia now planned to launch.

Forming the northern border of the Polish Salient until it turned north near Lomja, the German-Russian (Polish) frontier ran generally between the Niemen and Narew Rivers. A few kilometers west of the frontier lay the chain of the Masurian Lakes (*See Atlas Map No. 25*), a series of freshwater obstacles running south from Angerburg to Johannisburg. Patrolled by German craft and guarded by the central fortress of Lötzen, the lakes channelized advancing armies into two avenues of approach—through the 40-mile wide Insterburg gap north of the lakes and through Russian Poland to the south. The northern gap was cut by forests, marshes, and peat bogs that delayed the movement of horses, gun carriages, and wagons. South of the lakes, the second avenue extended from Bialystok to Mlava, northwest of Warsaw, along the edge of the salient.

In 1914, the Masurian Lakes region represented a formidable barrier to movement, very much like a large rock in the center of a mountain stream that divides the stream into two parts until the obstacle has been bypassed. While circumventing the lakes to the north and south, major forces would find contact most difficult, and mutual support against a foe engaging one wing or the other would be virtually impossible.

The Initial Russian Advance

While the German advance through Belgium was gaining momentum—Liège's forts had at last fallen—Rennenkampf's army passed the frontier into East Prussia and at once brought psychological pressure to bear on Eighth Army's commander. The Second Army, the left wing of the Northwest Army Group, was still struggling toward the border east of Niedenburg. Preliminary Russian cavalry thrusts had drawn the I German Corps (General Hermann von François) and a cavalry division close to the frontier as Rennenkampf crossed. General Prittwitz, an individual of dubious military reputation who had been appointed to command the Eighth Army over Moltke's protests, endeavored to execute the planned Eastern Front strategy: Germany would trade space for time in East Prussia, while precluding decisive engagement with superior Russian forces until the Western Front had been stabilized and more troops could be spared. In tactical terms, this basic strategy translated into a series of successive delays along such defensible obstacles as the Angerapp, Alle, Passarge, and Vistula Rivers, yielding segments of East Prussia slowly and at great cost to the Russians.

Prittwitz had a difficult task at best. Although his Eighth Army was better trained, better led, better disciplined, and superior in quality of armament and communications, the Russian superiority in numbers was overwhelming. Tales of Russian brutality and disregard for property colored the rumors rife in the German ranks. The Eighth Army was sub-

General Hermann von François

ject to assault from both the east and southeast, with the likelihood that unless its commander kept his wits, his troops were in danger of being pinned against the Masurian Lakes or pushed into the fortress of Königsberg, thereby enabling the enemy to march unopposed toward Potsdam. Further, German flank security depended on the tenacity and fighting ability of the Austro-Hungarians, a significant unknown in the equation.[11] Finally, Prittwitz appreciated that his was a secondary theater, and that he could expect little assistance.

Prittwitz' problems multiplied when one of his corps commanders decided to undertake an unauthorized offensive. (*See Atlas Map No. 25.*) On August 17, the fractious but patriotic François, in utter disregard of his orders to avoid decisive engagement, threw his corps against the first three Russian corps to cross the frontier, mauling the Russian center but risking encirclement and annihilation at Stallupönen. Eighth Army headquarters was incredulous at this preemptive attack by François; Prittwitz quickly dispatched his chief of staff to order François to break off the action immediately.[12] Although the battle was indecisive militarily, the ferocity of the German assault had a marked psychological effect on Rennenkampf, heightening his sense of caution. Henceforth, he would slow the pace of First Army's advance, thereby contributing significantly to the German victories against Samsonov's Second Army in the days to come.*

As the Russian offensive unfolded, perceptive German officers detected a fatal flaw. The poor state of training in the hastily mobilized Russian divisions and the low literacy level of the peasant soldiers resulted in an inability of Russian signal troops to master the intricate encryption systems required for secure communication over the new wireless radio system. Since they were equally bereft of a good field telephone system, the Russians resorted to broadcasting instructions "in the clear," to the delight of German wireless intercept teams. The net result was that Germany's Eighth Army Headquarters and Russia's subordinates were simultaneously informed of *Stavka's* plans.

Bolstered by this knowledge and by the entreaties of the aggressive François, Prittwitz elected to attack with three corps against the Russians at Gumbinnen on the twentieth. Despite initial German success against the Russian center, Rennenkampf's forces held; by dusk, Prittwitz was faced with the choice of either withdrawing or digging in for the night preparatory to resuming the attack on the following morning. Events elsewhere would influence his decision.

Prittwitz knew that Samsonov's Second Army was tramping across the Polish Salient, but he calculated that its

---

*Rennenkampf was of German ancestry. He was also a personal and professional enemy of the Second Army Commander, Samsonov. There have been serious accusations that he either actively assisted the German side by providing information or passively allowed the enemy to capitalize on his lethargy.[13]

advance would be slow and that it could not strike his flank for several days. During his attack on Rennenkampf on August 20, however, he had been shocked to discover, through reports from aerial reconnaissance, that Samsonov's columns were approaching Mlava, the southeastern gateway to East Prussia, and advancing west of the Masurian Lakes. Moreover, he was deceived by conflicting intelligence reports into believing that yet a third Russian army was on the march. Presumably, this force could enter the German homeland and emerge at Deutsch-Eylau and Allenstein, well to the rear of Prittwitz' troops in Gumbinnen.[14]

This combination of the threat from the south and the tenuous nature of the situation in the north put Prittwitz in a state of extreme anxiety. His principal staff officers, Chief of Staff General Ernest Grünert and Lieutenant Colonel Max von Hoffman (the operations officer), advised him that the situation did not warrant drastic action and that it would be expedient to allow the situation to develop. Despite these recommendations, Prittwitz panicked and decided that a desperate move was required to avoid destruction by the combined forces of Samsonov and Rennenkampf. Thus, he rang up Moltke's Headquarters in Berlin and reported that he was ordering the Eighth Army to withdraw without delay behind the Vistula, with no guarantees that he could even hold on that line.[15]

Following his urgent call to Berlin, Prittwitz was eventually calmed by his staff and became more rational. Grünert and Hoffman demonstrated the absurdity of retreat and began to devise a plan whereby the Germans could exploit their superior lateral communications, Samsonov's inability to move rapidly, and Rennenkampf's ignorance of German strengths and dispositions. Prittwitz then consented to the operation that would become known as the "Tannenberg maneuver," and abandoned his plans for a general retreat. However, an irony resulted from his vacillation. Entranced by his staff officers' proposal, the general failed to inform them that he had already called Moltke. Thus, on the evening of the twentieth, when Prittwitz approved of the new operation, the staff did not think to advise Supreme Headquarters that the decision to retreat had been countermanded and that a coordinated German offensive was now being planned. Meanwhile, in Berlin, Moltke was ignorant of Prittwitz' change of heart and had decided to rid the Army of Prittwitz and his Chief of Staff. They were dismissed, and a new commander, General Paul von Beckendorff und Hindenburg, was recalled from retirement. A chief of staff was also chosen—the well respected and competent Major General Erich Ludendorff, newly famous for his role in the capture of Liège. Additionally, to confirm that the situation was not as grim as Prittwitz had originally stated, Moltke's staff officers bypassed the Eighth Army Headquarters and contacted their opposite numbers at corps

**Hindenburg, Ludendorff, and Hoffman
in East Prussia, 1914**

and division level on the Eastern Front to assure themselves that Prittwitz' panic was not justified.

The new commander, Hindenburg, had a good reputation as a solid commander in the Franco-Prussian War and provided a strong image of leadership. His Chief of Staff, the energetic Ludendorff, was the personification of German military genius. By virtue of the consistency of their views and mutual affection, the pair, only recently acquainted, soon came to be known as a team—Hindenburg-Ludendorff, or H-L. Arriving by train at the ancient Marienburg Fortress on August 23, they would breathe new life into the efforts of the Central Powers in the East. En route, they had already approved the concept of the southward deployment that Hoffman had initiated. Thus, the new command team entered the field, approving a plan of battle that had already been determined.

A German Offensive

The essence of the Tannenberg maneuver was to be an amalgam of mass, surprise, and economy of force. Briefly, the scheme formulated by Hoffman and sanctioned by the command team was this: their movements concealed behind the Masurian Lake region, the bulk of the German forces (I, XVII, and I Reserve Corps) were to be transported southward to join the XX Corps near the southern border of East Prussia. A small force (one cavalry division) would remain behind to slow the advance of the Russian

First Army into East Prussia. (*See Atlas Map No. 25.*) The objective was to envelop Samsonov's Second Army and defeat it quickly, before Rennenkampf could react or accelerate his progress. If this phase were successful, the German Eighth Army could reconcentrate in the Insterburg gap and defeat the Russian First Army in turn. It was a hazardous plan in which the German advantages of excellent lateral communications and well-trained forces would be balanced against Russia's numerical superiority. The high command gambled on several assumptions: that Rennenkampf would not hasten his western advance and thereby discover that only a cavalry division lay to his front; that, upon learning of Samsonov's plight, Rennenkampf could not or would not react quickly enough to come to the Second Army's relief;* that the crude state of Russian electronic communications would continue to give the Germans timely knowledge of Russian plans and dispositions; and that a rapid and bold attack in the south would catch Russian leaders by surprise. Although they would prove to be correct—or lucky—on all counts, neither Hindenburg nor Ludendorff could be certain that any of the premises would hold, thus adding to the audacity of the stroke. The decision making process, however, was not as instantaneous as many accounts might suggest.

Before the arrival of H-L in the theater, Hoffman had already issued to the corps commanders the movement plans for the envelopment of the unsuspecting Samsonov, who was then advancing along the northern edge of the Polish Salient. (Shortly, the Russians intended to swing to the

---

*Hoffman had knowledge of a fist fight that had occurred between Samsonov and Rennenkampf in the Russo-Japanese War on the station platform at Mukden. He surmised that this enmity had persisted for 10 years and that Rennenkampf would not be inclined to rush to Samsonov's assistance.[16]

**Russian Sharpshooters in Action Against
Germans in East Prussia**

north toward Allenstein in order to envelop the German Eighth Army.) On August 21, François' I Corps was to use the circuitous but excellent railroad to move from Insterburg to Marienburg and Deutsch-Eylau. It would then march southeast, taking positions on the right flank of General Friedrich von Scholtz' XX Corps by August 25. While a partial solution to Germany's problem, this maneuver could not accomplish the destruction of an entire Russian army. As the locomotives transported François' veteran troops south, Ludendorff pondered the wisdom of also sending XVII Corps (General August von Mackensen) and I Reserve (General Otto von Below) southward, as planned, to oppose the Russians at Bischofsburg. On the twenty-fourth, he opted for this bolder course, and the regiments of those two units began a forced march to the south, leaving Rennenkampf's army unattended save for the aforementioned cavalry division.

The Battle of Tannenberg

An early morning interception of Russian radio traffic indicated that Ludendorff's decision had been correct, for it disclosed that Rennenkampf intended to continue eastward at a very slow rate; indeed, he had already taken one day off on the twentieth to rest his troops. Thus, the plan of maneuver began to take shape: I Corps, supplemented by *Landwehr* troops, would be on the German right, in position for a thrust at the Russian left flank; XX Corps would slowly withdraw into the German center to lure the Russian XV and XXIII Corps deeper northeastward in search of a quick and easy victory; I Reserve and XVII Corps would descend from the north, the latter sideslipping to the east to form the German left, thus creating an inverted "U" around Samsonov's army. In the next phase, as opportunity permitted, the German flank units would maneuver to encircle the Russians and annihilate them. An attack was ordered by Ludendorff for August 26, when all units would be in position. (*See Atlas Map No. 26.*)

After François had delayed the initial assault—again in violation of written orders—to permit his artillery to detrain and move into position, I Corps began the action. Despite the delay, François took Seeben, the corps' objective, by 1:00 p.m. Although ordered to proceed eastward that day and take Usdau, he again defied his superiors and delayed the assault until the twenty-seventh,* allowing his corps time to consolidate. Scholtz' XX Corps held its own on the twenty-sixth, when it hesitantly committed only one division. This tentative maneuver caused Scholtz to miss an

---

*In his account of the battle, Hoffman suggests that this was a wise decision. Had the ordered attack failed, Samsonov could have extricated his army, nullifying the German victory of the ensuing days.[17]

opportunity to take the advancing Russian XV Corps in the flank. To the north, I Reserve and XVII Corps sent Samsonov's VI Corps fleeing southeastward, and moved ominously toward the Russian XIII Corps. Although H-L had now cast the die, Moltke was apprehensive about the outcome and worried that Rennenkampf would turn southwest behind the lakes. He therefore ordered Colonel von Tappen to telephone Ludendorff at his field headquarters, offering reinforcements from the Western Front. Ludendorff protested that added troops were not required and that, if sent, would arrive too late. In any event, Moltke insisted that the transfer take place. Thus, three corps were withdrawn from the German right wing in France, depriving it of vital combat power at a critical moment. Nor did these three corps participate in the Battle of Tannenberg.

Acting in accordance with his own perception of the situation, François captured Usdau on August 27. This resulted in a penetration of the Russian left and isolated the I Corps from its flank corps, the XXIII, which was positioned west of Niedenburg. François then moved part of his corps south against Samsonov's I Corps and punished its remnants, which were falling back from Soldau. On the left, the Russian VI Corps was fleeing eastward ahead of Mackensen's XVII Corps, which now turned to the southeast. Although victory was still not assured, the net was closing around the Russian center. Only the situation in Scholtz' sector remained in doubt.

Ludendorff ordered François to send a division north to bolster the XX Corps and, for the fourth time in as many weeks, François chose to disregard his superior's instructions. Without an acknowledgment or explanation, François ordered his troops due east toward Niedenburg on the twenty-eighth. Scholtz, left to his own devices, spent the day plugging holes wherever Russian attacks threatened to overrun his positions.

Meanwhile, in Russian Second Army Headquarters, Samsonov was unaware that his army was on the brink of disaster. On August 27, he ordered that an attack to the northwest be launched the next day. The friction of war and poor communications blinded him to the fact that both of his flank corps (I and VI) had been so roughly handled that any attack was doomed from its inception.

August 28 was the day of decision. (*See Atlas Map No. 27.*) Scholtz' XX Corps held its ground in front of the limited Russian advance. In the afternoon, the Germans struck the Russian XXIII Corps flank, which disintegrated; its commander fled in terror. The annihilation of the corps took place just east of the tiny village of Frankenau. François, mesmerized by success, drove stolidly onward toward Niedenburg. Although he did divert one division toward Lahna, his main course of movement showed that he had again disregarded two orders from army headquarters to

Russians Surrender During the Battle of Tannenberg, 1914

swing northeastward to assist XX Corps. As the army staff's perception of the Russian plight became clearer, François' orders were changed, directing him to continue toward Niedenburg exactly as he was doing. To the east, I Reserve and XVII Corps were able to provide little support as, to evade pursuit of the fleeing Russian VI Corps, they were countermarched by Ludendorff back toward Allenstein and Passenheim, respectively. Despite the grumbling in the ranks that resulted from these frequent changes in orders, two German corps were now in the rear of the Russian XIII Corps, which was endeavoring to move southwest to link up with the collapsing XV Corps; steadily, Scholtz and François tightened the noose. As Cyril Falls observed in *The Great War*, "It was like herding stock into a corral, and the head cowboy was François."[18]

The twenty-ninth and thirtieth were almost anticlimactic days. Inept generalship, fatigue, despair, and communications failures combined to preclude vigorous Russian counteraction. The Russian soldiers, in a state of stupor, stood in their hastily prepared positions, awaiting their fate—death or capture. One 15-kilometer-wide escape alley was found along the swift-running Omulev River in the direction of Ostrolenka. However, this corridor could not accommodate all the transports and soldiers endeavoring to make the passage, and many men died along the roadside. From Usdau to Ortelsburg—wherever Russians moved, in seven of the eight principal compass points—they found exultant Germans with rifles poised. Artillery rounds slammed every road intersection with despairing regularity. The three Russian interior corps (XV, XXIII, and XIII) were literally destroyed as the Russian Second Army died in the fastnesses of the trans-border region. General N.N. Martos, Commander of the XV Corps, was taken prisoner, as was the commander of the XIII Corps. Samsonov, retreating with his staff, found the sheer weight of responsibility for the debacle too much to bear. In a nighttime tragedy near a small rural village, he took unannounced leave of his subordinates and ended his life with a pistol shot. A replay of Hannibal's Cannae had materialized in East Prussia.

By conservative estimates, the Germans captured 500 guns and took between 55,000 and 75,000 prisoners, having left 70,000 Russians dead in the ditches and forests of Tannenberg.* The Germans lost from 10,000 to 15,000 men. There was little time for resting on laurels, however; Rennenkampf's army was still in East Prussia, and could at any moment move on Königsberg or the Passarge crossings.

During the Tannenberg encirclement, Rennenkampf had inched his First Army westward through the Angerburg gap, unaware that he was opposed only by a cavalry screen. Nor was he aware that trains arriving from France and Germany were disgorging fresh German troops eager for a chance to do battle. By the end of the Tannenberg battle, the Eighth Army had been augmented by the XI Corps, the Guard Reserve Corps, and the 8th Cavalry Division. Russian troop strength in the northwest had been reduced by about 50 percent, while German strength had been increased by about the same amount. It was a far more formidable and inspired army that turned on Rennenkampf than had moved on Samsonov two weeks earlier. The Russians still held the numerical edge (24 versus 16 divisions), but this factor had been discounted by events on the battlefield.

The outcome was almost predictable. Jolted by the news of the disaster, Rennenkampf abandoned any previous plan he may have had for a vigorous advance into Prussia and began to dig in. On the German side, morale soared as a consequence of the great victory over Samsonov's army. Lax Russian communications security continued to provide the Germans with all the information that H-L needed to finalize the Eighth Army plan for a repetition of the success in the south. German enthusiasm was moderated, however, by the knowledge that the Austro-Hungarians had suffered alarming reverses in Galicia and Serbia. Conrad pleaded for German assistance in the form of a thrust toward Warsaw to draw off Russian strength south of the Polish Salient, but the Germans demurred for the time being, seeing Rennenkampf as the most immediate threat. Still, Hindenburg was fearful for his own right flank as he moved northwestward against the Russian First Army.

Rennenkampf anchored his army along strong natural obstacles, rivers in the north and the Masurian Lakes in the south. (*See Atlas Map No. 28.*) The German scheme of maneuver called for a wide envelopment of the Russian southern flank, while holding attacks pinned the majority of Rennenkampf's divisions in place. Interestingly, the bulk of the German divisions were committed to the secondary (holding) mission, while H-L assigned two of the most aggressive German commanders (Mackensen and François) the enveloping mission. Their two corps were to sally forth from the southern lakes region south of the fortress of Lötzen. Moving in a wide sweep to the northeast, and then to the north, they would strike behind Rennenkampf's army so as to sever the roads leading to Vilna.

The first action following the German advance occurred on September 7, when one of François' divisions scattered a Russian force at Bialla. By the ninth, the Germans were pressing all along the front. In the center, the Russians battled them to a standstill; but Rennenkampf, noting that his left flank was in danger, elected to initiate a withdrawal. By September 13, he had fallen back to the Russian border, thereby restoring the situation essentially to what it had been at the initiation of the advance into East Prussia a month earlier. The month's campaigning cost the Russian First Army 145,000 men and 200 guns. Estimates of German losses in this First Battle of the Masurian Lakes have ranged from 10,000 to 30,000 men.[19]

Prussia had been cleared of Russian forces, the First Army had experienced very heavy losses, and the Second Army had been destroyed and would not be reconstituted for many months. The Czar could replace the private soldiers, but not the trained officers and non commissioned officers. Two great victories in as many weeks buoyed Germany's confidence in its Eastern Front forces and served to offset the disquieting bulletins of Moltke's failures in the Marne battles. H-L had established a reputation for success that would be used by the German state to mask stalemate elsewhere.

Russian failures at Tannenberg and Masuria were not entirely due to the incompetence of the field commanders. Rennenkampf and Samsonov's tactical mistakes were equaled by the strategic blunders of Marshal Jilinsky, commander of the Northwest Army Group. In response to the urgings of the French for an early offensive, Jilinsky had not counseled his superior, Grand Duke Nicholas, to defer all movements until mobilization was complete and the logistical base established for a large-scale maneuver. Further, he had directed that two large armies approach East Prussia in a poorly coordinated fashion, virtually isolated from each other by restrictive terrain obstacles. He had compounded Samsonov's problems by urging too rapid an approach march over marginally trafficable terrain. His arbitrary orders had worn down Samsonov's troops, who had to undertake sustained combat against fresher German forces.[20] Finally, his intelligence and communications networks had been so poor that he was unaware of the oppor-

---

*The battlefield of Tannenberg was so named by Hindenburg in his dispatches to the Kaiser. Tannenberg was selected as the official name of the campaign to give it historical significance. In 1410, Polish and Ruthenian armies had defeated the German Order of Teutonic Knights in a pitched battle near the same area.

tunity that arose between August 26 and August 30 to push Rennenkampf's army forward to the southwest. This maneuver would have foreclosed the German action, possibly saving the bulk of Second Army and forcing the Germans to separate their forces.

In September 1914, soldiers in the German Eighth Army could breathe easier. To the southeast, however, other Russian armies were inflicting grievous losses on the armies of the Austro-Hungarian Empire.

Operations in Galicia, 1914

From the Austro-Hungarian viewpoint, the Eastern Front was of secondary importance. Vienna's first concern was to assault and punish the recalcitrant Serbs. After that, the bulk of the Empire's combat power could be employed against adversaries who ranked lower on Austria's scale of priorities: Italy, Rumania, and Russia. Despite Vienna's immediate concern, however, Conrad appreciated the ominous threat to the Empire presented by Russian armies surging across the Vistula. For this reason, he had hoped that the German effort in the East would be greater and more closely coordinated with that of Austria. When these supportive efforts failed to materialize, Conrad had to deal with Russia largely alone, never quite being able to concentrate his force on either front (Serbia or Galicia).

The Austrian Situation

Initially, Conrad activated the Dual Monarchy's Plan B, which called for the launching of three armies across the Danube and Save Rivers against Serbia. (*See Atlas Map No. 24b.*) Under this plan, three additional armies in Galicia were to face eastward in position to defend against a Russian offensive against Austria. However, the abysmal failure of the first Austrian invasion of Serbia, the surprise early Russian advance into East Prussia, the decision of Italy and Rumania not to enter the war on the side of the Central Powers, and the assembly of large Russian forces between Lublin and the Dniester, all convinced Conrad that Plan B had to be abandoned in favor of Plan R. This plan required the transfer of one army from the Serbian front to Galicia. There were additional factors bearing on this critical decision to go on the offensive in Galicia. First, the depth of defensible terrain north of the Carpathian Mountains was shallow, and it would be practical to increase maneuver room for future operations. Second, the Austrians wanted to regain prestige following the Empire's humiliating defeat by the Serbs. Finally, Conrad was probably a victim of the same weakness that affected the Czar and his Commander-in-Chief, the Grand Duke

Field Marshal Conrad von Hötzendorf

Nicholas of Russia—he wanted to be a good ally. By undertaking an offensive against the Russians, he hoped to draw a considerable amount of Russian attention and strength to the southeast, thus relieving pressure on East Prussia. If the Austrians were successful, Germany could hold that region with the modest Eighth Army, thereby enhancing German chances of success on the Western Front.

By contemporary European military standards, the Austrian Army should have given a better account of itself than it did. Modeled along German lines, it had a nice balance among the combat arms of infantry, cavalry, and artillery. The Austrian Skoda armament plants in Pilsen were as efficient as the German Krupp works. In fact, the Austrians provided a substantial number of the heavy howitzers and mortars to the Germans on the Western Front. Austrian railway construction units, hospitals, and signal and pioneer companies were organized, trained, and mobilized. There was also a rudimentary air force, and the Austrian Navy was capable of providing considerable gunfire and limited amphibious support.

While not immediately obvious, it became evident during the first Austrian clashes with the Serbians that national diversity was the fundamental weakness of the Austrian Army. There was a plethora of ethnic groupings—over a dozen were incorporated in the armed forces.[21] The pluralism of the Austro-Hungarian state was a decisive factor in both political and social areas, and seriously affected the Army's operational planning. While German units from Prussia and Bavaria were different in some ways, they were literate and had ethnically similar backgrounds. The linguistic and cultural diversities of Austria, however, rendered command and control extremely difficult. The social and cultural rivalries, and the resulting political conflicts, were extremely debilitating to a united military effort. There was innate hostility between Teuton and Slav, while the Magyars despised the Rumanians. Slovenes, Serbs, Croats, and Poles constituted the bulk of the forces, but most of the command positions went to persons of German ancestry, and German was the language of command.

The superficiality of the training that the officer corps received resulted in another deficiency. Although there were officer training schools, the emphasis was on theory rather than practice. Austrian maneuvers in prewar years often consisted more of parades for the Emperor's benefit than of realistic exercises in combat training. The war game, terrain ride, and rigid training schedule of the German *Kriegsakademie* were not incorporated into the programs of Austrian service schools. As in some other monarchial armies, military promotion was more often based on birthright than ability. Innovation by junior officers and non commissioned officers was suppressed by the smug apathy and conservatism that permeated the senior ranks and imperial court.

Finally, the link that tied Austria to Germany was politically weak. Still smarting from his defeat at the hands of the Prussians in 1866, Emperor Franz Joseph was no Germanophile. The constant martial warnings of Conrad, however, had kept the pot simmering and worn down the old Emperor's resistance to Kaiser Wilhelm. Throughout his long reign, Franz Joseph had spent much of his time and energy holding his empire together in defiance of internal and external pressures that threatened to rend it asunder. It was Conrad, the late Franz Ferdinand, and Berchtold, the Austrian foreign minister, who had bound Austria to Germany. A younger emperor might have fended off the insistent saber rattling of his subordinates and avoided war. But Franz Joseph, two years from death, lacked the energy to withstand the pressure.

Russian Victory in Galicia

Operations in Galicia, which initially were characterized by an offensive esprit on both sides, began as one large meeting engagement all along the frontier.* Expecting the Austrians to attack due east from fortress Lemberg (*See Atlas Map No. 28*), General Nikolai Ivanov, the Russian Southwest Army Group Commander, had positioned his forces in depth to absorb an initial Austrian blow between Dubno and Proskurov. His Third and Eighth Armies would defend

---

*An offensive operation is termed a meeting engagement when opposing forces move to contact and engage before either side can adequately plan to attack or defend.

against the Austrian attack, while two other armies, the Fourth and Fifth, would strike due south to position themselves between the attacking Austrians and Cracow, taking, in turn, the key Austrian fortresses of Przemysl and Lemberg. If this maneuver proved successful, the Austrian forces would be isolated from their bases and vulnerable to destruction. Assuming their destruction, the reunited four Russian armies would then clear the Carpathian passes leading to Budapest and Vienna.

Conrad's plan, however, did not conform to Ivanov's estimate of Austrian intentions. On August 23, the Austrian main attack was launched by the First and Fourth Armies. Moving from positions west of Lemberg to the northeast, this main effort effected a head-on strike against Russia's Fourth and Fifth Armies, the encircling wing in the Russian plan. Thus, it caught them poised for their own strike southward. Meanwhile, rather than advancing eastward, the Austrian right-flank armies adopted a defensive posture; this confounded the *Stavka,* which had planned for the Russian left opposing them to be on the defensive. As the next days' actions unfolded, the situation was analagous to a revolving door, with the Austrians making limited gains in the northwest while the Russians seized the initiative in the south and pushed back the Austrian right.

This period, from August 23 to September 26, constituted the First Galician Campaign, and chronologically unfolded in this fashion:

August 23 to 25: The Battle of Krasnik, a clash between the Austrian First Army and the Russian Fourth Army, resulted not only in an Austrian victory but in the relief of the Russian Fourth Army commander. To halt the Austrian advance, Ivanov directed the Fifth Army to wheel south and west to strike the Austrian First Army's flank; in the meantime, he urged the Eighth and Third Armies, north of the Dniester River, to move forward against the Austrian Third Army.

August 26 to 30: This period comprised days of success and failure for both sides. To the northeast, the Russian Fifth Army, in response to the order from Ivanov, was maneuvering when the Austrian Fourth Army slammed into the flank of the Russians and gained initial success in the opening action of the Battle of Komarov. The battle then degenerated into a four-day soldiers' battle, with the Russians experiencing increasingly greater losses each day. On the southern flank, the Russian Third and Eighth Armies, gathering momentum, barreled into the weak Austrian right (Kovess Group and Third Army) in the Battle of Gnila-Lipa. Despite the respite offered by a two-day Russian halt caused by inadequate roads, the Austrian Third Army Commander could not unify his separated units in time to dig in and stop the overpowering Russian advance.

August 31 to September 11: The Austrian Fourth Army Commander attempted a double envelopment of the Russian Fifth Army, but soon became a victim of friction of war. Each of his enveloping flank corps commanders acted not upon his orders, but upon erroneous information. Fearing that his corps was about to be enveloped by the Russians, each of these corps commanders ordered a withdrawal. This wholly negated the effects of the Austrian Fourth Army's assault upon the Russian Fourth Army and left the Austrian First Army well forward and isolated, with only light forces on the flank. In the south, the Russian advance had proceeded westward, driving the Austrian Third Army before it. By September 2, the Austrian line was west of Lemberg, and that fortress was in Russian hands. The two fronts were becoming commingled.

The Russian drive now threatened the rear of the Austrian Fourth Army. Conrad accordingly directed the Fourth to break contact with the Russian Fifth Army and turn about and attack the Russian Third Army. This, it was hoped, would relieve pressure on the Austrian Third Army, which was now falling back on Przemysl. On September 5, that encounter occurred in the Battle of Rava-Russka. In the northwest, the Austrian First Army was still pressuring the Russian Fourth Army. However, with the Austrian Fourth Army's about-face, a 40-mile gap had opened between the two left-flank Austrian armies; immediately, the Russian Fifth Army pushed into the gap. The Austrian Fourth Army managed to turn eastward in the face of the advancing Russian Third, while, in the south, the Russian Eighth Army continued to pound at the disintegrating Austrian Third Army. As the success of the Russian Fifth Army became apparent, Conrad ordered a general withdrawal.

September 12 to 26: The 100-mile withdrawal was generally orderly. It was halted about 50 miles east of Cracow on the Dunajec River, leaving the Austrian forces occupying a narrow corridor between the Vistula and the Carpathians. The Russian pursuit was slow and tentative; otherwise, there might have been a desperate struggle for the passes to the interior of Austria-Hungary.

Although badly battered, the Austrian armies were still intact. Almost all of Galicia was in Russian hands, except for the fortress of Przemysl, which had been invested but was still holding. Austrian morale was at a low point because the first offensive against the Russians had achieved the same abysmal results as had the offensive against Serbia. From the German viewpoint, Silesia was now vulnerable to invasion by Russian armies. (*See Atlas Map No. 28.*) This possibility, coupled with the serious situation on the Austrian front in Galicia, led the new German Chief of Staff, General Erich von Falkenhayn, to conclude that Germany must reinforce its ally. Since the only immediate source of troops was in his theater, Hindenburg, who agreed

with Falkenhayn's assessment, created the Ninth Army from units withdrawn from the Eighth. In a large-scale movement involving 750 trains, he then shifted the new army to the vicinity of Chenstokhov.

Vast Space for Maneuver in the East, 1914 to 1915

On September 22, while the German Ninth Army was en route to its designated assembly area, the *Stavka* decided to reinforce success in Galicia by launching an offensive from the Polish Salient into Silesia. (*See Atlas Map No. 29.*) First, however, the Grand Duke Nicholas had to realign his armies. Realignment was needed to relieve the crowded conditions in Galicia, where logistical difficulties were mounting; to strengthen the Northwest Army Group; and to build up sufficient forces in the center to drive on Breslau-Glogau-Posen. This adjustment was in its early stages when, on September 28, Hindenburg's Ninth Army launched its offensive—a drive designed to seize crossings over the Vistula from Warsaw to the San River.

The Campaign of Lodz

The German offensive, which was supported by Conrad's forces in the south, reached the line of the Vistula by October 9, but then slowed against stiffening resistance. Although in possession of a captured Russian order that revealed the *Stavka's* plan for the invasion of Silesia, Hindenburg continued to push into the teeth of the buildup. After reaching a point 12 miles from Warsaw, he recognized that his army was in danger of being enveloped from the northwest. Finally, on October 17, he ordered a withdrawal and the execution of a meticulously prepared demolition plan that was designed to impede Russian pursuit. On November 1, back on the line from which the offensive had been launched, Hindenburg faced the bleak prospect of defending against four Russian armies that were preparing to move on Silesia. He could not expect much help from the Austrians, who had by then also withdrawn back to the initial line.

Hindenburg pondered further strategy to prevent the encirclement of any of his forces and to halt a Russian drive into mineral-rich Silesia. Upon the advice of the brilliant Colonel Hoffman, Hindenburg adopted a maneuver similar to that used at Tannenberg. He elected to move the Ninth Army surreptitiously to the northern tip of the Polish Salient and then strike the enemy's flank as he drove for the Silesian frontier. (*See Atlas Map No. 29.*) By mutual agreement with

Conrad, the Austrian Second Army would move from the Carpathians to fill the gap left by the departing Germans in the vicinity of Noworadomsk. This decision was made on November 3, two days after Falkenhayn had designated Hindenburg Commander-in-Chief of the Eastern Front. The German Chief of Staff had come to recognize that the complexities of exercising command over nine armies on two fronts were creating an unmanageable situation. With this realignment of command responsibility, Hindenburg turned over command of the Eighth and Ninth Armies to Below and Mackensen, respectively. Then, between November 4 and 10, the efficient Germans completed the movement of the Ninth Army. Mackensen's army, buffered by fortress troops stripped from Silesian cities, was now ready to strike between the Russian First and Second Armies, which were confidently advancing with the mission of protecting the northern flank of the Russian main attack.

What followed was the campaign that culminated in the Battle of Lodz. It commenced on November 11 and continued until December 6, when the Russians evacuated Lodz and abandoned their plans to invade Silesia for that year. (*See Atlas Map No. 29.*) Combat was characterized by a series of slugfests between small units, encirclements, daring escapes, night marches, and pitched battles in the snow. While a victory was claimed by the Germans, Lodz was at best a tactical standoff. Moreover, although the efficacy of German reserve formations was clearly demonstrated, there was a lack of the precise execution that had been demonstrated at Tannenberg. Strategically, however, the battle was a German victory, since the Russians were forced to abandon their plans to invade Silesia. At year's end, the German Army in the East could boast of several accomplishments. It had halted and reversed three Russian invasions; although greatly outnumbered, it had demonstrated superior organizational, tactical, and logistical skills; and it had proved itself master of the battlefield terrain, demonstrating strategic and tactical mobility over vast spaces that enabled its numerically inferior units to outmaneuver and outfight the Russians.

Taking Stock of the Situation

As 1914 ended, several situations were becoming apparent in German military circles. First, the Schlieffen-Moltke strategy, which had been designed to achieve a quick victory, had undergone an obvious change. The descent from mobile to trench warfare and the parity in combat power on the Western Front gave considerable credibility to a growing number of general staff officers who now believed that victory might come first on the Eastern Front rather than in France. The vastness of Russian Poland and Galicia fur-

nished maneuver room unavailable in Flanders and the Vosges Mountains. Additionally, the Russian High Command seemed to disregard any of the obvious limitations of warfare. They repeatedly ordered their armies forward in open order against prepared positions, with no concern for the attendant human sacrifice. When the Germans were on the offensive, there was little evidence that Russian commanders had learned much about defensive tactics and procedures, despite the German example. Almost like little children, the simple Russian peasant soldiers attacked in the face of superior firepower with predictably dire results.

Considering these factors, a growing number of senior officers in the German Army—the so-called "Easterners"—believed that the main strategic effort should be launched across the Vistula to knock Russia out of the war. The fact that the majority of high commanders remained "Westerners" led to a schism in the General Staff Corps. On the one hand, Falkenhayn, the army commanders on the Western Front, and key general staff officers wanted the East to remain a secondary theater. In contrast, Hindenburg, Ludendorff, Hoffman, and Mackensen argued that Russian tactics were unlikely to change, and that if more German forces were committed in the East, the Russian Army would continue to hurl itself in poorly planned and executed attacks that would eventually result in self-destruction. Reinforcing his arguments with fresh victories, Hindenburg prevailed over Falkenhayn. When the Kaiser agreed that offensive success in 1915 appeared most promising in the East, Falkenhayn was told to make that the theater of decision.[22]

Another important influence on German thinking in 1915 was the Austrian defeat in Galicia. At the beginning of the year, the Austrian offensive had failed. Russian counterthrusts had laid waste to Galicia, which was now almost devoid of Austrian forces; only Przemysl remained invested. The armies of the Dual Monarchy had been pushed back into the Carpathian Mountain passes. The Austrian debacles in Serbia and Galicia, the latter of which required reinforcement by German forces, led to Germany's growing disenchantment with her Austrian ally. Coalition with Vienna was producing more debits than credits. While it appeared necessary to continue to shore up Austrian positions in the south to prevent catastrophe, the German General Staff increasingly desired that Conrad's armies carry a greater share of the war effort.

For the Russians, the outlook was mixed. Their armies in the south were clearing a way to the Carpathian passes in winter warfare and appeared capable of eventually thrusting toward Vienna. In East Prussia and Poland, however, the outcome of past operations led the *Stavka* to believe that those areas would be unproductive in the immediate future. The penalties of inadequate prewar planning and a hasty mobilization were being levied upon the Army. Moreover,

Russian Reinforcements Move to the Front

the shortage of rifles and small arms ammunition was keenly felt; indeed, shoulder weapons were in such short supply that certain leaders proposed arming infantry units with long-handled axes![23] The paucity of artillery ammunition at the war's opening had been exacerbated by losses, expenditures that were considerably heavier than originally estimated, and a poor distribution system. In some divisions, the rate of supply was only four rounds per battery per day.[24] The best of the experienced junior officers and non commissioned officers had perished at Tannenberg, Lodz, and Lemberg. Motor vehicles and aircraft, never available in abundance, became fewer through attrition in combat and poor maintenance. Still, a strong loyalty to Mother Russia underlay reasonably high troop morale, and the Russian masses in the heartland continued to provide replacements to fill the ranks of the battalions that had been decimated by the Germans. The Czar's formations were battered, but not yet broken.

Winter Campaigning at Both Ends of the Front

The preparatory moves in 1915 were highlighted by German organizational and troop changes. To support an Austrian counteroffensive that was designed to relieve a Russian threat of invasion through the Carpathians, Falkenhayn directed the formation of the Southern Army. Commanded by General Alexander von Linsingen, this force was to operate with the Austrians. Fearing that Russia would again advance into East Prussia, Hindenburg formed yet another army, the Tenth, using four corps that had recently arrived in the theater. This army was positioned on Hindenburg's left wing, near Tilsit.

In terms of the overall German strategy for the war, schism in the high command was making itself felt. In response to a plea from Conrad, Falkenhayn directed that the Central Powers' main effort be made in the south, while Hindenburg argued that a decisive victory could be achieved

**General Aleksiei A. Brusilov, the Best
of the Russian Commanders**

in the north against the Russian Tenth Army, which had commenced a probe into East Prussia. Coincidentally, the Russians were themselves creating a new Twelfth Army that, teamed with the Tenth, might be able to seize East Prussia. Consistent with the poor quality of their intelligence operations, the *Stavka* was not aware that Hindenburg had formed a new army east of Königsberg.

The Austro-German Carpathian counteroffensive was a failure. Unable to gain the momentum to force the Russians to retreat, the Austro-German force fought for the snowy passes from January through March. General Aleksiei A. Brusilov, perhaps the best of the Russian field commanders, tried to pull his army forward, although Austrian tenacity in the mountains and the notoriously poor Russian logistics system prevented his entry onto the Hungarian plain. For their part, the Austrians sought to relieve beleaguered Przemysl, which grew weaker daily as the effects of the Russian investment became more acute. It finally capitulated on March 18. The surrender of Przemysl removed most of the incentive for Austria to continue frontal assaults through the passes to relieve the fortress. This, in turn, permitted her to concentrate forces on the Hungarian plains, thereby deterring a Russian

invasion. Exhausted by the rigors of winter combat in mountains, both sides settled into a stalemate wherein infantrymen glowered at each other from snow-covered entrenchments and exchanged an occasional shot. Thus ended Conrad and Falkenhayn's inglorious Carpathian offensive.

In the north, H-L were preparing to justify their recommendation that decisive results were to be found there, rather than in the Carpathians. Again, around the Masurian Lakes (*See Atlas Map No. 30*), another planned double envelopment on the model of the Battle of Cannae* was in the planning stages.

Using the Ninth Army east of Warsaw in a ruse to divert Russian attention to that sector, the Germans undertook the first experiment in gas warfare on January 31, 1915. The gas artillery shells, of which 18,000 were fired, had no apparent effect on the soldiers in the Russian trenches. Presumably, the frigid temperatures nullified the physical effects of the gas. The artillery attack, however, did have the secondary effect of drawing Russian attention away from the Insterburg area, thus permitting the Eighth and Ninth Armies to ccmplete their preparations in relative secrecy.

On February 7, the offensive opened, with the Eighth Army immediately achieving success. A day later, the Tenth Army attacked in the meanest of winter weather encountered in any campaign of the war. The heavy snow and freezing temperatures made movement difficult, resulting in isolated troops and uncoordinated action. Artillery support was sporadic on both sides due to the difficulty of displacing artillery under the wintry conditions. Nevertheless, the weather and the initiative favored the Germans, who took a series of objectives approximately in keeping with their tactical timetable.

The Tenth Army reached Stallupönen on February 11; Lyck fell to the Eighth Army on the fourteenth. The axis of advance was littered with abandoned Russian guns and wagons. Still, the Russian Tenth Army evaded encirclement, slipping to the southeast toward the Augustów Forest. A sudden thaw turned the Bobr River lowlands into a sea of mud, denying entry to the Eighth Army. This prevented further advance and saved the Russians from annihilation in the nearly trackless forest. While most of the Russian survivors escaped to the east and south of the forest, the Germans managed to isolate the XX Corps and practically destroy it. Besides those Russians missing or killed in action, about 60,000 were taken prisoner. The Russian Tenth Army had suffered the same fate as the First and Second before it.

---

*Throughout World War I, German professional thought concentrated on the double envelopment. Many tacticians referred to this maneuver in their writings and memoirs. An obvious reason was Schlieffen's prewar treatise, *Cannae Studies*. This examination of the classic battle of annihilation and its relation to rapid and decisive victory was popular throughout the army's high command.

In March, the Germans, now inside Russian territory, reverted to the defensive north and west of Augustów. The German defense of this new line against a Russian counterattack provided the capstone for the entire operation. Although the whole winter campaign in the north was another brilliant tactical victory, in a strategic sense, the Second Masurian Campaign was not significant. Russia was still very much in the war.[25]

The Central Powers Press Their Advantage in the East

The spring (March-April) of 1915 witnessed several events that were to influence German strategy in the East and, ultimately, the outcome of the war. First, the continued Russian presence in the Carpathians forced Conrad to seek a new solution following the failure of his January offensive. Second, it appeared likely that Italy would abandon its neutral posture and enter the war on the side of the Triple Entente. This development would require a further dilution of Austrian strength to permit the manning of a third front. Without strong assistance from Germany, Austria appeared incapable of regaining Galicia. Finally, despite the severe defeat that she had suffered in the Second Masurian Campaign, Russia had moved the newly formed Twelfth Army against Memel and Courland, the former of which was located just inside the German boundary on the Baltic. While these areas were not strategically significant, Russia's incessant probes into East Prussia clearly demonstrated that the threat to German soil could only be ended by pushing the Russian Army far to the east. The combination of these factors led H-L to the conclusion that a general offensive would be in order for the summer campaign. Such an offensive, it was hoped, would rid the Carpathians of Russians and restore the buffer territory of Galicia to the Dual Monarchy. It would also deliver Prussia from the continuing fear of "hordes of Cossacks" and guarantee an advantageous tactical situation to Germany by driving the Russians from the Polish Salient.

As might have been expected, Falkenhayn and Hindenburg proposed conflicting plans for the summer campaign, as they engaged in another round of strategic jousting. While the Chief of Staff had reluctantly accepted the thesis that the Eastern Front was, for the moment, paramount, he was more sensitive to the problems of his ally than was Hindenburg. Conrad favored a penetration launched across the Dunajec River toward Przemysl and Lemberg to force the Russians to leave the Carpathians. H-L, still the proponents of offensives to first secure the frontiers of Prussia, rather than Austria, counseled Falkenhayn to agree to a deep thrust into Russia proper toward Kovno and Vilna.

The advance would then turn south and trap the Russian Second and Tenth Armies, which were positioned farther west. This, they argued, would not only impose the greatest number of casualties on the entrapped Russians, but would also force the Russians out of the Carpathians. Despite Hoffman's planning skills and Ludendorff's persuasiveness, Falkenhayn sided with Conrad and directed that the main effort be made in Galicia. The H-L plan for the north was relegated to the status of a minor clearing operation.

To assist the Austrian offensive, Falkenhayn activated the Eleventh Army, appointing Mackensen as its commander. By stripping infantry battalions and artillery pieces and crews from Western Front divisions, he was able to provide the Eleventh Army with ten infantry divisions and one cavalry division. This new army, along with the Fourth and Third Austrian Armies on either flank, gave the Central Powers considerable combat power in the offensive sector between the towns of Gorlice and Tarnow, 60 miles due west of Przemysl. Across the line, the Russian Fourth, Third, Eighth, and Eleventh Armies were positioned from north to south to counter the assault. (*See Atlas Map No. 31.*)

From April 27, when the German Tenth Army far to the north launched a diversionary attack into Lithuania, until the Germans arbitrarily called off the offensive in September, it appeared that the Central Powers could do no wrong. Whether by accident or design, through tactical virtuosity or as a result of Russian blunders, the Austro-German offensive achieved remarkable success.

On May 2, under Mackensen's operational control, the German Eleventh and Austrian Fourth Armies seized Tarnow, the first objective. They used the tactic of first creating a gap in the defenses with artillery fire and initial assault waves, then pouring reinforcements through the hole, and finally widening the shoulders of the penetration. The stunned Russian High Command appeared unable to react and did not reinforce the Third Army, in whose zone the penetration had been made. The remnants of this army fell back in disorder on Przemysl, with the Austro-Germans in pursuit. Dogging the fleeing Russians, the Central Powers' armies reached the San River on May 15 and gazed across at Przemysl. The fortress city was poorly defended; by early June, it had been retaken by the Austro-German force, which also captured Lemberg on June 22. The Russian armies, again trading men and space for time, fell back to the Bug River. The Carpathians were now cleared, and Galicia had been liberated.

The continuing strategic debate was now renewed between Conrad, Falkenhayn, and Hindenburg. Conrad implored Falkenhayn to continue the successful offensive. For his part, the German Chief of Staff believed that the offensive had accomplished its purposes and that the line should be stabilized east of Lemberg. From East Prussia, H-L again raised the issue of the northern drive on Vilna and gave their armies orders for a July 1 attack. However, Conrad was able to convince Falkenhayn that the most fortuitous course would be to continue the initiative begun by Mackensen. When the Kaiser approved this course of action, a frustrated Hindenburg had to cancel his maneuver. Accordingly, the offensive's second phase began on July 13, with the German Twelfth Army conducting a series of frontal assaults against the northwest lip of the salient. To insure that H-L would not seize the tactical initiative, Falkenhayn placed the Woyrsch Corps and the Ninth Army in a new Army Group, under Prince Leopold of Bavaria, who in turn received his orders from the German Chief of Staff. In effect, Falkenhayn had created a sub-theater in which Hindenburg had no command authority.

Thus, from Mlava, southwest of the Masurian Lakes, to Czernowitz, near Rumania, the armies of the Central Powers advanced on a broad front, achieving success whenever and wherever they struck. By the end of July, Lublin and fortress Ivangorod had fallen to Woyrsch; Warsaw followed on August 5. On August 19, the German Ninth Army took Novo Georgievsk, inflicting 80,000 Russian casualties. On the eighteenth, Kovno fell to the Tenth Army, whose northward advance kept apace with its sister armies but failed to move in the rapid fashion desired by H-L. Reeling from the incessant offensives all along the front, the Russians elected not to defend Brest-Litovsk, and retreated across the Niemen River into the inhospitable Pripet Marshes. The Polish Salient ceased to exist as such, and, by the beginning of September, German armies were entrenched in the soil of Mother Russia. Despite the scorched earth policy directed by the *Stavka,* the Russian withdrawal approximated a rout.

Secure in his belief that his own objectives had been accomplished, Falkenhayn unleashed Hindenburg in mid-August to execute his northern thrust. Although it was now too late to achieve the envelopment sought earlier in the summer, the Germans in the north pressed on, decreasing their rate of advance in accordance with the poor Russian communications net, the lengthening lines of supply, and the approaching winter. Remembering the vicissitudes of Napoleon Bonaparte a century earlier, the Germans and Austrians elected to halt the advance at the end of September along a line running north-south from Dvinsk to Khotin on the Dniester. This line, with minor adjustments, was held until the end of 1917, when Russia left the war.

The breakthrough at Gorlice-Tarnow and its aftermath are a tribute to Germany's superior ability to plan and coordinate. The Germans also recognized and adapted to the logistic exigencies of the campaign. At the same time, the results of the campaign must call forth another condemnation of Russian generalship and organization: a lack of fore-

sight before the war, a lack of cooperation by senior commanders during battle, and a failure of the staff to consider the hardship and casualties inflicted on the soldiers. Ultimately, the Russians became the victims of their near absence of military professionalism and their social and administrative systems. It was clear that they were no match for their enemies, who had recognized the demands of twentieth century warfare and had prepared for them.

Clearly, the outcome was a tremendous victory in the strategic sense for the Central Powers. The specter of invasion had been dispelled, and the Russian homeland had been invaded. The *Stavka* confronted the task of reconstituting the demoralized, shattered armies with the diminishing manpower and material assets of Russia. Although not as obvious in late 1915, perhaps the greatest indirect benefit to Germany of the year's campaigning was the relief of the Grand Duke Nicholas and the assumption of field command by his nephew, Czar Nicholas. This not only resulted in the loss of the Grand Duke's military capabilities and experience, but also amounted to a psychological blow to the morale of the officers of the Army, with whom he had enjoyed great popularity. This action, along with the political turmoil existing in St. Petersburg and the public despair at the events of the year, removed yet another prop from the tottering Russian Empire.[26]

Mountains, Heroics, and Determination in Serbia

From 1914 to 1915, tiny but defiant Serbia was a political pawn and a strategic target of the Central Powers. Implementing a plot that was to become the most celebrated direct cause of World War I, Serbian nationalists, allegedly directed by the Belgrade government, assassinated Archduke Franz Ferdinand and his archduchess in June 1914. Coming after years of friction between Belgrade and Vienna, this was the last straw for the Austrian war party. Conrad and Count Leopold von Berchtold were determined to punish the little kingdom whose minions had assaulted the Dual Monarchy's royal family. Rejecting a servile response to their ultimatum, the Austrians needed only a guarantee from Kaiser Wilhelm to hold Russia at bay before attacking Serbia.[27] The Kaiser acquiesced without considering the ramifications, thus setting off the chain of events that would throw all of Europe into the caldron of total war.[28] Although Serbia's meek response to Vienna seemed to negate the basis for Austrian hostilities, war commenced on July 29 when an Austrian flotilla on the Danube began a bombardment of Belgrade. Even Kaiser Wilhelm was taken aback by Austria's tenacity following Serbia's conciliatory response,[29] but his second thoughts came too late.

As pointed out earlier in this chapter, Conrad ordered Plan B into effect upon the declaration of war on Serbia. When Russia came to the defense of the Serbs, however, the Austrian strategic situation changed. In implementation of Plan R, Conrad grudgingly directed the transfer of the Second Army from the Balkan Front to Galicia. Thus, six days after the implementation of Plan R had commenced, most of the Second Army began moving to the northeast, leaving only two army corps (from the Second Army) on the Serbian Front.

To General Oskar Potiorek, the Austrian commander, conquest of the "pig farmers" of Serbia appeared simple. A more perceptive understanding of his enemy and the terrain would have better prepared him for his task. The Serbian Army was small but tough. Organized into three armies that comprised 12 divisions, its 200,000 soldiers were largely veterans of the Balkan Wars and were accustomed to hardship.[30] They had only recently thrown off a Turkish yoke and were wary of Austrian influence. Loyal to their aging King Peter and responsive to their ill but competent commander, Field Marshal Voivode Radomir Putnik,* the Serbs massed east of the Kolubra River (*see Atlas Map No. 32a*), in a central position, to await the Austrian attack.

Potiorek's imperial battalions crossed the Save and Drina Rivers from Bosnia on August 12. The Serbs, having determined the nature of the threat, immediately swung northwestward with two armies in line (the Second and Third) and one in reserve (the First). Initially, Potiorek's 19 divisions achieved success in the Battle of the Jadar. By the eighteenth, however, the Austrian diversion of forces to Galicia was well under way, and the combat power of the two sides was approaching parity. The first invasion ended after a week of fighting, with the Austrians back at their starting point, although still on Serbian territory. In early September, Potiorek renewed the offensive (*see Atlas Map No. 32b*); after holding the Austrians in check for a week, Putnik withdrew his beleaguered forces to a new defensive line that ran from Belgrade to Uzhitse. Running short of ammunition, which was always scarce, Putnik awaited a third Austrian drive.

Time and patience were running out in Vienna, particularly in view of the Galician reverses. Nevertheless, Potiorek persuaded the Austrian High Command to sanction a new offensive on November 5. This time, the combination of rugged terrain and Serbian tenacity would defeat the Austrian Fifth and Sixth Armies. Although occupying the Serbian capital on December 2, the Austrians pushed too deeply into Serbian territory. Putnik's armies counterattacked the next day. Advancing with three armies abreast, the Serbs drove the Austrians back along the routes that they had earlier used. Serbia was cleared of all Austrians by December 15, and Potiorek was dismissed. In the words of Winston Churchill, the Serbs "had added to the Austrian annals this most ignominious, rankling and derisory defeat."[31] However, Serbia's respite was not long lived. Before the first days of 1916, the Central Powers would snuff out the flame of resistance in that unfortunate little kingdom.

During the first half of 1915, Serbia's importance as a strategic objective increased as a result of her location astride the land route to Turkey, which had joined the Central Powers in October 1914. By mid-1915, Turkey was pinning down half a million Allied soldiers, and the Central Powers determined to supply her with the ammunition and guns she needed to continue performing this valuable task. Allied naval supremacy denied all but occasional use of the Mediterranean, and Serbia blocked the use of the Berlin-Constantinople railroad. Thus, Serbia became the object of German as well as Austrian attention.

Hungry for postwar territorial gains, Bulgaria had observed the events of 1914 and 1915 as a neutral while deciding which alliance to join. Germany's economic bid, reinforced by H-L's impressive gains in Poland and by the failure of the Allies to open the Dardenelles, proved the most attractive. On September 6, 1915, Bulgaria joined the Central Powers. Serbia promptly became the objective of common interest for Bulgaria and her allies.

---

*Putnik suffered from chronic asthma. To ease his discomfort, the temperature and humidity in his command post were rigidly controlled. He was frequently carried about the battlefield on a litter.

**King Peter of Serbia Observes His Army in Action
Against Austrian Troops, 1914**

The plan for the subjugation of Serbia in late 1915 was carefully thought through and well coordinated. By common consent, a tripartite invasion force of 16 divisions was formed, of which Germany and Austria were to provide 6 each and Bulgaria 4. Mackensen, the German Eleventh Army commander, was surreptitiously ordered to Bosnia to finalize the planning and command the invasion force. Falkenhayn also directed that Eleventh Army headquarters be transferred to the command of General Max von Gallwitz, and demanded that H-L provide the bulk of the German divisions for the operation. This generated another exchange of messages, establishing a vehement difference of strategic opinions that could be resolved only by the Kaiser. Hindenburg was pursuing his pet project of a deep encircling movement in north Poland from Kovno to Vilna. Providing units for operations in Serbia would erode his combat power considerably. While his objections about the transfer were vociferous at the time, he later admitted that his interests were parochial and that Falkenhayn had a broader perspective.[32] Despite his objections, the forces were transferred, with Germany providing not six but ten divisions because of Austria's depleted manpower and the fact that five Austrian armies were already engaged east of the Bug River. As invasion became imminent, England and France implored Serbia to offer Bulgaria immediate Macedonian territorial concessions in order to stave off attack. The nationalistic Serbs declined, electing to fight as long as their capabilities permitted.

Mackensen's plan was a masterpiece of coordinated staff work based on voluminous data on terrain and order of battle, much of which had been compiled by Lieutenant Colonel Hentsch of Marne Campaign notoriety. Most laudably, it was also simple. (*See Atlas Map No. 33.*) Two armies—the Austrian Third and the German Eleventh—would attack Serbia across the Save and Danube Rivers. A few days later, another two-army attack would be launched from Bulgaria.

On October 7, Mackensen sent the German Eleventh and Austrian Third Armies across the water barriers in boats, gaining success from the outset. Two days later, Belgrade was occupied and the Serbian Army started a retrograde movement to the interior, destroying depots and bridges as it went. On the eleventh, the enveloping arm of the offensive, the Bulgarian First and Second Armies, swarmed across the eastern Serbian frontier. The First Army was expected to squeeze the Serbian Army between itself and the Austro-German force moving south from the river line. The Second Army swung south to block reinforcement from Greece, Serbia's vacillating, erstwhile ally, and from Allied forces that had recently landed (October 5) at Salonika.

Mackensen ordered a general advance to commence on October 18. Squeezed by the combined forces and blocked from using the route to Salonika, the three disintegrating Serbian armies changed direction to the southwest, passing through the town of Prichtina, where the dependents of the troops were finally abandoned. Weakened by the ravages of a typhus epidemic, exhausted to the point of collapse, and down to a few cartridges per man, the soldiers of King Peter struggled into the mountains of Montenegro and Albania. There, in mid-November, they faced longtime tribal enemies even more brutal than those in pursuit. Ultimately, the remnants reached the Adriatic coast. With 100,000 killed and wounded and 160,000 captured, the pitiful vestiges of Putnik's armies were ferried by Allied ships to the island of Corfu.[33] There, the survivors languished in refugee camps until they were re-formed to join the Allied Front in Salonika.

A Recapitulation and Assessment

By November 1915, the nature of warfare that characterized the Eastern and Western Fronts suggested not two different theaters, but two different wars. The vast distances from the Baltic to Bukovina swallowed up whole army groups, while formations in France were ranged shoulder-to-shoulder along the fire steps of the trench systems. In Galicia and Poland, offensive gains were measured not in yards, but in miles. Mobile warfare was still the order of the day—cavalry sweeping and reconnoitering in its traditional role, infantry conducting wide and deep movements, and artillery striving without success to saturate the front.

In the East, the most dominant theme from the opening days of August 1914 was German military professionalism. Years of training, an efficient school system, the adaptation of modern weaponry, and a rational plan for the amalgamation of Reserves and Regulars gave the Germans an edge that Russian patriotic fervor and numbers could not match. The shattering specter of Tannenberg seemed to lurk in the background of all Russian planning.

Russian failures were attributable to a number of causes, one of which was the perpetuation of an officer corps that emphasized royal lineage and nepotism over ability. In a system that placed greater stock in staff and school assignments than command, it is no wonder that the Russian armies foundered against their more skillful adversaries. The comparison of command personalities—Samsonov, Jilinsky, and Rennenkampf versus François, Mackensen, and Ludendorff—is a vivid one that does much to explain what was wrong with the Czar's armies.

Against the Dual Monarchy, the Russians performed much better, suggesting that the Austrians suffered from many of the same problems. There may be considerable validity in this conclusion. However, in light of Austria's superior mobilization readiness and technological experience, the Austrians should have done better than they did.

Serbia was the most unfortunate of victims. Its small size, lack of resources, and dearth of industry dictated that its role would be brief and unhappy.

As operations continued in the East, both sides sought to achieve strategic superiority. Maneuver forced the geographical areas of operations to expand, which in turn demanded more forces to control the terrain. More forces, in turn, required more room to maneuver. In August 1914, Germany had one undersized army east of Posen; by March of 1915, there were three, plus one independent corps; by September, there were no less than seven armies, ranging from the Baltic to Galicia. The Russians expanded in similar fashion, not only putting new armies in the field, but also rebuilding those that had been decimated in combat.

Finally, despite the distances, the victories, the ever-growing rifle strength, and the enormous Russian losses, German strategists realized that this could not be the decisive front. As Marshall Kutusov had demonstrated in 1812, there was limitless opportunity for Russian retreat even farther into the interior. Germany had baited the bear in its den. It now had to support its allies and continue to inflict damage on the Russian Army while awaiting its collapse from exhaustion.

Notes

[1]Letter from Engels to Sorge, London, January 7, 1888, in Friedrich Engels, *Letters to Americans 1848–1895* (New York, 1953), pp. 194–195.

[2]A.A. Brusilov, *A Soldier's Notebook, 1914–1918* (Westport, Conn., 1971), pp. 7–30; N.N. Golovin, *The Russian Army in the World War* (New Haven, 1931), pp. 30–44. These are two excellent references on the shortcomings of the Russian Army at the outbreak of war, recounting the mobilization planning, initial moves, characteristics of officers and troops, and underdeveloped logistic system.

[3]Winston S. Churchill, *The Unknown War* (New York, 1931), p. 142.

[4]Norman Stone, *The Eastern Front, 1914–1917* (New York, 1975), pp. 33–34.

[5]T. Dodson Stamps and Vincent J. Esposito (eds.), *A Short Military History of World War I* (West Point, N.Y., 1950), p. 144.

[6]Churchill, *Unknown War,* p. 118.

[7]Sir Alfred Knox, *With the Russian Army, 1914–1917* (New York, 1921), p. 47.

[8]Sir Edmund Ironside, *Tannenberg: The First Thirty Days in East Prussia* (London, 1925), pp. 1–9.

[9]*Ibid.*, pp. 22–23.

[10]Knox, *Russian Army,* p. 111.

[11]Erich Ludendorff, *Ludendorff's Own Story* (2 vols.; New York, 1919), I, 90.

[12]Major Ward H. Maris, Lecture: "François, Prittwitz and Gumbinnen" (Fort Leavenworth, Kansas, USAC&GSC, 1937), pp. 23–27.

[13]C.R.M.F. Cruttwell, *A History of the Great War, 1914–1918* (Oxford, 1936), pp. 45–46.

[14]General Max von Hoffman. "Tannenberg As It Really Was" (U.S. War Dept. translation of monograph, 1933), p. 6. This was allegedly the Tenth Army, which had not yet begun to move on August 20.

[15]Max Hoffman, *The War of Lost Opportunities* (New York, 1925), pp. 20–23.

[16]Basil H. Liddell Hart, *The Real War, 1914–1918* (Boston, 1930), p. 109.

[17]Hoffman, "Tannenberg As It Really Was," pp. 23–25.

[18]Cyril Falls, *The Great War* (New York, 1959), p. 56.

[19]Churchill, *Unknown War,* p. 224.

[20]Liddell Hart, *Real War,* pp. 110–111; Knox, *Russian Army,* pp. 82–86.

[21]Great Britain, Imperial General Staff, *Handbook on the Austro-Hungarian Army in War* (London, 1918), p. 3.

[22]Vincent J. Esposito (ed.), *The West Point Atlas of American Wars* (2 vols.; New York, 1959), II

[23]Golovin, *Russian Army,* pp. 127–128.

[24]*Ibid.*, p. 145.

[25]Stamps and Esposito, *World War I,* p. 153.

[26]Brusilov, *A Soldier's Notebook, 1914–1918,* pp. 170–171.

[27]John Keegan, *Opening Moves: August 1914* (New York, 1971), p. 44.

[28]*Ibid.*, p. 46.

[29]Stamps and Esposito, *World War I,* p. 33.

[30]*The Times History of the War,* Vol. 2 (London, 1915), pp. 283–285.

[31]Churchill, *Unknown War,* p. 269.

[32]*Ibid.*, p. 334.

[33]Stamps and Esposito, *World War I,* p. 222.

Deadlock and Attrition on the Western Front, 1914–1916

4

This Western-front business couldn't be done again, not for a long time. The young men think they could do it again but they couldn't. They could fight the first Marne again but not this. This took religion and years of plenty and tremendous sureties and the exact relation that existed between the classes. The Russians and Italians weren't any good on this front. You had to have a whole-souled sentimental equipment going back further than you could remember, you had to remember Christmas and postcards of the Crown Prince and his fiancée, and little cafés in Valence and beer gardens in Unter den Linden and weddings at the Mairie, and going to the Derby and your grandfather's whiskers . . . . This was a love battle—there was a century of middle-class love spent here . . . . All my beautiful lovely soft world blew itself up here with a great gust of high explosive love . . . .

F. Scott Fitzgerald, *Tender Is the Night*

As the gray masses of the German Army fell back from Paris and the Marne, their broken chief, General Helmuth Graf von Moltke, succumbed to the reality of the situation in his headquarters in Luxembourg City. His health and nerves shattered, he was in a pitiable state. Kaiser Wilhelm could delay replacing him no longer; on September 14, he ordered the Minister of War, General Erich von Falkenhayn, to take over the direction of operations. At Moltke's request that he remain as a figurehead chief due to impressions that might be formed abroad as a result of the German defeat, however, the change was not widely known. On November 3, the Kaiser would formally relieve him and appoint Falkenhayn to the post of Chief of the General

Staff. Formalities aside, as Chief Quartermaster, Falkenhayn in effect exercised the full authority of the Chief of the General Staff in mid-September.

Falkenhayn was strong willed and determined to end the series of blunders that had prevented a rapid German victory. He now attempted to revive the stalled Schlieffen Plan on a more modest basis by massing strength on his right flank with which to turn the Allied left.[1] Thus, even before the deadlock on the Aisne had ended, a new phase, erro-

General Erich von Falkenhayn

**Field Marshal Sir John D.P. French,
Commander of the BEF**

neously dubbed "the Race to the Sea," evolved. The opposing sides were not racing to the seacoast, but were frantically attempting to outflank each other. As the armies extended northwards, they met, clashed, and then dug into the series of static trench lines that would characterize the Western Front for the remainder of the war. (*The dates and locations of the major engagements in this series of maneuvers are shown on Map 10.*)

Sir John French's British Expeditionary Force was particulary sensitive to the gradual movement of conflict toward the Channel seaports. In order to protect British lines of communication and the routes and bases that future reinforcements would use, French felt that the BEF should be positioned on or near the Allied left flank. Consequently, in early October, the BEF moved from the Aisne battlefield to the line extending from Ypres to La Bassée.[2]

King Albert and his tiny Belgian Army, hastily reinforced by three British Marine Brigades, remained under siege in Antwerp. There, Albert tied down a considerable German force until October 7, when he successfully retreated to the Allied lines.[3] After flooding the lowlands

south of Nieuport, the Belgians fortified the Yser River and canal line, thus blocking any German attempt to sweep down the coast. The Belgians clung to this small portion of the trench line in Belgian territory for the remainder of the war.

The Specter of Trench Warfare

A key component of Falkenhayn's strategy for gaining decisive results in the West was his plan to outflank the Allies and cut them off from the seacoast before they could fully mobilize or reinforce their armies. In this endeavor, time was important, since Falkenhayn's numerical superiority on the Western Front was dwindling rapidly. The British were being reinforced with Indian units and their last Regular Army divisions. However, the Germans did have five newly organized reserve corps with which to make a final attempt to turn the enemy's positions. Ignoring Hindenburg's pleas for reinforcement in the East, Falkenhayn determined to break through the thinly held line to seize the ports of Dunkirk, Calais, and Boulogne.[4] The attacking forces were amply supported by the powerful artillery from the Antwerp siege train. But the 17- to 20-year-old volunteers in these five corps were virtually untrained. Their patriotic enthusiasm could not compensate for this lack of training and experience or for the poor leadership of the new units.

On October 31, the assault began on a narrow front stretching from the Messines ridge to Gheluvelt. After bitter fighting, the Germans drove the British Cavalry Corps off the ridge and then managed to break through General Douglas Haig's I Corps at Gheluvelt. After a brief pause, they, in turn, were driven back by fierce counterattacks that Haig mounted by assembling all able-bodied troops, regardless of unit or assignment. Then the German volunteers were thrown into the mincing machine in an attempt to retrieve victory from defeat. For the last time in the war, enthusiastic volunteers sang patriotic songs as they assaulted entrenched defenders head-on. The toll of dead was appalling and has been described as "The Massacre of the Innocents at Ypres." More than 130,000 of Germany's potential leaders and officers were lost. In holding the tenuous Ypres salient, however, the flower of the British Regular Army— "The Old Contemptibles"*—lost 50,000 men and passed into history.[5] Although the lists of dead and wounded in this battle would soon be eclipsed, what would later be known as the First Battle of Ypres continued to hold special signif-

---

*"The Old Contemptibles" was the proud nickname of England's original expeditionary force. The name had its origin in Kaiser Wilhelm's reference to the BEF as "a contemptible little army."

icance. It introduced the armies of the West to the horrors of modern positional warfare.

The successful defense at Ypres and the Yser River in October and November was truly an Allied effort. British, French, and Belgians cooperated in warding off the vigorous assaults by the initially superior German forces. To coordinate the entire battle, General Joseph Joffre had dispatched General Ferdinand Foch to Flanders. Signaling the tentative Allied approach to military cooperation, Foch had no real command authority over the Belgians or British. However, he did control the flow of French reinforcements, and through his strong personality influenced the British to cooperate.[6]

The Battles of the Yser and First Ypres, which were curious admixtures of open and positional warfare, marked the stagnation of warfare on the Western Front. As winter closed in, scattered rifle pits and trench sections were interconnected, drained, and deepened. Both sides constructed bombproof dugouts along the entire front and placed barbed wire entanglements, fastened first to wooden stakes and later to iron corkscrew pickets. (*See Atlas Map No. 11.*) The character of the war had changed—a 450-mile front now stretched from the Channel coast to the Swiss frontier.

The initial series of trench lines that were constructed in the winter of 1914–1915 bore little resemblance to the elaborate field fortifications of later years. The line initially consisted of either a frontline ditch able to conceal a man or, when the ground water level was too high, a compensating parapet. Two or three hundred yards to the rear lay the support line trench. An area soon referred to as "No Man's Land" separated the opposing positions by 30 to 800 meters.

From the outset, German techniques and construction were superior to those of the Allies. While all forces had anticipated an offensive, mobile war in 1914, only the Germans had actually instructed their troops in defensive tactics and supported them with medium and heavy artillery. Moreover, they had immediately available trench stores such as barbed wire, hand grenades, and trench mortars, while the British and French had to improvise until their factories could provide those materials necessary for the new method of warfare.

In general terms, the Allied commanders enforced a policy of establishing their frontline at the point of farthermost advance without regard to fields of fire, terrain, obstacles, or observation. Compounding this error, Joffre and French vigorously insisted that ground, once gained, must be held at all costs, and that if lost, it must be regained by immediate counterattacks. In their more methodical manner, the Germans constructed deep belts of wire obstacles, concrete pillboxes, and well-sited trenches. They also prepared immense dugouts that were used to shelter platoons and companies when they were not manning the front. These dugouts were also used to protect and conceal large bodies of troops prior to an assault.

Artillery fire played an increasingly important role on the stabilized battlefield. The guns were dug into fixed positions to the rear and were carefully registered upon a limited number of targets. Aerial observers soon became vital in locating targets of opportunity behind the enemy lines. As the defenses solidified, the type and caliber of the ammunition that was used changed radically from prewar estimates. Light, mobile pieces firing shrapnel shells were excellent for the open warfare envisioned by prewar leaders. Such

British 13-Pounder Guns Mounted on Revolving Pedestals for Employment as Antiaircraft Weapons

**A Wounded Soldier is Carried from
the Trenches to the Rear**

pieces, however, were virtually impotent against the entrenchments and obstacles on the front. Thus the call went to the rear for more and heavier caliber guns that could fire high explosive shells. Because the consumption of ammunition dwarfed all estimates, a shortage of shells became chronic to both sides.*

To the individual soldier, life in the trenches varied from uncomfortable monotony to abject misery. The variables that influenced his condition were the construction and maintenance of the trenches themselves, the weather, and enemy activity. If the opposing lines were in close proximity, the front was usually immune from the incessant pounding of artillery; but then this was replaced by constant dueling with rifle and hand grenades, mortar fire, sniping, and trench raids. During periods of low visibility, No Man's Land became a flurry of activity. Wiring parties, intelligence-gathering patrols, and burial teams were dispatched to maintain an offensive spirit. Infantry units were rotated on tours of frontline duty, which varied according to the activity in their sector and the availability of replacements. When offensive actions were planned, the troops were rehearsed in a rear area for the open warfare that the high commanders expected after the rupture of the enemy lines.

*As an example, the British available supply rate for field guns was based upon the experience of the Boer war—10 rounds per gun per day. In December 1914, the required supply rate was 50 rounds per gun per day. In fact, only 6 rounds per gun per day got to the front.

Large masses of cavalry were retained in the rear, especially by the British, for the exploitation of breakthroughs, which would not come until 1918. Both sides periodically used cavalry units in a dismounted role, however, as an economy of force measure in the line. The breakthrough, which was the goal of all commanders on the Western Front, was an illusive dream. The main lines would not shift more than 10 miles in either direction until the Germans voluntarily evacuated the Noyon salient in early 1917.

A break into the enemy's trench position was always possible if the commanders were willing to expend the necessary materiel and manpower. The defender could counter such a break-in by resorting to strategic mobility—that is, he could rapidly shift reinforcements to a threatened area by using the highly developed railroad network or trucks. The attacker, however, was hampered by the lack of tactical mobility—the legs of the assaulting infantry provided the only mobility for the offense. The relative inflexibility of the supporting fires limited gains to the maximum range of the artillery pieces until they could be displaced forward. As the attack progressed, however, the defender's artillery became more concentrated as it fired on pre-registered barrage locations. Finally, the ubiquitous machinegun, placed in covered and concealed positions, gave the defender a tremendous firepower advantage until the light assault gun was developed.

While problems of mobility, logistics, and fire support slowed the attack as it penetrated the enemy lines, the defender was able to fall back on previously prepared or sited positions. He could reinforce his front more rapidly than the attacker, who lost momentum as his penetration slowed and ground to a halt. Not until the introduction and perfection of the tank was the attacker able to take advantage of tactical mobility. In the meantime, countless assaults were mounted with little or no result, save for the expenditure of hundreds of thousands of lives. This method of warfare would dominate the military operations on the Western Front until the last year of the war.

Frustration in 1915

Despite the failure of his plan to win decisively in the West, Falkenhayn remained a "Westerner." Although he continued to believe that the war would ultimately be decided on the Franco-British front, he now reconciled himself to the fact that the war would be a drawn out and arduous affair. In order to prepare the homefront for the long ordeal ahead, Dr. Walther Rathenau took charge of Germany's economic mobilization. This scientist and industrialist organized an efficient distribution system of vital raw materials to the war industries. In reaction to the shortages created by the

British naval blockade, Rathenau directed the development of many substitute, or *ersatz*, materials.[7]

Opposing Strategies

Falkenhayn felt that while victory could not be achieved in the East, the opportunities for maneuver in the near future lay on the Eastern Front. The team of Hindenburg, Ludendorff, and Hoffman had achieved brilliant success in the East with only moderate reinforcement. This fact, coupled with the dire situation of his Austro-Hungarian ally, forced Falkenhayn to shift the focus of his attention to the East. He decided to perfect his defensive positions in the West and shift sufficient force to the East to exploit success and relieve Russian pressure on Austria-Hungary. This plan required the further development and refinement of the excellent German railroad network to permit the rapid transfer of troops between two main fronts. With these somewhat ambiguous objectives, Falkenhayn hesitantly led the German nation into the second year of the war.[8] Meanwhile, across the western trench barrier, the Allies began to awaken to the problems of waging a coalition war.

No unity of command existed on the Allied side. The British armies in France and Flanders had been ordered "to coincide most sympathetically with the plans and wishes of [the French] but remain an entirely independent command." However, because the French had thus far made the greatest military contribution as well as the greatest sacrifice, the British High Command surrendered the initiative for planning to General Joffre.[9] The British were now rapidly reinforcing their expeditionary force with Dominion forces from Canada, Australia, and New Zealand, while volunteer "New Armies"* were being formed and trained in England. Yet, although Great Britain's military contribution increased and later became dominant,[†] she never achieved a corresponding voice in the higher direction of the Allied strategy.

The French were determined to drive the German forces from the Noyon salient. (*See Atlas Map No. 11.*) The reality that the enemy remained in possession of one-tenth of France's territory made any other military objective politically unrealistic. Joffre proposed mounting converging offensives on both the northern and southern faces of the salient in 1915. These assaults in Artois (vicinity of Arras)

*Rather than impose a draft, the British Government decided to build its military forces on an entirely voluntary basis. This system worked haphazardly until January 1916, when conscription was finally adopted. The new formations were distinct from the Regular or Territorial Forces and were called the New Armies or Kitchener's Armies.

†While the British Army never exceeded the French Army in either number of divisions or number of troops, it was the most militarily significant force after the French Army Mutinies of 1917.

**A Stern Lorn Kitchener Enjoins His Countrymen
to Enlist in the "New Armies"**

and Champagne (vicinity of Rheims) would directly threaten the enemy's lateral communications, forcing him to react. When these operations were successful, a northward thrust from the Verdun-Nancy area would decisively defeat the retreating Germans.[10] This basic strategy was perfectly sound, and was used to end the war in 1918. Even more important to the French than this military strategy, however, was their insistence that the major effort of the Allied coalition be made on the Western Front. Although British political and naval leaders were fascinated with the idea of conducting strategic operations on the periphery of the Central Powers, her military commanders generally accepted the French point of view.

The French resumed their attacks in the Champagne sector on February 15. Gains were insignificant, but the commanders doggedly insisted on prolonging the assaults until March 30. As a result of this insistence on reinforcing failure, the French took more than 240,000 casualties. In April, a subsequent failure of French arms occurred during the attempt to reduce the German-held salient around St. Mihiel. The purpose of this operation was to remove the threat of German operations around Verdun. The defending garrisons easily beat off the French assaults in the wooded and broken terrain. The only significant result of these unsuccessful operations was that the heavy casualties sustained by the French prevented them from cooperating with the

British in the planned offensives on the northern face of the Noyon salient.

The second phase of Joffre's strategy called for a combined Franco-British offensive in the Arras sector. Part of the plan called for the expanding BEF to relieve French units of portions of their trench line in Flanders. When Field Marshal French found himself unable to relieve the French divisions as planned, General Foch, the local commander, cancelled his portion of the operation. Thus the combination of heavy casualties in the Champagne offensives and responsibility for longer defensive lines kept Joffre's plan from being implemented. Despite the inability of the French to participate in the combined offensive, the British commander decided to attack alone at Neuve Chapelle. The reasons for Sir John's decision may have included a desire to display British arms after four months of rebuilding and reorganization and to foster an offensive spirit in his army. In any event, the Battle of Neuve Chapelle was so isolated and lacking in support that it seemed doomed to failure.

The Battle of Neuve Chapelle

Ironically, through the advantage of surprise and the benefits of meticulous preparation, General Douglas Haig's First Army just barely missed achieving the tactical breakthrough that the much larger French offensive never approached. The front for the attack was extremely narrow (2,000 meters) and was designed to reduce the small salient

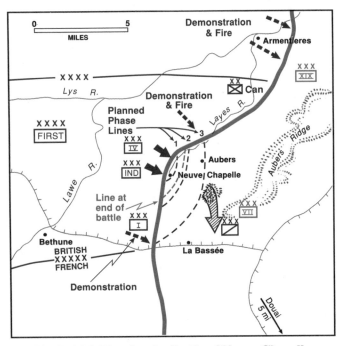

The British Plan for the Battle of Neuve Chapelle, March 10–13, 1915

around the village of Neuve Chapelle. Once the southern portion of Aubers Ridge was secured, the planners hoped to launch a second offensive to break out onto the Douai plain and menace the German communications system.

Planning was thorough and complete.* Large-scale (1:5000) maps and aerial photographs made the commanders of all assault units familiar with their sectors of responsibility. The three assault brigades conducted extensive rehearsals of the operation behind the lines. Haig's tactical planning stressed both surprise and concentration of combat power. He would gain surprise by the use of feints and demonstrations on both sides of the main attack. Concentration of power would be achieved by massing 40,000 men supported by 62 light artillery batteries against the six German infantry companies and twelve machineguns that defended the narrow front. Behind this assault, Field Marshal French controlled two cavalry corps with which he planned to exploit the expected breakthrough. However, British intelligence officers accurately estimated that local enemy reserves could reinforce the threatened sector within four hours, and that up to 16,000 army reserves could be shifted to bolster the defenses within 36 hours.

Due as much to a shortage of artillery ammunition as to Haig's desire for surprise and secrecy, the preparatory bombardment was to be violent but brief (35 minutes). These fires were designed to destroy the enemy wire obstacles and prevent the transfer of reserves. The shortage of heavier caliber artillery, however, prevented the preparation from seriously damaging the German defensive breastworks and shelters. During the assault, three designated phase lines were to be used for coordination of artillery supporting fires. Colored flares, fired from Very pistols, were to signal the shifting of these fires from one line to the next.

The attack commenced at 7:30 a.m. on March 10. Complete surprise was achieved, and the first objectives were promptly secured. However, the attackers soon began to bog down. Artillery support, tied to a rigid schedule, could not be adjusted, and the advancing infantry had to seize their assigned phase lines in unison. Because there was no field radio communication to assist coordination, the small unit commanders had great difficulty shifting their supporting artillery fires. The succeeding waves of attackers quickly became entangled with the assault troops, and all had to await the lifting of their own artillery. With no enemy to their front, the attackers waited until 2:50 p.m., when they received orders to continue the advance. During this delay, the Germans transferred local reserves into the gap; when the assault actually resumed at 5:30 p.m., the machineguns

---

*An example of the growing respect for British military competence was shown when General Joffre forwarded a translation of Haig's operations order for Neuve Chapelle to all French staffs as a model of how field instructions should be imparted to subordinates.

and artillery of the defenders broke the back of the assault.[11]

Upon assessing their failure at Neuve Chapelle, the Allied generals were unable to recognize that their near success had come from achieving surprise. Instead, they blamed their repulse on an inadequacy of artillery support. Thus began the cry for more artillery shells and longer, more intense preparatory bombardments. However, a little over a month after the battle, the Germans would supplement artillery preparations with a new weapon that would offer great promise as a solution to the tactical stalemate.

Poisonous Gas Is Used at Ypres

The first successful use of lethal gas as a weapon of warfare occurred during the Second Battle of Ypres (April 22–May 25, 1915). Prior to this time, tear gas grenades and artillery shells had been employed by both sides. The one previous use of asphyxiating gas (by the Germans against the Russians) had failed because of the extremely cold weather, which had prevented the gas from vaporizing.[12]

Although the attack at Ypres was in the way of an experiment, it nevertheless had both tactical and strategic objectives. Tactically, the German Fourth Army desired to reduce the vulnerable Ypres salient, while Falkenhayn's strategic motive was to deceive the Entente Powers and cloak the movement of large forces to the Eastern Front in preparation for the Gorlice-Tarnow offensive. Despite these important goals, the Germans were completely un-

prepared to exploit the great initial success that the attack achieved.

One of the manifestations of the German Supreme Command's lack of faith in the new chemical weapon was its failure to provide adequate facilities for dispensing the chlorine. Dr. Fritz Haber, the scientist in charge of the program, had to release the gas from commercial cylinders and depend upon the prevailing winds to disperse the vapors. This means of employment dictated the initial emplacement of the cylinders on the southern face of the Ypres salient to take advantage of the southerly winds predicted for the area. But the Germans meteorological service had misjudged the wind direction, which continued to blow from the north throughout February. Consequently, the equipment and gas units had to be shifted to the northern face of the salient between the end of March and mid-April. This unusual activity did not go without notice.

Prisoners taken on the southern face of the salient in March gave full details of the strange metal cylinders stored in the frontline trenches, as well as their method of discharge. The French commanders who received this intelligence did not bother to inform the British commanders who relieved them in the line. More convincing evidence of the impending gas attack came on April 13, when a German deserter described "tubes of asphyxiating gas . . . placed in batteries of twenty . . . along the front."[13] The obliging informant even carried a crude respirator mask, which had been issued to protect the assault troops. Again, the French chain of command either ignored or failed to disseminate this information of a new method of attack.

In one respect, Falkenhayn's refusal to provide additional reserves for the offensive aided in the surprise effect it achieved. Aerial reconnaissance by the British Royal Flying Corps failed to disclose any of the unusual preparations or large troop concentrations that normally preceded an attack. On April 17, a British trench raiding party captured several of the gas cylinders. This conclusive evidence was still not enough. General Horace Smith-Dorrien did not issue a general warning or institute any precautionary measures. One of his corps commanders did pass on a warning of the possibility of the use of gas "for what it was worth." The attitude of all Allied commanders toward the possible danger to their units seems to have been conditioned by the fact that such means of warfare had been outlawed by the Hague Convention and was deemed "ungentlemanly."

On the morning of April 22, 1915, the German Fourth Army began a conventional artillery preparation. At 5:30 p.m., technicians released an ominous green cloud of chlorine gas from 5,000 cylinders. The cloud engulfed the portion of the line manned by French African Territorial

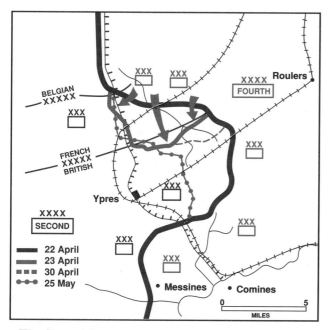

The Second Battle of Ypres, April 22–May 25, 1915

**Infantry Attacks in Waves Behind a Cloud
of Asphyxiating Gas**

troops; the French promptly fled in panic, leaving four miles of the northern face of the salient undefended. The Germans easily occupied nearly half the salient with negligible casualties before the Canadian defenses and those pockets remaining from the gas cloud halted the advance.

Surprised by their own success, the Germans lacked sufficient reserves to exploit the breakthrough. During the night, British troops reconstructed defensive positions and reinforced the area for effective counterattacks. The German opportunity for victory had passed quickly. The British, who had improvised protective gas masks of damp cloth, were able to nullify a second gas attack on May 1.[14] With Ypres, chemical warfare became a permanent weapon in the arsenals of both sides. Technology quickly spawned new protective devices and means of delivery, but never again would the surprise effect of this weapon come so close to achieving victory.

Italy Enters the War and Strategies Change

Although Italy had been allied with Germany and the Austro-Hungarian Empire in 1914, she had resisted the war fever that gripped the rest of Europe and had declared her neutrality when hostilities commenced. Because the military terms of the Triple Alliance were purely defensive in nature, she was legally justified in this action. The alliance with Austria and Germany had been made as a matter of convenience and necessity, not friendship; in reality, Italy's hatred of Austria was intense, having its origin in years of oppression under the Hapsburgs. After opting for neutrality, Italy then negotiated with the two alliances, advising the Central Powers of the price of continued neutrality and seeking territorial aggrandizement from the

Allies. When the Allied promise of Trieste and the Trentino exceeded any Austrian offer, Italy agreed to intervene on the Allied side. Her entry into the war on the side of the western allies on May 23, 1915 was the one bright spot in an otherwise depressing year for the Anglo-French partnership, providing a spiritual boost to the Allied cause. Italy's geographical position and military shortcomings, however, would combine to make her contribution of dubious value. (*See Atlas Map No. 14.*)

Although she flanked the Central Powers, Italy's borders with Austria were guarded by the southern slopes of the Alps, which meant that only along the narrow, extremely rugged front on the Isonzo River could an offensive against Austrian territory be mounted. Since political factors dictated that Italian troops had to be used against the Austrians, no thought was ever given to reinforcing the French or British lines on the Western Front. Thus, the Italian commander, General Luigi Cadorna, planned his main efforts on the Isonzo front, attacking toward Trieste, a historic goal of the "Irredentist" movement.* During his initial advances, Cadorna was opposed by second line Austrian forces, which slowly withdrew back to frontier defenses. There, as on the other fronts, the defense hardened and gained the ascendency. During 1915, Cadorna fought the first four of the many Battles of the Isonzo.[15] Paying dearly for its lack of artillery support and poor choice of objectives, the Italian Army suffered nearly 280,000 casualties in exchange for negligible gains.

Among the agreements for Italy's entry into the war was the first formal Allied statement about military cooperation. The treaties signed in London required the conclusion of a "Military Convention" between all Allied general staffs in order to decide upon the appropriate plans to be implemented against Austria-Hungary. With this limited mandate, Joffre began combined military planning.

On July 7, 1915, the first Inter-Allied Military Conference was convened at Joffre's headquarters in Chantilly. The assembled military leaders now realized the necessity for, at least, developing a timetable that would govern the coordination of their independent activities. However, this first attempt failed to produce any specific agreements except ". . . a general [one] that each national army should be active in its own way" and a call for a series of similar conferences.[16]

The second conference was held on December 6–8 between the military representatives of France, Russia, Great Britain, Italy, and Serbia. Joffre forcefully proposed that all armies deliver "simultaneous attacks with their maximum forces on their respective fronts as soon as

---

*This strong Italian political movement was aimed at redeeming territory inhabited by Italians but under foreign control.

Joffre and Haig Discuss a Problem with a Skeptical British Minister of Munitions, David Lloyd George

they [were] ready." Only the minimum forces required for defense would be maintained in secondary theaters. Another proposal was to acknowledge the war of attrition—"the continual wearing down of the enemy"—that was already a reality. The representatives of the other Allied armies agreed unanimously with Joffre's plan and added in their communiqué that "the decision of the war can only be obtained in the principal theaters [the Russian front, Franco-British front, and Italian front]. . . The decisions should be obtained by coordinated offensives on these fronts."[17]

On the Franco-British front, Joffre specifically envisioned a combined offensive on both sides of the Somme River. While the French would provide the larger share of the combat power for this operation, the growing British Army would test its new volunteer forces during the campaign. The newly appointed British commander, General

Sir Douglas Haig, while wishing to conduct an offensive in the north around Ypres, acquiesced in Joffre's plan.* The Somme offensive was provisionally scheduled for the late summer of 1916.

Meanwhile, the German General Staff had made plans to seize the initiative in the West. Under the growing control of Erich von Falkenhayn, the Central Powers had made not a few gains in 1915. Successes in the East included the reoccupation of Russian Poland and most of Galicia. The Russian Army had been badly mauled, and the Germans felt that it would not be a serious threat for a long period of time. Elsewhere, the polyglot Allied force that had landed at Salonika, in northern Greece, had been effectively neutralized, and tiny Serbia had finally been crushed. The British amphibious force was being withdrawn from Gallipoli after its abortive invasion attempt. Even in Mesopotamia, the weak Turkish Army had checked and was now besieging the British at Kut-al-Amara. Only at sea were the fortunes of the Central Powers in danger; the naval blockade was beginning to cause shortages among the civilian population and hamper military operations. Reverting to the western orientation that he had abandoned in 1915, Falkenhayn now felt that his resources would allow him to achieve decisive results against the French.

Falkenhayn anticipated his adversaries' planned offensive for 1916. He would shift his main effort from the East to the West. He viewed the French nation as war-weary and militarily weak after suffering nearly two million casualties, of which more than one million were dead or missing.[18] Therefore, he fixed upon the British Empire as Germany's "arch enemy in this war." Believing, however, that he could not build up the necessary superiority to defeat the British directly, Falkenhayn's solution was to strike at the French Army, "England's best sword," and bleed it to death. The objective he chose was the psychologically key fortress complex of Verdun.† The Germans struck on February 21, 1916, dislocating all previous Allied military plans. Falkenhayn had assessed his enemy correctly—the French would sacrifice their entire army in the defense of this area, and thus would not be able to cooperate with the British in the Somme offensive as planned.[19]

---

*Prior to this conference, Joffre had been elevated from Commander-in-Chief of the Armies of the Northeast to the command of all French armies. This move was obviously taken to increase his prestige among the Allied generals.

†The fortress of Verdun had fallen into German hands during the Franco-Prussian War of 1870–1871. Following this humiliation, General Sere de Rivières was charged with the rehabilitation of the frontier defenses. The fortress complex of Verdun was chosen as the cornerstone of the new system, and the French Government spent huge sums on its continued reinforcement. The public, however, was not aware of the downgrading of the Verdun defenses in 1914–1915, and would have been shocked if this supposedly impregnable fortress were to fall to the enemy. Falkenhayn hoped that the seizure of Verdun would complete the demoralization of the French people and bring into power political elements more disposed toward a negotiated peace.

The Inferno of Verdun: February 21–December 15, 1916

Verdun was an ancient fortress area. (*See Atlas Map No. 12.*) Even after the Franco-German War of 1870, it was considered a valuable blocking position in the Meuse River valley. Prior to 1914, it had been continually reinforced as the striking power and range of modern guns increased. But after the reduction of fortified areas such as Liège, Namur, and Maubeuge in 1914, the French had downgraded Verdun's importance. Additionally, the immediate need for heavier artillery during the early stages of the war had led to the stripping of large caliber guns from the fortress area. The removal of weapons from the forts continued through January 1916, and the empty casemates served as troop billets. Meanwhile, the defenders manned a single trench line three miles from the fortress line, with only one usable secondary trench system provided as a reserve position.

The German Crown Prince, whose Fifth Army was given the mission of assaulting Verdun, desired to attack simultaneously on both sides of the Meuse River. Falkenhayn, wishing to minimize his losses, initially ordered that the attack be confined to the east bank of the Meuse. Bad weather delayed the initial attack from February 12 until the twenty-first. During this grace period, the German buildup was detected, and Joffre began to reinforce the threatened sector. Falkenhayn massed 1,400 guns on an eight-mile front to support the attack.

At 7:15 a.m. on February 21, the heaviest artillery preparation yet unleased during the war signaled the attack. Each hour, guns poured 100,000 shells into the small front. Three German corps launched the attack, each division attacking with two regiments on line and one in reserve. Objectives were limited and were to be seized only after the artillery had destroyed all enemy resistance. After the initial bombardment, scouting parties probed forward to test the defenses. If the destruction had not been complete, a second bombardment was ordered. In no case were infantry troops to attempt an overthrow of strongpoints with frontal assaults. The attacking troops carried flamethrowers and grenades in order to more quickly force the defenders from their positions. They also carried trench stores, such as light mortars, barbed wire, screw pickets, and entrenching tools, to assist them in establishing temporary defensive positions against counterattack or surrounding enemy strongpoints that could not be reduced. When a strongpoint could not be blasted away, it was bypassed and encircled. Thus, a precisely coordinated attack that substituted weight of metal for human lives had evolved.[20]

Despite the heavy support and deliberate tactics employed by the attackers, the results of the initial assault

Aerial Views of Fort Douamount at Verdun, Before the German Assault *(top)* and Afterwards *(bottom)*

were disappointing. For a combination of reasons, the offensive had overrun only the frontline trenches by the end of the first day. Foremost among the reasons for these limited gains was the narrowness of the assault frontage and Falkenhayn's failure to provide a supporting attack west of the Meuse. As a result, French artillery pieces were able to enfilade the advancing German lines from across the river. The spirited resistance of the French was another important factor in limiting German successes.

Coordinated defensive efforts by the outnumbered French soon ceased to exist above company level. Small unit commanders displayed determination and leadership, thwarting a major break in the defenses. Moreover, the orders of the unflappable Joffre that any commander who voluntarily surrendered ground would be court-martialed, stiffened resolve. Meanwhile, the French High Command sped reinforcements to the vulnerable point. In spite of the heroic efforts of the defenders, the reserve trench line fell on February 24. By that evening, the local commander, General Langle de Cary, had decided to evacuate the Wöevre plain and the entire east bank of the Meuse. Joffre reacted characteristically by replacing him with General Henri Pétain.

Upon assuming overall charge of the defensive sector, Pétain was faced with a critical supply problem. Heavy German fire had restricted communications with the front to one rail line and a parallel road from Bar-le-Duc. Moving reinforcements into the line would be meaningless unless these men could be supplied and fed. This single line of communication, later immortalized as *La Voie Sacrée* (The Sacred Way), soon was improved and efficiently scheduled. As many as 6,000 trucks passed into Verdun each day.

Pétain organized his defenses into four corps areas, each of which was provided with separate artillery support. Local counterattacks were ordered whenever appropriate, and while they regained little lost ground, they did succeed in startling the Germans, who thought that the French had been beaten. The German advance slowed. Again, the tactical mobility of the offensive had been stopped by rapidly constructed defenses. A phrase coined on the field of battle—"*Ils ne passeront pas!*" ("They shall not pass!")—fully described the grim determination of the French *poilu** to carry out his orders to the death.

Until the end of February, German losses had not been heavy. Faced with a check on the east bank, Falkenhayn now decided to expand the battle, and attacked west of the Meuse on March 6. Encouraged by the optimism of the German Crown Prince and his staff, Falkenhayn was determined to push on. A battle of attrition was in prospect. Meanwhile, Pétain had wisely reinforced this new zone, and conditions now appeared to be equalized between the two sides. Moreover, bad weather had grounded the aggressive air formations that previously had given an advantage to the Germans. The defenses again held. On both sides of the Meuse, fighting settled into the familiar pattern of trench warfare.

Pétain adopted a policy of rotating divisions through his defensive sectors in relatively short intervals. By the end of June, 65 French divisions had been through the hell that was Verdun while the Germans had used only 47, each of which endured a longer period in the line. The success of Pétain's policy showed that soldiers who must be exposed to continuous danger and artillery bombardment will maintain their mental and physical resiliency over a longer time if they are allowed specific amounts of rest in the rear and regular periods of leave. Exposure to prolonged trench warfare conditions produced a new phenomenon—shell shock, a mental condition characterized by erratic, often hysterical behavior. Another benefit of Pétain's troop rotation policy was the boost that it gave to the morale of French units. All knew that the heavy punishment and high number of casualties that had to be endured would be shared equally.[21]

The brutal fighting continued until December 15, 1916.

*The French private soldier.

The battle culminated in a series of methodical counterattacks. Directed by a rising military commander, General Robert Nivelle, these regained much of the lost territory for the French. The results of this battle—the longest in modern history—were truly staggering. The French casualties totaled approximately 542,000. But the strategy of attrition can be a two-edged sword, and Germany suffered nearly 434,000 casualties. Falkenhayn had discovered, too late, that battles in this war often assumed a character and will of their own when the commander could not shut down a battle after its initial failure.

Partly as a result of his miscalculation, the Chief of the German General Staff was replaced by Field Marshal Paul von Hindenburg and his ever present first quartermaster general, Erich von Ludendorff. This team would direct the war efforts of Germany, indeed of the Central Powers, for the remainder of the war. Another influence on Falkenhayn's replacement was the loyal response of the British to the predicament of the French at Verdun. The British would assume the major role in the planned offensive on the Somme River and attempt to relieve the German pressure on the French.

First Battle of the Somme: July 1–November 19, 1916

The original plans for the Somme offensive, it will be remembered, had called for the French to make the main effort while the British played a subsidiary rote. Falkenhayn's attack at Verdun reversed these roles, and the reasons for the offensive were altered. Instead of applying pressure on the Germans, the Somme offensive was now designed to relieve presure on the French at Verdun. (*See Atlas Map No. 13.*)

The location and tactics employed at the Somme are open to serious criticism. Joffre claimed to have chosen this area because it had been quiet since 1914. This may have been true, but this period of inactivity had allowed the Germans time to reinforce and methodically develop a defensive position. In truth, Joffre probably wanted the attack there, at the junction of the French and British forces, to insure British cooperation. Haig had desired an attack in Flanders utilizing an amphibious end run; but once he agreed to the Somme attack, he became a loyal and enthusiastic supporter.

The British plan of attack was ambitious. The British Fourth Army under General Henry Rawlinson would make the main attack, supported by the French Sixth Army to the south. After penetrating the German lines and seizing the high ground to the rear, the gap would be widened and developed. With the flanks secured, the main effort would turn north and, after decisive gains, all available cavalry units would conduct the exploitation. The main attack was to be supported by secondary attacks, demonstrations, and feints.

In implementation, these plans were to prove most disappointing. The Royal Flying Corps established air superiority over the battlefield. The British ground forces, now swollen with half-trained conscripts, watched the preparatory bombardment begin at dawn on June 24. However, the assault was delayed from June 29 to July 1 because of bad weather. Despite the extra days of preparation, the German wire and defenses were not seriously harmed; the British still lacked the heavy artillery necessary to counteract the improved defenses. Additionally, the number of malfunctioning rounds among the new high explosive shells seriously hampered the preparation for the attack.

At 7:28 a.m. on July 1, the French and British infantry climbed from their trenches and began the harrowing advance. Although the French employed a creeping artillery barrage in front of their forces, British artillery-infantry coordination was still crude. Once the artillery fire lifted from the German trenches, the machinegunners left the protection of their dugouts, zeroed in their weapons, and extracted their toll in lives. The heavily burdened British infantry soldier advanced slowly across the 500 meters of No Man's Land. The battalion attack formation comprised four lines, each separated by 100 meters, the troops being spaced every three paces. As the withering machinegun fire began, however, the soldiers bunched up and the lines became intermingled. The casualties on that first day were at the heaviest rate ever sustained by the British Army—60,000 men.

In his isolated headquarters, Haig completely misunderstood the first day's action. He deluded himself that "Reports . . . seemed most satisfactory."[22] In fact, none of the objectives had been attained, and the only result had been the blooding of the "New Armies." The British commander ordered the attacks to continue until November 18. He remained confident that he could achieve tactical success and a breakthrough with one more offensive. Another reason for Haig's determination to keep up the offensive was Joffre's insistence that it was vital to divert German attention while the French consolidated their position and reclaimed ground lost in the Verdun battle.

On September 15, after two months of mutually destructive attacks and counterattacks, British tanks made their unimpressive entry onto the field of battle. While they overran some German positions, these new machines were mechanically unreliable, and the British had not adequately developed a doctrine for their integration with infantry units. Of the 49 tanks employed, only 18 were able to cross the line of departure. Despite their failure to retrieve victory on the Somme, however, the new weapons proved their

Ponderous British Tanks Make Their Disappointing Debut on the Somme Battlefield

shock value and promised to be the means for regaining tactical mobility. The British High Command immediately ordered 1,000 of the new machines, and all armies began assessing the value of this revolutionary weapon.[23] Uncharacteristically, while the Germans recognized the potential of the tank, the weapon's faltering start made them slow to produce their own tanks or develop antitank tactics.

The great attrition battles of Verdun and the Somme confirmed the wasteful and immobile nature of warfare on the Western Front. Once again, it was illustrated that a break into the enemy's defensive positions could be achieved if a commander was willing to expend the resources. But the ultimate goal of a penetration, the rupture of the enemy's entire defensive system, proved illusive. In reaction to their heavy losses in the defensive portions of these battles, the Germans developed and field tested a method of "elastic" defense, which will be fully discussed later. In fact, the failure of many German commanders to adhere to the new elastic doctrine during the latter stages of the Battle of the Somme resulted in increasingly heavy casualties. Commanders who either could not or would not abandon the old policy of holding forward positions at all costs subjected their soldiers to the murderous fire of the enemy's artillery. The use of the airplane as an effective ground support weapon was also confirmed in these battles. Perhaps the greatest lesson of these battles, however, was the close relationship between events all along the trench line. Commanders on both sides now visualized the entire Western

Front as a single battle zone. The ability of both sides to shift combat power rapidly from one sector to another made it much more difficult to achieve effective surprise. It also proved the efficacy of countering enemy initiatives in sectors unaffected by direct assault.

The Asiago Offensive

Concomitant with the great battles on the Western Front, Austria attempted a decisive operation against Italy. Obsessed with a hatred of Italy, the Austrian commander, Field Marshal Conrad von Hötzendorf, was determined to divert the combined military operations of Germany and Austria against this old foe. Falkenhayn, of course, was most unsympathetic to this view, since he had already decided upon his battle of attrition against the French at Verdun. Although refused German assistance, Conrad persisted with his plan to attack in the Trentino, behind the main Italian armies on the Isonzo front. Falkenhayn, equally determined, plunged into battle at Verdun without Austrian cooperation. This situation is a clear illustration of the fact that the Central Powers, like the Allies, suffered from difficulties in coordinating military operations in a coalition war.

Conrad's plan, in what came to be known as the Asiago Offensive, was to drive through the mountain passes of the Trentino, seize the northern Italian plain, and, in so doing, trap the Italian armies on the Isonzo and Carnic fronts.[24] (*See Atlas Map No. 14.*) Because of the sensitivity of the Italian commander to the possibility of such a move and the difficulties involved in assembling the Austrian strike force of 15 divisions, Conrad could not hope to achieve surprise.

General Cadorna ordered his First Army to prepare its defenses in depth against the expected Austrian offensive. The First Army commander chose to ignore these directions and conducted local operations to improve his front. Consequently, when Conrad's blow fell on May 15, 1916, the First Army was unprepared and off balance. Considering the rugged nature of the terrain, the Austrians made excellent initial gains. However, although they reached the Arsiero-Asiago line, they were unable to break out onto the Asiago Plateau. Cadorna now displayed the finest qualities of determination and efficiency under extreme pressure. Utilizing his superior lateral communications, he shifted more than half a million troops into the threatened area by June 2 and contained the Austrian drive.

In response to the requests of the panic-stricken Italian Government, Russia mounted an attack in Galicia under General Brusilov on June 4. Although this action did not materially affect Conrad's Asiago Offensive, it did force the transfer of Austrian units and guns to the Eastern Front after June 8. This, in turn, weakened the Austrian Trentino and

Isonzo fronts. Thus, when Cadorna mounted counterattacks, he was able to regain more than half of the ground lost to enemy attacks. Another significant result of this complex series of events was the comparative success of Cadorna's Sixth Battle of the Isonzo on August 6–17.

The Balance Sheet for 1916

The year 1916 ended on a note of frustration and with a benumbing tally of casualties on both sides. The Allies were able to divert and finally check the German offensives on the Western Front, but the prospect of final victory appeared distant, if not unattainable.

At sea, the Royal Navy imposed an increasingly more restrictive blockade on the Central Powers.[25] Items originally omitted from the list of contraband items, such as copper, oil, and cotton, were gradually added. The blockade became total in March 1915, when foodstuffs were finally banned from trade. All goods on neutral ships destined for the enemy were purchased by the British, and the ships returned empty. This method of restriction, while irritating to the neutrals, was never as inflammatory as the German naval tactics.

The German response to the blockade was a modern version of commerce raiding—a submarine campaign. The underwater boats inflicted severe damage upon both naval and commercial vessels. The mounting tonnage sunk by the U-boats and the deaths of noncombatants caused by the surprise attacks became excellent subjects for British propaganda in the neutral states—especially the United States. However, the German Government was careful to appease American anger. The sinking of the Cunard Liner, *Lusitania,* in May 1915, with the loss of more than 100 American lives, nearly ruptured the uneasy relationship between Germany and the United States. But when the Germans realized the seriousness of President Woodrow Wilson's reaction, they retreated to an apologetic stance and guaranteed the safety of noncombatants. Later, after the sinking of the *Sussex,* a cross-Channel steamer, President Wilson demanded that Germany either abandon all submarine attacks upon commercial vessels or face the severance of diplomatic relations. The Germans then repentantly promised not to attack any commercial vessel without adequate warning. It would not be until 1917 that the leaders of the German Government would feel secure enough to commence unrestricted submarine warfare and bring the United States into the war.

In the East, the loyal Russian ally mounted an abortive offensive at Lake Narotch in an effort to draw German forces away from the critical Verdun battle. This operation, which began on March 18, 1916, was poorly planned and mismanaged. At a cost of more than 70,000 casualties, the

**Hindenburg, Kaiser Wilhelm II, and Ludendorff—
the Final Command Team of the Central Powers**

Russians provided the besieged French with little relief. Another related campaign on the Eastern Front, the so-called Brusilov Offensive (June-August 1916), was mounted in response to pleas from Italy to relieve pressure created by the Austrian Asiago Offensive. While Brusilov achieved some success, his attack came just as the Austrian forces were grinding to a halt and the threat to the Italian Army was being contained. To add to the apparent futility of the Allied military situation, a combined task force of the Central Powers overwhelmed Rumania after she had joined the Allied cause. The Italians contributed little towards military victory in their repeated offensives on the Isonzo River. In fact, they only narrowly averted disaster themselves when the Austrian Asiago Offensive just failed to cut off and trap their main armies.

On the Western Front, the British conducted their first major offensive on the Somme River. They accepted heavy losses in order to deflect German combat power from the Battle of Verdun. Falkenhayn removed Verdun's priority on ammunition when the Somme artillery preparation began, and only 10 days after the opening of the infantry assault on the Somme front, the Germans made their last attack at Verdun. From this point forward, they maintained a defensive posture at Verdun while fighting the British to a draw on the Somme. Perhaps the most portentous result of the year's operations was the relief of Falkenhayn as the Chief of the German General Staff by the team of Hindenburg and Ludendorff, who were more disposed to seek a solution in the East.

Despite a marked numerical superiority and the crushing economic weapon of naval blockade, the Allies had been unable to move toward victory. They had merely succeeded in negating the enemy's actions on the Western Front.

Notes

[1] Erich von Falkenhayn, *The German General Staff and Its Decisions, 1914–1916* (New York, 1920), pp. 17–19.

[2] James E. Edmonds (ed.), *History of the Great War: Military Operations, France and Belgium, 1914* (2 vols.; London, 1925), 406–407. This British official history is hereinafter cited as *BOH, 1914*.

[3] C.R.M.F. Cruttwell, *A History of the Great War, 1914–1918*, 2nd ed. (Oxford, 1936), pp. 94–96.

[4] Philip Nearne, *German Strategy in the Great War* (London, 1923), pp. 42–43; Falkenhayn, *German General Staff*, pp. 10–19. For an opposing view of Falkenhayn's motives in this strategy, see Wolfgang Foerster, *Count Schlieffen and the World War*, trans. by C.G. Bowen (Berlin, 1921), pp. 11–14.

[5] Cyril Falls, *The Great War* (New York, 1959), pp. 79–80.

[6] Ferdinand Foch, *The Memoirs of Marshal Foch* (New York, 1931), pp. 117–139.

[7] Frank P. Chambers, *The War Behind the War, 1914–1918* (New York, 1939), pp. 144–156.

[8] Basil H. Liddell Hart, *A History of the World War, 1914–1918* (London, 1930), pp. 179–180; Falkenhayn, *German General Staff*, pp. 43–53, 58–71.

[9] "Instructions to Sir John French from Lord Kitchener," in Edmonds, *BOH, 1914*, I, 499–500.

[10] "Instructions of General Joffre to Field Marshal French, December 27, 1914," in James E. Edmonds (ed.), *History of the Great War: Military Operations, France and Belgium, 1914–1916* (6 vols.; London, 1922–1938), I, 66–69, hereinafter cited as *BOH, 1914–1916*; *Les Armées Française dans La Grande Guerre* (Paris, 1931), II, 681–682, hereinafter cited as *FOH*.

[11] Edmonds, *BOH, 1914–1916*, I, 74–109.

[12] Reichsarchiv, "The Gas Attack of the Fourth Army at Ypres" in *Der Weltkrieg, 1914 bis 1919*, trans. by Army War College (Berlin, 1925), III, 3. The gas was xylyl bromide dispensed from artillery shells.

[13] Liddell Hart, *History of the World War*, pp. 175–177.

[14] Falkenhayn, *German General Staff*, p. 94; Edmonds, *BOH, 1914–1916*, I, 187–192.

[15] Falls, *The Great War*, pp. 141–146.

[16] Edmonds, *BOH, 1914–1916*, II, 87–89.

[17] "The Plan of Action Proposed by France to the Coalition," trans. in Edmonds, *BOH, 1914–1916*, III, App. I, 1–5.

[18] *FOH*, III, 602.

[19] "Memorandum from Gen. von Falkenhayn to the Kaiser, December 25, 1915," in Falkenhayn, *German General Staff*, pp. 239–250.

[20] T. Dodson Stamps and Vincent J. Esposito (eds.), *A Short Military History of World War I* (West Point, New York, 1950), pp. 163–165.

[21] Lord Moran, *The Anatomy of Courage* (London, 1945), pp. 75–84.

[22] Robert Blake (ed.), *The Private Papers of Douglas Haig, 1914–1919* (London, 1952), p. 153.

[23] Basil H. Liddell Hart, *The Tanks* (2 vols.; New York, 1959), I, 79.

[24] Vincent J. Esposito (ed.), *A Concise History of World War I* (New York, 1964), pp. 165–167; Cruttwell, *Great War*, pp. 449–453.

[25] Cruttwell, *Great War*, pp. 187–203.

Peripheral Operations

5

This is one of the great campaigns of history. Think what Constantinople is to the East. It is more than London, Paris, and Berlin rolled into one are to the West. Think how it has dominated the East. Think what its fall will mean. Think how it will affect Bulgaria, Greece, Roumania, and Italy, who have already been affected by what has taken place. You cannot win this war by sitting still.

Winston S. Churchill
First Lord of the Admiralty

The Great War came to be known as the World War because, ultimately, 36 nations were drawn into the hostilities. Unlike World War II, however, the Great War's principal battles were confined to the European Continent.* Due to the dominant position of the British Navy and the extensive British and French colonial empires (*See Atlas Map No. 1*), the Central Powers had little opportunity to seek military victory outside of the European theaters of operation.

Despite this fact, campaigns and battles were fought the world over—on the high seas, and in colonies in Asia, Africa, and the Pacific Ocean. Referred to as peripheral operations, these military and naval actions of the Great War are often relegated to a lesser position of importance. Nevertheless, some of these operations were critical. For example, the Battle of Jutland determined the single constant of the war—the control of the oceans by the Entente Powers. Other operations, such as the tenacious resistance of German colonial forces in East Africa, created a great drain on Allied resources and earned admiration for the skillful defenders, but never seriously affected the outcome of the war.

*The Library of Congress classification for works concerning World War I remains: "European War, 1914–1918."

Most of the peripheral operations were initiated without adequate analysis of the human or material resources required to achieve success. Some of these operations were undertaken without their advocates defining what would constitute success within the framework of the war as a whole. Finally, these battles on the periphery of the war were clearly influenced by the vagaries of politics and national ambition. While the same can be said of the continental campaigns, it is easier to discern these influences in the isolated, peripheral campaigns.

Although most of the peripheral operations were undertaken with the belief that they would bring the Great War to a swifter conclusion, the reverse effect was universal. Drawing troops and materiel away from the decisive theaters, these operations prolonged the inevitable defeat of the Central Powers. Most significant, the peripheral campaigns were to have a great effect upon the postwar reallocation of territory and the perception of non-Europeans about the fragility of European society and the colonial empires that this society had spawned.

Occupation of the German Colonial Empire, 1914–1918

On August 5, 1914, one day after having declared war on Germany, the British began planning the capture of German colonies throughout the world. The purport of such operations was to prevent German ships from gaining access to ports and to protect adjacent Allied colonies from the threat of invasion. This, however, was only a rationalization for the traditional British strategy of acquiring enemy colonies either for use as bargaining tools during peacetime negotiations or as a means of enlarging the British Empire.[1]

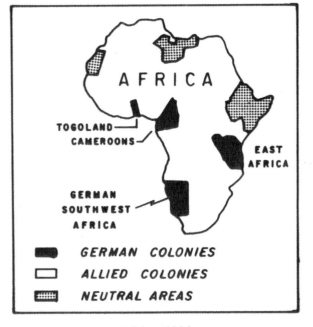

Africa, 1914

On August 7, without waiting for instructions, four companies of British-led native troops and a detachment of French-led Senegalese troops invaded German Togoland, which surrendered 20 days later. Togoland harbored the radio station that coordinated the operations of German surface raider ships in African waters. Its capture, therefore, greatly contributed to the Allied effort at sea.

On August 10, when all British regular troops were withdrawn from South Africa for employment in France, the white civilian inhabitants promptly formed four small detachments and invaded their northern neighbor, German Southwest Africa. After the capture of all ports, however, the invasion was halted because of a rebellion back in South Africa. By the time the campaign was resumed in January 1915, the South Africans were 50,000 strong. A slow march into the dry interior, relieved occasionally by a skirmish, brought victory on July 9, 1915. South African units were then transferred to German East Africa and Europe.

The invasion of the Cameroons began on August 20, 1914, with French columns moving west from French Equatorial Africa, and British and Belgian columns moving east from Nigeria. One month later, an Allied amphibious landing seized the colony's ports, but the Cameroonian Army, consisting of 12 companies, resisted until January 1916.

By early November 1914, New Zealanders, Australians, and Japanese had cleared the Pacific Ocean of all German colonies. Sailing to the Solomons, Rabaul, the Marshalls, the Carolines, and the German portion of New Guinea, they accepted the surrender of the German colonial governments. Resistance was offered only in the Chinese province of Shantung, where, in early September, the Japanese mounted a 23,000-man expedition against this German colony. On November 1, they attacked the principal fortress, Kiao-Chau, by digging the first parallel as dictated by eighteenth century methods of siegecraft. The following night, the second parallel was dug, reducing No Man's Land to 300 yards. Four nights later, the besiegers overran the redoubts; the German garrison surrendered at dawn.

In most cases, operations against German colonies were worthwhile. Although the conquests of the Cameroons and Southwest Africa required more than 11 months, the ports of all colonies had been captured and made unavailable to commerce raiders by November 1914. Because the colonial and constabulary troops employed in these campaigns would not, in any event, be transferred to the Western Front,* the colonial operations had little effect on the war in Europe. With the seizure of these colonies, the Allies deprived Germany of colonial areas the size of France, Germany, and Austria-Hungary combined—a total of 6,421,295 square miles—at a cost of only 991 British, French, and Belgian battle and disease casualties, 350 of whom died. Native black casualties, on whom poor records were kept, were between 12,000 and 20,000.

One colonial campaign, however, was not so successful. It became a quagmire, canceling the low cost of all the others. In German East Africa, Lieutenant Colonel Paul von Lettow-Vörbeck and his 15-company constabulary took the offensive and raided neighboring British Uganda. For the rest of the war, more than 130,000 British, Belgian, Portuguese, and African troops chased Lettow-Vörbeck across German and Portuguese East Africa; however, they were never able to corner their quarry, whose force never exceeded 3,500 Germans and 12,000 natives. When the armistice was signed in 1918, Lettow-Vörbeck's tenacity had cost the Allies over $360 million, 48,328 dead of wounds and disease, 13,892 wounded, and more than 350,000 cases of malaria, sleeping sickness, dysentery, and pneumonia. Because of Lettow-Vörbeck's elusiveness, all the forces freed by the quick completion of the other African colonial campaigns were used as reinforcements in East Africa, the only exception being one South African brigade that was sent to the Western Front.[2]

The Ottoman Empire— Key to the Expansion of War

The weak and faltering Ottoman Empire had been a major factor in European diplomatic and military developments

---

*The Allied leaders felt that native troops could not be used on the cold, wet Western Front.

Enver Pasha, War Minister of Turkey

throughout the nineteenth century. At the time of the assassination of the Archduke Francis Ferdinand in Sarajevo, the Ottoman Turks had many enemies, most of whom coveted the Turkish provinces. Known as the "sick man" of Europe, through the years Turkey had lost power and influence—both as a result of war and as a consequence of the establishment of suzerainty in the Middle East by several European nations. (*See Atlas Map No. 42.*)

In 1909, a band of military officers known as the Young Turks finally secured power from the corrupt sultanate and established a government under the Committee of Union and Progress. Acting as a corporate government, the Young Turks planned to revive the Pan-Islamic domination over all the former lands of the Ottoman Empire. This was in direct conflict with the interests of Russia, France, and Great Britain, all of whom had benefited from Turkey's declining power. On the other hand, Germany, a late entrant in the colonial race, saw Turkey's new-found national spirit as an opportunity to gain influence in the Middle East. Accordingly, Germany's military leaders and diplomats actively courted the Young Turks, and in 1913 established an extensive military mission headed by Lieutenant General Liman von Sanders.[3]

Although Turkish leaders may have mistrusted Germany's motives, they accepted her assistance. Turkey clearly perceived that neighboring Russia, her historic enemy, posed the greatest threat to Turkish interests. For

centuries, the czars had coveted Constantinople and the route to the Mediterranean Sea running through the narrows of the Dardanelles and the Bosporus. Through this path lay Russia's only warm water outlet to the world. Formerly, England, the preeminent sea power, had found it in her national interest to act as the Turkish Sultan's protector in order to prevent a stronger power from threatening the routes to India and Asia through the Mediterranean and Suez Canal.[4] Although in 1911—three years before the Great War commenced—England still acted as patron and adviser to the Turkish Navy, she refused a formal request for an alliance. To the Turks, therefore, German assistance was very welcome.

On August 2, 1914, a secret treaty between Germany and Turkey was signed, obligating the signatories to join together if either one was at war with Russia.[5] However, Germany's failure to secure victory in the Battle of the Marne and Austria's defeats in Serbia and Galicia caused the suspicious Turks to delay entry into the conflict until they felt assured of joining the winning side.

The Flight of the Goeben and Breslau

Before the war, the Turkish Government had contracted with British shipyards to build Turkey's first two dreadnought-class battleships. These were nearing completion on the eve of war. Since the ships had been financed by donations from the Turkish people, they served as a symbol of national pride. However, on August 3, 1914, Great Britain commandeered these battleships for her own fleet, which was then preparing for war. Moreover, rather than apologizing, the British Government made a vague promise to provide compensation at a later date. Turkish popular opinion promptly hardened against England.

On the next day, August 4, Great Britain gave Germany the ultimatum that was to bring about a state of war. Two German ships, the battle cruiser *Goeben* and the light cruiser *Breslau,* were on that day cruising in the Mediterranean Sea, closely shadowed by a British battle cruiser squadron.[6] The British squadron was charged with protecting French transports ferrying colonial troops from North Africa to Europe. As night fell, the *Goeben* and *Breslau* steamed away from the British; by midnight, when hostilities commenced, they were out of range.

Realizing that escape from the Mediterranean was out of the question, Vice Admiral Wilhelm A.T. Souchon, commander of the *Goeben,* decided to harass the French North African ports of embarkation. After shelling Bone and Phillipville, he set course for Turkey. Narrowly avoiding the strong British squadron several times,[7] the two ships fi-

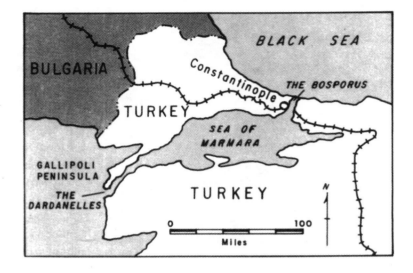

The Dardanelles and Bosporus Straits

nally slipped into the Dardanelles straits.* Using this turn of fortune to best advantage, Germany then presented the two ships to the Turkish Navy as replacements for the battleships seized by the British. Although Admiral Souchon and his crews went through the formalities of entering the Turkish Navy, they continued to man the ships.

Shortly thereafter, in a plot in which Turkish War Minister Enver Pasha participated, Turkey was plunged into the war.[8] On October 28, the *Goeben* and *Breslau,* now renamed and flying the Turkish ensign on their jack staffs, led a battle fleet into the Black Sea. The next morning, the Turkish ships began bombarding the Russian ports of Odessa and Sevastopol, in the process sinking several Russian ships. As a result of this act, Russia and her allies declared themselves at war with Turkey. In this manner, German seamanship and diplomacy had achieved a far-reaching victory without battle. For the remainder of the war, the Allies would be unable to transfer war supplies to the poorly equipped Russian Army. More important, and to the advantage of the Central Powers, a belligerent Turkey insured that several active fronts would expand the war and consume the resources of the Allies.

The state of the Turkish Army in 1914 was not one to inspire confidence. It had not won a significant victory in the twentieth century, although it had been involved in three wars. Morale was low. The Army was six months behind in pay. Troops were ill-fed and physically unfit. Although company grade officers were competent, field grade and flag officers were generally ignorant of their duties. There were only three rays of hope: first, Sanders had placed German officers into many of the critical command and staff slots by the end of 1914; second, the Anatolian Turk was as hardy a

soldier as any in the world, stoically accepting conditions that would have driven other armies to mutiny; third, Turk soldiers, unlike those of Great Britain and Germany, had had recent experience in the conditions of modern war.

The Army consisted of 36 divisions, and Turkey raised 70 more during the war. A Turkish division was very light, usually not even approaching its authorized strength of 9,000 infantry and 36 guns. Movement of these divisions was a logistic nightmare. The Turkish railway system consisted of one standard gauge railroad that ran from Constantinople, the site of both of Turkey's munitions factories, to Baghdad. A narrow gauge system went on to Gaza. (*See Atlas Map No. 42.*) However, the main road contained three significant gaps: one through the Taurus Mountains, one through the Adana Mountains, and one of 240 miles from Ras-al-Ain to Samarrah. Troops destined for the Caucasus also had a 250-mile march after detraining at Ras-al-Ain.

Mesopotamia

By 1914, the British Royal Navy had nearly completed the conversion of its capital ships to the use of oil rather than coal. The fleet was now dependent upon this fuel, which came principally from the refinery on Abadan Island[9] at the head of the Persian Gulf. (*See Atlas Map No. 43.*) In October 1914, prior to Turkey's entry into the war, the British colonial government in India dispatched its 6th Poonah Division to the Persian Gulf for the purpose of protecting the refinery.

Mesopotamia is a giant river plain lying between the high mountains of Persia (modern-day Iran) and the deserts of Saudi Arabia. (*See Atlas Map No. 42.*) The great rivers, the Tigris and the Euphrates, not only drain the area but also provide the main arteries of transportation. All permanent

---

*This was in direct violation of international treaties that forbade warships from transiting the straits.

The Abadan Oil Refinery

settlements of any size are on the shores of these two rivers, with Baghdad, the major city, 415 miles up the Tigris from Abadan Island. The rivers overflow each spring when the mountain snows melt, inundating lower Mesopotamia extensively. In fact, many of the marshes thus created never dry up. In 1914, the entire area was infested with fleas, mosquitoes, and filthy dogs; notorious for its mud and searing sun; and plagued by jaundice, malaria, yellow fever, and cholera.

Four days after war was declared on Turkey, the 6th Division landed at Fao. (*See Atlas Map No. 43.*) The Turkish reaction was slow; by the time 1,500 troops had been sent from Basra, the Anglo-Indian force was in control, supported by gunboats on the Shatt-al-Arab estuary. When the British attacked the Turkish trench line at Sahil, the defenders broke and ran, losing many of their number and leaving Basra undefended.

The success of the Anglo-Indian force against feeble Turkish resistance encouraged the British and Indian Governments to order a further advance inland to Qurna,[10] at the confluence of the Tigris and Euphrates Rivers. Following light resistance, Qurna fell on December 9, 1914. The oil refinery, the original objective of the operation, was now 50 miles behind the front and Indian forces controlled the only route to the island. The local commander and the British Government considered the campaign successfully concluded. Later, however, unwise political decisions would cause this tactical front to be reopened.

The Caucasus Mountains

Enver Pasha, the young war leader of Turkey, had been a prominent soldier in the series of lost wars that had marked the decline of the Ottoman Empire. Despite this record, he fancied himself a brilliant military strategist. With his nation at war, he planned a decisive campaign against Turkey's ancient enemy. Russia.[11] The campaign was to take place in the Caucasus Mountains, which defined the border between the two countries. (*See Atlas Map No. 42.*) The Germans encouraged this plan because it would tie down Russian troops far from the action on the Eastern Front.

Having concentrated 95,000 men in the Caucasus, on December 21, 1914, Enver Pasha led his poorly equipped and ill-prepared troops forward against the equally unprepared Russian forces. The objective was to destroy the Russian Caucasian Army and open South Georgia to invasion. It was hoped that this victory would be followed by a general Moslem uprising in the southern provinces of Russia. Pasha disregarded the treacherous mountain terrain, which rises to an average of 6,500 feet—several peaks reach 16,000 feet—and the weather, which keeps the area snowbound for six months each year. Consequently, the Turkish commander led his army to quick destruction. Even the hardy Turkish peasant could not live off the land in sub-zero temperatures. Soldiers on both sides fought savagely, but adept Russian generalship in the defense and the merciless cold soon reduced the Turkish force to less than 18,000 men. By mid-January, Enver Pasha admitted defeat and quit the field.[12] The grave results of this foolish campaign, undertaken without proper planning or logistical support, sapped the Turkish Army's offensive strength for the remainder of the war.

In January 1916, after the British had completed their evacuation of the Gallipoli Peninsula, 22 Turkish divisions were freed for employment elsewhere. General Erich von Falkenhayn, the Chief of the German General Staff, refused an offer of 20 of these divisions to reinforce the Western Front, and recommended that they be employed within the Ottoman Empire. Accordingly, Enver Pasha ordered two divisions to Mesopotamia and two to the Greek frontier near Salonika, dispersed ten divisions on coast-watching missions in Turkey, and sent the remaining divisions to the Caucasus Front.

The Russian commander on the Caucasus Front, General Nikolai N. Yudenich, anticipated that the Turkish forces facing him would be reinforced as soon as the British evacuated Gallipoli. When his careful study of the situation convinced him that none of the Turkish divisions was likely to appear on his front before late March, Yudenich decided to seize the initiative and attack before the arrival of the Turkish reinforcements. The Grand Duke Nicholas, recently relieved as Russian Commander-in-Chief and now Viceroy of Transcaucasia, approved Yudenich's concept, whereupon the general set about obtaining adequate winter clothing for his troops. (*See Atlas Map No. 42.*)

The Russian attack on January 17 took the Turkish Third Army by surprise and ripped the front wide open. A month later, Yudenich captured Erzurum, an important Turkish fortified base located 50 miles from the point of the initial attack. The continued Russian success goaded an angry Enver Pasha into ordering the seriously depleted Third Army to launch a counteroffensive in May, before all of its reinforcement divisions had arrived; after slight success, the attack collapsed. After strengthening his force with troops brought to the front via the Black Sea and through the previously captured Turkish port of Trebizond, Yudenich renewed his offensive, winning a crushing victory at Erzincan in July. This battle climaxed the collective actions that eliminated the Turkish Third Army as an effective force; it had suffered 35,000 casualties, about half of which had been taken prisoner. The Turkish Second Army, farther to the southeast, waited until all the Gallipoli divisions had reached the front before launching an offensive in August; in this instance, Yudenich managed to contain the attack after it made moderate gains.[13] Once more, the promise of a successful Turkish offensive had been nipped in the bud. Although Yudenich was able to penetrate as far south as Lake Van by the end of August 1916, the Russians were handicapped by the poor road network and the fact that the Caucasus, which was a secondary theater for Russia, received only limited reinforcements.

There were no other significant operations on the Caucasus Front for the remainder of the war. In April 1917, the outbreak of the Russian Revolution caused the Czar's army to disintegrate. Although the troops in the Caucasus resisted the summons of Vladimir Lenin and Leon Trotsky more strongly than did those on the Eastern Front, Yudenich's command was paralyzed by insubordination. The Cossacks led the troop exodus to their homes, erroneously believing that the farms were to become theirs as free peasants.

Egypt 1914–1915

The British-controlled Suez Canal—an early Turkish military and economic objective—was defended by Anglo-Indian troops from its west bank. (*See Atlas Map No. 42.*) The British domination of the Mediterranean forced the Turks, under the command of German Colonel Kress von Kressenstein, to approach the Suez Canal overland through the Sinai Desert. In January 1915, about 20,000 Turkish troops began their march across the desert, literally dragging the field guns, boats, and bridging materials that were to be used in the assault.[14] Any chance of gaining surprise was lost when the attacking columns were discovered by British aerial reconnaissance flights as they approached the canal.

The Turkish columns reached the east bank of the canal on February 2. Waiting for them were about 70,000 British troops, including five recently arrived, half-trained Indian divisions. The Turks, however, were undeterred by the disparity of numbers; under the cover of darkness, they launched rafts carrying assault forces. These were engaged by British machinegun teams, which sank the rafts and killed many of the troops. The next day, the Turks made another attempt to cross. Under fire from British artillery and French and British gunboats, the Turks suffered heavily. Although three boats managed to reach the far shore, the troops in them were quickly killed or captured. The British commander, General Sir John Maxwell, then ordered the Indian infantry across the canal. The Turks, who had by now begun their retreat, were quickly driven back into the desert. They were not pursued.

The Indirect Approach—The Easterners vs. The Westerners

As previously discussed,* the military plans and strategy of Great Britain at the outbreak of war were based upon two major premises. First, while protecting the home islands, the Royal Navy would insure free passage of reinforcements and supplies for the Allied armies on the Continent. Second, the small standing army (the BEF) would support the French plan of attack, thereby honoring British commitments and securing a quick victory. Surrendering the choice of military options in order to support a continental ally was a surprising course of action to adopt, as it was in direct conflict with traditional British strategic policy. Having depended upon naval superiority for defense of the home islands since the defeat of the Spanish Armada in 1588, the British had been reluctant to maintain a large professional army and refused to institute conscription. With the notable exception of the colonial wars and peacekeeping missions, throughout the nineteenth century the British Army had remained of secondary importance in comparison with the Royal Navy.

During the eighteenth and nineteenth centuries, whenever a European power threatened to dominate the Continent, England had reacted with what has been called a "blue water strategy." The initial step was to enforce or gain naval supremacy by defeating or blockading the rival fleet(s). This allowed England to restrict or cut off the enemy's trade while her own ships transported goods and troops freely. Meanwhile, allied with one or more continental powers, England would provide money and supplies to sustain ground campaigns that would resist and, eventually, exhaust her enemies. If an enemy power had colonial pos-

*See Chapter 2, Page 25.

sessions, these would also be seized. When circumstances appeared favorable, England, in combination with her allies, would intervene with troops on the Continent, either to defeat her enemy or to negotiate a peace from a position of strength. The colonial possessions were often used as bargaining chips in the peace negotiations.

In contrast to the "blue water strategy," the Army had begun to develop a new strategy in the early years of the twentieth century. The Imperial General Staff, which had come into being as a result of the Haldane reforms following the Boer War, began planning for future wars, just as it was expected to do. As a result of study and war games at Camberley, the staff determined that the most dangerous general war situation would occur if France fell because of a strong German attack through Belgium. Since the French Army could not cover the Belgian border adequately, the critical place for deployment of the British Army would be on the French left. The Army strategy, which was known as "continental," called for the six British divisions to move to the Continent at war's outbreak and form on the left of the French line. This "continental" strategy prevailed over the "blue water strategy" in 1911, when the Committee of Imperial Defence* chose it for use in wartime.

In the mistaken belief that the war would be concluded quickly and decisively in the Allies' favor, the Imperial General Staff committed the BEF to the French battle plan. When defeat and deadlock occurred on the Western Front, the immediate reaction of the British War Cabinet was to reinforce the BEF with all available regular troops from the colonies as well as trained soldiers from Canada, Australia, and New Zealand. Lord Kitchener began a massive program of building "New Armies" of volunteers who, in time, would be sent to Europe. Additionally, the woefully inadequate production of arms and military equipment was recognized, and a vigorous program was begun to supply the enormous requirements of the war. From the outset of the war, Great Britain was tied to defeating the principal enemy, Germany, on the Western Front.

England, however, was the only power that possessed the capability to conduct large-scale operations against the Central Powers elsewhere. The "blue water strategy," which later became known as the "Eastern Strategy," would periodically rise to the fore as an alternative approach. This was especially true whenever the appalling toll of dead and wounded mounted in France with little apparent progress, or when shortages of military supplies and ammunition prevented large-scale offensive operations in Europe.

---

*Like the general staff, the British Committee of Imperial Defence (CID), was a product of the post-Boer War reform movement. A very high level governmental committee, the CID was created to coordinate national policy with military means and thereby determine national strategy.

The Dardanelles and Gallipoli

As 1914 ended with a bloodly stalemate in France, members of the British War Council, led by First Lord of the Admiralty Winston Churchill and First Sea Lord Admiral John Fisher, began pressing the Government to return to the traditional British strategy of the indirect approach. David Lloyd George, a shrewd Welsh politician who served as Chancellor of the Exchequer, agreed that Great Britain needed to apply its growing power away from the caldron of the Western Front and provide the public with victories to sustain morale. He was interested in defeating one of Germany's weaker allies—Austria or Turkey. This energetic group was given the support it needed to carry the day by the Secretary of State for War, Field Marshal Kitchener. He expressed the view that the German trench line in France could not be broken until the arms and munitions industries had begun to supply sufficient artillery to support trench warfare.[15] Therefore, if the British were to succeed anywhere in the near future, it would have to be outside of Europe.

The final impetus to action against Turkey came from the Russians. The Russian Commander-in-Chief, Grand Duke Nicholas, was extremely concerned about the Turkish offensive in the Caucasus, and requested a British demonstration against Turkey to prevent her from reinforcing the Caucasus Front.[†] Given Allied fears over Russia's strength following her massive defeat in East Prussia, the British Cabinet was disposed to honor the request.

The Naval Expedition

Because there were no troops at hand, a naval operation was the only option that could threaten and perhaps breach the Dardanelles. Such an operation had been studied by the British Admiralty and the Imperial General Staff on numerous occasions prior to the war.[16] These studies had concluded that a purely naval operation could not succeed, and that a joint army-navy amphibious operation was necessary.

On January 3, 1915, Churchill, anxious to act on the Cabinet's direction, cabled Vice Admiral Sackville Carden, Commander of Naval Forces in the Aegean Sea, to ask if his naval elements could force the straits with ships alone. Replying that the Dardanelles could not be "rushed," Carden submitted a plan for a methodical reduction of the

---

†Unfortunately, Russia was ambivalent toward Allied assistance in Turkey. She desired a demonstration to divert attention from the Caucasus area, but did not want an Allied invasion for fear that Russian claims to Turkey and the Dardanelles would be forfeited. Russia blocked the possible assistance of Greece in defeating Turkey for the same reason. Thus, the halting and gradual approach to the Dardanelles and Gallipoli was due as much to Russian self-interest as British indecision.

Turkish defenses. He stated that large caliber guns on aging battleships could pound the forts guarding the straits while minesweepers cleared channels through the mine belts. Carden estimated that this method would allow the naval expedition to reach Constantinople within a month. Having heard what they wished to hear, Churchill and the remainder of the War Council ignored the findings of previous studies and supported Carden's plan. Another influence on this decision was the example of the German heavy guns that had reduced the sturdy forts at Liège and Namur.

Thus began the most controversial and frustrating campaign of the war. Operations against the Dardanelles would always seem just beyond the grasp of the Allies. With great hope for decisive results, more troops and resources would be drawn into the campaign, only to be squandered through inaction or lack of coordination.

On January 13, 1915, the British War Cabinet directed "a naval expedition in February to bombard and take the Gallipoli Peninsula with Constantinople as its objective."[17] This ambiguous order revealed the Cabinet's lack of understanding of the capabilities of a naval force operating without supporting invasion troops. It also proved that the British underestimated the Turkish Army, expecting, or perhaps hoping, that it would crumble under only slight pressure. Both miscalculations would lead to the gradual application of military and naval power without success.

Under the skillful direction of German Lieutenant General Limon von Sanders, the Turkish Army had been revitalized since 1913. Following a disastrous performance in the Balkan Wars, it had been provided with subsidies for pay, furnished with weapons and equipment, and given training under German methods. Because of the increasing possibility of war, Sanders mobilized the Army to a full strength of 36 divisions by the end of September 1914. With the British Mediterranean squadron's casual bombardment of the defenses of the Dardanelles in November (*See Atlas Map No. 44a*), the Turkish Army was alerted to the intentions of the Allies.[18]

In command of an Anglo-French naval squadron of 12 predreadnought battleships, one new super dreadnought (the *Queen Elizabeth*), and auxiliary ships and minesweepers, Admiral Carden planned to destroy the Dardanelles' forts at Cape Helles on the Gallipoli Peninsula and Kum Kale on the Asiatic shore. The key to the campaign was the narrows, where the shores were only a mile apart and 20 forts were concentrated to guard the passage. During the three weeks it took to assemble the naval force, the Turks reinforced the forts, deployed mobile artillery batteries along the shore, and reinforced the belts of mines that extended across the straits.

As directed, the British commander opened the campaign on February 19, shelling the forts at Cape Helles at long range. When no fire was returned, the ships closed to within three miles of shore. Then, just as the British became convinced that the Turks had fled, shore batteries returned the fire, and the Allied squadron withdrew. The next day, storms set in, delaying the return of Carden's ships until February 25. This time they silenced the forts in two days and then sent Marine landing parties ashore to destroy enemy guns. Following this, the fleet sailed into the straits.

Although the methodical advance continued, it was hampered by bad weather, accurate Turkish artillery fire against the improvised wooden minesweepers, and enemy minefields. The British persevered, however, and planned to make a major assault on March 18 that would break through the Turkish defenses. On the eve of this assault, Admiral Carden suffered a nervous collapse and was replaced by Rear Admiral John de Robeck, who pressed the attack, thinking that all the mine belts had been cleared. Unknown to the British and French, however, a week earlier a Turkish minelayer had sown a new line of 20 mines parallel to the shore. The French battleship *Bouvet* struck this belt and sank immediately, with a loss of 700. Sailors watched in disbelief, thinking that a Turkish artillery round had exploded in the ship's magazine. Two hours later, the battle cruiser *Inflexible* hit a mine, followed in rapid succession by the battleships *Irresistible* and *Ocean*. Confused and fearing a barrage of free-floating mines or torpedoes, de Robeck ordered a retreat* back to his base on the island of Lemnos.[19]

An Amphibious Landing

When the operation to force the Dardanelles had first been discussed, Kitchener had stated that he could not spare any ground troops. Later, however, he relented, conceding that a few divisions might be found. Designated and assembled, those divisions were in the process of being concentrated in Egypt and Lemnos while the naval operations were proceeding. Known as the Mediterranean Force, they were commanded by General Ian Hamilton, a Boer War favorite of Kitchener. Hastily briefed before leaving London for the Dardanelles on March 13, Hamilton had been instructed that his force was not to be used until the Navy had been thwarted in its every effort to force the straits. Hopefully, his troops might only be used to destroy already neutralized Turkish forts and batteries.

---

*It is now generally accepted that the Turkish defenders were badly hurt by the March 18 assault. A determined British attack in the next few days probably would have forced the straits. De Robeck, of course, could not have known this. Moreover, it is doubtful that a naval raid on Constantinople would have had major consequences. Supplying such a raiding fleet in the Sea of Marmara would also have been very difficult.

Hamilton had arrived at the Dardanelles just in time to see the costly March 18 assault. Concluding that the Navy could not alone force the straits, he so advised Kitchener on March 19. Although de Robeck seems to have intended to renew his attack after refitting, Hamilton apparently convinced him that a joint ground-sea effort would be necessary. By supporting this view in a message to the Admiralty on the twenty-third, de Robeck effectively undercut an aggressively confident Churchill, who then had to concede to the change in plans.[20]

Hamilton and his small staff began feverish preparations in the face of difficult conditions. The quartermaster had no experience regarding amphibious supply consumption upon which to base his plans. Weapons were scarce. Naval intelligence officers had almost no information concerning the Turkish troop dispositions. Maps were practically nonexistent. There were not enough ships, and joint planning with de Robeck on how best to use the ones available began very late. Yet somehow Hamilton managed to get his entire force of 5 divisions into 77 ships and concentrate those ships at Lemnos by April 21.

The four-week lull following the naval attack had been put to good use by the Turks. Because preparations for the landings were now obvious, Sanders sent seven divisions into the Dardanelles area, fortified defenses around the beaches, and intensified training. Although defensive operations would be severely hindered by the primitive road network and the inability to move by water, Sanders placed his forces in centrally located assembly areas where they could react as quickly as possible to any landings.

The task facing the Allied attackers was by no means new. Throughout history, armies have been landed by ship on hostile shores. Until 1815, armies had fought as compact bodies formed in ranks. The problem to be solved by an amphibious commander then was to pick a landing point where the enemy army was not formed in ranks on the beach and to unload his army and arrange it in battle formation faster than the enemy army could march to the landing beach and attack.

The British at Gallipoli were well prepared to solve this classic problem. A large supply of barges was on hand. These unpowered boats were to be towed by motorboats. The tows, each with a string of four or five barges, would in turn be towed by battleships to within 3,000 yards of shore. Guide boats would lead the tows to the correct beach. After discharging their troops, the tows were to move 1,500 yards out to sea. There they would meet trawlers and destroyers carrying the second wave, transfer the second wave, and return to the beach.

Unfortunately for the Allies, machineguns and barbed wire had altered amphibious warfare as much as they had land warfare. Armies no longer needed to be formed in ranks on a small piece of ground before offering effective resistance. A small unit with machineguns could delay and disorganize a landing force, and such small units could easily be placed at all likely landing beaches. Fire support techniques were not sufficiently developed to allow the landing force to direct naval gun fire against a target as small as a machinegun. Twentieth century amphibious warfare, then, posed two problems: the new one of overcoming initial resistance on the beach, and the old one of getting troops ashore faster than the defender could mass. Hamilton had solved only the old one.

The British amphibious plan called for a series of landings, feints, and demonstrations. The French division was to conduct a feint by threatening a landing on the Asiatic shore at Kum Kale. (*See Atlas Map No. 44b.*) The Royal Naval Division was to sail up to the base of the peninsula in a demonstration against Bulair. The British 29th Infantry Division would conduct the main attack at Cape Helles, while the ANZAC (Australia-New Zealand Army) Corps was to land 12 miles up the peninsula and conduct a supporting attack.

On April 25, the attack began as planned. The French division and the British Naval Division achieved their goals of diverting enemy forces from the main attack. Although the ANZAC Corps landed a mile farther north than planned, it initially met no opposition. As the troops began moving inland, however, they encountered General Mustapha Kemal's* division, which quickly reinforced the area and contained the invaders. By noon, the situation at ANZAC Beach had stabilized.

At Cape Helles, the 29th Division landed, dispersed across five beaches that were designated S, V, W, X, and Y. At three beaches—S, X and Y—there was only light resistance. But at W Beach on the end of the Cape, the defenders

---

*Kemal would later be known as Atatürk, the father of modern Turkey.

British Troops Are Towed to Cape Helles

were well entrenched, the landing area was mined, and the beach was protected with barbed wire, which in turn was covered by enfilading machinegun fire. The British infantry were towed in rowboats to a point just short of the shore, where they were cut loose to glide onto the beach. The Turkish defenders held their fire until the attackers were ashore, and then opened with devastating effect. Despite heavy casualties, small groups got through; and the British now had a toehold on W Beach.

On V Beach, which was to be the location of the main assault, an old collier, the *River Clyde,* had been converted into a crude infantry landing craft to supplement the towed boats. Two thousand infantrymen were to disembark through doors cut in the bow of the ship. But V Beach was skillfully defended by a dug-in company of Turks with four machineguns. As the landing craft beached and small craft were positioned to make a ramp to the shoreline, the defenders' machineguns opened fire. While trying to leave the *River Clyde* and reach the beach, 70 percent of the first 1,000 troops became casualties. By mid-morning, the landing at V Beach had collapsed; the few survivors huddled inside the *River Clyde* or under the heights, which remained dominated by the Turkish defenders.

Although he could clearly observe the slaughter and stalemate on W and V Beaches, Hamilton chose not to influence the operation by ordering the shifting of troops between beaches. In his operational plan, he had placed all the Cape Helles landings under the 29th Division commander, and now scrupulously refrained from interfering with the latter's conduct of the battle. Unfortunately, the division commander was handicapped by poor communications, and therefore could not exercise effective control. Nor did the lower level commanders display the necessary initiative required to link up the beaches and advance to the high ground against an enemy who was outnumbered 6 to 1. Thus, when the British attacked on succeeding days, they made only minimal gains against the defenders, who had been promptly reinforced in the interim. Lady Luck had smiled briefly on the British, but the key commanders had missed the opportunity to court her.

By May 8, the Gallipoli beachheads had coalesced into trench lines. As in France, maneuver was no longer possible. The troops were exposed to the elements, particularly the hot sun, and were very short of supplies. Lack of transport made it difficult to evacuate the wounded. Disease, spread by flies and fleas, soon began to take its toll of Allied soldiers, and hospital rolls mounted.[21]

The failure of the landings and the subsequent stalemate were blamed on the principal architects of the Dardanelles operation. The Cabinet fell, bringing about a change in the British Government. Admiral Fisher resigned in protest over the weakening of the Grand Fleet in order to reinforce the Gallipoli area; Lloyd George became Minister of Munitions. Winston Churchill, having been relegated to an insignificant Cabinet post, went to serve in the army on the Western Front.

Renewal of the Assault

Lord Kitchener, who had originally opposed the entire Dardanelles operation, now became its principal supporter. He told the Government that the troops would suffer up to 50 percent casualties in any evacuation attempt.[22] Since a continuation of the stalemate was out of the question, he recommended that Hamilton be reinforced and that a new attempt to secure Gallipoli be undertaken. As if to emphasize the importance of this new theater, the War Council was actually renamed the Dardanelles Committee. As far as the British were concerned, Gallipoli remained the principal theater of operations throughout the summer. Five new British divisions were sent to Gallipoli, and Hamilton's command received priority on ammunition and supplies.

Hamilton planned to use his new forces to make a landing at Suvla Bay. (*See map on page 87.*) This landing was expected to outflank the Turkish defenders to the south and draw them away from ANZAC Beach, from which the British would launch the main effort. Hamilton also ordered supporting attacks at Cape Helles to pin down the enemy. The ANZAC Corps's objective was the Sidi Bahr Ridge, which dominated those Turkish forts and artillery sites that controlled the Narrows.

The assault resumed on August 6. Although the secondary attack at Cape Helles made only minor gains, it did manage to immobilize the Turkish defenders. The ANZAC main attack was launched at night and became disoriented; resumed the next morning, it failed to reach the heights of Sidi Bahr Ridge. To the north, the supporting attack at Suvla Bay missed yet another opportunity to make the Gallipoli Campaign a success. There, the British IX Corps landing surprised the Turks and was virtually unopposed. Unfortunately, the corps consisted of new units that were poorly led, and, as a result, did not capitalize on the enemy weakness. After two days of ineffective efforts, Lieutenant General Sir Frederick Stopford, the IX Corps commander, was ordered to move inland and seize the high ground. By then, however, Sanders had used the intervening two days to transfer two Turkish divisions south to oppose Stopford and prevent movement from the Suvla Bay front.

The British Withdrawal

Although operations on Gallipoli continued for the next few months, nothing broke the power of the defense. In

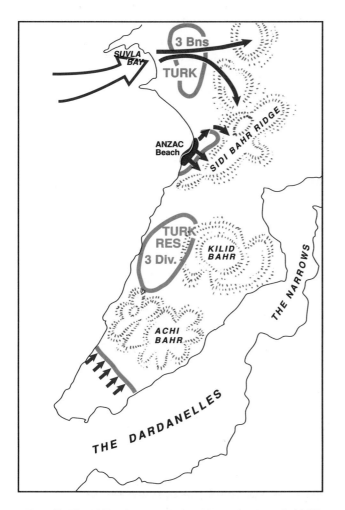

The Gallipoli Peninsula, Allied Plan, August 6, 1915

Salonika, 1915–1918

Another campaign that diverted substantial resources from the principal European Theater operation was launched in Greece in October 1915. Following three unsuccessful Austrian invasions, the Central Powers were determined to conquer Serbia. If that country could be crushed, territorial concessions could be used to bring Bulgaria into the war as a member of the Central Powers. This chain of events would, in turn, secure the Berlin-to-Constantinople railroad (see *Atlas Map No. 2*), and thereby allow shipment of war supplies to Turkey. These were sufficient reasons for Germany to offer Austria assistance in defeating Serbia.

At this time, King Ferdinand of Bulgaria felt confident that it lay in his interests to join the Central Powers. The British had failed in Gallipoli, and the concessions offered by Germany seemed real; the Allies offered only territory in Greece, which was not theirs to give. Therefore, Bulgaria signed a treaty of alliance with Germany and mobilized its forces.[23] (*See Atlas Map No. 33.*)

Appreciating Serbia's plight, the British and the French Governments sought to assist the gallant Serbs in defending against the impending fourth invasion. Both nations, however, also had less worthy reasons for assisting the Serbs. The French apparently desired to find a job for General Maurice P. Sarrail. A radical socialist who had been relieved from the Western Front by Joffre, Sarrail was now in Paris, fomenting political opposition. The British, on the other hand, sent help at the insistence of Lloyd George, Bonar Law, and other Cabinet members who saw another active theater near Turkey as a way to force evacuation of Gallipoli.

Greece had thus far maintained a tenuous neutrality in the war. King Constantine was in favor of Germany and the Central Powers, while Prime Minister Venizelos was pro-Allied. Greece, moreover, did have a treaty of mutual defense with Serbia, which bound her to support Serbia in the event of an attack by Bulgaria.[24] However, the treaty contained a provision that required Serbia to commit 150,000 troops against Bulgaria for it to be effective. Confronted with strong attacks from Austrian and German armies in the north, a force in such strength could not be spared for employment against Bulgaria.

Ostensibly for the purpose of assisting Serbia, the French and British made arrangements with Venizelos to move units being evacuated from Gallipoli through the Greek port of Salonika. On October 5, two days after the first Allied troops landed, Venizelos was forced to resign,[25] and Greece remained neutral. From the onset, confused command arrangements, poor coordination, and political maneuvering doomed Allied operations in Salonika. The French and British forces were dispatched too late to be of

October, Hamilton was relieved by General Charles Monro. In November, Kitchener traveled to Gallipoli to assess the situation firsthand. He advised the Government to end the campaign and withdraw the Allied forces.

The evacuations of the enclaves began in December and continued through January 9, 1916. Surprised and slow to react, the Turks did little to interfere with these professionally conducted evacuations. Contrary to dire predictions, not one life was lost, nor one soldier left behind. This was the only well executed British operation of a campaign that cost both sides more than 200,000 casualties each. The question of the lost opportunities in the Dardanelles and Gallipoli Campaigns has been debated endlessly. Without demeaning the dedicated and effective defensive actions fought by the Turkish forces, it is fair to say that the British lost several very real chances of achieving victory through the lack of realistic planning, the failure to coordinate properly, and the mistaken attempt to apply force gradually.

any assistance to the Serbs, who, along with many civilian refugees, were pushed back into Albania. In December 1915, the remnants of the Serbian Army were shipped to the Island of Corfu. After the Serbs were reequipped and reorganized, they reembarked on French and British ships for Salonika, where they joined the disorganized multi-national force.

Despite the failure of the Allies to achieve any military or political objective, French and British political leaders would not evacuate the Allied army in Salonika. Following Gallipoli, these leaders dreaded the stigma of another evacuation and defeat.* Therefore, the Balkan Front, like many other poorly conceived military operations, gained a life of its own, demanding resources for no foreseeable purpose.

The *Armées Allies en Orient* (Allied Army in the East), as Sarrail's force came to be known, grew in size to four French and five British divisions and an additional 100,000 Serbians. In 1916, the Allies mounted an offensive to assist Romania when it entered the war. (*See Atlas Map No. 39.*) The operation was unsuccessful. In fact, little of importance

occurred on this front until the Central Powers began to collapse in the fall of 1918. The Balkan Front was an expensive sideshow that drained 300,000 to 600,000 Allied troops from much more important areas of operations.[26] Since these forces were contained by 150,000 Bulgarian troops, Salonika was jokingly referred to as "the largest internment camp in the world."

The Battle of Jutland,† May 1916

For nearly two years after the beginning of the war, the British Royal Navy performed its duty as the dominant surface fleet. Once it had swept the few German surface warships off the oceans of the world, it established an open blockade of the Central Powers. By intercepting transport vessels bound for Germany and forcing them into British ports where their cargoes could be purchased, the Royal Navy effectively cut off trade between the Central Powers and the rest of the world. Although this open blockade was highly resented by neutral traders, such as the United States, and was not recognized by international law, im-

---

*Both the British Admiralty and Imperial General Staff had advised the Cabinet against offering assistance to Serbia, and thereafter consistently recommended the evacuation of Salonika.

†The Germans call this the Battle of Skagerrak. It was fought over a large area of the North Sea about 70 miles west of the North Jutland coast.

The Grand Fleet Patrols the North Sea

proved technology had made the close blockade impossible.* Therefore, short of unrestricted submarine warfare, the open blockade was the only effective alternative available to a superior surface fleet.

Having failed to interdict the transport of the British Expeditionary Force to France or to prevent the reinforcement of the Entente Powers from their colonies, the German High Seas Fleet sat in the protection of the Jade Anchorage. (*See Atlas Map No. 45a.*) The British Grand Fleet had remained intact since its mobilization a week before the outbreak of war in 1914. Despite isolated surface commerce raiders and an increasing number of German submarines (*Unterseeboot,* or U-boats), the British fleet held a position of preeminence on the high seas. Since England could depend upon the French for support in the Mediterranean and the Japanese for protection of British trade in the Pacific, the British Grand Fleet was able to remain concentrated in its base, Scapa Flow, in the Orkney Islands.

Admiral Sir John Jellicoe, ever mindful that "he was the only man on either side who could lose the war in an afternoon,"[27] controlled four squadrons of dreadnought-class battleships, a battle cruiser squadron, two cruiser squadrons, and a light cruiser squadron. The strategy of the German commander, Admiral Reinhard von Scheer, was to attempt to surprise and trap a portion of the Grand Fleet in battle, thus evening the odds of the engagement. Scheer sent cruisers on raids to shell the English coast, hoping to lure small contingents of Jellicoe's force into a surprise surface engagement or into uncharted minefields. Jellicoe, on the other hand, kept his superior force intact while attempting to interpose it between part or all of the German fleet and its secure anchorage. These conservative strategies led to a year and a half of stalement and frustration, although by default the British profited; they controlled the world's sea lanes.

Having broken the German naval code, the British were able to monitor radio frequencies and read Scheer's radio traffic. On May 31, 1916, Scheer sent five battle cruisers under Vice Admiral Franz von Hipper to sea as bait for a trap. He then followed with the main fleet at 40 miles, out of visual contact. Alerted by intercepted radio transmissions and spies in Bremerhaven, Jellicoe ordered his fleet to sea.[28] He sent Admiral David Beatty with six battle cruisers and four battleships to act as scouts for the Grand Fleet, which trailed him by 70 miles. (*See Atlas Map No. 45b.*)

The two lead battle cruiser squadrons sighted each other at 3:15 p.m. on May 31. Hipper turned south, trying to make Beatty believe that he was running for port when he was really luring him into range of Scheer's battleships. Throughout the engagement, German gunnery and the survivability of German ships proved superior to that of the British. Beatty's squadron lost two ships to long-range fire, but continued to pursue Hipper. After an hour and ten minutes, Beatty spotted the rest of the High Seas Fleet, lying in wait; he then turned north, chased by the entire German fleet.

After another hour and a half, Scheer spotted Jellicoe's main force, realized that he was now the hunted, and turned to the west. (*See Atlas Map No. 45c.*) Jellicoe then steamed south in an attempt to cut off the Germans from their anchorage. At 7:17 p.m., the two fleets engaged, as Scheer led his ships directly into the heavy fire of the British guns. This was the most critical point in the battle because the Germans were in danger of sustaining heavy losses.[29] To extricate himself, Scheer turned all of his ships about independently. As a cover for this dangerous maneuver, his escorting destroyers laid down a dense smokescreen while other ships fired torpedoes at the British line. Jellicoe, always fearful of a torpedo attack, directed each of his ships to turn 45 degrees, thereby allowing the Germans to pull out of range. Scheer then sailed behind the Grand Fleet and returned safely to the Jade Anchorage.

This sole major fleet engagement of the war resulted in a tactical victory for the Germans and a strategic one for the British. Scheer had sunk 14 of the 151 British ships while losing only 11 of his 99 ships engaged.[30] Although the British were chagrined by this relative balance, they retained control of the seas and continued the successful and debilitating blockade of the Central Powers.

Ironically, this last battle of surface fleets was unaffected by submarines, mines, or torpedo weapons. Naval and land-based aircraft also failed to contribute to the outcome. Never again would huge dreadnought battleships rule the waves, but in their last engagement, the big guns and superior numbers determined the result.

The German High Seas Fleet did sally forth from its safe harbor several more times during the war, but without effect. The Germany Navy surrendered the initiative on surface waters to the British. As the war progressed, the German fleet began to deteriorate and morale dropped as more and more of the best sailors were impressed into the service of the U-boat fleet.

Mesopotamia, 1915–1918

As previously described, at the urging of the British Cabinet, the Indian Government had dispatched a small expedition to secure the flow of oil from the Anglo-Persian

---

*In a traditional close blockade, a fleet patrols just off the enemy ports, forcing inward-bound ships away and engaging ships trying to depart from the enemy port. Because of the effectiveness of the submarine, the torpedo boat, and floating mines, this type of close blockade had became too costly by 1914, and the open blockade was substituted.

pipeline. The relative ease with which Turkish resistance was overcome in capturing Qurna, however, tempted political leaders and military commanders to confuse the ability to continue the advance into Mesopotamia with the desirability of doing so. Militarily, the Government of India was neither prepared nor organized for expanding the initial operation. Certainly a rational assessment of such a campaign[31] could only show that an advance up the rivers of Mesopotamia would not seriously affect Turkey, much less bother Germany or Austria-Hungary. Meanwhile, for four months, the Indian 6th Division defended British oil interests from a central position. (*See Atlas Map No. 46.*) During this time, Lieutenant General Sir Arthur A. Barrett dispatched a brigade to Ahwaz to fend off a Turkish attempt to cut the oil pipeline.

Lord Hardinge, the Viceroy of India, visited the Anglo-Indian troops in February 1915 and returned with an overly optimistic view of the military situation. Enthusiastically, he then scraped together enough troops to form an incomplete infantry corps under General Sir John E. Nixon, assigning that general the mission of occupying the entire province of Basra. This was expected to counter the Turkish 37th Reserve Division, which had reinforced the area. While these plans might seem ambitious, the British calculated that the imminent naval assault on the Dardanelles and Russian pressure in Armenia would preclude the Turks from offering strong resistance.[32]

On April 11–13, in the Battle of Shaiba, Nixon beat back a determined Turkish offensive at the western approaches to his base at Basra. The complete defeat and dispersal of the Turkish forces left the Anglo-Indian base secure. Sir Beauchamp Duff, the Commander-in-Chief of the Indian Army, then instructed Nixon to retain control of all of lower Mesopotamia and to secure the oil pipeline. He was also authorized to begin planning an advance on Baghdad. Nixon promptly requested the assignment of Major General Charles V.F. Townshend to replace Barrett, who had fallen ill.

By April 24, the British Secretary of State for India, Austin Chamberlain, began to suspect that Nixon had overly aggressive plans. Chamberlain's suspicion had been aroused by Nixon's request for more combat troops, especially cavalry. Chamberlain wired the Viceroy that "no advance beyond the present theater of operation will be sanctioned." Aside from the military futility of advancing into Mesopotamia, Chamberlain knew that further operations could not be supported because of the impending invasion of the Gallipoli Peninsula, which would draw all troops and supplies that could be spared from Northeastern France. Unfortunately, in his wire to Hardinge, Chamberlain negated the effect of his good advice by adding that an advance to Amara might benefit the Allied effort by insuring the security of the pipeline.[33]

Under the incompetent Nixon and the self-serving Townshend, events moved toward a British disaster. The two men continued their requests for reinforcements and permission to seize Amara. Reluctant to overrule the military men in the field, the Indian Viceroy and the political leadership in London finally sanctioned the advance.[34]

On May 31, Townshend began his advance with an attack on the Turkish position north of Qurna. (*See Atlas Map No. 46.*) Because of extensive marshes between the attackers and the defenders, the Anglo-Indian force had to pole forward in native flat-bottomed boats, many of which were shielded with iron boilerplate. Once their position had been breached, the Turkish defenders panicked and fled. Townshend and less than 100 soldiers then boarded five river gunboats and relentlessly pursued the beaten enemy all the way north to Amara. By the time the remainder of the 6th Division had caught up with its vanguard, Townshend had captured 2,000 enemy troops and sunk three gunboats. This romantic and astonishing victory had the unfortunate effect of confirming the contempt with which most British soldiers regarded the fighting qualities of the Turks.

Along with the capture of Nasiriyeh on July 22, Townshend's seizure of Amara led to Nixon's plea for permission to seize Kut-al-Amara, which lay 40 miles north of Amara on the Tigris. (*See Atlas Map No. 47a.*) Forced to acknowledge Nixon's previous success, Chamberlain gave his grudging approval. Townshend's reinforced 6th Division then continued its advance upriver from Amara. However, signs of the strain on the limited logistical support system of the Anglo-Indian force were becoming evident. The inadequate field hospitals could barely treat those soldiers suffering from the elements and disease, much less the wounded. Thus, the 450 casualties from the Battle of Nasiriyeh were given a foretaste of the horrible conditions that would later develop.[35] The improvised river fleet upon which the attacking column depended exclusively was stretched thin as the British line of communication became longer than that of the defending Turks.

When Townshend's division arrived in front of Kut on September 24, it confronted a well fortified defensive system. (*See Atlas Map No. 47b.*) The only weakness in the Turkish position was that it lay astride the Tigris River, with the only bridge being five miles upstream (behind the Turkish position). Townshend capitalized on this lack of Turkish lateral mobility by ordering two of his brigades to conduct a demonstration on the right bank to draw the Turkish reserves. When the Turk Commander, Nur-ud-Din, placed his reserve 37th Division south of the Tigris, Townshend moved the two brigades back north of the river on the night of September 27. The Anglo-Indian divisions then attacked and successfully enveloped the Turkish left flank. Unfortunately, the long march, debilitating weather, and lack of water left the attackers and their horses too weary to pursue the Turks.[36] About two-thirds of the Turkish defenders withdrew in good order up the Tigris to positions at Ctesiphon.

The lure of Baghdad—only 40 miles away—now became irresistible. The British Government viewed the seizure of the fabled city as second in importance only to that of Constantinople. After Townshend's 320-mile advance up the Tigris, one more battle against the oft-defeated Turks seemed a reasonable risk—even if Baghdad could not be secured, once captured. Finally, political objectives decided the issue. To impress the Arab tribes and to provide a victory for the English people when all else attempted in 1915 had failed, the War Council telegraphed the Viceroy: "Nixon may march on Baghdad if he is satisfied that force he has available is sufficient for the operation. . . . Two divisions [from France, to assist in the occupation] will be sent as soon as possible."[37]

Unfortunately, Nixon's force was woefully inadequate, although he had concealed that fact from his superiors. By November, the Anglo-Indian force in Mesopotamia had suffered severely. The heat in summer was debilitating, often remaining above 120 degrees for 10 hours a day. Bacteria carried by flies, fleas, mosquitoes, and water spread dysentery, diarrhea, malaria, typhoid, and cholera among the troops. Townshend's reinforced division could muster only 13,756 men. To add to all these problems, the morale of the troops was low due to boredom and lack of diversion.

The logistical situation was chaotic. Basra, the only port supporting the Anglo-Indian force in Mesopotamia, still had no wharves. Ships had to be unloaded at anchor by native boats, causing a delay in port that averaged six weeks. Many critical items were not available, including water purification equipment, ice, ambulances, and vegetables. There were insufficient river boats to support Townshend, who required more than 200 tons of supplies daily, but received only 150. Because of low water in November, only six small steamers could traverse the Tigris, and these could not carry full loads. Lack of fodder made wagon transport impractical, but no plans were made to build a railway up to the front. Finally, the Arab's nasty habit of murdering guards when stealing supplies required large numbers of combat troops to secure the line of communication.[38]

Despite these problems, on November 22, 1915, Townshend, using essentially the same scheme of maneuver that he had used at Kut, hurled his sick, ill-equipped men against an equal number of strongly entrenched Turks at Ctesiphon. Although the enveloping force managed to penetrate the first and second lines of trenches, the British lacked the strength to turn opportunity into victory. Nur-ud-Din successfully counterattacked. The day's battle cost Townshend 4,600 casualties and Nur-ud-Din 9,500. The following day, Townshend collected his wounded from the battlefield while Nur-ud-Din received reinforcements.[39] The British began withdrawing, with the Turks in aggressive pursuit. Seven days later, upon reaching Kut with his exhausted division, Townshend accepted siege.

The Battle of Ctesiphon changed the military and political situation dramatically. Now that the British had a sizable force trapped, they began to scrape together reinforcements for its rescue. The two Indian Divisions arrived from France in January 1916, and the 13th Division from Gallipoli disembarked in February. Nothing, however, was done to solve the logistical and sanitary problems. In fact, the arrival of three new divisions further burdened the facilities, complicating the logistical task. These three divisions immediately encountered the same debilitating conditions that had weakened the 6th Division.

Kut held out for five months. In a series of bloody attacks, the relieving force suffered 23,000 battle casualties in its efforts to rescue the 13,000 men trapped there. Nevertheless, it was unable to force its way into the town. The surrender, which followed in April 1916, shocked the British public. Never before had such a large English force been captured. Its nearest parallel was the surrender of Cornwallis with his 7,000 men at Yorktown, during the American Revolution. Consequently, the British Government relieved India of its direction of the war, subsequently changing all the principal commanders and giving the needs of the theater more sympathetic attention.[40]

Fortunately, in August 1916, the competent General Sir Stanley Maude assumed overall command in Mesopotamia. Maude energetically attacked his logistical problems. All through the hot summer months, the Turks and English faced each other but did not fight. Behind the lines, though, the British were improving logistical support by building a port with wharves, procuring flat-bottomed steamboats, laying a railroad and a water pipeline, and importing gasoline-powered trucks. The logistical system that had delivered only 150 tons of supplies per day to Townshend at Ctesiphon in November 1915 would often deliver more than 2,000 tons per day to Baghdad in July 1917.[41] Although 11,000 sick men were sent back to India during each summer month of 1916, by July, replacements exceeded disease casualties for the first time.[42]

In December, the Allied line of communication was more than sufficient to support the Tigris Corps below Kut. Moreover, Maude now had 48,500 troops on line, as opposed to Turkey's 12,000. Although his orders clearly stated that "no fresh advance to Baghdad can be contemplated,"[43] they did not exclude offensive action. Maude therefore began a methodical limited operation against his enemy on the right bank. (*See Atlas Map No. 47c.*) By moving cautiously and maximizing the use of his artillery, he was not likely to trap

Turkish Trenches at Sannaiyat

and destroy the Turks, but he could advance with minimal casualties. After two months of battle, the right bank was cleared at a cost of only 3,700 casualties.

At this time, Maude faced a problem. The Turks still held the left bank at the seemingly impregnable position in the Sannaiyat defile. The year before, assaults launched there in the attempt to relieve Kut had been bloody failures. By occupying the right bank, however, Maude had forced the Turks to weaken Sannalyat in order to spread forces all along the left bank and prevent a river crossing. On the morning of February 22, 1917, one brigade assaulted the Sannaiyat position, forcing the Turk commander, Kara Bekr Bey, to commit his reserve. Two nights later, Maude launched his main attack across the Tigris, upstream of Kut, immediately compromising the entire Turkish force on the left bank. The Turks began to withdraw.

Sensibly, Maude stopped the pursuit when he began to outrun his supplies. However, because of his sound logistical organization, he was able to extend his line of communication within 10 days. By that time, the extent of Maude's victory had become apparent to the War Cabinet. Since December, he had captured 7,000 of Kara Bekr Bey's 12,000-man corps. On March 4 with the opportunity to regain lost prestige beckoning, London granted Maude permission to capture Baghdad. He did so on the eleventh. Within six weeks, British units controlled all the river, rail, and road approaches to Baghdad, and fighting ceased for the sum-

mer. In 1918, the British would continue to push slowly up the Tigris, reaching Fat-Ha by the war's end. (*See Atlas Map No. 42.*)

The campaign in Mesopotamia must be regarded as one of the major strategic errors of the war. While the original task of protecting the Royal Navy's oil supply was vital, this was easily accomplished from Qurna. Baghdad was a political objective that offered nothing except the hope that its capture would impress the Moslems in India and the Arabs in Mesopotamia. Its seizure necessitated a 415-mile-long line of communication, requiring over 350,000 men in order to keep 50,000 combat troops at the fighting front north of Baghdad. The Turks opposing the advance never exceeded 50,000 men, an economy-of-force measure that must have delighted the German General Staff. The total cost of the campaign to the British was 16,000 killed, 13,000 dead of disease, 51,000 wounded, and 13,000 either taken prisoner or missing. Additionally, 975 out of every 1,000 men were hospitalized sometime during their stay in Mesopotamia.[44]

Egypt and Palestine, 1916–1918

The Egyptian Theater of Operations remained quiescent during both the Gallipoli Campaign and the siege of Kut-al-Amara. Operations on Gallipoli precluded either side from providing resources for actions on the Suez Canal front.

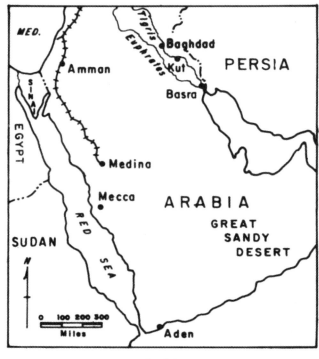

Arabia

With the evacuation of Gallipoli in December 1915, however, the British turned to improving the defense in Egypt. (*See Atlas Map No. 48.*) One rather obvious improvement was the transfer of the defensive line to a location east of the canal. The strongly entrenched position that the British established eight miles east of the canal prevented Turkish artillery from firing on the waterway.

During the inactive period, the High Commissioner for Egypt began negotiations with Hussein, the Sherif of Mecca, in an effort to encourage the population of Arabia to revolt against the Turks. The effort was successful. In October of 1915, Hussein agreed to join the Allies in return for material assistance and a vague promise of Arab independence after the war.

It was almost a year before actual fighting erupted. Then, in June 1916, Hussein's men expelled the Turks from the holy city of Mecca. The Arabs then moved north against Medina, but were unable to take it. While observing Arab

Wire Mesh Road in the Sinai Desert

operations in front of Medina, an English staff officer, Captain T.E. Lawrence, concluded that the Arab light cavalry could never challenge the well armed Turks in positional warfare. He convinced Feisal, third son of Hussein and field commander of the Arab Army, to use his forces to spread propaganda and to raid the long Turkish line of communication into Medina. This tactic was immediately successful. The Turks were compelled to stop offensive operations south of Medina and to scatter troops all along the Hejaz railway.[45] Lawrence of Arabia, as T.E. Lawrence came to be known, remained with Feisal, becoming one of his principal advisers. Unlike other British advisers, Lawrence dressed in Arab garb and adopted their customs, which increased his influence with the Arabs.

In March 1916, General Sir Archibald Murray assumed command of the newly designated Egyptian Expeditionary Force (EEF). Within a month, he wired London to request permission to move to El Arish on the far side of the Sinai Desert, explaining that he could defend the canal with one less division by using El Arish as a flanking position. Granted permission to advance, Murray began his slow crossing of the Sinai, fighting one battle and several skirmishes during the next 10 months.

Unlike Nixon in Mesopotamia, Murray developed a solid logistical foundation. As his divisions advanced, he constructed a standard gauge railway, laid a 12-inch water pipeline, created roads by laying wire mesh on the desert sand, and used 35,000 camels to cover the gap from railhead to frontline. The rate of construction—about 15 miles per month—determined the force's rate of advance, for Murray kept his main body within 20 miles of the railhead. On December 21, 1916, the EEF entered El Arish without a fight. Murray's mission was as good as accomplished, for no Turkish force could attack the canal without first capturing El Arish. Moreover, that town was located at a strong position and could be supplied from the sea.[46]

T.E. Lawrence in Arab Garb

Murray's success soon caused London to consider expanding his mission. On December 7, 1916, David Lloyd George, a strong "Easterner," replaced Asquith as Prime Minister. Time had only strengthened Lloyd George's distaste for warfare on the Western Front. The casualties in France were excessive, while the results were infinitesimal. The British Empire was being drained of manpower and materiel without a single significant victory since the Battle of the Marne. A master politician, Lloyd George felt that in order to keep hope alive in England he must have an identifiable victory. Consequently, two days after assuming office he asked the Chief of the Imperial General Staff (CIGS) to determine how Murray's success could be exploited. After a series of telegrams, Murray understood that although his mission was to defend Egypt, he was to "be as aggressive as possible with the troops at your disposal" and to advance beyond El Arish.[47]

After protesting without success that he needed two more divisions to fulfill his new role, Murray advanced beyond El Arish toward Gaza, the next major Turkish stronghold. His Gaza attack on March 26, 1917 failed on the brink of success because of the friction of war.* Nevertheless, Murray's official report of the battle was optimistic. He implied that he had won the battle by saying that "the operation was most successful" and by exaggerating Turkish casualties.[48]

Elated at this news, which followed Maude's capture of Baghdad by only two weeks, the War Cabinet directed Murray to capture Jerusalem. Murray, shocked by this new mission, reiterated his need for two more divisions. Denied these reinforcements, he loyally prepared to do the job with the troops on hand. His plans for the Second Battle of Gaza (April 17) lacked sophistication. A frontal attack failed badly against improved Turkish positions. Murray was relieved and called home.

It is instructive to compare Nixon's campaign in Mesopotamia with that of Murray in Egypt. Nixon had advanced with a force too small and ill-equipped, supported by an inadequate logistical system. Having deceived his government into approving the advance on Baghdad, he failed, with disastrous consequences for 35,000 men. Murray also advanced with an inadequate force, but it was superbly equipped and supported by a solid logistical system. He had foolishly, but unintentionally, deceived his government into ordering his advance; then he tried to have the decision changed. He loyally executed his orders and failed, but suffered only 6,444 casualties. Both men were relieved for their failure, but Murray served both his country and his men far better.

The War Cabinet now had to decide whether to continue the offensive into Palestine or to resume a purely defensive posture in Egypt. There was really little choice. Although the Second Battle of Gaza had been a failure, its cost had at least been considerably less than the 79,732 men lost during April in the Nivelle Offensive in France. This disaster further convinced Lloyd George to fight in places other than France.

Another decisive factor was Turkey's assembly of a sizable army at Aleppo in preparation for the recapture of Baghdad. Since Great Britain could reinforce Palestine faster than Mesopotamia, the general staff favored an offensive toward Jerusalem as the best method of countering Turkish attempts to retake Baghdad. Finally, the Westerners in the government would lose nothing. The Chief of the Imperial General Staff would not consent to reducing British strength on the Western Front, while the Easterners would not consent to shipping any more troops there. In a compromise solution, two divisions were shipped from Salonika to Palestine, "where they would at any rate enjoy a better climate and be under British control."[49]

General Sir Edmund Allenby, formerly the commander of the Third Army in France, replaced Murray in June 1917. Before Allenby left London, Lloyd George told him that he wanted Jerusalem as a Christmas present for England. At about the same time, Falkenhayn, the former chief of the German General Staff, arrived in Turkey to command the *Yilderim,* a force of two Turkish corps and the German Asia Corps that was assembling at Aleppo preparatory to advancing on Baghdad. In mid-September, *Yilderim* was redirected

A Camel-Borne Ambulance

---

*The cavalry, not understanding the infantry's progress, withdrew to water their horses, thereby exposing the infantry to flank attack.

to Palestine to counter Allenby. The Asian Corps, which consisted of three battalions of infantry and two of artillery, was the largest force ever sent by Germany to Turkey; its size illustrates how little it cost Germany to stiffen the Turks so that they would occupy a million British troops. Falkenhayn and Allenby would soon clash in Palestine.[50]

Allenby's first objective was Gaza. Since the Second Battle of Gaza, Turkey had strengthened her position and extended it to Beersheba. (*See Atlas Map No. 49.*) The weakness of the position lay at Beersheba, which was manned by only 5,000 Turks in a single trench. Allenby developed a plan based on surprise and deception. He gave every indication of planning to assault Gaza, but instead struck Beersheba on October 31, 1917. The surprise was complete, even to catching Falkenhayn away in Jerusalem. The first day's action culminated in the capture of Beersheba by a cavalry charge. During the next five days, Allenby concentrated on rolling up the flank from Beersheba to Gaza. When a stubborn defense prevented progress, he converted his supporting attack to the main attack and smashed through at Gaza, whereupon the enemy withdrew to avoid entrapment.

Allenby pursued with difficulty. Because the lightly equipped, hardy Turk could outmarch the British Tommy, Allenby's infantry was ineffective as a direct-pressure or encircling force. On the other hand, the EEF contained a high percentage of cavalry (3 cavalry to 10 infantry divisions). While the cavalry lacked sufficient firepower to trap the Turkish force, it was able to harry the retreating elements, preventing reorganization, capturing rear guards, and spreading demoralization among the Turks. For example, one serious Turkish attempt to defend Junction Station

ended as soon as Allenby's infantry arrived at the position and assaulted it. Its capture was almost a formality.

As Allenby pushed on, Falkenhayn was forced to cover both Jerusalem and Jaffa. By thus splitting his force, he enabled Allenby, after a stiff fight in the Judean foothills,* to capture Jerusalem on December 8. On the eleventh, Allenby humbly made his official entry into the Holy City on foot. The English people received their Christmas present at a total cost of 18,000 casualties.

Now that Allenby's mission was complete, the Government had to set him a new task. Quite naturally, the debate between the Westerners and the Easterners erupted again. While the basic arguments were old, there were significant new factors: Russia had just collapsed, and America had entered the war nine months before. The Westerners argued that with Russia out of the war, Germany was sure to transfer troops to the Western Front and seize the initiative. It was folly to leave good troops in Palestine; no matter how successful Allenby might be, it was still 900 miles from Jerusalem to Constantinople, and Turkey would never sue for peace while her German ally was winning in France. Besides, the main purpose of defeating Turkey—that of obtaining a supply route to Russia—was no longer a factor. Finally, the valuable shipping being used to support British troops in Turkey was needed to bring American troops to the front.

The Easterners argued that Germany's impending offensive on the Western Front would prove unsuccessful.[51] The

---

*As the EEF left the desert and entered the craggy Judean Hills, camels became useless. But a farsighted staff officer had ordered 2,000 donkeys prior to the Third Battle of Gaza. These animals enabled the advance to continue after camel transport had become impractical.

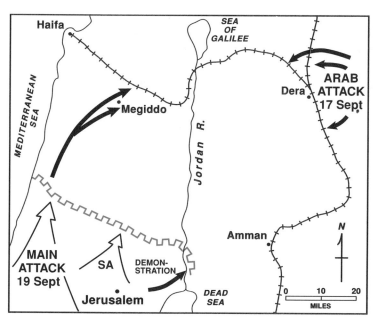

Allenby's Concept of Operations, 1918

Allies had failed to break the trench systems when they enjoyed numerical superiority in 1917; the Germans would fail in 1918. The Western Front was only a meat grinder that consumed everything fed into it. It was much better to use valuable manpower to force Turkey from the war, defeat Bulgaria, and, finally, attack Austria.[†]

The crux of both arguments was the assessment of Allied ability to hold the line in France. The Prime Minister, being an Easterner, ordered Allenby to continue his drive toward Damascus and then Aleppo, the capture of which would trap Turkish forces in Mesopotamia. (*See Atlas Map No. 42.*)

Events conspired to delay the resumption of the offensive for nine months. Exceptionally heavy winter rains made maneuver impossible. More important, the Westerners' prediction about the German offensive in France proved all too correct. When Ludendorff attacked on March 21, 1918, the Allies were soundly defeated, and large sections of the Western Front reeled back 40 miles. As a direct result, Allenby received orders to transfer to France two complete divisions and enough separate battalions to constitute three more. These units were replaced by Indian divisions from Mesopotamia and by newly formed battalions from India. In turn, the new Indian units required training and acclimatization during the summer, further delaying Allenby's plans.

Allenby used this delay to formulate a plan for the Battle of Megiddo, one of the most successful battles of World War I, and one of the few operations in which the horse cavalry played a role.[52] Allenby's plan was the reverse of the one used in the Third Battle of Gaza. (*See Atlas Map No. 50a.*) After deceiving the Turks into expecting an attack on the inland flank, the British would attack the sea flank. Allenby used the time available, therefore, not only to plan, but also to implement his deception plan. He confined aggressive combat actions to the Jordan Valley, where the Australian cavalry seized a bridgehead over the Jordan River and made two large raids toward Amman. These activities posed a credible threat to the railway at Amman, which still supported Turkish troops in Medina; indeed, by September 1918, Sanders, now elevated from adviser to army commander, had a third of his troops deployed east of the Jordan.

Meanwhile, Allenby had moved troops from the east to the west, but had concealed the move well. His deception measures included placing 15,000 stuffed canvas horses in the Jordan Valley and establishing dummy headquarters complete with credible radio traffic and miles of supporting telephone lines. Lawrence and his Arabs spread news that

vast amounts of fodder would soon be purchased near Amman. Troops marched east in daylight and returned to their starting point by truck at night, only to march east again the next day. Mules pulled sleds around the Jordan Valley, kicking up great clouds of dust. On the sea flank, however, troops were billeted in camps twice as large as necessary so that units arriving from the Jordan Valley could occupy existing facilities without being noticed.

Allenby massed 50 percent of his infantry, 75 percent of his cavalry, and 70 percent of his artillery on only 25 percent of his front. The unsuspecting Turks faced 38,000 rifles, 9,000 sabers, and 383 guns with only 8,000 infantry and 130 guns. The outcome of the battle was decided before the first shot could be fired.

Allenby's plan was simple and bold. (*See Atlas Map No. 50a.*) XXI Corps, on the left, would conduct the main attack with the infantry and artillery. XX Corps, in the center, would launch a supporting attack. The right flank unit, Chaytor Force, would stage a demonstration with its reinforced cavalry division. Arab horsemen would cut the rail lines in the vicinity of Dera, paralyzing rail movement into and out of the battle area. Once the main attack had penetrated Turkish lines, the cavalry was to pass through, avoid contact with isolated Turk units, and seize defiles from which to block the escape of the enemy army.

Allenby's concept shows his excellent grasp of the principles of mass and surprise. He also deserves credit for his emphasis on coordination and use of combined arms. His artillery support of the infantry was based on a rolling barrage controlled by forward observers, not an unusual situation. However, many other aspects of combined arms coordination were new. Cavalry liaison officers waited at infantry division headquarters to ease the passage of the cavalry through the lines, while engineers went forward with the infantry to prepare routes through the barbed wire. To prevent masking supporting fires,[*] cavalry routes of movement were coordinated with the artillery. Armored cars were also integrated into horse cavalry divisions. The Royal Navy assisted with fire support and in the supply of the exploiting cavalry. The Royal Air Force performed its now standard missions of controlling the skies and harassing the retreating Turks. The air arm also performed some less glamorous tasks, such as bombing wire communications to enemy headquarters and flying supplies to Arab irregulars in the enemy rear. Finally, Allenby successfully coordinated the actions of the most difficult of all units, the irregular forces. The Arabs, advised by Lawrence, not only attacked on schedule, but also facilitated the success of the deception plan by spreading rumors.[53]

[†]The phrase used to describe this strategy was "knocking out the German props." Of course, Turkey and Bulgaria were not props upon which Germany leaned. In fact, the opposite relationship existed. The phrase used in World War II to make the same scheme seem atractive was "soft underbelly of Europe." Both terms are misleading.

[*]Fire is said to be "masked" when weapons are firing at a target and friendly troops enter the target area, thus making possible the injury of friendly personnel and forcing the fire to be lifted.

Having made careful and intelligent preparations, Allenby was virtually assured of victory. The only question was how decisive his victory would be. At 4:30 a.m. on September 19, the artillery and Navy fired a sudden, intense 15-minute preparation in the area of the main attack. The infantry assault that followed shattered the enemy front. The 60th Division on the coast had advanced four miles and crossed the El Faliq River by 7:00 a.m. Shortly thereafter, the cavalry passed through, racing north. (*See Atlas Map No. 50b.*) By midnight, one division controlled the pass near the little village of Megiddo. At 5:30 a.m. the following morning, another division dispersed the Turkish headquarters at Nazareth, forcing Sanders to flee in his pajamas. The supporting attack logically picked up momentum as the main attack succeeded. By September 21, the Seventh and Eighth Turkish Armies had ceased to exist, and 25,000 prisoners were in British hands. Allenby spent the next six days rounding up fleeing Turkish columns. Only a part of the Turkish Fourth Army managed to escape on foot, through Dera, prior to the army's capture by the Arabs on September 27.

In the remaining few weeks of the war, British forces ranged deep into Turkish territory. Allenby ordered his cavalry onto Damascus, which fell on September 31. About 1,500 cavalry and a few armored cars continued the chase for 200 miles, advancing beyond Aleppo. There, the British received their only setback of the battle from a hastily organized unit that had been thrown together by Mustapha Kemal, the man who had been the bane of the British at Gallipoli.[54] This minor setback was overcome, however, and two days later, on October 28, Turkey asked for an armistice. Her Palestinian army had been destroyed, her Mesopotamian army was trapped, the Salonikan front had collapsed, Arabs from Aleppo to Mecca were in revolt, and even Germany was retreating.

The Logic of the Indirect Approach

At first glance, the melange of battles and campaigns categorized as peripheral operations seem unrelated and dissimilar. Upon closer examination, however, they have two factors in common, the Battle of Jutland excepted.

First, they were all begun without thorough analysis of the probable consequences and costs. If unsuccessful initially, they were continued, even though they contributed nothing to the defeat of Germany. The colonial campaigns began spontaneously and lasted long after all German colonial ports had been captured—even into 1918, in the case of East Africa. Gallipoli was the only campaign terminated once it had failed decisively. The campaign in Mesopotamia quickly grew from a strategically sound effort to protect oil sources to an overly ambitious attempt to capture Baghdad, ultimately absorbing 400,000 men. The Salonikan front occupied another 600,000, with no practical military benefits. Turkey and Russia fought savagely in the remote Caucasus Mountains, where neither had any hope of obtaining a decisive advantage. In Egypt, the British retained their sense of proportion for two years, but by 1917 the goal of defending the Suez Canal had escalated to that of capturing Jerusalem.

The second common factor among these campaigns was that the Allies fought them with leftover forces. The Dardanelles used battleships due to be scrapped. The Mesopotamian Campaign was fought with the Indian Army, old officers, obsolete artillery, and minimal logistical support. Black Africans, who were considered unsuited for duty in France, captured the German colonies. Salonika was fought with French colonial divisions under the command of a relieved general. In 1918, Palestine was stripped of combat-experienced British battalions and filled with untrained Indian battalions. Russia used regional regiments in the Caucasus.

These two common factors were the result of committee-made decisions. Committee members who win important arguments often concede on minor points in order to promote harmony within the committee. This is exactly what happened in the British Cabinet. The Westerners usually won the major strategy debates because once the BEF was in France in 1914, it could neither be withdrawn nor left unsupported. England never varied from a Continental strategy, except for three months during operations in Gallipoli. But to maintain stability within the Government, the Easterners were allowed to try their strategy with those resources that were left over. Even though committee members might have been against making new commitments, they were not prepared to bring down the Government, so they compromised and allowed half-hearted measures. Unfortunately, these half-hearted measures usually resulted in larger commitments than those originally envisioned. It was, perhaps, inevitable that the peripheral operations of the Great War violated the principles of economy of force and objective. Since British and French societies determined their national strategies by democratic methods, however, competing demands often had to be accommodated in order to maintain unity.

The debates over strategy continued in the press and in government long after the Great War was over. Military analysts still asked if the war could have been won with fewer casualties if the BEF had been employed in peripheral operations rather than in France. Even with the BEF in France, they questioned if the war would have been shortened if sufficient strength had been committed to open the Dardanelles or to save Serbia. Conversely, others wondered if the war was lengthened because the resources required for an early victory had been frittered away in secondary theaters. Was the seizure of Jerusalem and Baghdad necessary to provided much needed victories for a war-weary populace, or did their capture just prolong a war of attrition, thereby heightening later disillusionment with the war?

Despite the logic of applying military might at the decisive point, the people of Europe would continue to reject this harsh reality in the inter-war years.[55] Pacifists and Easterners would insist that national security could be bought cheaply. Unfortunately, this was a delusion that would cost the world dearly in 1939.

Notes

[1]James E. Edmonds, *A Short History of World War I* (London, 1951), p. 394.

[2]Brian Gardner, *On To Kilimanjaro* (Philadelphia, 1963), p. 265; Cyril Falls, *The Great War* (New York, 1959), p. 243.

[3]Frank P. Chambers, *The War Behind the War 1914–1918* (New York, 1939), pp. 59–60.

[4]Francis Bertie to Edward Grey, November 6, 1912, in *British Documents on the Origins of the War, 1898–1914* (London, 1934), IX, 108–109.

[5]"Treaty of Alliance Between Germany and Turkey. August 2, 1914," in Louis L. Snyder, *Historic Documents of World War I* (Princeton, 1958), pp. 86–88; Cyril Falls, "Turkish Campaigns," in Vincent J. Esposito (ed.), *A Concise History of World War I* (New York, 1964), p. 187.

[6]Barbara W. Tuchman, *The Guns of August* (New York, 1962), pp. 141–151.

[7]C.R.M.F. Cruttwell, *A History of the Great War, 1914–1918* (Oxford, 1940), pp. 70–72.

[8]A. Emin, *Turkey in the War* (London, 1930), pp. 69–75.

[9]Cruttwell, *Great War*, p. 339.

[10]A.J. Barker, *The Bastard War: The Mesopotamian Campaign of 1914–1918* (New York, 1967), pp. 33–36.

[11]Frank G. Weber, *Eagles on the Crescent* (London, 1970), pp. 62–66.

[12]Winston S. Churchill, *The Unknown War* (New York, 1931), pp. 269–271.

[13]Correlli Barnett, *The Great War* (New York, 1979), p. 57; Esposito, *Concise History*, pp. 205–207.

[14]Archibald P. Wavell, *The Palestine Campaigns* (New York, 1931), pp. 28–33.

[15]Winston S. Churchill, *The World Crisis* (2 vols.; New York, 1923), II, 95–100.

[16]Robert R. James, *Gallipoli* (London, 1965), pp. 9–11.

[17]Maurice P.A. Hankey, *The Supreme Command, 1914–1918* (2 vols.; London, 1961), I, 266–267.

[18]James L. Stokesbury, *A Short History of World War I* (New York, 1981), pp. 116–117.

[19]George H. Cassar, *The French and the Dardanelles* (London, 1971), pp. 104–105. Much debate has taken place over this decision. Although the Turkish troops were relatively unscathed, they were nearly out of ammunition. If even a modest landing force had been available, there is little doubt that the shores at the Narrows could have been secured. By the time sufficient troops arrived, the Turks had substantially reinforced the defenses.

[20]C.F. Aspinall-Oglander, *Military Operations, Gallipoli* (2 vols.; London, 1932), I, 75; Alan Moorehead, *Gallipoli* (New York, 1956), pp. 79–92.

[21]Edmonds, *Short History of World War I*, p. 114.

[22]Moorehead, *Gallipoli*, pp. 301–302.

[23]Churchill, *Unknown War*, pp. 332–333.

[24]Alan Palmer, *The Gardeners of Salonika* (New York, 1965), pp. 18–19.

[25]Frank P. Chambers, *The War Behind the War*, p. 81.

[25]Falls, *The Great War*, pp. 310–314.

[27]Churchill, *World Crisis*, II, 612.

[28]Geoffrey Bennett, *Naval Battles of the First World War* (London, 1968), p. 176; William James, *The Code Breakers of Room 40* (New York, 1956), pp. 117–118.

[29]Holloway H. Frost, *The Battle of Jutland* (Annapolis, 1936), pp. 346–347.

[30]Bennett, *Naval Battles*. p. 243.

[31]Cruttwell, *Great War*, p. 341.

[32]*Ibid.*, pp. 339–342.

[33]Barker, *The Bastard War*, p. 60.

[34]*Ibid.*, pp. 63–69. The Viceroy's instructions to Nixon directed him to: ". . .submit a plan for the occupation of the Basra Vilayet (province) which includes Amara. . . ."

[35]Arnold T. Wilson, *Loyalties: Mesopotamia 1914–1917* (New York, 1930), pp. 61–63.

[36]Russel Braddon, *The Siege* (New York, 1969), pp. 75–76.

[37]F.J. Moberly, *The Campaign in Mesopotamia, 1914–1918* (4 vols.; London, 1923–1927), II, 28.

[38]Barker, *The Bastard War*, pp. 146–152.

[39]*Ibid.*, p. 115.

[40]Moberly, *Mesopotamia*, III, 24.

[41]Barker, *The Bastard War*, p. 360.

[42]Moberly, *Mesopotamia*, III, 35.

[43]"CIGS GEN Robertson to C-in-C India 30th September, 1916," in Barker, *The Bastard War*, p. 276.

[44]Edmonds, *Short History of World War I*, pp. 114, 393.

[45]Wavell, *Palestine Campaigns*, pp. 54–55.

[46]*Ibid.*, pp. 38–42.

[47]Moberly, *Mesopotatnia*, III, 259–261.

[48]*Ibid.*, p. 322; Cyril Falls, *Armageddon: 1918* (New York, 1963), p. 10.

[49]Wavell, *Palestine Campaigns*, pp. 88–90; William Robertson, *Soldiers and Statesmen, 1914–1918* (2 vols.; London, 1926), II, 143.

[50]Wavell, *Palestine Campaigns*, pp. 96–98.

[51]*Ibid.*, pp. 174–176.

[52]Falls, *Armageddon*, p. ix.

[53]*Ibid.*, pp. 35–49.

[54]*Ibid.*, p. 154.

[55]Theodore Ropp, *War in the Modern World* (New York, 1962), p. 311.

War in the East, 1916–1918   6

. . . particular attention should be given to Marx's extremely profound remark that the destruction of the military and bureaucratic apparatus of the state is "the precondition of any real people's revolution."

V.I. Lenin, *State and Revolution*

For the soldiers of both the Central Powers and the Allies, the winter and spring of 1916 on the Eastern Front was a period of relief from the battles of attrition in Galicia, the Balkans, and northwest Poland. In St. Petersburg, Czar Nicholas II seemed indifferent to the Supreme Command, the control of which he had wrested from his uncle, Grand Duke Nicholas. The Czar preferred to dabble in the peripheral affairs of state and household intrigue. Being neither a military man nor an effective leader, he left the management of Russia's military effort to the *Stavka* and the Chief of Staff, General Mikhail Alexeyev. This staff had evolved into a group of inept military pessimists.

Still, Russia's strategic picture was not totally bleak. The chronic artillery and small arms ammunition shortages had been remedied. Despite the reverses of 1915, troop morale was still reasonably high. Domestic rifle production had been increased to 100,000 per month, while 1,200,000 new weapons had been received from abroad.[1] Training had improved, and despite the severe losses suffered at Tannenberg, Masuria, and Lodz, the mammoth Russian manpower pool remained plentiful. A few able commanders, such as General Aleksiei A. Brusilov, soon to be promoted to command of a front, were still serving. The Czar's unsophisticated army had few airplanes or tanks and only a very rudimentary system of communications; its strength lay in the hearty infantry and cavalry soldiers who, instilled with a love of Mother Russia, poured through the depots to fill the ranks.

Political life in Russia remained turbulent, however, reflecting underlying dissatisfaction with the Government's conduct of state affairs in general and the war in particular. Entrance into the war in 1914 had given the Czar a brief respite from the pressures exerted by liberal reformers, socialists, and anarchists of every stripe, who sought liberation from the onerous autocratic system that had dominated Russia for centuries. For a time, the euphoria that accompanied the march toward Prussia in 1914 had silenced hostility toward the Romanovs. However, rampant inflation, unemployment, and the brutal measures of Minister of Interior Alexander Protopopov against striking workers brought dissent back to the surface.[2]

The Strategic Prospect

As 1915 closed, Russian leaders cast about for a workable military strategy. (*See Atlas Map No. 34.*) Most of the field commanders were pessimistic about the prospects for a successful offensive in the coming year, and were anxious to avoid responsibility for undertaking one. This was particularly true of Generals Alexei N. Kuropatkin (North Front) and Alexei E. Ewarth (West Front), both of whom faced skillful and vigorous German defenders. The prospects for an offensive against the Austro-Hungarians were more promising, despite the fact that the armies of the Dual Monarchy had been stiffened with German divisions. The commander of the Southwest Front, Nikolai Y. Ivanov, was aware of this, and was not eager for another march into Galicia. As Commander-in-Chief, the Czar took little part in decision making. Between the *Stavka* and the field commanders there was virtually no communication. As a result, the component elements of the army groups did not know how their missions fit into the overall scheme of operations.[3] Lethargy characterized Russian military thinking

The Easterners: Hindenburg Flanked by Ludendorff and Hoffman (center figures)

throughout the winter months, while political events propelled the Empire toward the abyss of 1917.

In Berlin and Vienna, the strategic situation was also ambiguous. Despite the gains made against the Russians in 1915 and the success of the Turks in repelling the Allied invasion of Gallipoli, the strains of multi-front warfare were beginning to be felt by the Central Powers. Falkenhayn and the general staff concluded that Germany did not have the resources to continue offensive operations everywhere. On the other hand, it was recognized that a defensive strategy would not yield decisive results. The controversy between the Easterners (Hindenburg, Ludendorff, and Hoffman) and the Westerners (Falkenhayn, the Crown Prince, and Prince Rupprecht of Bavaria) continued, with the Kaiser vacillating in view between the two factions. Falkenhayn sought to create a truly unified command whereby the Kaiser would become *de facto* Commander-in-Chief of coalition forces, with a centralized direction of operations emanating from him through the German General Staff. The Austrians refused to relinquish that degree of sovereignty, however, and the inefficient system of coordination continued.[4] With regard to a German strategy for 1916, the Westerners' philosophy ultimately prevailed. The assault on Verdun, intended "to bleed France white," was adopted, to the consternation of H-L, who found themselves temporarily relegated to a subordinate role.[5]

Domestic pressures were being felt by the German High Command also. Despite his forcefulness, Falkenhayn could not mute the criticism of the war effort that sprang from liberal elements in the *Reichstag*. The British naval blockade was having a cumulative effect on the civilian population, many of whom were seeking sustenance through food supplements and *ersatz* goods. The works of liberal poets and writers, such as Lersch, Baumer, and Remarque, reflected the weariness of trench warfare, contributing to the growing disillusionment of the civil populace.

Still, military professionalism in the Germany Army remained high. While corners might be cut with regard to civilian requirements, sufficient supplies still reached the troops in the field. Some flaws were evident in the German system, however. For example, many competent junior officers and non commissioned officers went unrewarded. This was a manifestation of the caste system that had been inherited from Prussia. Birthright and wealth counted for more than demonstrated competence in the commissioned ranks. New officers were selected from noble families and promoted ahead of deserving non commissioned officers, who were denied entrance to commissioned ranks.[6]

Despite its earlier defeat in Galicia, morale had improved in the Austro-Hungarian Army following the conquest of Serbia. Overestimating their capability, Austrian military leaders looked southward for new operational opportunities. The most likely target was Italy, which had entered the Allied camp on May 23, 1915. Ignoring Falkenhayn's demand that Austrian divisions be sent to Poland so that German units could be shipped to the West for the Battle of Verdun, Conrad commenced unilateral planning for an offensive in the South Tyrol. As resentment of being patronized by the Germans increased in Austrian military circles, Conrad also refused to provide Austrian artillery units for the Western Front.

Military Operations, 1916–1917

The month of March 1916 marked a brief change in the fortunes of the Russian Army. One cause for this was Brusilov's elevation to the command of one of the three principal army groups, the Southwest Front,[7] replacing the incompetent Ivanov. Brusilov's manner and attitude contrasted sharply with those of his fellow commanders. He was energetic, aggressive, and not subject to the fits of pessimism that gripped his contemporaries. He did not view his German adversaries with the same awe as did the others, and had faith in the fighting capabilities of his soldiers. He had demonstrated that when inspired, well-led, and properly supplied, Russian troops were equal to the challenge.

In his first meeting with the Czar Brusilov informed his Emperor in clear terms that the Russian Army must adopt an offensive attitude and abandon its defensive mentality.[8] Nicholas' reaction was one of consternation:

> This positive and uncompromising statement somewhat embarrassed the Emperor because his temperament rather inclined him to prefer vague and indefinite situations . . . .[9]

As in previous years, the Russian leadership responded to entreaties from France to launch an offensive in order to relieve pressure on the Western Front. Falkenhayn's attack on Verdun had opened in February, and the initial successes of the German Crown Prince's Army led the French to ask for yet another diversionary offensive in the East. In March, the Northern Army Group had commenced a short-lived offensive against the Germans near Lake Narotch which was easily contained by the Germans. As usual, Russian casualties were heavy, approximating 70,000.[10] Elsewhere, the Eastern Front was characterized by static trench warfare. Russian and German troops languished in murky dugouts and squalid towns, awaiting the next round.

On April 14, a Russian War Council assembled in Mogilev, Supreme Headquarters in the field. A dolorous atmosphere prevailed as the conference opened. Generals Kuropatkin (North Front commander) and Ewarth (West Front Commander) advised the Czar to continue the policy of "defend and wait," reinforcing their views by pointing out the shortage of artillery ammunition and other materiel. Brusilov, supported by General Sergei Mikhailovitch, the Inspector General for Artillery, insisted that an offensive was in order and that his army group was capable of bearing the main effort if required. Brusilov's eloquent presentation gained the reluctant support of the Czar and the other senior officers around the table. There was weak but unanimous agreement for a summer offensive on all fronts. Brusilov's recollections regarding the capabilities of his peers suggest the reason for his strong desire for offensive action:

> Ivanov belonged to the company of star performers who, under Kuropatkin, had successfully lost the Russo-Japanese war, and Evert [Ewarth] was another of the actors in that painful exhibition. I have always been nervous of generals of the Kuropatkin school, and I think that if at the outbreak of war their activities could have been confined to the back areas we should have been all the better off.[11]

With the strategic issue resolved, Brusilov returned to the headquarters of the Southwest Front to prepare his armies for an offensive.

The Brusilov Offensive

Brusilov's concept of operations (*see Atlas Map No. 35a*) envisioned an attack on a broad front of 280 miles, preceded by an intense artillery preparation. He planned for a main attack against the Germans in the direction of Kowel, with supporting attacks directed at Lemberg in Galicia and Czernowitz in Bukovina. If the offensive were successful,

Czar Nicholas and His Generals Discuss Russian Strategy at the Mogilev Conference, April 1916

the Austrians and Germans would be channeled into the Carpathian passes and Silesia. The Germans might then be forced either to shift forces from north to south or to shuttle more troops from the Western Front to Galicia, thus relieving pressure on the French at Verdun.

Unlike those of his military colleagues who lacked tactical finesse, Brusilov was able to incorporate an elaborate deception plan into his campaign scheme. Wishing to confuse the enemy as to the location of his main attack, he directed each of his army commanders—those of the Seventh, Eighth, Ninth, and Eleventh Armies—to create an active sector in his area of responsibility. He ordered the forward movement of troops, the intensification of artillery fire, and the increase of aerial reconnaissance activity. The German and Austrian staffs were therefore faced with the problem of guessing which of four areas the Russian main attack would emanate from. Brusilov further strengthened his plan by insuring that each of the 25 corps also created active sectors, thereby compounding the intelligence collection problem for the enemy. From mid-April until June, digging went on in earnest, artillery ammunition was stacked in locations all along the front, and assault troops moved up behind the main lines. Brusilov's professional methods became evident to his subordinates throughout the spring. He insisted upon extensive map reconnaissance* and rehearsals. Each corps commander was to develop detailed operations plans, which Brusilov personally reviewed. He became a tireless overseer of the planning process, insuring that as little as possible would be left to chance when the assault opened.[12] The preparations for this offensive served as the premier exam-

---

*Commanders perform map reconnaissance, which involves the detailed study of a terrain map, in order to familiarize themselves with the intended site of an operation.

ple of Russian military skill; Brusilov's efforts were cited by Winston Churchill as being marked by "exceptional energy and comprehension."[13]

According to the *Stavka's* plan, the Southwest Front's offensive was to be accompanied by a simultaneous attack by Ewarth toward Warsaw. Both advances were scheduled for late June 1916. The operation was accelerated, however, by circumstances over which the Russian planners had no control—on May 15, Conrad launched the Asiago offensive by sending his Austro-Hungarian forces southward, renewing operations along the Trentino River in the South Tyrol. This action annoyed Conrad's German allies. Falkenhayn, seeing the German efforts at Verdun beginning to flounder, had asked the Austrians to provide divisions for employment in France. Ludendorff was equally desirous of keeping as many Austrian units as possible in Galicia and Bukovina. Nevertheless, Conrad's operation effectively disrupted Allied plans. His initial success in the Trentino quickly led Italy to request aid. The Russians were asked to commence operations at an earlier date in the hope that the Austrians would return some divisions to Galicia.

After a series of frantic telegrams from the *Stavka*, Brusilov agreed to advance the starting date for his offensive to June 4. He agreed despite the fact that Ewarth could not attack until June 14. Alexeyev, the Russian Chief of Staff, feared that Brusilov's scheme was too ambitious and suggested that he revert to the steam-roller technique of massing all the assault forces in one sector. Brusilov, however, vehemently defended his original multi-axis plan.[14]

Brusilov's offensive (*see Atlas Map No. 35b*) opened in the early hours of June 5, following an effective day-long artillery preparation that tore wide gaps in the enemy wire. Russian assault troops were quick to exploit the opportunity created by their gunners. During the first day, the two flank armies advanced 10 miles. Progress against the Austrian forces was more rapid than that against the Germans, who resisted fiercely and surrendered territory more slowly. The Russian Eighth Army achieved breakthroughs west of Rowno and Dubno.[15] Russian achievements were impressive; by noon on June 6, they had captured 900 officers, 44,000 men, and 77 guns. Three days later, these numbers had increased substantially.[16]

The armies of the Southwest Front continued advancing, but Brusilov was still deprived of the assistance of Ewarth's supporting attack, now postponed until July 3. The Germans were not hesitant to capitalize on Ewarth's hesitation. Falkenhayn and H-L began to shift German divisions from the north and west, using the efficient railway system that always gave the Germans the edge in strategic mobility.

A limited German counterattack along the Stockhod River in July yielded partial success, but Brusilov moved on.[17] By the end of July, he had achieved a major triumph:

An American Cartoon Exaggerates the Renewed Health of the Russian Army

his bag included 8,255 officers and 370,000 enlisted prisoners, 496 guns, and 400 automatic weapons.[18] It was Russia's greatest success of the war.

With each mile that the Russian infantry plodded westward, however, they marched farther from their source of supply. Meanwhile, German reinforcements poured into Galicia. With the reluctance of Kuropatkin and Ewarth to press vigorous attacks to the north, Brusilov was unable to sustain the momentum of his offensive, and it predictably ground to a halt. Stiffening the Austrians with their own troops,[19] the Germans stopped the drive well east of the final objectives—Lemberg and Kowel.

Although it failed to achieve sustained strategic effect, the Brusilov offensive was noticed in other quarters. Smarting from tactical failures at Verdun and the Somme, Falkenhayn could not survive this latest humiliation. Relieved as Chief of Staff in late August, he was replaced by Hindenburg, who went to Berlin accompanied by his alter ego, Ludendorff. The two were to guide Germany's military fortunes until the war ended in November, 1918.

The ultimate check of Brusilov's initially successful offensive highlighted the lack of ability and cooperation among the members of the Russian General Staff and High Command. As such, it had a disheartening effect on an army already disillusioned by repeated failure. A cloud of despair descended upon the ranks and soon spread to the civilian populace in the urban centers of Russia.

In those centers, there was already political unrest that would intensify in the early weeks of 1917 as the Russian people sought relief from the autocratic administration of the Romanovs.

The Rumanian Campaign

To the southwest, the Balkan kingdom of Rumania, watching the battles raging back and forth, weighed the advantages and disadvantages of entering the war. A combination of factors, one of which was the initial success of the Brusilov offensive, decided the issue.[20] On August 17, 1917, Rumania stated her intention to declare war on Austria-Hungary in 10 days. Unfortunately for Rumania, she had waited too long. If her operations against Austria had been concurrent with Brusilov's drive, her chance of success would have been greatly improved. Once the 1916 Russian offensive was halted, however, it was comparatively easy for the Central Powers to mass forces for a coordinated operation against the small Rumanian Army.[21]

Rumania entered the war with a small, poorly trained and equipped peasant army. It was deficient in artillery, ammunition, and knowledge of combined arms tactics and gunnery. The high command was inept and more familiar with the techniques of parade ground maneuvers than those required by a force in the field.[22] Nevertheless, the Rumanian High Command launched its troops across the Transylvanian Alps against the Austrians. Had it been a one-on-one engagement against the Austrians or the Bulgarians, the outcome might have been more even, but, as it turned out, an effective coalition effort insured that Rumania's tenure as a belligerent would be brief.

The Rumanians took the offensive in the late summer. Three Rumanian armies (the First, Second, and Fourth) advanced into Transylvania on the night of August 27, 1916. Another army, the Third, was in a reserve position in the vicinity of Bucharest; by September 15, this army was reinforced by Russian divisions in the Dobrudja. (*See Atlas Map No. 36.*) In addition, Brusilov had reluctantly sent his Ninth Army into Bukovina to back up the Rumanian advance into Transylvania.[23] Control of Russian forces passed to the King of Rumania as titular Commander-in-Chief.

Rumania's strategic concept was predicated not only on Russian support, but also on the initiation of a new Allied drive on Bulgaria from the Allied base in Salonika, Greece. This sortie was part of Rumania's Plan A, which called for

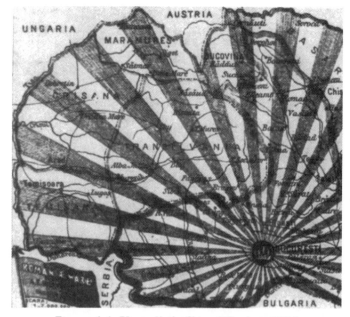

Rumania's Unrealistic Grand Design, 1916

the defensive against Austria and an offensive effort south into Bulgaria to link up with the Allied drive. Plan B involved a large-scale offensive into Transylvania and a defensive in the south. Unwisely, Rumania implemented a combination of these two plans. Moreover, the Salonika-based thrust against the Bulgarians gained little, and had no effect on operations in Rumania.[24]

The Central Powers had expected Rumania's declaration of war, and responded immediately. Anticipating the opening of a new front, the military leaders of Germany and her allies had commenced planning on July 28 to determine strategy and calculate the number of troops that should be furnished by the respective coalition partners.[25] The resultant force was comprised of divisions from Germany, Austria, Turkey, and Bulgaria. The strategy consisted of a three-pronged offensive that would first drive the Rumanians back across the Transylvanian Alps, and then compress them from three directions for annihilation between the mountains and the Black Sea. Interestingly, the ex-Chief of the German General Staff, General Erich von Falkenhayn, was selected to command the combined force, and would therefore execute the plan that he had approved a few weeks earlier. His task as commander of one of the major elements (the Ninth Army) was to drive the Rumanian First and Second Armies through the Transylvanian passes, pursue, and turn eastward toward Bucharest. The Austrian First Army was to push the Rumanian Fourth Army east of the Alps into Moldavia and then turn southward. The secondary effort, which was to be accomplished by Mackensen's veteran army from Galicia in concert with Bulgarian divisions, consisted of a drive northeastward from Bulgaria across the border into the Dobrudja. Mackensen was to block the Rumanian avenue of retreat and seize the port of Constanza.

Initially, the Rumanians made limited gains against the Austrians in Transylvania; but by September 18, the attack had stalled. On September 1, Mackensen had entered the Dobrudja and captured the Danubian fortress of Turtukai. As he advanced, the Rumanians panicked. Quickly shuttling divisions from Transylvania to the south, they were able to push Mackensen back a few miles. However, this shift of Rumanian combat power also eased the pressure on Falkenhayn's army; on September 18, Falkenhayn launched his counteroffensive.

The Rumanians were finding themselves successively more isolated from their allies. There was no help from Salonika, and the Russian forces in Rumania and Bukovina were not strong enough to balance the combat power of the Central Powers. Finally, the necessary supplies were not arriving from Russia. Mackensen continued to apply pressure in the Dobrudja, and Falkenhayn's Ninth Army began to seize the passes controlling the routes into Transylvania. (*See Atlas Map No. 37.*) The Rumanian High Command then began to reconsider its ill-conceived invasion. After deliberation, it was decided to renew the Transylvanian offensive while simultaneously using the national reserve (the Third Army) to make a river crossing at Rahovo and get behind Mackensen's army, thereby forcing him to abandon the line south of Cernavoda. The crossing, which commenced on October 1, was aborted by a flood and by the forces that Mackensen had left on the south bank of the Danube to guard against such a contingency. Shortly thereafter, the drive by Falkenhayn into the northern passes resulted in another reshuffling of the dwindling Rumanian forces from the Dobrudja back to Transylvania.

Thereafter, notwithstanding the onset of winter and a consequent slowing of operations, the Germans and their allies took pass after pass, driving the Rumanians ahead of them toward Bucharest. Mackensen took Constanza and Cernavoda in the Dobrudja. On November 23, his troops crossed the Danube near Sistova, and in three days advanced to within 30 miles of the capital. (*See Atlas Map No. 38.*) Despite a gallant counterattack mounted against Mackensen on December 1, the fate of Rumania was sealed.

Falkenhayn's troops entered Bucharest on December 6. The dispirited Rumanian Army, having lost an estimated 350,000 troops, dissolved during a halfhearted effort to link up with Russians to the northeast.[26] The ill-fated Allied attempt to send relief forces from the Salonika base to Rumania was contained by Bulgarian forces in the summer of 1916. (*See Atlas Map No. 39.*)

Archduke Frederick and General Falkenhayn Inspect Austrian Troops at the Front, 1916

In mounting a model campaign against Rumania, the Central Powers reaffirmed the validity of as many of the principles of war as the Rumanians had violated. The classic operation involved multilateral planning and produced an offensive on three axes that merged into one sustained drive against the Rumanian Army. The Rumanians vacillated between offense and defense on two fronts that were not mutually supportive. The Germans massed their combat power and operated on secure lines of communication, while the Rumanians required external sea lanes and support from Salonika to survive. Mackensen's appearance in the Dobrudja on September 1 surprised the enemy, causing the Rumanian strategists to shift troops from their primary offensive to reinforce a secondary effort. Mackensen safeguarded his rear by leaving forces along the Danube to guard against a possible turning movement—one that the Rumanians attempted in early October. Finally, the success of the Central Powers can be attributed to the excellent planning and execution of the campaign by several national forces under a unified command. In contrast, Rumania's allies were poorly informed of her war plans. The leaders of the Central Powers were precise and methodical, leaving little to chance; in opting for war, the Rumanians took a foolish gamble based on faulty assumptions. The execution of the Rumanian Campaign confirmed Falkenhayn's assessment of the capabilities of his allies and enemies.

1917: The Last Battles on the Eastern Front

In 1917, the march of events led to a shuffling in the Central Powers' command structure on the Eastern Front. When Hindenburg replaced Falkenhayn as German Chief of Staff, Hindenburg's post of commander of German armies in the East was nominally assumed by Field Marshal Prince Leopold of Bavaria. In accordance with the German method of command, however, the daily conduct of operations was delegated to the sagacious veteran of three years' work on the Eastern Front: Max von Hoffman, now promoted to Major General and assigned as Leopold's chief of staff. On November 20, 1916, Austria's aging Emperor Franz Joseph died and was succeeded by the Archduke Charles. While he did not relieve Conrad, Charles was determined to get Austria out of the war by one means or another as soon as circumstances permitted. This policy naturally resulted in acrimonious exchanges with the Germans.

In Russia, an ominous political revolution was taking form. In February,* the month of the first revolution and the beginning of the short-lived experiment with popular government (the Provisional Government), many of the old faces (Ewarth, Ivanov, and Kuropatkin) disappeared from the scene. More staff changes would follow in the ensuing weeks, which were marked by violent eruptions across the

*By the old style Russian calendar, which lagged 13 days behind the one adopted in 1918, the accepted date of the first Russian Revolution is February 27, 1917.

length and breadth of Russia. In the late spring, Alexander Kerensky, a politician turned soldier, assumed duties as Minister of War. Kerensky implored the reliable Brusilov—now Russian Commander-in-Chief—to make one more attempt to keep Russia in the war. In a July offensive, similar to the one of the previous year, Kerensky launched the armies of the Southwest Front into Galicia. (*See Atlas Map No. 41b.*) As had happened previously, early gains were achieved by the Russian Army; however, the Germans and the Austrians absorbed the blow and counterattacked on July 19, driving the dispirited Russians out of Galicia. Their momentum probably could have carried them deep into the Caucasus as the Russian troop units—hungry and rent by revolution—literally disintegrated. Eventually, lengthening communications caused logistics to prevail and halted the counteroffensive. As the Russian soldiers dug in, many were faced with the dilemma of obeying either their appointed officers or their newly elected military leaders in the Soldiers Committees (Soviets) that had been established from company to national level in Petrograd.*

With the front in southern Poland stabilized, the German High Command looked about for new conquests. In early August 1917, Ludendorff called Hoffman and reopened the old idea of an offensive in the Baltic region that would cross the Dvina River and seize Riga.[27] Irrespective of past differences with H-L, Hoffman, always the professional, concurred, and planning commenced for a joint operation against Riga and the Baltic Islands at the mouth of the Gulf of Riga. (*See Atlas Map No. 40.*)

For the ground operation, Hoffman selected the veteran Eighth Army commanded by General Oskar von Hutier. Ludendorff chose General Hugo von Kathen to lead the amphibious forces that would carry out landings several weeks after Hutier seized Riga. The amphibious operation was not considered essential to the success of Hutier's drive, and was included largely in order to give the High Seas Fleet, also infected with revolutionary ideas, a productive mission. Because it had as an objective a port less than 300 miles from Petrograd, this joint maneuver posed a strategic threat to the Russians.[28]

On September 1, following an artillery and gas preparation fired by 170 artillery batteries, Hutier's troops established a bridgehead against General Vladislav N.K. Klembovski's Twelfth Army. The Russians abandoned their positions before noon. Success came so quickly that the Germans were not prepared to exploit it. On September 3, 1917, the Eighth Army literally strolled into Riga, unopposed. Although it took longer, the naval operation was no less effective. With one infantry division and a cycle-infantry brigade, supported by 19 capital ships, Kathen's

A Russian Officer, with Drawn Sword, Exhorts Troops to Turn Back the Central Powers, 1917

*Petrograd was the new name for the capital of St. Petersburg.

German Artillery Moves Up to Support the Assault on Riga, 1917

joint task force landed on October 12 on the north side of Oesel Island. Quickly, troops moved south and east, taking the shoreline opposite Moon Island. The next day they occupied Moon and Dagoe Islands, which were defended by a hapless Russian admiral named Atvater. The amphibious operation was successfully concluded on October 20.

With respect to the tactics employed in the assault, Hutier's success at Riga has been the subject of considerable debate among military analysts. Some ascribe to Hutier the innovation in assault tactics that nearly enabled Germany to win the war in 1918. It has been suggested that Hutier, while commanding the Eighteenth Army on the Western Front in the German breakthrough in March 1918, put into practice the tactical methods developed at Riga.[29] In fact, Hutier and his artillery commander, Colonel Georg Bruchmüller, carefully coordinated the artillery support of the advancing infantry to allow light mobile troops to penetrate to the rear of defense positions and restore movement to the battlefield.

Hutier's tactics have been briefly described as "offensive with limited objectives." Theoretically, the defending enemy troops were to be subjected to a short, violent artillery preparation to preserve surprise; then the artillery fire would be placed to the rear of the objective position to prevent the frontline positions from being reinforced by reserve formations. Having moved stealthily to assault positions as close to the enemy as possible, German special shock troops, or *Sturmbattaillon* (Storm Battalions), armed with grenades, automatic weapons, flamethrowers, and light mobile artillery, would advance rapidly. Throwing themselves upon the dazed defenders, the *Sturmbattaillon*

would rapidly build up local superiority. Success was achieved by a combination of surprise and the rapid shifting of artillery support, which could move from counterbattery to assault fire, and then be shifted to seal the penetration. This technique was termed the *Feuerwalz* (Firedance).[30]

Analysis of Hutier's successful Riga campaign does not sustain the thesis that these novel assault tactics were employed. Hutier's name was never linked to doctrinal innovation by his contemporaries in the German Army. It was the Allies, primarily the French, who credited Hutier with developing the tactics exhibited in March of 1918 after rehearsal at Riga in 1917. In fact, it was the German General Staff's dissemination of lessons learned during battle that created this step in the evolution of tactics. German infiltration assault tactics were an offensive adaptation of techniques developed by the Germans in the trenches of the Western Front in 1915 and 1916.[31] The elastic defense in depth was discovered to have offensive ramifications, and thus was applied in the last German drives of 1918.

At Riga, in September 1917, there was no surprise. Having expected Hutier's assault as early as August 20, the Russians began to withdraw from their bridgehead southeast of the Dvina River. On the same day, General Klembovski began to withdraw supplies from Riga. The German artillery assault was ferocious, but most of the rounds fell on unoccupied terrain north of the river. Although the Germans crossed the river and took their first day's objective, they then commenced to mill around without further guidance on the next phase of operation. The leading divisions brought along heavy baggage; they were not lightly armed storm troops.[32] Riga was not taken by new tactical methods. It was given away by the Russians despite a relatively sluggish performance by Germans using evolving tactics. Riga is more significant for being the last campaign on the Eastern Front in which Russia fought as a member of the Allies.

Revolution and Truce in the East

The political revolution that occurred in Russia in 1917 had profound effects, not only upon that unfortunate nation and the warring powers in Europe, but also upon the entire world. The downfall of the 300-year-old Romanov dynasty and the accession to power of a very militant group that espoused Marx' Communist ideology would shape world events for the remainder of the century.

The history of the Revolution is a long and bloody one, marked by violence, repression, and tragedy. It is a complex tale of absolutism versus human aspirations, war weariness, and intrigue. Revolution flowed from the autocratic and administratively backward conditions in czarist Russia. It was provoked and brought to the fore by the horrors of modern war, just as Marx and Engels had predicted.

A history of the Revolution should commence with the earliest reform attempts of Czar Alexander II. In 1861, that Emperor established a system of local courts and provided for locally elected governments in the provinces, thus affording a debt-ridden and impoverished peasantry a draught of human rights.[33] Almost as if he had instituted his reforms while sleepwalking, Alexander soon swung back to conservatism, enforced by repression. This pendulum served to stir unfulfilled expectations in many breasts. The 1870s became a decade of terrorism as intellectual radicals and students, preaching the slogan of "Land and Liberty" to a rural population still burdened by redemption dues[34] and heavy taxes, sought reform in violence. The leaders of the movement were shot or imprisoned, but not before Alexander was himself assassinated.

Vladimir I. Ulyanov (Lenin), a name inextricably linked with the international Communist movement, appeared as the leader of a new party (the Bolsheviks) that was dedicated to the overthrow of imperialist and capitalist regimes everywhere. A multitude of new liberal and socialist movements had appeared in Russia, but the Czar's brutal secret police forced them into clandestine operations. The Russo-Japanese war of 1904–1905, in which the Russians were soundly defeated, did much to fan the sparks of revolution, ultimately leading to the first attempt on the part of the liberals to take control. On January 9, 1905 ("Bloody Sunday"), striking workers and their families marched unarmed on the Winter Palace in St. Petersburg to petition the Czar for redress. Czar Nicholas turned his police and Cossack cavalry loose on the mob, killing and wounding hundreds.[35] Bloody Sunday was followed by several months of violence, strikes, and unrest, as well as a short-lived sailors' mutiny at Kronstadt Naval Base. Recognizing the need for some reform, the Czar issued a manifesto on October 17, 1905 in which he decreed the establishment of the first *Duma,* or representative assembly, and granted a wider franchise and certain other civil liberties.

The *Duma* was made up of a number of splinter parties that represented diverse political movements. These included the Bolsheviks, perhaps the most extreme in their desires for total revolution; the Mensheviks, a more moderate offshoot of the Marxist movement; the Constitutional Democrats, or Cadets, a group that espoused socialism and land reform measures; and a number of other factions ranging from moderate to reactionary. They found almost as much to quarrel about among each other as with the Czar. The first *Duma* was short-lived, and its successional assemblies did not achieve useful reform.

The outbreak of World War I brought a patriotic fervor to Russia, temporarily muting popular unrest. With the exception of the Bolsheviks, who were soon arrested and sent into exile, all parties in the *Duma* voted to support the war effort.[36] Despite military setbacks, popular support for the war effort remained high throughout 1914 and 1915. Had the Russians achieved success or a negotiated peace with Germany in those years, the Revolution might have been forestalled. However, lack of ministerial stability, the failure of Brusilov's offensive in 1916, and a breakdown in food distribution and rail services brought renewed demands for peace and bread.

The first Revolution began almost unnoticed. On February 23, 1917, a few workers in St. Petersburg went on strike and demonstrated in the streets, but they were quiet and dispersed without incident. On February 26, 200,000 strikers were in the streets, but most of the Cossacks ordered out to disperse the crowds refused to charge. Mutiny spread. One garrison regiment in the capital shot its commander and joined the mob in the streets. They then proceeded to break into the Czar's metropolitan arsenal and seize 40,000 rifles.[37] General Ivanov, with a force west of the capital,

Vladimir I. Ulyanov (Lenin) in 1920

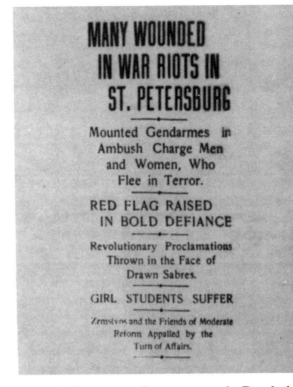

A British Newspaper Comments on the Revolution in Russia, 1917

responded to pleas of assistance from the royal court and marched to the relief of the Government. When he reached the suburbs, his troops began deserting.

When the *Duma* met in the Tauride Palace on February 27 to deliberate, it found itself meeting alongside a newly formed body, the Workers' and Peasants' Soviet. This Bolshevik-inspired organization was established to accomplish Lenin's purpose—the violent transfer of all power to the people. What occurred in those confusing days of February and March propelled the forces of social change. Under considerable pressure, the Czar abdicated, and Russia became a republic. The *Duma* and the Petrograd Soviet created the first Provisional Government under Premier Prince G.E. Lvov, a moderate liberal.

A popular hero and Socialist revolutionary, Alexander Kerensky, was named Minister of Justice.

Before it implemented its broad program of reform, the Provisional Government began to dismember the Russian Army, the one organization that might have allowed it to survive. By the promulgation of General Order Number 1 on March 1, the Government destroyed all remaining discipline in Russia's armed forces. The March 1 document provided for the election of committees (Soviets) in all army units. Designed to rule the units that they served, these committees were ordered to obey the Petrograd Soviet rather than their appointed military officers. The order

also abolished saluting and the rendering of honors to military superiors.[38] These moves clearly eroded the discipline and authority necessary for an effective military organization.

The German General Staff also plotted to encourage the revolution that weakened Russian military operations. It arranged for Lenin and fellow Bolsheviks to travel from Switzerland across Germany to Finland in sealed railway cars, thereby expediting the return of the most radical of the revolutionaries. In addition, Leon Trotsky, perhaps the most articulate of Lenin's lieutenants, returned from his exile in New York City.

A great debate arose concerning Russia's role in the war and her relationship with her allies. Moderates favored continuing the war as long as possible, while the Bolsheviks urged that Russia sue for peace and let the Revolution move forward.[39]

In the First Congress of Soviets, Kerensky, elevated to the position of War Minister, rode out dissent against a continuation of the war. In June 1917, he directed Brusilov to undertake a new offensive in Galicia. As previously recounted, in this repetition of Russian attacks in other years, the thrust through Austrian lines soon lost its impetus. By July 19, an Austro-German counterattack had contained the Russian offensive. Stimulated by the Bolsheviks and the depressing military bulletins, 200,000 people went into the streets of Petrograd, shouting "All Power to the Soviets" and "Down With the Provisional Government."[40]

Although in August the Government restored some

The Petrograd Soviet of Soldiers and Workers, 1917

measure of control, the Revolution could not be contained. A reactionary military coup attempted by General L.G. Kornilov appeared to gain support, but was thwarted by Kerensky, who forced the general's resignation. On the pretense of arriving to defend the capital, Bolsheviks and sailors from Kronstadt poured into Petrograd and gained support from the army garrisons in the city. September was a time of unrest and uncertainty, as demands for an armistice became more insistent. At the front, the Soldiers' Soviets condoned the murder of unit officers. The sailors of the Baltic Fleet solidly supported the Bolsheviks, who gained more political support as each day passed. On August 31, power effectively changed hands when the Bolsheviks gained control of the Petrograd Soviet. On September 25, Trotsky was elected Chairman of the Executive Committee. A Military Revolutionary Committee was established in the Petrograd Soviet for the purpose of serving as a sort of Bolshevik general staff. A week later, Kerensky tried to raise a relief force to enter the city and restore the Provisional Government, but he was too late. On October 25, the Reds, as the Bolsheviks were called, seized the State Bank, the railroad stations, and the Winter Palace, in which the remaining ministers of the Russian Government were barricaded. Kerensky fled. Petrograd belonged to the Bolsheviks; the rest of Russia was to follow.[41]

One of the first acts of the Bolsheviks was a call for a cessation of the war. On November 8, in a Decree of Peace that was addressed to all belligerents and was made without prior consultation with Russia's erstwhile allies, the Bolsheviks called upon the world at large to declare a just and democratic peace without territorial annexations of any kind.[42] The Allies were stunned, not only by the collapse of established power in Russia, but also by the unrealistic Soviet proposal. The Central Powers were no less confounded, but were relieved over the prospect that the Russian Army would soon cease to be a threat. This would enable the transfer of German units to the West.

Lenin and Trotsky, not concerned with Allied reactions to the decree, attempted to establish contact with the Germans through Soldiers' Committees at the front. Ensign Nikolai V. Krylenko, a former Russian corporal, was entrusted with command of the Army and was also charged with establishing contact with the German General Staff. After some fumbling, he was successful; on December 2, 1917, a three-man Soviet Peace Mission entered the German lines at Dvinsk, setting the stage for a future conference at Brest-Litovsk in Poland.[43]

Prior to an analysis of results of the negotiations at Brest-Litovsk, which continued through March 1918, it is necessary to understand the strategic positions of Russia and Germany at the end of 1917. Russia was in a state of internal chaos. Hunger and poverty were rife; there was no opera-

General Max von Hoffman *(left)* **Leads the Delegation of The Central Powers at Brest-Litovsk, 1917**

tional transportation system; reactionary "White Forces" were organizing throughout the country in an attempt to re-establish the monarchy. The Russian Army had all but ceased to exist as an effective military force. The Bolshevik offer of world peace without compensation was completely unrealistic and would not be considered by any of the other belligerents. The Red leadership was naive in believing that the rest of Europe was on the brink of revolution. They thought that all of Europe would soon emulate the Russian example and that the warring powers would then cease hostilities, declare peace, and return to the prewar status quo. The forces of the Central Powers were deep inside Russian Poland and had every intention of establishing a security zone between their own frontiers and Russia—a zone that would include western Poland, Courland, and Lithuania.[44] The Germans had 80 divisions to enforce their desires. Austria-Hungary would have agreed to the Russian terms, but did not have the freedom of action to do so. Bulgaria and Turkey appeared ready to follow any course set by the Germans.

The Brest-Litovsk Conference convened on December 12, and an agreement was soon reached on an armistice that would extend for several weeks. The delegates to the conference formed a polyglot assemblage: Hoffman and Foreign Minister Richard von Kühlmann from Germany; minor military representatives from Austria, Turkey, and Bulgaria; and a Russian delegation that included Adolf Joffe, Lev B. Kamenev, Madame Byzenko, a Red Army non commissioned officer, a sailor, a worker, and a peasant.[45]

Bolshevik tactics depended on the wearing down of their adversaries with rhetoric. They berated their opponents with pompous speeches, hoping perhaps to prolong the meetings until the chimerical world revolution. Throughout most of these tirades, Hoffman and his colleagues listened patiently, agreeing in principle with some rather ambiguous Russian propositions and rejecting others. Finally, it became evident that the Russians seriously expected German and Austrian forces to retire to the frontiers of August 1914.[46] In response, on December 24, Hoffman leveled his stern gaze at Joffe and declared bluntly and without reservation that the Central Powers had no intention of withdrawing from territories already occupied.* This clear statement shocked not only the Bolshevik delegation but also Count Czernin, the Austrian negotiator, who was seeking a settlement for war-weary Austria under almost any conditions. He promptly and peremptorily countered Hoffman's words with a proposal that the Soviets and Austrians negotiate a separate peace. Hoffman led Czernin aside and coolly suggested that if Czernin desired to consummate a separate peace with the Bolsheviks, Germany would remove the 25 divisions that were then supporting the Austrians in Galicia. Realizing that Austria could not stand alone, Czernin let the issue die.[47]

Joffe requested a recess in order to return to Petrograd and acquaint Lenin and Trotsky with Hoffman's interpretation of "no annexation." The recess was granted. There then ensued an acrimonious debate in the Petrograd Soviet over the future of the negotiations. Lenin's view was realistic—settle for what Russia could get now and hope that the longed-for revolution in central Europe would invalidate the unfavorable terms. Trotsky's more idealistic view prevailed—continue negotiations only on the basis of the principles of the Red Revolution. The obvious weakness in this position was that the Bolsheviks, having destroyed the Russian Army, had no effective instrument with which to enforce their position. Baron von Kühlmann drolly summarized the Russian alternatives: "The only choice they have is as to what sort of sauce they shall be eaten with."[48]

When the conference reconvened at Brest-Litovsk on January 9, 1918, Trotsky, replacing Joffe as chief of the Russian delegation, reiterated the Bolshevik line. Hoffman refuted the argument in blunt, realistic terms. This time, however, he further confounded the Soviets by announcing that the Central Powers were prepared to sign in a separate peace with the anti-Bolshevik Ukrainian national government, which then held political power in that rich and fertile

Leon Trotsky in 1918

region. This was followed by another adjournment and further debate between Trotsky and Lenin. The Bolshevik reaction was to promulgate an even more incredible and unrealistic proposal: "no war—no peace." In short, this meant that the Russians would neither fight nor sign a treaty of peace on German terms. The Bolsheviks unilaterally declared Russia out of the war without agreements or provisions for concluding hostilities.

On January 30, when the conference reconvened and Trotsky announced this decision, it was Hoffman's turn to be astounded: "Unprecedented!" he exclaimed.[49] He then proceeded to sign a separate peace with the Ukrainian *Rada,* and on February 16, 1918, he notified the Soviet Government that the Central Powers would resume military operations in two days.

On February 18, German divisions once again rolled eastward in the easiest assault of the war. Platoons and squads riding on railroad flatcars seized whole towns and districts against token opposition. (*See Atlas Map No. 41a.*) Lenin's worst fears of more war and more losses of territory were realized. After further debate in Petrograd, the Russians reluctantly agreed to sign the treaty. Then the German General Staff deferred their reply, enabling their divisions to advance to Narva, within 100 miles of Petrograd.* Fin-

---

*The Germans had viewed the Russian proposal for "peace without annexations" in the light of self-interest. German policy makers decided that Poland, Lithuania, and Courland desired independence from Russia and closer affiliation with Germany. Thus, the Germans would not annex, but would grant autonomy to these areas; the areas would remain under German "protection."

---

*This threat precipitated the movement of the political capital inland to Moscow.

ally, Hoffman responded to Russia's frantic calls for a resumption of the conference so that an end could be put to the huge losses of territory, population, and industry occasioned by the German drive.

The Russians finally signed the Treaty of Brest-Litovsk on March 3, 1918, and for them the Great War was over.[50] It would take the final defeat of the Central Powers on the Western Front to nullify the territorial and material gains that German military power had wrested from the idealistic and disorganized Bolshevik Government.

Notes

[1]Winston S. Churchill, *The Unknown War* (New York, 1931), p. 360.

[2]John S. Curtis, *The Russian Revolutions of 1917* (Princeton, N.J., 1952), p. 28.

[3]Stanley Washburn, *The Russian Offensive* (London, 1937), pp. 77–80.

[4]Walther Hubatsch, *Germany and the Central Powers in the World War, 1914–1918* (Lawrence, Kans., 1963), p. 67.

[5]Churchill, *Unknown War,* pp. 366–367.

[6]Hubatsch, *World War,* p. 69.

[7]A.A. Brusilov, *A Soldier's Notebook, 1914–1918* (Westport, Conn., 1971), p. 204.

[8]*Ibid.*

[9]*Ibid.,* pp. 210–211.

[10]Churchill, *Unknown War,* p. 359.

[11]Brusilov, *A Soldier's Notebook, 1914–1918,* p. 277.

[12]*Ibid.,* pp. 222–234.

[13]Churchill, *Unknown War,* p. 359.

[14]*Ibid.,* p. 361.

[15]Washburn, *Russian Offensive,* p. 10.

[16]Brusilov, *A Soldier's Notebook, 1914–1918,* pp. 241–243.

[17]Washburn, *Russian Offensive,* p. 15.

[18]Brusilov, *A Soldier's Notebook, 1914–1918,* p. 256.

[19]Berhard Schulz, *Revolutions and Peace Treaties 1917–1920* (London, 1967), p. 256.

[20]Hubatsch, *World War,* p. 74. Other factors in the decision were Allied promises of postwar territorial concessions in Transylvania, Bukovina, and the Banot; the German failure at Verdun; and abandonment of the German drives on Salonika.

[21]Vincent J. Esposito (ed.), *The West Point Atlas of American Wars* (2 vols.; New York, 1959), II, 37.

[22]Brusilov, *A Soldier's Notebook, 1914–1918,* p. 262.

[23]*Ibid.,* p. 265.

[24]Esposito, *West Point Atlas,* II, 37–38.

[25]James B. Agnew, "The Improbable Alliance," *Parameters,* II, (USAWC, 1972), 28.

[26]Hubatsch, *World War,* p. 75.

[27]Max von Hoffman, *The War of Lost Opportunities* (New York, 1925), p. 188.

[28]*Ibid.,* p. 191.

[29]Laszlo M. Alfoldi, "The Hutier Legend," unpublished monograph, (USAMHRC, December 1974), p. 6.

[30]*Ibid.,* p. 191.

[31]Timothy T. Lupfer, "The Dynamics of Doctrine: Changes in German Tactical Doctrine During the First World War," *Leavenworth Papers No. 4* (Combat Studies Institute, Fort Leavenworth, Kansas, July 1981), passim.

[32]James E. Edmonds, "Hutier's Rehearsal," *The Army Quarterly,* VIII (April-July 1924), 18.

[33]Curtis, *Russian Revolutions,* p. 7.

[34]*Ibid.,* pp. 11–13. "Redemption dues" were crop quotas imposed by landlords on renter peasants; they often approximated 75 percent of the annual crop. This added to the burden of low productivity of Russian agriculture. Hand tilling measures were in effect, and one-third of the fields lay fallow each year.

[35]*Ibid.,* p. 16.

[36]*Ibid.,* p. 22.

[37]*Ibid.,* p. 30.

[38]*Ibid.,* p. 36.

[39]*Ibid.,* p. 29.

[40]*Ibid.,* p. 43.

[41]*Ibid.,* pp. 32–75.

[42]George F. Kennan, *Russia Leaves the War* (New York, 1967), p. 322.

[43]*Ibid.,* p. 104.

[44]S.L.A. Marshall, *World War I* (New York, 1971), p. 322.

[45]Hoffman, *Lost Opportunities,* p. 197.

[46]*Ibid.,* pp. 205–207. The Russians also demanded that the proceedings be publicized, that no more German troops be transferred from the Eastern Front, that Bolshevik propaganda be permitted in Germany, and that the Germans remove their troops from the Moon Bay Islands in the Baltic. Hoffman and Kühlmann agreed to the first two proposals and rejected the last two. Hoffman had no problem with the troop movement pledge, for he had already given the orders to move all the forces required by Ludendorff to the Western Front.

[47]*Ibid.,* pp. 208–210.

[48]Kennan, *Russia Leaves War,* p. 228.

[49]Hoffman, *Lost Opportunities,* p. 226.

[50]Kennan, *Russia Leaves War,* p. 368.

The Search for Mobility on the Western Front, 1917

7

Since the chance of success of an attack by tanks lies almost entirely in its novelty and in the element of surprise, it is obvious that no repetition of it will have the same opportunity of succeeding as the first unexpected effort. It follows, therefore, that these machines should not be used in driblets (for instance, as they may be produced), but the fact of their existence should be kept as secret as possible until the whole are ready to be launched, together with the infantry assault, in one great combined operation.

LTC E.D. Swinton, *Notes on the Employment of Tanks*

As the third full year of the Great War dawned, Europe was in the grip of destructive total war. On December 12, 1916, the German Government had issued a proposal for a peaceful resolution of the hostilities.[1] The Central Powers were careful to deny any moral responsibility for the war, and threw the opprobrium for continuing the killing onto the Allied Powers.* The response of the Allies marked the changed nature of modern warfare—they rejected the proposal out of hand. Aside from the obvious fact that the nebulous "peace proposals" indicated that Germany would retain much of the territory that her armies had captured, the real reason for the rejection was that the societies of Western Europe had sacrificed too much to accept a negotiated peace.[2] Politicians and soldiers alike no longer saw a resolution of the conflict except by defeating the enemy on the battlefield.

The scope and intensity of the war had increased in 1916. Societies were being more efficiently organized to satisfy the maw of total war. National passions were now inflamed, and any who spoke of negotiation or conciliation were regarded as traitors. This stoic acceptance of continued sacrifice, however, was not accompanied by blind loyalty to the leaders who had conducted the war up to that point. The promotion of Sir Douglas Haig to the rank of Field Marshal on New Year's Day, 1917, was the single reaffirmation of faith in the wartime leadership.

Shortly, many of the principal characters would pass from the scene. Four months earlier, Falkenhayn had been replaced by the team of Hindenburg and Ludendorff. In England, the coalition government of Prime Minister H.H. Asquith had fallen on December 5, 1915 and been replaced by that of David Lloyd George. On December 12, 1915, the French Cabinet had been reconstituted under M. Aristide Briand as Premier. On that same day, perhaps the most profound change had occurred when General Joffre was effectively replaced by a young general, Robert Georges Nivelle.* Although the honor of appointment as a Marshal of France was bestowed upon the departing Commander-in-Chief, he was promoted out of his job and became a technical adviser to the Government.[3] His relief mirrored the dissatisfaction of the French people with the costliness and frustration of the war. Significantly, Nivelle was given command of only the Armies of the North and Northeast, rather than all French forces.†

*While this was the only move for peace by one of the principal belligerents, it was made during a time of intense diplomatic maneuvering to define war aims and possible peace terms.

*Marshal Joffre later became an important public relations asset for the French Government. When the United States entered the war, he led the French delegation that guided and advised the Americans on their war preparations. He was received as a military hero by the United States Congress and public, thus magnifying France's influence upon United States military policy.

†Joffre had run the military areas with authoritarian control. His elevation to Commander-in-Chief of all French armies merely confirmed his power and independence from political control. Fearing a further dilution of their war powers, the French politicians selected a relatively junior general who would be more malleable.

Civilians Learn New Ways to Participate in the War

Elsewhere, change was also in the winds. The aged Emperor Franz Joseph of Austria-Hungary had died on November 20, 1916 at the age of 86. His successor, Charles, realized that a rapid peace settlement was the only way to salvage his decaying inheritance.[4] In the United States, a change of policy, rather than actors, was the order of the day. President Woodrow Wilson, who had been re-elected in November on a platform of "He Kept Us Out of the War," severed diplomatic relations with Germany on February 3 in reaction to the reinstitution of unrestricted submarine warfare. He would lead his nation into the war on April 6, 1917.[5]

The unremitting casualty rolls from the Somme and Verdun battlefields added to the growing war weariness in France. The British nation, experiencing its first massive losses, endured the sorrow, but also questioned the effectiveness of a political and military leadership that would allow such Pyrrhic victories.

A False Promise of Success

The new leader of the French Armies was a recent hero of the Battle of Verdun. Nivelle was a charming and forceful speaker, able to converse fluently in accentless English.*

Perhaps because Lloyd George was not used to such clear military discussion, he accepted Nivelle's leadership and proposals without reservation.[6] The general's main proposal was to mass French forces for one final breakthrough of the German line. (*See Atlas Maps Nos. 16a, 16b and 16c.*) Basically, he planned to apply on a grand strategic scale the methods that had proven tactically successful at Verdun. He foresaw a decisive battle on the Western Front that would destroy the enemy's main arms and achieve the elusive breakthrough that other military leaders had been unable to produce. He wanted to pin down the major portion of the enemy line, with British assistance, and then shatter the front on the Chemin-des-Dames ridge with a massive attack. Nivelle felt that his method would achieve a breakthrough on the Chemin-des-Dames and thus turn the entire German line. The main attack was to be supported by the British attack at Arras and holding attacks by the French on both sides of his main thrust. This was reminiscent of the plans and doctrine of August 1914, and the attack, as he envisioned it, would break through within 24 hours. He promised that if success were not achieved within 48 hours, the offensive would be halted. This plan was a drastic change from that agreed upon in November by Nivelle's predecessor.[†] While it required an extension of the British line by more than 20 miles, it also placed the principal burden of battle squarely on the French.[7]

Field Marshal Haig offered to begin his relief of the French line on February 1, and indicated that after the first increment (eight miles), the rate of relief would depend upon the reinforcements he received. In addition, Haig asked Nivelle to agree that if his attempt to achieve a breakthrough failed, the French would take over some of the British line to allow the long delayed northern operations to continue into the summer.[8] Affronted by the mere suggestion that his program might fail, Nivelle appealed to his government to press the British for more complete conformity to his desires.

At a Franco-British conference in December, Lloyd George had emphasized his support of Nivelle's plan, but he later told Haig that no British reinforcements could be expected. Before the next conference was held, the British Prime Minister met with the author of the new plan and was converted to its complete support. Lloyd George welcomed the vision of a decisive end to the war, especially if it imposed no heavy burden upon his nation. His desire to win

---

*It is significant that Lloyd George was advised by two military men, Haig and Robertson, who were inarticulate in personal conversation. Not until General Henry Wilson replaced Robertson as Chief of the Imperial General Staff (CIGS) in 1918 did Lloyd George have a military adviser who could match the politicians' art of persuasion.

† Joffre and Haig had agreed upon a continued strategy of attrition on the Western Front. The main burden was to be borne by the British in 1917. The other Allies were to mount offensives on their respective fronts in order to prevent Germany from reinforcing in the West.

"on the cheap" blinded him to the fact that the plan before him was merely a repeat of policies that had failed miserably in the past two years. At the second conference on the proposed plan, the Prime Minister agreed to send Haig two divisions from the home island defense force, in addition to four others. With this reinforcement, it was agreed that by April 1 the British could take over the full 20 miles of trenches, as requested by Nivelle. The strength of the British Army would now be increased to 62 divisions in France.[9] With this expansion, however, another serious problem arose.

Franco-British Squabbling

The growth of the British forces in northern France had placed a heavy strain upon the rail network that served the Army's needs. In line with his policy of utilizing civilian expertise whenever advantageous, Haig had appointed Eric Geddes as the Director-General of Transportation for his armies.* Geddes implemented an extensive program of coordinating rolling stock in the British sector. The technical details of the logistical network were being dealt with, and additional rolling stock was being sent from England. However, for the immediate needs of the expanding front, the British were still heavily dependent upon French facilities.[10]

On January 24, Haig explained to Nivelle that his current capacity of 150,000 tons of supplies per week would have to be increased to 250,000 tons for an effective implementation of the spring offensive plans. The French viewed these requirements as excuses for postponing the attack. This incident of inter-Allied distrust illustrates a simple but basic problem in combined military operations. The very difference between the French and British standards of living caused the British soldier to expect more food, ammunition, and other classes of supply† than his French counterpart. Thus, the British logistical plans were on a different scale than those of the French. As the size and duration of the operations increased, these differences became magnified. Nivelle, failing to understand the problem confronting his combined command, actually felt that the British were inflating their requirements as an excuse for not participating in the operation.[11]

Nevertheless, Nivelle proposed to supplement the British supply system and to improve the northern transportation network so that it could carry 200,000 tons each week. Haig agreed to compromise on this supply plan. At a later con-

*Geddes was a civilian railway expert and former manager of the North Eastern Railway System in England. He was later appointed First Lord of the Admiralty to organize and coordinate the anti-U-boat campaign.

† Because of the great variety of goods, like items were grouped into "classes of supply." For example, Class I included those items consumed at a uniform rate. Food was a Class I supply.

Supplies for British Forces are Unloaded

ference between the two commanders, the French general extended his assurance of assistance to the promise that the offensive would not begin until all British requirements had been met. This completely satisfied Haig, and there appeared to be no further technical problems in the way of the planned offensive.

Haig, however, took one military exception to Nivelle's plan. He insisted that Vimy Ridge (*see Atlas Map No. 16b*) be included as an objective in the British portion of the operation. He argued that his forces could not operate successfully east of Arras without first securing this dominant terrain feature to their left rear. The French refused to believe that the British could secure Vimy Ridge; Foch had attempted this twice without success. Despite the skepticism of the French, Haig pressed his demand and finally received permission to modify his operational plans. With all evident problems disposed of, there now appeared no further reason for high-level discussion. Surprisingly, however, Lloyd George scheduled a full-scale Franco-British conference to be held at Calais on February 26. The reason given for this meeting was the need for additional talks on the British supply problems.

The Calais Conference convened on February 26, 1917, and its results were to color the political and military coordination of Franco-British affairs for the remainder of the war.[12] From the outset, the British Prime Minister allowed his revulsion with the policies of his own commanders to so warp his appreciation of the military situation that he seriously compromised what little unity of effort there had been up until that time. An even more critical result of David Lloyd George's decisions at this conference was that he bound the main Entente armies to a foolhardy military plan that would nearly lose the war within three months.[13]

The purported focus of the conference—the transportation problems behind the British lines—was quickly brushed aside and the technical matters referred to a committee of experts. Lloyd George then turned to his real reason for calling the conference. He asked Nivelle and Haig to speak frankly of any disagreements they had over the coming operations, indicating that he was not interested in technical military points but in the highest level of military cooperation on the Western Front. Lloyd George then asked Nivelle to place in writing a guide to the military command structure that he felt should be instituted on the Western Front. At last, the conflict between the British political and military hierarchies was exposed, leaving an opening for the French to gain ascendency in the alliance.

Lloyd George had previously informed the French Government and the *Grande Quartiers Général* (GQG) that he was willing to allow the British forces in France to be placed under General Nivelle's command. At that time, he had expressed both complete confidence in Nivelle's plan and the feeling that, to insure success, Nivelle had to command all Allied troops in the coming operations. But, he noted, these sentiments could not be expressed publicly, because Field Marshal Haig's reputation with the British public and in the Army was too great. Deviously, however, the Prime Minister intimated that secret orders to the British Commander-in-Chief, making him subordinate to Nivelle, would be possible.[14] Accordingly, the French had prepared a detailed formula for a reorganization of the high command; in response to Lloyd George's invitation, Nivelle presented it when the conference reconvened.[15]

France's formula exploited all the weaknesses that Lloyd George had exposed. The memorandum called for insuring "unity of command on the Western Front from the 1st of March 1917" by granting the French General-in-Chief "authority over the British forces operating on this front, in all that concerns the conduct of operations and especially: the planning and execution of offensive and defensive action; the dispositions of the forces . . . the boundaries between . . . formations [and] the allotment of material." The British commander would carry out "the directives and instructions of the French Commander-in-Chief" and otherwise would only decide "questions of personnel and general discipline in the British Armies."[16] The French commander would control the British forces through a chief of staff at GQG who would directly supervise the British General Staff and Quartermaster General, bypassing the British commander. The ultimate humiliation was that this arrangement was to be permanent; even if Nivelle were replaced, it could only be modified by a new combined Franco-British directive.

The British military ranks were shocked by this proposal. They had not been told of the preconference maneuvering or even informed of the general topics of discussion. In fact, they had purposely been kept unaware of Lloyd George's plans. Such a situation left Haig and General William Robertson, the Chief of the Imperial General Staff, bitter toward their Prime Minister and distrustful of the ally with whom they had loyally cooperated. General Robertson vowed that he would resign his position rather than allow the British armies to be placed in such a subordinate role. Haig, while smarting under this blow of ingratitude, publicly held that the higher command system was a political, not a military concern, and that it was therefore not within the realm of his responsibility.[17]

The French proposal was even too drastic and specific for Lloyd George. As a result, a second command proposal was drafted. Besides endorsing the 1917 war plans of Nivelle, this proposal gave the French Commander-in-Chief "general direction" of the campaign, while reserving for the British commander the option of appealing to his government if his forces were endangered. This hastily prepared compromise was approved, but its imprecise nature soon became a source of friction.*

The day after the conclusion of the Calais Conference, GHQ received from Nivelle a peremptory order that all instructions issued by Haig to his army commanders had to first be cleared by the French headquarters. This obvious attempt to meddle in the internal operations of the British command may have been caused by Nivelle's desire to embarrass Haig and force him to resign, or may have resulted from the French officer's imperfect understanding of the final limitations of the Calais Agreement. In any event, Haig protested to his government that he was being treated unfairly and that the relationship with Nivelle should be further defined. At this point, the association between the French and British High Commands became spiteful and sank to the lowest point in the war.[18]

The result of Haig's protest was a second conference, held in London on March 13, to more precisely define the command relationship between the two generals. The resulting agreement reaffirmed the British commander as a coequal and instructed "the French Commander-in-Chief [to receive] from the British Commander-in-Chief information as to his operation orders as well as all information respecting their execution."[19]

When asked to approve this agreement, Sir Douglas Haig refused to give a blanket endorsement. Instead, he appended the following statement to the document before he signed.

---

*An extract of the Calais Agreement may be found in Annex B, Appendix 9.

I agree with the above on the understanding that while I am fully determined to carry out the Calais Agreement in spirit and letter, the British Army and its Commander-in-Chief will be regarded by General Nivelle as Allies and not as subordinates, except during the particular operations which he explained at the Calais Conference.

Further, while I also accept the Agreement respecting the functions of the British Mission at French Headquarters, it should be understood that these functions may be subject to modifications as experience shows to be necessary.[20]

This endorsement is interesting for several reasons. First, Haig's principal objection to any modification in the command arrangement that had previously existed between General Joffre and Haig had apparently been more one of form than reality. He insisted that he be recognized as an ally and not as a subordinate, when he had, in practice, readily subordinated himself and his forces to the wishes of the former French commander. Another key to Haig's attitude is seen in his pragmatic approach to the liaison system between GHQ and GQG. Haig wanted to insure that he would retain control of his general staff sections and the Quartermaster General's activities. The most obvious exception that Haig took to the previous negotiations, however, was that he viewed any direct subordination of British forces to French command as a temporary expedient—he agreed to conform to General Nivelle's wishes only for the forthcoming spring offensive.

This exchange of proposals and counterproposals did nothing but exacerbate the latent distrust between the French and British High Commands. Ironically, the command structure soon became unimportant in comparison with the disastrous course of events on the battlefield. In any event, the British headquarters did conform to Nivelle's plan, with the inclusion of Vimy Ridge as an objective, and loyally carried out all instructions from the French Commander-in-Chief.[21]

German Preparations

Throughout the period of recrimination and confusion over Franco-British military coordination, the German chief of staff in the West, General Erich Ludendorff, had been working to nullify the effect of Nivelle's planned offensive. The German forces were ordered to pull back to a new defensive line. The fortifications behind the Noyon salient, a part of the new *Siegfried Stellung,** had long been suspected by Allied intelligence services of portending a voluntary withdrawal. Indeed, during the Calais Conference, which

had committed the Allies to Nivelle's attack, the frontline troops reported that the Germans had begun a general withdrawal. Ludendorff's decision to voluntarily surrender territory was a break with the concepts of the generals on the Western Front. While it risked certain psychological hazards, the military advantages of the decision cannot be denied. The vulnerable Noyon salient was traded for a much shorter line and this, in turn, increased the defensive power of the German positions. The move was also an economy-of-force measure in that it freed units for possible offensive actions.[22] (*See Atlas Map No. 16a.*)

The construction of the Hindenburg Line had begun five months earlier. This huge task required the concentrated efforts of civilian, military, and impressed prisoner labor. The new positions were more of a defensive zone than a line. The construction exploited lessons that had been learned in the past on the Western Front. Care was taken to accurately site and protect automatic weapons positions. Reverse slope positions on dominating terrain provided excellent artillery observation from behind the front.

The German retirement to the Hindenburg Line began on February 25, 1917. Security measures and the required logistical support caused it to last until April 5. In order to impede Franco-British reaction to the withdrawal, a deliberate policy of devastation was implemented in the Noyon salient; buildings were leveled, road networks were blocked and cratered, and water and food supplies were either contaminated or destroyed.

In addition to preparing a new defensive line, the Germans readied a tactical surprise for the Allies. The growing intensity of combat during 1916, coupled with the superiority of the Allied artillery of all calibers, had convinced the Germans that it was no longer feasible to conduct the main defensive battle in the forward zone of the battle area.[23] Investigations of the failure of the rigid defensive system at Verdun against the French counterattacks in October and December of 1916 and experience on the more mobile Eastern Front were the basis of the new flexible, or elastic, defensive system.[†]

Ludendorff, the guiding spirit of the German command team, was not wedded to the inflexible defensive tactics of many Western Front generals. He realized that the doctrine of holding terrain at all costs was as expensive for the defenders as for the attackers. In the German General Staff, Ludendorff also possessed a responsive instrument with which he could rapidly and effectively transmit his ideas to the commanders on the Western Front. The first edition of the new instructions was distributed in mid-December 1916, and revisions followed as experience was gained in battle.

The elastic defensive doctrine employed by the Germans

*This position was known to the Allies as the Hindenburg Line.

†The Germans also incorporated defensive lessons learned in the latter stages of the First Battle of the Somme. Their great success on the Chemin-des-Dames in April 1917 confirmed the validity of the new doctrine.

had as its object the prevention of a breakthrough while inflicting maximum losses on the attacker. Since some terrain could be lost in this system, the bulk of the defender's resources did not have to be placed on the frontline. Accordingly, the leading edge of the defensive zone was lightly outposted with just enough strength to repel minor enemy probes, provide advanced warnings, and delay and disorganize a major offensive. Rather than fortifying the forward areas with trench networks, the Germans established a series of mutually supporting strongpoints to take maximum advantage of machinegun and artillery fire.

Behind the outpost line to a distance of one kilometer lay the main defensive zone of three trench systems. The forces that manned these positions were given great latitude to maneuver within their sectors, to mount local counterattacks, and to develop the situation. Behind these forces lay the specifically designated counterattack (*eingrief*) divisions, which were provided in approximately the same strength as the forces in the main battle zone. The emphasis on counterattack units that could inflict damage on the attackers before they could adequately prepare their defenses and the provisions for moving them were the precursors of the "mobile defensive" doctrines of the Second World War. This system proved devastatingly effective when properly executed. The only problems that were encountered in its adoption were the refusal of certain commanders to change their methods and the adjustment of the new doctrine to varying types of terrain. The most sincere compliment paid to these new defensive tactics came from the Allies who officially adopted the elastic defense during the battles of 1918, when they were forced onto the strategic and tactical defensive. This new concept would soon be tested by Nivelle's offensive.

Nivelle's Offensive

After the conclusion of the London conference that resolved Franco-British command structure differences, Allied planning for the offensive proceeded at a rapid pace. At the same time, the German withdrawal to the Hindenburg Line accelerated. Nivelle's two planned holding attacks were seriously affected by the enemy actions, but the main attack on the Chemin-des-Dames was not. After having promised an end to the war after one more offensive, Nivelle was now trapped by his own publicity campaign. Maintaining an air of optimism, he refused to modify his plans to conform to the changed conditions.

Coincidentally, the firm support that Nivelle had enjoyed, especially from his own government, was being rapidly eroded. The Briand Government fell on March 17, 1917, and the new ministry, headed by M. Alexandre Ribot, had as its War Minister Paul Painlevé, a skeptic about the soundness of Nivelle's plans. Painlevé inquired among the army group commanders about the plan and found that the subordinates who would have to carry out the orders also had serious misgivings.[24]

To add to Nivelle's problems, it became apparent that there would be no cooperative efforts from the other theaters of war to divert the enemy's reserves. The tottering Russian Army would make no offensive efforts until the end of June, and a weak offensive by the Allies in Macedonia had ended on March 23, after having lasted only 12 days.[25] The British had sent the Italian Army 10 batteries of howitzers* in hopes of spurring an offensive on that front.[26] However, General Cadorna, fearing an Austro-German attack after the fall of Rumania and the beginning of the Russian Revolution, did not launch his offensive until after Nivelle's had failed. There appeared to be no chance of the cooperation that had been in effect under Joffre's direction. To complete this chain of bad omens for the success of the spring offensive, the Germans captured a set of operational plans for the main attack. Faced with these mounting obstacles, Nivelle nevertheless persisted with his plans without any substantial changes. Meanwhile, the Germans had fully perfected their system of elastic defense and would provide the final ingredient in the failure of Nivelle's vaunted offensive.

The purpose of the first phase of the Battle of Arras, which was conducted from April 9 to 14, was to divert enemy attention and forces away from the main French attack on the Aisne River. Unfortunately, the sector chosen for the attack was heavily fortified and contained not only the new defenses of the Drocourt-Quéant Switch Line,† but the older positions as well. (*See Atlas Map No. 16b.*) Adding to the difficulty of attacking in this area was the fact that enemy positions on Vimy Ridge dominated the entire area and were considered impregnable.

The British First and Third Armies were to attack simultaneously, with the latter, under General Edmund Allenby, making the main effort. The First Army, commanded by General Henry Horne, had to secure Vimy Ridge in order to protect the left flank of the main attack. If both of these operations proved successful, Haig envisioned expanding the fighting to the south using General Hubert Gough's Fifth Army. Finally, if a breakthrough was achieved, the British commander planned to exploit it with horse cavalry reserves.

---

*In addition, a liaison team was sent to Italy to coordinate plans for British reinforcement of the Italian Army in the event of an Austrian victory on the Isonzo front.

† This new line was just being completed. It was an alternate line about seven miles to the rear of the old positions, which were still occupied by the Germans. The Drocourt-Quéant line was designed as a fallback position in the event that the British made gains in the vicinity of Arras. Such British success, without a German fallback position, would allow Haig's forces to outflank the Hindenburg Line.

Against the wishes of the local commanders, who planned a surprise artillery hurricane barrage, GHQ ordered a conventional four-day bombardment by the heaviest concentration of guns yet assembled in the war.* Sixty tanks were available for the attack; again, however, as he had done at the Somme eight months earlier, Haig distributed these among the corps commanders as infantry support weapons rather than massing them for maximum effect.

The tactical disposition of the British and Canadian troops in the vast tunnel and cave complex under the town of Arras provided the assaulting waves of troops with welcome protection. Additionally, fresh divisions were available at critical moments to exploit success. The soldiers, thus protected from the "wastage" of the front in well lit and ventilated underground shelters, had extremely high morale and operated with great efficiency.

The attack commenced at 5:30 a.m. on April 9 against defenders who were demoralized by the heavy artillery preparation. The German Sixth Army commander had refused to adopt the new elastic defensive doctrine because he felt that he had to hold the dominating Vimy Ridge. As a result of this decision, his forces sustained heavy frontline casualties from the intense artillery preparation. By evening, the British had capitalized on their momentum by "leapfrogging" fresh divisions through those that had been spent, thus achieving excellent results. The Canadian Corps took Vimy Ridge, and due east of Arras the British 4th Division reached the enemy's final defensive line. That evening, General Allenby ordered the capture of all remaining defenses and the preparation of the cavalry for their mission of exploitation. However, once again the initial success of the break-in could not be parlayed into a breakthrough.

Bad weather coupled with the readjustment and reinforcement of the German defenses held the succeeding attacks to minor gains. The Fifth Army's attempts to extend the offensive to the south were also failures. The Germans, immediately reinforcing the threatened sector, relieved the Sixth Army Chief of Staff. His replacement, Colonel Lossberg, was an excellent tactician who instituted the elastic defensive measures that might have prevented the heavy initial German losses.

A second phase of the battle was opened on April 23, after Nivelle's offensive had failed. With no real strategic goals, the continuation of the Arras offensive merely served the purpose of diverting enemy attention from the defeated French. The results of the first phase of the Battle of Arras had been encouraging—the Allies had captured Vimy Ridge, along with 200 guns and 13,000 prisoners—but the

The Canadian Corps Goes Over the Top During the Battle of Arras, April 1917

final cost of 150,000 casualties was a high one to pay for operations in a diversionary sector. The battle, however, did provide an encouraging prelude for Nivelle's main effort on the Chemin-des-Dames in the Second Battle of the Aisne.

Despite all of the trouble involved in continuing with his final breakthrough to victory, General Nivelle persisted. Ignoring the skepticism of his allies, the doubts of his political superiors, and the defensive preparations of the enemy, Nivelle pushed forward with the grand assault on the Chemin-des-Dames ridge. He inspired his troops with a feeling of invincibility, and they were led to believe that the time for an end to the futility of trench warfare had finally come.†

Nivelle had initially achieved eminence through his superb tactical battles at Verdun. He had developed and successfully applied a method of artillery-infantry coordination that inexorably regained all of France's lost territory around the ancient fortress city. However, the tactical method developed by Nivelle was based upon limited objective assaults by specialized infantry teams operating behind a precisely coordinated artillery barrage. When he was given the chance to command on the Western Front, his method was transformed into a massive headlong rush against one of the German's most heavily fortified defensive areas. (*See Atlas Map No. 16c.*)

Huge stocks of artillery ammunition were stored for use in an overwhelming attack of the forbidding steep and wooded ridges that the Germans had meticulously fortified. The assault force of 28 divisions was to be under the con-

---

*This was prolonged for one additional day to aid Nivelle, whose attack had been delayed by weather.

† Nivelle's final message before the assault is revealing: "The Hour has come! Confidence! Courage! *Vive La France!*"

General Robert Georges Nivelle

trol of Generals Alfred Micheler and Charles Mangin. These troops and their supporting units were rigorously trained and continuously inspired to believe in their ultimate success. The unprecedented preparations for the offensive and Nivelle's own propaganda efforts impressed not only the soldiers but the entire French nation. Not since August 1914 had expectations for a rapid end to the war been so high. Once again, they would prove groundless.

The Germans were also expectant. Their intelligence system had accurately pieced together the entire plan for the offensive. To prepare for the French offensive, the new system of elastic defense was completely implemented. This meant that the frontlines were held with a minimum of manpower so that the effect of the heavy French artillery preparation would be nullified. Machinegun strongpoints were reinforced, and troop assembly areas were located on the reverse slopes of hills while taking full advantage of the limestone caves in the area. An additional army was positioned in the vicinity, and counterattack divisions were placed throughout a defensive zone 20 miles in depth.

On the cold and snowy morning of April 16, the long awaited offensive began. At 6:00 a.m., the frontline divisions of the Fifth and Sixth Armies attacked with an élan and esprit reminiscent of the Battles of the Frontiers. By 8:00 a.m., most of the forward German positions had been occupied. It soon became obvious, however, that the heavy

artillery bombardment had failed to silence numerous German machinegun positions. As the rolling barrage passed by, the machinegunners emerged from their covered protection and manned their weapons. Moreover, the broken and wooded terrain slowed the advancing infantry and severely hampered the support they could receive from the accompanying tanks. After 2:30 p.m., the snow squalls turned to rain, and the Germans implemented their plans for a counterattack. By evening, many of the attacking units had been thrown back to their line of departure. In all, less than 10 square miles of captured terrain remained under French control. The vaunted Nivelle offensive had failed all along the line.

The French commander renewed his attack the next day. In fact, the offensive continued until May 7, showing once again that battles—even those that commanders promise to terminate in 48 hours—achieve a life of their own and cannot be halted at will. The French Army lost 135,000 men, but the real casualty was the morale of the troops. Although Nivelle's offensive ultimately captured 20,000 German prisoners and 147 guns, it had not achieved the desired *percée,* or breakthrough. The French *poilu* had been promised decisive victory once too often; he reacted sharply to this final example of the futility of frontal assaults. In the wake of defeat and disappointment came the nightmare of mutiny in the French Army.

On the night of April 21, while the 1st Colonial Infantry Division was being transferred to the rear, the French troops demonstrated their disgust with the slaughter. They screamed at the fresh troops moving up to the front: "Long live peace! We're through with killing!" Although the officers reported the incident, they were powerless to discipline the entire unit.[27] This mild but ominous act was the first of 119 acts of "collective indiscipline" that would come close to forcing France out of the war.[28]

The British Assume the Burden

During the period of the mutinies, which would last until mid-September, 54 French divisions were affected. The acts of mutiny ranged from outright demonstrations against the war and attacks on officers to situations in which units merely informed their superiors that they would defend their positions but nothing else.[29] Following the disappointing results of the Nivelle offensive and the disastrous mutinies that ensued, the Government felt it necessary to replace the Commander-in-Chief. The new commander of the Armies of the North and Northeast was General Henri Phillipe Pétain, the first hero of Verdun. Faced with an enormous problem of leadership in a precarious military situation, Pétain reacted with admirable common sense. He immediately began a program of informing the troops of his intentions while clearing away all of the remnants of the discredited Nivelle regime. The new commander promised defensive activity while he rebuilt his forces. Even when the French returned to the offense, Pétain stated: "The equality of the opposing forces does not for a moment permit us to envisage the rupture of the front. . . . Attacks in the future will be mounted economically with infantry and with a maximum of artillery."[30] The new commander visited between 80 and 90 divisions, explaining his program to the senior officers and then speaking to the assembled troops. Although he authorized a program of ruthless punishment for mutineers, in practice he applied this extreme weapon with great selectivity. Many of the leaders of the rebellions were transferred, and their sentences of death or long imprisonment were commuted. He stressed active leadership by the junior officers, and made it clear that the old *"Système D,"** or the former sloppy methods of preparation, lax supervision, and excuses, would no longer be tolerated

---

*Système D got its name from the verb *débrouiller,* meaning "to disentangle." This referred to the practice of muddling through with a minimum of effort.

General Henri Phillipe Pétain

when men's lives were at stake. Gradually. Pétain's measures restored the faith of the French troops in their leaders, but the Army would bear the scars of this episode for the remainder of the war.

Pétain favored a military course of "limited liability" and planned to await the arrival of the American Army before continuing offensive operations. As a result, while the French Army turned inward to heal its mutiny-riddled spirit, it passed the total military initiative to the British for the remainder of the year.[31] Under these conditions, Haig commanded without external restraint upon his authority until the following November.[†] After more than two years of conforming to French military strategy, the British would finally conduct their northern operations.[32]

The Third Ypres Campaign was undertaken for numerous and complex reasons. (*See Atlas Map Nos. 17a. 17b, and 17c.*) Besides diverting German attention from the perilous condition of the French, perhaps the most compelling reason for its conduct was the Royal Navy's inability to counter the full-scale German submarine campaign that had begun earlier in the year. The unrestricted U-boat campaign was causing irreplaceable losses in merchant shipping. Most naval authorities believed that the submarine pens at Ostend and Zeebrugge, Belgium were the home bases of these raiding vessels. Admiral Sir John Jellicoe, suffering from the strain of three years' command of the British blockade of the Continent, added his plea for the Army to relieve the mounting pressure. The First Sea Lord disclosed to the War Cabinet that unless the menace of the underwater boats was neutralized by the seizure of their home ports, Great Britain would be unable to continue the war into 1918.[33] The Royal Navy viewed the objective of seizing the Channel ports and countering the U-boat threat as the single most important goal for British land operations. It was also obvious that if command of the seas were relinquished, the anticipated support of the new ally—the United States—would be severely restricted. Another consideration that affected Haig's decision to carry on with the planned offensive was that American military power could not be brought to bear on the Western Front for another 6 to 12 months. Therefore, any Entente initiative had to be supplied by the British armies. Yet another factor was that the British Government, led by Lloyd George, was pressing its unrealistic dreams of winning the war through victories on the Italian Front or in the Middle East.[34] This strategic concept always threatened to draw British strength to subsidiary theaters. Haig, unalterably opposed to this view, feared that

---

† General Henry Wilson, the chief British liaison officer at GQG, wrote on June 28, 1917: "The French Army is in a state of indiscipline not due to losses but to disappointment." He urged his superiors to continue offensive pressure on the northern portion of the line in order to provide the French with time to rebuild their armies.

if he did not utilize his battle-ready forces they would eventually be siphoned off.[35] A final consideration in Haig's decision to proceed with the northern operations was not military in nature, but was caused by the political realities that had brought the British Empire into the war—her commitment to restore Belgium as a sovereign and neutral state.

Before any operations could be launched from the Ypres salient, the dominating terrain of the Messines-Wytschaete ridge had to be secured. (*See Atlas Map No. 17a.*) General Sir Herbert Plumer's gallant Second Arms, which had held the vulnerable positions within the salient for two years, was given the mission of initiating the long-awaited northern operations. The Battle of Messines stands out as the most complete local success of the war. Certainly, one cannot deny that it was a most meticulously prepared setpiece operation—similar in nature to the breaching and occupation of a medieval castle. Eighteen months prior to the attack, 24 mine shafts had been projected under the German frontline positions.[36] Each tunnel ended in a chamber that was packed with high explosives and fused for later detonation. Additionally, the Royal Flying Corps gained and maintained air superiority throughout the battle; its observation of the 17-day artillery preparation greatly assisted the destruction of German field and medium artillery positions. (In this particular operation, the battlefield destruction caused by the long preparatory fires was not considered a detriment to the infantry advance since the total distance to be covered was small and no exploitation in that portion of the front was planned.)

When Zero Hour came at dawn on June 7, 19 of the sunken mines were simultaneously exploded by 500 tons of explosive.* The sound was so loud that it was heard in London. The crest of the Messines-Wytschaete ridge was virtually shorn off by the explosions. At this signal, the artillery increased the tempo of its fire and added a mixture of poisonous gas and smoke. As might be imagined, the demoralization of the German frontline troops was matched by their heavy casualties. The British Second Army went over the top, supported by a small number of tanks and a new weapon, the Levens projector, which hurled canisters of asphyxiating gas into the enemy positions. Success was complete and the troops rapidly secured their limited objectives. With the dazed enemy unable to mount an effective counterattack, the ridge stayed in British hands.[†] Thus the first phase of the northern operations came to a successful con-

clusion with the result that the British Cabinet endorsed their continuation, providing the French Army supported the offensive. This approval, given without knowledge of the true condition of the French Army, insured that there would be a Third Battle of Ypres.

From its inception, the planned operation in Flanders had been plagued by postponements, misconceptions, and bad luck.[37] Forced to wait until the summer by the need to support the Nivelle offensive, Haig now waited an additional seven weeks between the brilliant stroke at Messines and the commencement of his main assault. (*See Atlas Map No. 17b.*) He began the operation with the heaviest artillery preparation of the war.* Starting on July 18, more than 65,000 tons of artillery shells were fired from 3,091 guns onto the poorly drained battlefield.[38]

The bad luck came in the form of the heaviest rains recorded in 30 years. These delayed the assault until July 31, by which time the combination of rain, mud, and shell craters made the zone of advance a morass.[39] The misconceptions that impaired the conduct of the campaign included the overly optimistic intelligence reports of Haig's Intelligence Officer, Brigadier General John Carteris. These reports indicated that Germany was within four to six months of being unable to maintain her armies in the field, and that the units being released from action on the Eastern Front could not be transported rapidly to the West. Haig selected General Hubert Gough to command the initial phase of the British offensive, believing that Gough's youth and optimistic view of the possibility of a breakthrough would outweigh the experience and familiarity with the terrain possessed by Plumer.

The infantry assault began on July 31. Gough's Fifth Army attacked with nine divisions, supported by attacks on both flanks made by Plumer's Second Army and the French First Army under General Pierre Anthoine. The German defenses, commanded by Crown Prince Rupprecht of Bavaria, had been completely adapted to the new elastic method and took full advantage of the bad weather and the warning provided by the long preparation. The massive and obvious preparations for the Third Battle of Ypres had the unplanned bonus of drawing German divisions from the Eastern Front to Flanders, rather than reinforcing the front opposite the weakened French Army. While this movement greatly decreased the possibility of British success in the campaign, it did keep the Germans reacting to the Allied initiative, thereby contributing to the secrecy of the plight of the French.

---

*One mine had been destroyed by German countermining efforts, one had been flooded in 1917, and three were not used.

† While it is rarely noted, tunneling and mining operations were a complementary function in many sectors of the line and were also employed in other theaters. They were conducted by both sides for morale and psychological reasons as well as for their tactical value. The mining of Messines ridge was only the largest and most successful of hundreds of similar operations.

*While reference to increasingly heavy artillery bombardment may appear repetitious, the growing dependence of the western Allied armies on the weight of artillery fire must he understood. In part, due to the lack of success of the Third Ypres preparation, this doctrine declined and was replaced by one that emphasized violent, but brief, surprise preparations.

The Fifth Army made some progress in the north, advancing about two miles, but the main attack, with the objective of securing the Passchendaele ridge, was repulsed. Heavy rains continued, delaying the next attempt until August 16. This second assault was even less successful than the first. The lightly outposted German defenses, which took maximum advantage of automatic weapons and negated the British superiority in artillery support, again proved their worth. The horrible conditions endured by the British attackers and the frustration of being unable to obtain tangible results induced Haig to replace Gough with Plumer. But he persisted with the offensive. Continually advised by his intelligence personnel that the German defenders were about to crack, Haig wished to at least secure the first stage objective of controlling the Passchendaele ridge before the winter ended operations. Plumer began a series of methodical limited objective advances. These well coordinated bites into the defensive works caused the Germans, in turn, to drift back to the older concept of defending heavily in the forward areas in order to retain terrain. The result of this reversion to the older method was that the defenders suffered increasingly under the weight of the preparatory fires of the attackers.[40] Finally, on November 6, the Canadian Corps seized the ruins of the village of Passchendaele. The British line was ordered to consolidate the ridge and go into winter defensive positions.

The seizure of the Passchendaele ridge was an arduous task, costly in men and materiel to both attacker and defender. It did not achieve the announced objectives, but it did divert the attention of the Germans from the faltering French line and continue the depletion of German strength. Ludendorff commented on these results:

> . . . the costly August battles imposed a great strain on the Western [German] troops. I myself was placed in an awkward predicament. The state of affairs in the West appeared to prevent the execution of our plans elsewhere, our wastage had been . . . high.[41]

The casualties suffered by the attacking British forces, while not as great as those in the First Battle of the Somme, seemed an extreme price for the barren tract of five miles that the campaign had secured. To the soldier who struggled on that field, and to later critics of World War I generalship, particularly that of Field Marshal Haig, Third Ypres or Passchendaele remained the lasting symbol of the futility of the war on the Western Front.

Faltering Allied Coordination and a German Initiative in Italy

Throughout 1917, there was virtually no inter-Allied cooperation or coordination. The French Army, under General Pétain, continued its moral and physical rearmament in near secrecy.* The Italians were concerned with their static front on the Isonzo River. The Russians were being effectively eliminated from the war by a combination of German victories and internal revolution. The prospective American armies were being raised and trained, but they would not be ready for field duty for at least six months. The only active front was that of the British in Flanders. Although this activity kept the Germans from seizing the initiative in a more vulnerable theater, there was little reason to attempt coordination until the French and Americans were capable of effective action.

Joffre's attempts to bring about cooperative Allied efforts during the first two years of the war had proved frustrating, particularly to the civilian leadership. Accordingly, the Allied politicians had retrieved their rightful control over the conduct of the war and instituted their kind of unified command—subordination of the British Army to French generals. In a very short time, however, the politicians' solution had proved to be an even bloodier failure. As a result, there would be no effective military cooperation until defeat confronted the alliance in March 1918.

Disillusioned by the failure of the Nivelle offensive in April 1917, Prime Minister Lloyd George had shifted his support from the Westerners[†] to a new strategy that would insure that the British Armies would no longer suffer heavily on the Western Front. As we have seen, his attempts to transfer the main effort of the western Allies to the Italian Front failed. Chastened by his ill-starred adventure into grand strategy and politically weakened on the homefront, Lloyd George withdrew from active direction of combat operations. The end result of this debate between the Easterners and Westerners was a victory for the latter, and the generals had conducted the Third Battle of Ypres.

A more lasting result of renewed interest in Italy was the formation of a planning staff under General Ferdinand Foch to prepare for an emergency transfer of combat power to Italy. This seemed a prudent step, since the German Army was now capable of transferring divisions to support the faltering Austro-Hungarian Army. Men and materiel were being released from active campaigning on the Eastern Front. Despite the sidetracking of Lloyd George's strategy

---

*It is one of the miracles of the First World War that the efficient German intelligence system was unaware of the French Army mutinies until after they had been quelled. One can only speculate as to what might have happened if they had broken through the French lines during the summer of 1917.

† In general terms, an Allied "Westerner" was a person who felt that victory could only come from success on the Franco-British Front and that either a large majority or all of the Allied combat power should be concentrated there. An "Easterner'" was one who felt that victory could be achieved by either destroying Germany on the Russian Front or by forcing Germany's allies out of the war.

of "knocking the props out" from under the Central Powers, the Franco-British-Italian cooperation and staff planning boded well for the future of combined operations.

General Luigi Cadorna still sought victory on the Isonzo front. (*See Atlas Map No. 14.*) Although Cadorna's forces had made only meager gains in the 10 battles fought on this river and had barely staved off defeat in the Austrian Asiago offensive of 1916, the Italian High Command stubbornly insisted on fighting the Eleventh Battle of the Isonzo. At long last, decisive results appeared in the offing. In August 1916, the Italian Second Army gained the first substantial success since the Sixth Isonzo. The Austrians were pushed back beyond their final defenses on the Bainsizza plateau. The Italians suffered nearly twice the number of casualties that they inflicted on the enemy, but a tangible result could be shown for the sacrifice—the objective of Trieste was finally within reach. Because Cadorna's forces had outrun their logistical support, however, some time was required to redeploy their artillery support forward.

This defeat left the tottering Austrian forces near collapse. The new Austrian Chief of Staff, General Arz von Straussenburg,* appealed to his ally, Germany, for immediate assistance.[42] In response, Ludendorff ordered his Fourteenth Army, under General Otto von Below, to attack on the Isonzo front. The combined forces of the Central Powers totaled only *35* divisions (7 German and 28 Austrian) against Cadorna's 41 on the main front. Secondary attacks were to be conducted by the Austrian Second and Tenth

---

*In February 1917, Conrad von Hötzendorf had been relieved by Emperor Charles and made an army group commander.

General Luigi Cadorna

Armies on both flanks of the main attack. Again, the principle of surprise would be required to achieve success.

Preparing for continued offensive operations, Cadorna was completely unaware of the enemy's concentration and plan. The small town of Caporetto would lend its name to one of the most dramatic battles of the war, and would keep it from being known merely as the Twelfth Battle of the Isonzo.[43] (*See Atlas Map No. 15.*) Deeply discouraged, the Italian troops were weary of continual offensive actions that had brought meager gains at high costs in men and materiel. Communist and pacifist propaganda had been distributed among many of the units. But the deterioration of morale in the military forces merely reflected the general state of war weariness in Italian society.[†]

Finally sensing an enemy attack, Cadorna ordered defensive preparation in depth all along the front. Believing the Caporetto sector of the Second Army to be far too rugged for a major offensive thrust, he placed his reserves behind the Third Army. To compound this error in intelligence evaluation, the aggressive Italian Second Army commander ignored the order to prepare defenses. The stage for a great disaster had been set.

In its attack at Caporetto, the Austro-German Fourteenth Army used a new form of offensive tactics that had been developed by the German General Staff. The heart of these new tactics were surprise and rapid tactical movement designed to pierce and disorganize the enemy defensive.[44] At 2:00 a.m. on October 24, 1917, the massed Austro-German artillery opened a sudden and surprise bombardment of mixed gas, smoke, and high explosive shell. The assault was launched six hours later under the cover of driving rain and ground fog. The storm troops had been trained to bypass strongpoints in the Italian defenses and allow specialized teams of bombers or flamethrowers to mop them up later. These tactics would be further refined and play a decisive role in the German offensives of 1918.

The effect upon the frontline Italian troops was devastating. Completely unprepared for these mobile and fluid assault tactics, most frontline defenders either surrendered or began a precipitate withdrawal. The Italian division and corps commanders had made no contingency plans for mutual support, and the main reserves were located far to the south. By evening, the Austro-German attack had gained 10 to 12 miles, completely captured or routed an entire army,

---

†Various attempts have been made to compare the situation of the Italian troops with that of their French counterparts during the mutinies of April-September 1917. It must be remembered that propaganda played a much smaller part in the Italian demoralization. Also, the Italian problem virtually solved itself after the Central Powers had seized large portions of Italy. In both cases, however, a new commander, who understood the mood of the troops, was an essential factor in the solution of the problem.

General Armando Diaz

and forced Cadorna to order a general retreat to the line of the Tagliamento River.

By October 31, the Italian Third and Fourth Armies had retired in relatively good order to the Tagliamento defensive line. Fortunately, the pursuing enemy began to suffer from the problems of tactical mobility, and their pace slowed. Unable to achieve surprise in seizing crossing sites over this defensive line, the Germans conducted a deliberate attack at Cornino on November 2, outflanking the Italian line and forcing Cadorna to order a further retreat to previously prepared positions on the Piave River. This was Cadorna's final action, as he was later replaced in command by General Armando Diaz.

By November 10, as the Italians were forming on the Piave River, four French divisions that had been rushed to Italy's aid began to move forward from Mantua.* The total aid sent to the Southern Front amounted to six French and five British divisions. With this added support and a resolve to defend their country, the Italians held the new defensive line. Although the Italian Army had suffered a grievous defeat, both the nation and the Army were galvanized into heroic action to defend their home-

land.† While disaster stalked the Allies in Italy, the British would conclude the year with their own battle of tactical mobility and provide another key to the solution of strategic stalemate on the Western Front.

Cambrai: The Promise of a New Instrument

Although the term "lightning war" was not coined until the Second World War, the year of 1917 ended with a battle of mobility and shock action equal to any of later years. The Royal Tank Corps, under Brigadier General Hugh Elles, had recommended a tank-infantry raid on the Hindenburg Line west of Cambrai as early as August 3, 1917. Elles and his chief of staff, Colonel J.F.C. Fuller, realized the futility of employing the new weapon of tactical mobility on the muddy Flanders plain. The area around Cambrai, however, was ideal tank country—firm, rolling terrain.

At Cambrai, the plan was to employ tanks in massed formations with close infantry support. Rather than using the new shock weapon as an infantry support weapon in "penny packets," a combined arms assault would be mounted, with mutual support provided by each element. The raid was to be strengthened by a surprise hurricane artillery barrage fired from weapons that had not been previously registered. Unfortunately, when this plan for a rapid but

† Another significant result of the great Central Powers' victory in Italy was the realization by the western Allies that a greater coordination of their military efforts was required. This led directly to the establishment of the Supreme Allied War Council (SWC). This organization is discussed in detail in Chapter 9.

Tanks and Infantry Train for the Cambrai Assault

*The Italian casualty figures for this battle indicate the poor state of morale: KIA—10,000; WIA—30,000; POW—293,000; deserters—400,000.

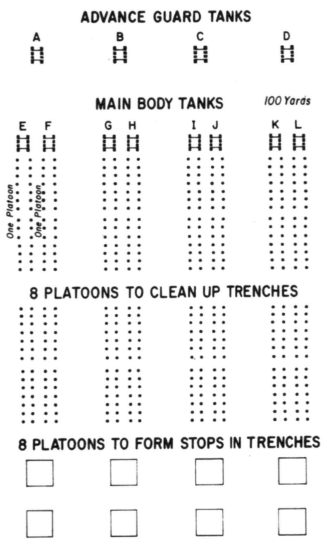

ADVANCE GUARD TANKS

A   B   C   D

MAIN BODY TANKS   *100 Yards*

E F   G H   I J   K L

One Platoon   One Platoon

8 PLATOONS TO CLEAN UP TRENCHES

8 PLATOONS TO FORM STOPS IN TRENCHES

The Method of Tank-Infantry Cooperation Prescribed by the British Third Army for the Battle of Cambrai, November 20–30, 1917

The Germans were completely surprised at 6:20 a.m. on November 20, when a sudden deluge of artillery fire poured onto their positions. Simultaneously, nine battalions of tanks, closely followed by their assigned infantry, surged forward from assault positions. General Elles led the attack in his own tank, with flags flying.[45] The leading tanks flattened the protective barbed wire of the German defensive system and dropped fascines* into the trenches in order to cross the wide barriers. By the time the following tanks and infantry reached the main defensive zone, the demoralized enemy had either fled or surrendered.

Only in the left center of the attack sector were the British formations checked. This was due to the refusal of one infantry division commander in the vicinity of Flesquières to support the tanks closely with infantry. More than half the tanks lost in action on the first day were lost in this area. Conversely, the infantry was left to mount uncoordinated frontal assaults against German machinegun positions without tank support. Despite this check, the advance had exceeded three miles by evening. The seemingly impregnable Hindenburg defensive zone had been breached.[46] Exhausted tank crews and infantry began their refueling and resupply operations. Of the reserve, only one squadron of Canadian cavalry had been committed, but its vulnerability to automatic fire was confirmed and it was forced to withdraw.

The next day, attempts to continue the advance at Bourlon failed, and the offensive began to lose its momentum. At the same time, the German High Command was rushing reinforcements to contain the attack. It was at this point that the lack of reserves and the refusal to limit the operation's objectives were exposed as errors in judgment. The battle

*Fascines are bundles of sticks used either as obstacles or, in this case, to fill ditches.

modest thrust was presented to Haig and his staff, it was expanded into a possible first step in a major breakthrough that was to secure a stunning victory over the Germans at year's end. (*See Atlas Map No. 17c.*) This expansion of the original plan proved most unfortunate since adequate reserves were unavailable, the troops either having been expended at Third Ypres or presently manning the defenses in Italy. The only real reserve available was the large body of horse cavalry, which, inexplicably, was never employed.

The security measures employed were superb. Low-flying aircraft were used to mask the inevitable noise associated with the assembly of the tank force. An additional 600 guns for the initial preparation were infiltrated into position, and their targets were selected from map charts. Even the infantry soldiers of the six attacking divisions were unaware of plans for the assault until two days before Z-Day.

The Aftermath of the Battle of Cambrai

shifted back and forth until November 24, when the British finally captured the contested Bourlon Woods and ridge. But this was to be the final advance. The Germans counterattacked on the thirtieth, using the new infiltration method of attack. Supported by massive strafing attacks by aircraft, the German infantry streamed through the thin British defenses in the south. Although the defenses in the north held, General Sir Julian Byng decided to pull back in order to straighten his lines.

The Battle of Cambrai cost both sides equally in terms of casualties and territory lost. The great elation of the British people over the initial victories of their armies on November 20 turned to doubt and disappointment after the successful German counteraction 10 days later. While the British commanders tended to blame the political leaders at home for their own inability to exploit the gains of the tank-infantry forces, they failed to realize that their persistence in the Third Battle of Ypres and their optimistic intelligence estimates were even more responsible. Despite the recriminations that followed the battle, there was little doubt that its tactical lessons would be of great value. The dawn of a new age of combined arms operations based upon tank-infantry-artillery cooperation had come. The element of surprise had returned to the battlefield. Most important, the tank and the German infiltration assault tactics had restored mobility to warfare on the Western Front. 1918 would be a year of exploitation of open warfare and tactical mobility by both sides.

Notes

[1]C.R.M.F. Cruttwell, *A History of the Great War, 1914–1918* (Oxford, 1934), pp. 359–375.

[2]Pierre Renouvin, "The Role of Public Opinion, 1914–1918," in George A. Panichas (ed.), *Promise of Greatness* (London, 1968), pp. 443–445.

[3]E.L. Spears, *Prelude to Victory* (London, 1939), pp. 24–30.

[4]Edmond Taylor, *The Fall of the Dynasties* (Garden City, N.Y., 1963), pp. 272–276.

[5]Walter Millis, *Road To War, America 1914–1917* (Boston, 1935), pp. 333–343.

[6]Robert Blake (ed.), *The Private Papers of Douglas Haig, 1914–1919* (London, 1952), p. 28.

[7]"Plan of Action Proposed By France To The Coalition," December 6, 1915, translation in James E. Edmonds (ed.), *History of the Great War: Military Operations, France and Belgium, 1914–1916* (6 vols.; London, 1922–1938), V, App. I, 1–5.

[8]John H. Davidson, *Haig: Master of the Field* (London, 1953), pp. 26–27.

[9]John Terraine, *Ordeal of Victory* (New York, 1963), p. xvii.

[10]Llewellyn Woodward, *Great Britain and the War of 1914–1918* (London, 1967), p. 257.

[11]Abel Ferry, *La Guerre Vue d'en Bas et d'en Haut* (Paris, 1916), translation in Spears, *Prelude to Victory*, p. 540.

[12]Lord Beaverbrook, "Two War Leaders: Lloyd George and Churchill," *History Today* (August, 1973), 546–553.

[13]The details of the military and political preparations are drawn from Spears, *Prelude to Victory,* passim.

[14]Telegram, Commandant Bertier de Sauvigny to General Nivelle, February 19, 1917, in Frederick B. Maurice, *Lessons of Allied Cooperation: Naval, Military and Air, 1914–1918* (London, 1942), p. 81.

[15]Translation of French memorandum, February 26, 1917, in James E. Edmonds, Cyril Falls, and Wilfred Miles, *History of the Great War: Military Operations, France and Belgium, 1917* (3 vols.; London, 1947), I, App. I, 62–63. Hereinafter referred to as *BOH, 1917.*

[16]*Ibid.*, p. 63.

[17]Blake, *The Private Papers of Douglas Haig*, pp. 198–212.

[18]Basil H. Liddell Hart, *Reputations: Ten Years After* (New York, 1928), p. 129.

[19]Edmonds, *BOH, 1917,* I, App. I, p. 66.

[20]*Ibid.*

[21]Letter, Haig to Nivelle, in *The Diaries and Papers of Field Marshal Sir Douglas Haig,* National Library of Scotland, H. 176.

[22]For details of the German withdrawal from the Noyon salient (OPERATION ALBRICH) see Erich Ludendorff, *My War Memories, 1914–1918* (2 vols.; London, 1919), II, 3–11; Spears, *Prelude to Victory,* pp. 204–228.

[23]Cruttwell, *Great War,* pp. 410–411; Edmonds, *BOH, 1917,* II, 11–12 fn.

[24]Basil Collier, *Brasshat: A Biography of Field-Marshal Sir Henry Wilson* (London, 1961), p. 278.

[25]Max Hoffman, *War Diaries and Other Papers* (2 vols.; London, 1928), I, 181.

[26]"O.B. 2019, 8th April 1917," *Diaries and Papers of Haig,* H. 176.

[27]Richard M. Watt, *Dare Call It Treason* (New York, 1963), p. 176.

[28]Thomas D. Shumate, Jr., "The Allied Supreme War Council, 1917–1918" (unpublished doctoral dissertation, University of Virginia, 1952), pp. 12–13; Blake, *The Private Papers of Douglas Haig,* p. 242.

[29]Bently B. Gilbert and Paul P. Bernard, "French Army Mutinies of 1917," *Historian,* XXII (November, 1959), 24–41; G.A.M., "The Bent Sword," *Blackwood's Magazine,* CCLV (January, 1944), 1–8.

[30]*Les Armées Francaise dans la Grande Guerre* (Paris, 1925), V, pt. II, 85–87, quoted in Watt, *Dare Call It Treason,* p. 217.

[31]Davidson, *Master of the Field,* pp. 15–17; *Diaries and Papers of Haig,* H. 176; Paul Painlevé, *Comme J'ai Nommée Foch* (Paris, 1923), p. 143; and "Letter From the CIGS to F.M. Commanding-in-Chief, British Armies in France," January 1, 1917, in Edmonds, *BOH, 1917,* I, App. I, 9.

[32]C.R.M.F. Cruttwell, *The Role of British Strategy In the Great War* (Cambridge, 1936), p. 4.

[33]Davidson, *Master of the Field,* p. 13; Blake, *The Private Papers of Douglas Haig,* pp. 240–241.

[34]David Lloyd George, *War Memoirs of David Lloyd George* (6 vols.; Boston, 1937), III, 338.

[35]"Role Of The British Forces Should Russia Fall Out Of The War," Haig to CIGS, October 8, 1917, in James E. Edmonds (ed.), *History of the Great War: Military Operations, France and Belgium, 1918* (5 vols.; London, 1935–1947), I, App. I, 1–8.

[36]W. Grant Grieve and Bernard Newman, *Tunnellers* (London, 1936), passim.

[37]C.E.W. Bean, *The Australian Imperial Force in France* (12 vols.; Sydney, 1924), IV, 697.

[38]Edmonds, *BOH, 1917,* II, 138–139.

[39]Hubert Gough, *The Fifth Army* (London, 1931), 205.

[40]Reichsarchiv, *Der Weltkrieg* (Berlin, 1939), XII, 97.

[41]Ludendorff, *Memories,* II, 90–92.

[42]Luigi Villari, *The War On The Italian Front* (London, 1932), pp. 126–127.

[43]*Ibid.*, pp. 144–145.

[44]Erwin Rommel, *Infantry Attacks,* trans. by G.E. Kidde (Washington, 1944), pp. 168–207.

[45]Basil H. Liddell Hart, *The Tanks* (2 vols.; New York, 1959), I, 135.

[46]Paul von Hindenburg, *Out Of My Life* (2 vols.; New York, 1921), II, 89–90.

The Ludendorff "Peace Offensive," 1918

. . . it was the greatest military task ever imposed upon an army. I believe that I . . . am more than any one impressed by the immensity of the operation. . . . We must not imagine that this offensive will be like those in Galicia or Italy; it will be an immense struggle that will begin at one point, continue at another, and take a long time; it is difficult, but it will be victorious.

General Ludendorff to Kaiser Wilhelm

On November 11, 1917—exactly one year before the cessation of hostilities—the First Quartermaster General of the German Army, Erich Ludendorff, convened a council of war.[1] He chose as the location for the conference the headquarters of Prince Rupprecht's Group of Armies in Mons, Belgium. This town, which had seen bitter fighting during the earliest battles of 1914, completed the symbolic link between the beginning and end of the Great War. The subject discussed at the conference and the decisions reached by the *de facto* commander of the German Army* would lock events on the Western Front into what, in retrospect, seems an unalterable pattern leading to an inevitable end. The politico-military situation confronting Germany demanded decisive action.[2]

The transitional year of 1917 had closed with the Central Powers in a dominant military position. With the crumbling of Russia's forces in the East, the catastrophic defeat of Italy's Army in the Battle of Caporetto, and the damage in-

flicted by the submarine campaign on the British, Germany could gain military superiority on the Western Front for the first time since 1915. However, it was obvious that action had to be taken quickly to capitalize on this fleeting advantage.[3] It would be only a matter of time before the great American Army would become a decisive factor. The first American division had arrived in France six months before.

General Erich Ludendorff

*Those in attendance at this meeting also symbolized the final breakdown in the system of command in the Imperial German Army. The nominal commanders of the army—Kaiser Wilhelm, Field Marshal von Hindenburg, and the two royal army group commanders—were not even consulted on the topics of discussion, let alone invited to attend. The German General Staff's method of controlling operations through assistants and chiefs of staff was now exposed as the only real source of power during a time of critical choices.

American Troops Board Ships for Transfer Overseas

Others were being rapidly trained for frontline action.[4] Soon, a fresh army of more than a million men would confront the Germans.

Another important consideration was the fact that the Second Reich's allies were faltering and would soon be unable to render even the limited assistance that they had previously provided. The Austro-Hungarian Empire was now a weakened puppet of Germany; her polyglot Army was no longer capable of independent action, and had to be shored up with German divisions and staffs for any major action. Bulgaria was satisfied with her conquests and now wished only to end the war with her gains intact. Turkey was losing campaigns on all of her fighting fronts. The British Middle Eastern Expeditionary Forces were now ascendant, and it would be only a matter of months before Turkey would meet with final defeat.

The German High Command also realized that serious problems on the homefront required rapid and conclusive action. A series of weak political leaders at home, coupled with the privations suffered by the civilian population, had resulted in unrest and a disintegration of the fragile political unity that had supported the war effort. At the end of January, a widespread strike by one million workers resulted in rioting and looting. The influence of the Communist and pacifist elements was evident, since this action had been called by the Executive Committee of the Workers Councils. This was the first time that this title was heard in Germany.[5]

Germany Considers Offensive Options

The strategic planning conducted by Ludendorff and his advisers in response to these conditions presents an ideal case study of general staff procedures. Certain constants, or assumptions, were dictated by the commander in his initial guidance. The first of these was that the German Army could transfer 35 divisions and 1,000 heavy guns to the Western Front and thus achieve superiority in combat power; this, however, would be sufficient for only one major offensive. The second assumption was that this temporary superiority in arms had to be exploited at the earliest possible moment—before the American Army could affect the war. The last dictum was that the defeat of the British Army in France was to be the ultimate objective of the offensive. Like his predecessor, Ludendorff viewed the perfidious British as Germany's most important enemy, and believed that their defeat would be decisive. The defeat of the French, it was thought, would cause an Allied withdrawal into the interior of France, merely delaying the ultimate decision.[6] Instructing his advisers to plan within these three guidelines, Ludendorff asked for recommendations regarding the execution of the offensive.

Crown Prince Rupprecht's chief of staff, General Hermann von Kuhl, advocated that the main offensive be conducted by his group of armies in Flanders. He argued that

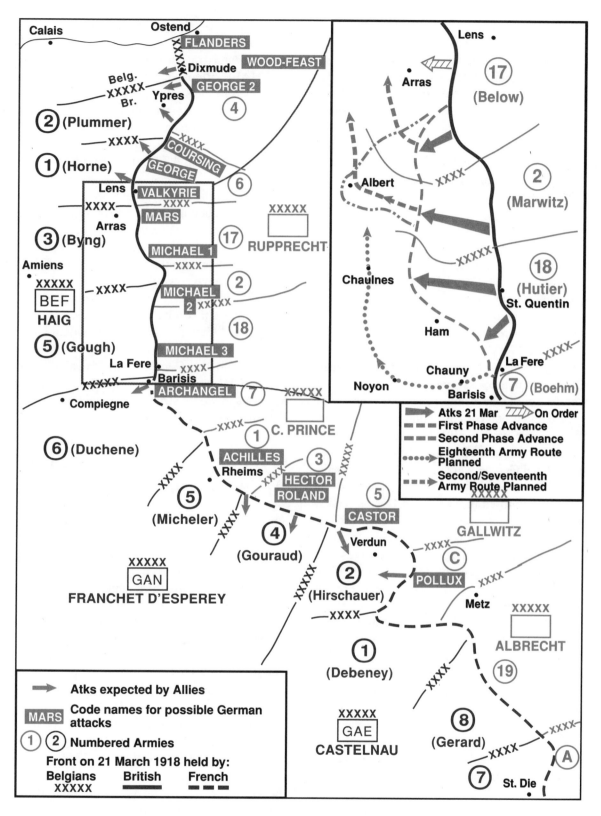

Plans for Ludendorff's *Friedensturm* (Peace Offensive), 1918

the heavy concentration of British divisions in the restricted northern portion of the line invited attack there in the direction of Hazebrouck. This plan was logical since an attack on Haig's armies in the north would pin down the strongest Allied force, capture their vital logistical bases on the Channel coast, and lead to either their destruction in detail or their withdrawal from the Continent. In line with these recommendations, Ludendorff authorized the preparation of Plans GEORGE 1 and GEORGE 2 (originally called ST. GEORGE). Because the extremely wet conditions on the Flanders Plain would continue until after April, however, Ludendorff felt that it was now too late in the year for the main offensive.[7]

Colonel von der Schulenberg, Crown Prince Wilhelm's chief of staff, countered the proposal by Prince Rupprecht's headquarters with one that placed his own organization in the principal role. He wished to attack on both sides of the Verdun salient—from the Argonne Forest and St. Mihiel. In his opinion, a partial victory over the British was all that could be hoped for. In addition, he sensed the war weariness of the French forces, even though the Germans remained ignorant of the mutinies that had ravaged the French Army. This proposal, moreover, sprang from the concept of destroying the weakest enemy first and hoping for a political and moral collapse, followed by a favorable negotiated peace settlement.[8] This last result was almost identical to that desired by Falkenhayn in 1916.

Lieutenant Colonel George Wetzell, Chief of the Operations Section of OHL, then presented his views. In his study, which was submitted in writing on December 12, 1917, Wetzell included an attack on the French around Verdun, but disagreed that a single main offensive could "succeed."[9] He recommended a series of offensives that would lead to the final objective, the defeat of the British. He insisted on the importance of attacking the French around Verdun to prevent their seizure of the initiative. Against the British, Ludendorff's G-3 advocated a two-phase plan of attack. The first move (later code named Plan MICHAEL 1, 2, 3) would be an attack along a wide front between Cambrai and St. Quentin. This would force the British to shift their principal reserves south, diverting their attention from the true objective. Following this initial assault, which would be strictly limited in its depth of advance, the main attack would begin in the direction of Hazebrouck. This final blow would pierce the weakened British front, create a flank, and allow the line to "be rolled up from the north."[10]

Faced with these widely diverse points of view, Ludendorff deferred his final decision. He held another interview with his principal advisers on December 27, but still he delayed the decision. Instead, he ordered plans drawn up for Operation ST. GEORGE, Operation MICHAEL, and two Verdun attacks—code named after the Gemini twins, Castor and Pollux—along with a multitude of smaller supporting offensives. A major supporting attack, Plan MARS, was added near Arras to capitalize on any success that the MICHAEL offensive might achieve. Thus, preparations continued to the stage of detailed written plans while the commander and his staff conducted a reconnaissance of the front. Finally, on January 21, 1918, Ludendorff announced his decision.

After surveying the front, discussing the operation with the army commanders, and weighing the influence of weather and the enemy's reinforcement capabilities, Ludendorff decided upon a compromise plan. This plan took into account all of the conflicting recommendations while adhering to his initial guidelines. The final German offensive of the war, popularly known as the *Friedensturm,* or peace offensive,* would basically be the same as Plan MICHAEL in that it would be launched on both sides of St. Quentin. Ludendorff held the other proposals in abeyance. Although this offensive would have to traverse the same terrain destroyed during the First Battle of the Somme and the German withdrawal during Operation ALBRICH in 1917,[11] it could be conducted soon (in March) and would strike at the junction of the French and British armies.

German Assault Tactics and Allied Manpower Problems

Aware of the difficulty of creating a decisive breakthrough on the Western Front, Ludendorff determined that a new tool was required to crack the strategic stalemate. The great successes achieved by the new German infiltration assault tactics during the counterattack at Cambrai and the Battle of Caporetto convinced Ludendorff that these methods would provide the tactical answer. The lessons learned during the preceding operations were culled by the general staff and disseminated in a series of pamphlets. Entitled *The Attack in Trench Warfare,* these pamphlets were compiled by Captain Geyer, an expert on infantry training and tactics.[12]

At the heart of these new tactics was reliance upon individual initiative at the lowest echelon of the attacking force and decentralization of authority. This method of command was necessary to impart continuing momentum to the surging waves of the assaulting infantry. The infantry vanguard, or storm troops, was organized into squads

---

*While this term, strictly speaking, should be reserved for the fifth German offensive (the Second Battle of the Marne), the attitude of the German Army and public was that this series of offensives would end the war quickly.

Trained Storm Troopers Carry Out German Infiltration Assault Tactics

around light machineguns. These squads were to advance as far and as quickly as possible into the enemy defenses in order to seize artillery positions and disorganize the static defenses. Instead of the infantry advancing at the pace prescribed by the artillery supporting fires, the leading elements were to determine the pace of the attack. Strongpoints in the enemy frontline defenses were to be neutralized with organic weapons or concentrated artillery fires. Once this was done, the assault elements could bypass these strongpoints and move quickly to the enemy's rear. In order to compensate for the necessary reduction of supporting fires, the assault elements were formed into small combined arms teams with bombers, light machinegun sections, pioneers,* and accompanying direct-fire artillery pieces. Many infantrymen carried the new 9-mm machine pistol, which gave each soldier a vastly increased rate of firepower.[13]

As the storm troopers moved through the enemy's first defensive positions, more heavily armed support elements advanced to mop up and reduce the defender's remaining strongpoints. Using light trench mortars, flamethrowers, and heavier direct-fire artillery, these teams of specialists could destroy all but the strongest pockets of enemy resistance. Following the support elements, ordinary infantry troops and reserves moved into the battle zone to relieve them and allow the continuation of the assault onto the next line of enemy defense. In all cases, reserves were used to reinforce success rather than to attempt to retrieve success from failure.

These tactics were a far cry from the mass-wave assaults that had been the hallmark of previous offensives. They obviously required a new mental attitude towards offensive operations on the part of commanders and troops. Healthy young men were screened for entrance into the specialized *Sturmbattaillion,* or assault battalions. Bachelors or childless married men were preferred for this duty because of the expected high casualty rates. Treated as elite organizations, these units had the finest food and equipment available, and were kept out of the frontlines until the last possible moment. In the rear of the battle zone, the general staff established regular training camps in which the storm troopers underwent rigorous combat training and patriotic indoctrination in the offensive spirit. Regardless of rank, all men were required to undergo this training, and were drilled constantly over terrain similar to that expected in their zone of action. Reserve groups of regimental officers and non commissioned officers were held at these training centers to be sent forward as immediate replacements for those lost in battle. As the number of men required for the massive assaults of 1918 increased, many of the storm troop battalions were broken down into training teams to act as cadres in the further training and indoctrination of regular infantrymen in the new methods of attack.

Tanks were not an important element in the German infiltration assault tactics. The high command knew that the strained German industrial system could not produce sufficient vehicles with the necessary capabilities. Therefore, they decided to rely little upon this new weapon. Interestingly, however, several companies of captured British tanks were employed in the assaults, although they had virtually no impact on the tactical battles to come.[14]

---

*Pioneers are engineers who are especially trained for road building, bridge construction, and demolition.

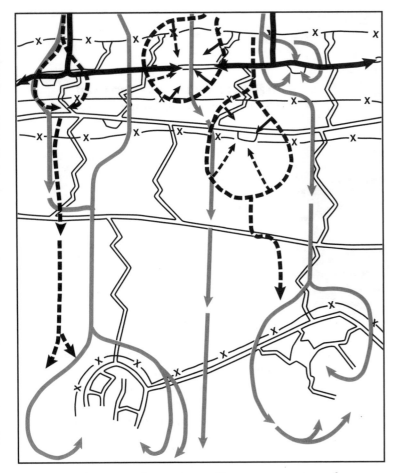

1. Hurricane barrage artillery preparation of poisonous gas, smoke, and high-explosive shell.
2. Storm troops infiltrate and bypass.
3. Support troops mop up centers of resistance.
4. Regular infantry troops and reserves clear trenches, relieve storm units.

German Infiltration Assault Tactics

The key supporting arm for the infantry was the artillery. General von Hutier's artillery chief, Lieutenant Colonel Georg Bruchmüller, had developed and refined the method of flexible and responsive artillery support first used on the Western Front by the British during the Battle of Cambrai. Bruchmüller became Ludendorff's principal artillery adviser for the remaining operations of the war. He directed the team of highly specialized general staff officers who planned and coordinated the activities of Ludendorff's "battering train," the heavy artillery reserves that moved in support of major offensives. This violent and demoralizing system of artillery support was

nearly as important to the success of the new tactical system as the teams of storm troops. Surprise was the cornerstone of the artillery support. The heavy concentration of guns of all calibers needed to support the initial attack was assembled either without the enemy's knowledge or before he could effectively react with counterbattery fire. The guns were infiltrated into the support line under the cover of darkness, many being positioned the night before the attack. Target data for the guns was developed from large-scale maps and visual reconnaissance; no registration firing was allowed.

The attacks usually were launched under the concealment of early morning darkness and ground fog. A brief but extremely violent artillery preparation preceded the advance of the infantry units. If possible, the squad-sized assault teams moved by covered routes right up to the forward edge of the defender's positions during the preparatory bombardment. These fires contained more poisonous gas and smoke rounds than high explosive shells. The killing and incapacitating effects of this mixture were nearly as great as that of high explosive shells alone, but left the battle zone relatively unscathed and facilitated the advance of the infantry. Of course, this lessened the wire-cutting effect of the bombardment, but the pioneer detachments assigned to the assault groups were responsible for making gaps in the defensive wire. As the assault pro-

Krupp's Famous 420-mm Howitzer, the "Big Bertha"

gressed, the rolling barrage of artillery fire was controlled by the fastest infantry elements, instead of the inverse situation that had prevailed in earlier offensives. The infantry used colored rockets and Very pistols to signal the shifting or lifting of the supporting fires or the firing of preplanned concentrations to neutralize strongpoints.

The fledgling air arm, too, was fully integrated into the new tactics. As soon as weather and light conditions permitted, aircraft supported the ground advance. In addition to scouting for long-range artillery targets and keeping commanders informed of enemy troop movements, the pilots maintained air superiority over the battlefield and bombed logistical and transportation centers behind the lines. By this time, light aircraft had become proficient in providing fire support to the advancing infantry. Low-flying machines sprayed the enemy with machinegun fire and dropped light bombs on strong centers of resistance. Like the supporting artillery, the pilots took their instructions from the infantry commanders who signaled to the planes by means of colored canvas panels or through their higher headquarters by means of a crude wireless radio communications system.

OHL recognized that the massive preparations for the spring offensives could not be completely concealed from the British intelligence services. Since tactical surprise was essential to success, however, orders were issued for preparations to continue for the numerous planned attacks and supporting operations all along the line. This deception plan deliberately misled major German unit commanders and staffs into believing that they would be participating in the main attack. This was done to insure their zeal in confusing the enemy. The cover story of numerous attacks also included a deception of the French civilian population in the occupied areas by announcing deportations from fictitious areas of assault. Special security officers were used to prevent leaks of information to the enemy. These officers censored personal correspondence, tapped telephone lines, and even monitored the conversations of soldiers on leave. Air superiority was tightened over the area of actual preparation; but, at the same time, Allied airmen were allowed to observe those portions of the line where deceptive movements were taking place.[15] Finally, a major German deception program was focused on convincing the French commander, the cautious and pessimistic Pétain, that the main attack was going to be launched against his portion of the front. A limited amount of extra ammunition was allotted to bombard Verdun, and units opposite the French were told to conduct a series of feints and demonstrations to indicate that a major effort would begin around mid-March. The plan proved so successful that when the great offensive came, Pétain refused to adequately support his ally to the north and nearly caused the collapse of the entire Allied front.

Meanwhile, across No Man's Land, the French and British Armies awaited the final enemy offensive in an atmosphere of guarded optimism. French and British commanders felt that cooperative defensive efforts would hold the enemy until the American Army could arrive in strength and turn the balance again in their favor. But beneath this veneer of confidence lay grave weaknesses in the fiber of the alliance and the disposition of its military forces. Throughout the war, the methods of coordinating the Allied military strategies had been haphazard and less than successful. Impelled by the catastrophic defeat of the Italians at Caporetto in 1917, however, the political leaders of the Entente Powers had finally acknowledged the need for a more precise method of coordinating their individual strategies. As the first of 11 French and British divisions streamed into Italy to bolster their ally, the heads of government met at the resort town of Rapallo, Italy to ratify a formal plan of action, which began with the establishment of the Inter-Allied Supreme War Council (SWC).[16]

At the meeting, David Lloyd George, Paul Painlevé, and Vittorio Orlando agreed to formalize their periodic conferences in order to provide strategic continuity. Each nation was to be represented on the council by its head of government and one other high ranking Cabinet member, usually the war minister. In order to provide the council with continuous and professional military advice, the charter of the new organization provided for a Board of Permanent Military Representatives to serve at Versailles. This body was composed of a prominent military leader, not necessarily the Chief of Staff or national Commander-in-Chief, from each Allied nation. The representatives' mission was to consider various courses of action open to the alliance, determine which resources were available, and then present detailed recommendations to the political body.[17] One unfortunate procedure adopted by the Military Representatives was to require that all of the notes presented to the Supreme War Council have the unanimous concurrence of the generals on the board. This feature tended to restrict the topics that the generals could consider and vitiate the effectiveness of their recommendations.[18]

As the disaster of Caporetto receded from immediate memory, the political leaders attempted once again to press their national interests at the expense of coalition unity. Lloyd George wished to restrict the flow of British resources into the caldron of destruction on the Continent. Mistrusting his leading military commander, he hoped that by cutting off resources of men and materiel, the ultimate social and economic cost of the war would be lessened. The French, under Georges Clemenceau, the newly installed Premier, viewed this attitude with alarm and fought Lloyd George's moves to divert his military resources to peripheral operations.[19] The Italian Government consistently refused to allow the Supreme War Council to consider questions involving operations in Italy. Orlando and his military adviser, Cadorna, looked at the new organization as applying exclusively to the Western Front. They did, however, hope to use it as a conduit through which they could receive additional military and financial support. Although the Belgians claimed that they could not constitutionally participate in the actions of the Council, a degree of cooperation was achieved by the appointment of a French general as King Albert's Chief of Staff. The newly joined Americans struggled to completely divorce their military cooperation from political considerations. The United States had chosen to enter the war as an associated power, not an ally. President Wilson agreed to allow General Tasker Bliss to sit on the Board of Permanent Military Representatives, but was only informally represented on the Supreme War Council by his itinerant colleague, Colonel Edward M. House.[20]

As the signs of the impending German offensive became more clear, the Board of Permanent Military Representatives called upon the Supreme War Council to authorize a centralized General Reserve. In the Joint Note No. 14, adopted by the board on January 25, 1918, they proposed that the Allies form a 30-division force under the control of an Executive War Board. This force was to be used for the general good of the alliance, thereby separating the reaction to the coming German offensive from purely national considerations. The French were asked to contribute 13 divisions, the British 10, and the Italians 7.[21] At face value, this proposal appears to have been logical and above political machinations; however, when it is placed in the perspective of the contemporary events that had spawned it, its true nature is revealed. The prime mover of the plan was General Ferdinand Foch, the French Chief of Staff who sat as the French military representative. He played upon the personal differences between the various political and military field commanders to assure not only unity of command on the battlefield but also increased power for himself. The proposal contained a system of command in which Foch, as the President of the Executive War Board, would control the disposition and commitment of the General Reserve. The national commanders would control the tactical employment of the reserve after it was put into action, but its withdrawal from action would again be Foch's decision. Pétain, Haig, and Diaz, as might be expected, resisted this method of limiting their prerogatives. The politicians approved the note on the General Reserve, but in a short time the field commanders would effectively destroy the plan.

The Allied defensive arrangements and dispositions on the Western Front had been well surveyed by the German planners. They knew that the bulk of Haig's forces were deployed on the northernmost portion of the line. Forty-six di-

General Ferdinand Foch, French Chief of Staff

visions manned the vulnerable and restricted sector that extended from Cambrai to the seacoast. (*See Atlas Map No. 18.*) General Hubert Gough's Fifth Army, with 12 infantry and 3 cavalry divisions, held the final 42 miles to the junction with the French line at Barisis. Under extreme political pressure, Haig had been forced to extend his line an additional 25 miles and to relieve the French of responsibility for the line to the south of the Oise River.* The relief took place during the period of January 10 to 30. As the Tommies took over their newly acquired trenches, they quickly understood why the French had been so anxious to be rid of them; they were in a "state of shocking neglect!" Sanitary facilities, the siting of weapons positions, and the construction of defensive zones were unacceptable. From the outset, then, Gough had to expend much of his effort in improving his defensive positions with his own limited resources.[22] Thus, by a quirk of fate, the German offensive MICHAEL 3 and the southern portion of MICHAEL 2 would strike one of the least prepared sectors of the Allied line. This deficiency in the south end of the British line was compounded by a more general misapplication of defensive doctrine by the Allies.

In the latter half of 1917, the Allied staffs had adopted a defensive doctrine similar to the one used by the Germans in

---

*Pétain and his political superiors had originally insisted that the British take over 55 miles of the line; the 25-mile distance was a compromise.

creating the elastic defenses that had stopped the Nivelle and Third Ypres offensives. This Allied concept called for defensive zones rather than a series of static trench lines. The forward zone was to be lightly manned with automatic weapons positions and was designed to delay and disorganize a major enemy attack. The principal defensive battles were to be fought in the battle zone and, if needed, a third or rear position was provided.[23] Unfortunately, this new doctrine was merely superimposed over the existing scheme of defense. Instead of being reconstructed, the forward zone was simply positioned on the labyrinth of trench lines. Many commanders reduced their frontline trench garrisons without supplementing the zone with strongpoints and automatic weapons. The Allied generals also placed less emphasis on special counterattack divisions than had the Germans in their elastic defensive doctrine. The greatest fault of the Allied employment of this new system, however, was that it had originally been designed by the German General Staff to counter the mass linear offensive attacks of the Allied armies, and would therefore prove of much less value against the newer German infiltration assault tactics.[24]

Manpower problems, too, burdened all Allied commanders, and the British in particular. When Haig was formally asked to contribute his share of 10 divisions to the Allied General Reserve on February 27, 1918, he refused. He pointed out that the sharply restricted flow of replacements his armies were receiving had actually reduced his total strength, while large numbers of fit troops remained on the home islands or were being diverted to peripheral theaters. He had control of only 10 reserve divisions in the entire BEF.[25] The growing shortage of British manpower had induced the War Cabinet to reduce each division in strength from 12 to 9 battalions.* As a final comment on the manpower difficulties of the Allied defenders, Pétain and Haig had still not received the 11 divisions that were to replace those that had been ordered south to aid the Italian Army. With these acute shortages confronting him and with his increased area of responsibility, Haig pinned his hopes for reinforcement on a cooperative understanding with Pétain.[27] He felt that the French, now recovering from their experience with mutiny, would support him with at least six divisions in the Fifth Army area when the expected attack came. Because he wished to control all of the forces engaged on his front, he preferred this arrangement to a more formal Allied General Reserve. In his resistance to the orders of the Supreme Allied War Council, moreover, Haig had the support of Pétain and Premier Georges Clemen-

ceau, both of whom distrusted the ambitious Foch.[28] Following Haig's example, Pétain and the Italians refused to contribute their share of divisions to the General Reserve. This rendered the Executive War Board and General Reserve useless.[29]

The German Offensives

The long-awaited German offensive came at 4:40 a.m. on March 21, 1918, as Colonel Bruchmüller presented his finest artillery overture to battle.[30] The British Third and Fifth Armies had accurately predicted the day of the offensive, but the immensity and concentrated violence of the 6,000-gun preparation was truly a surprise. Gas shells soaked the defender's artillery positions and forced the men to mask for hours before they were able to fire effectively in support of their forward zone of defense. Moreover, an extremely thick ground fog lay over the entire battlefield until 11:00 a.m. This condition greatly aided the assaulting teams of infantrymen when they began their infiltration of the defensive wire and strongpoints exactly five hours after the beginning of the bombardment. (*See Atlas Map No. 19a.*)

The First German Drive

By nightfall, the attackers had advanced through the forward zone of the Fifth Army, and in some localities had penetrated into the battle zone. The rear or support zone, which now became extremely important in checking the attack, hardly existed in this area. Chalk lines on the ground or a narrow band of barbed wire marked the trace of this final barrier, but work on its construction had not even been started by the over-taxed divisions of Gough's Army.[31]

The next two days also dawned in heavy ground fog, greatly assisting rapid advances by the German storm troops. Once the British defenders had been forced from their final trench positions, their inexperience in open warfare betrayed them and the commanders found it increasingly difficult to maintain a cohesive battle front. During the early afternoon of March 22, Gough ordered a retirement behind the Somme River. By the next day, Hutier's Eighteenth Army was well past its original limit of advance and was moving on Péronne. Farther north, the attackers were enjoying far less success as the Second and Seventeenth Armies, which were making the main effort, encountered the better prepared defenses of Byng's Third Army. The situation thus presented to Ludendorff was that his planned main attack designed to roll up the British line had faltered, while Hutier's supporting force had achieved success far beyond expectation. Now Ludendorff transposed to

---

*The British thus followed the 1917 example of the French and Germans in reducing the authorized strength of divisions from 5,000 to 9,000 men. This organizational change maintained the number of divisions, which perhaps reassured the public, but reduced the effectiveness of the units involved and caused unnecessary confusion at a critical moment in the war.[26]

the next higher level of operations his belief in following tactical success. The German technique of following tactical successes had proven itself, but now the high command proposed to allow its strategy on the Western Front to be dictated by the results of tactical battles. The mission of the Eighteenth Army was changed to exploit its initial victories to the southwest in the direction of Paris; the Seventeenth Army would continue its attack to the northwest; the Second Army, however, was ordered to move in the direction of the great rail center of Amiens. Thus, the three attacking armies were now directed to move on diverging axes. In order to implement this change of objectives, a wrenching shift in logistical support was required behind the lines.[32]

Although British defenders in the south resisted as best they could, they were overwhelmed by the weight of the German attack. A complete disaster for British arms seemed to be in the offing. Haig now called upon Pétain to send his promised reinforcements. When the two leaders met on the afternoon of March 23, Pétain promised to send sufficient forces to prevent the separation of the two Allied armies. Haig insisted that all available resources be concentrated in front of Amiens to prevent the complete rupture of the line.[33] However, when they met on the next day, Pétain was upset and anxious over the vulnerability of his own front, and continually referred to his orders to "cover Paris at all costs."[34] He felt that the British had been beaten and would now fall back to cover their Channel ports. Having been fooled by the German deception measures, he believed that the present attack was merely a prelude to the main blow, which would fall on his front in Champagne. Under these conditions of crisis, the informal gentleman's agreement between Haig and Pétain failed. Pétain wished to preserve his own forces, while Haig believed that the enemy could be stopped only by a united and resolute stand. The British field marshal reacted to what he considered Gallic treachery by telegraphing to his government the gravity of the military situation. He added a request that ". . . General Foch or some other determined" French commander be appointed to coordinate the defenses of the Franco-British front.[35] Once again, reverses on the battlefield had triggered action that hitherto had been impossible.

On the morning of March 26, in Doullens, the military leaders met with Lord Milner, the British Secretary of State for War, and French Premier Clemenceau to establish a unified command under General Ferdinand Foch. Haig recommended that Foch be empowered with the authority to coordinate all Allied armies on the Western Front.* Adver-

Field Marshal Douglas Haig Greets French Premier Georges Clemenceau at His Arrival at Doullens, March 1918

sity had finally brought about formal unity of command in the alliance's military structure.

Meanwhile, on the frontlines, the combat situation had begun to stabilize. Foch now directed French units onto the flank of the German salient, while British reinforcements began to arrive from the north. Coincidentally, the German infantry became bogged down by a combination of the poor trafficability of the old Somme battlefield and the troops' lack of tactical mobility.[36] Although the Germans had created a 10-mile gap between the French and the British forces, they lacked sufficient horses or mechanical transport to exploit this opportunity.

Now Ludendorff ordered the implementation of the MARS attack. Launched south of Arras, MARS was designed to support the stalled offensive on the Somme. These assaults were driven back with heavy casualties being suffered by some of the best of the remaining storm troop battalions. MARS was conducted in clear weather, and the stronger British defenses in this area easily held. In their determination to succeed, several German units reverted to the old shoulder-to-shoulder offensive tactics. Standing six ranks deep, these units only allowed the British machineguns and artillery barrages to extract their deadly toll more quickly. By April 5, Ludendorff decided that his grand assaults in Picardy must be suspended. He could not afford the men or the time necessary to conduct a battle of attrition.[37]

With his main attack in the Somme area checked, Ludendorff appears to have lost sight of his concept of considering tactical objectives before those of strictly strategic value.[38] While he had been firm in his final instructions that the MICHAEL offensives, supported by the MARS attack, were to be the key to victory, he had allowed the other planned

---

*Foch was later installed as the Generalissimo of all Allied armies on the Western Front, to include the American Army under General John Pershing. A copy of the protocol delineating Foch's final authority is contained in Annex B, Appendix 7.

operations to remain in existence. He now deviated from this resolution and chose a course very similar to that originally advocated by his operations chief, Wetzell. Whether he had always planned a following series of attacks as a contingency or was now succumbing to a feeling of depression, grasping at any opportunity for success, is unclear.

The Second German Drive

Ludendorff set his revised strategy in motion by authorizing the initiation of a second drive against the British Flanders defensive positions (code named GEORGE). Unfortunately, one vital difference existed between the situation that the Germans now faced and the series of coordinated attacks originally advocated by Wetzell. The MICHAEL offensives had not been strictly limited in scope, and more than half of the offensive combat power available had been expended in seeking the elusive breakthrough on the Somme. Also, a large garrison force would be needed to protect the vulnerable salient created by this brilliant tactical success. The German leaders no longer had sufficient reserves, and many of the well trained storm troop battalions now lay broken on the old Somme battlefield. These units had been the key to the first success. But having come to close to a final rupture of the enemy line, the German commander now deluded himself that he could still crumble the British defensives with just one more offensive. This was known as the Lys Offensive. (*See Atlas Map No. 18.*) Rather than revert to the defensive and conserve his remaining forces, he entered upon a course that would consume all of Germany's military strength, leaving his forces open to a fearsome counterstroke. It was precisely because his first operations had been so successful that he was now lured into this course of action. While he would achieve limited gains in his following four drives, they would become increasingly less decisive. None came close to cracking the resolve of the Allies.

By April 9, the "battering train" of 137 batteries of mixed artillery, which had produced such devastation during the Second Battle of the Somme, was transported north to Flanders. (*See Atlas Map No. 19b.*) Owing to the heavy losses sustained by the Germans in their first drive, the scope and frontage of the planned GEORGE offensives had to be reduced.* The second drive was made against General Henry S. Horne's First Army, from Armentières to the La Bassée Canal. Its initial objective was the Hazebrouck rail center, but Ludendorff never had a clear idea of his final objective,

and probably had in mind exploiting any success all the way to the coast. Again, his strategic goal was the destruction of the major portion of the British forces.[39]

Just as had occurred in the first drive, unexpected weaknesses in the British defenses greatly assisted the opening German moves. One of the two Portuguese infantry divisions that had been fighting on the Western Front under British control since 1916 happened to be manning the critical central portion of the attack frontage. These troops were of inferior quality, and had been retained in the line longer than usual because of the heavy fighting farther south. When the German attack came on the morning of the ninth, the Portuguese troops broke immediately and fled to the rear. Carrying only their weapons and some artillery with them, they left a gap of six miles in the line.[40] Within three hours, the advance elements of the German Sixth Army had reached the open country behind the final defensive system. It was only with the greatest difficulty that the adjoining British divisions were able to close this gap, but a significant penetration had been made. This encouraged Ludendorff to order a second blow around the Ypres salient farther north. This attack, launched the next day, succeeded in driving Plumer's Second Army back from the Messines-Wytschaete ridge.[41]

The German attacks now ground relentlessly forward all along the northern line. By April 12, the defenders had been pushed back halfway to Hazebrouck. Haig was now desperately pleading for assistance from Foch, and futilely searching for reserves in his own sector. Foch replied that the British should expect no further reinforcement from the French, but that he had every confidence in the tenacity of the British soldier in the defense.[†] In desperation, Haig issued his now famous "Backs to the Wall" order to his troops in which he instructed his men to stand their ground to the death.[42]

Finally, on the nineteenth, several French divisions from the *Détachement d'Armée du Nord* arrived to support the beleaguered British; however, they did not counterattack as requested. When they assumed a portion of the defensive line on Mount Kemmel on the twenty-first, the Germans quickly swept them off of this critical defensive position. In general terms, French assistance in the north was ineffectual, with the brunt of the defensive and counteroffensive burden being borne by Belgian and British units.[43] Yet the confidence of Foch and the German evaluation of the defensive capabilities of the British soldier proved all too correct. By April 29, the Germans had been forced to call off their offensive. Ludendorff began redeploying his

---

*Accordingly, the plan's code name was changed to GEORGETTE. This completed the transition of the plan's name with Teutonic thoroughness. It began as the heroic ST. GEORGE, was reduced to the mortal GEORGE, and ended in the diminutive GEORGETTE.

† When asked to send reinforcements to Haig's relief, General Foch replied: "*La bataille de Hazebrouck est finie!*" This response would have been received with the utmost incredulity by the exhausted British soldiers, who would struggle for at least another week in their effort to stem the German tide.

diminishing reserves of artillery and men south for another attempt at a breakthrough.

By now, the spirit and will of the German attackers had changed. The remnants of storm troop battalions and the regular infantry that had fought in the Lys Offensive were mere shadows of those that had so confidently assaulted in the first drive. If the same quality troops had been available for the second drive, there seems little doubt that the objective of Hazebrouck could have been taken. The troops of the April fighting were less disciplined and motivated. For the first time, pillaging and looting were reported as having significantly delayed the advance.* The poorly supplied German privates were amazed by the huge stocks of equipment, food, and liquor that they captured.[44] Drunkenness and acts of insubordination during the Lys Offensive were merely harbingers of the final disintegration of the German Army.

During the first two drives, the British suffered heavily. Their losses of 239,000 included 28,000 dead. These dire statistics convinced Lloyd George's government to reinstitute the flow of replacements to Haig's armies in France. Almost miraculously, the home islands were found to have 449,000 Category A men over 19 years of age.[45] In addition, boys of 18 years of age and older men previously exempted from service were pulled out of the British factories. Veterans wounded several times in the fighting were also added to the lists of those available for service in the BEF. British losses could be replaced. But the German Army, which had come so close to victory, had lost over 50,000 dead out of a total of 348,300 casualties; these losses were irreplaceable.[46]

Despite his recent checks and his dwindling combat power, Ludendorff persisted in his attempt to destroy the British armies in France. He instructed Crown Prince Rupprecht's staff to plan for a renewed offensive on the British positions in Flanders in mid-June. This operation was code named NEW GEORGE (later changed to HAGEN).[47] The purpose of this operation was to separate the British and Belgian armies, break through the British line on a wide front, and drive the BEF against the Channel coast. First, however, Ludendorff ordered diversionary attacks against the French front on the Chemin-des-Dames ridge in order to draw both Foch's attention and his reserves away from Flanders. This diversion, and two others, would be launched, but the HAGEN offensive would never be implemented; Ludendorff was running out of time.

*Isolated cases of looting had been encountered during the first German drive, but postwar investigation indicated that these had little effect upon its failure. More than the immediate tactical consequences of these acts, the discovery of well stocked enemy depots indicated to the German soldier that his leaders had been lying when they described the miserable conditions under which the Allied troops were living. Thus, these acts reflected the decline in German morale.

The Third and Fourth German Drives

The Chemin-des-Dames ridge, overlooking the Aisne River in the Champagne region, had seen bloody fighting both in 1914 and during Nivelle's disastrous offensive of 1917. The reason that this sector was selected for the first diversionary operation was that it was a naturally strong position in a sector that had remained relatively quiet for more than a year. It was now used by the Allies as an area for the recuperation of wornout divisions. In fact, a British corps, which had been broken in the first two German drives, was attached to the French Sixth Army for precisely this reason. Therefore, the Germans counted on the Allied garrison being unprepared for a major attack. A diversion here would also threaten Paris, hopefully causing the French to overreact and rush all available reserves to the south.

The local French commander, General Denis Auguste Duchêne, had completely ignored the directives of his superiors to establish a defense in depth. The accepted Allied doctrine of manning the forward positions lightly did not conform with this stubborn man's desire to hold every inch of sacred French soil. He used his friendship with Foch to circumvent Pétain's orders in the preparation of the defense.[48] This led to his refusal to allow any elasticity to his defensive planning and his insistence on the old rigid method of repelling an attack.

Once again, the Germans secretly positioned 30 divisions in the area of attack. The now accepted procedure of covering the preparations with elaborate deceptive measures in other sectors misled Foch into expecting a renewal of the Somme of Lys Offensives. On May 27, at 1:00 a.m., the violent German artillery bombardment commenced. Duchêne's heavily manned frontlines suffered grievously because of their commander's stubbornness. Before the first light of dawn, the German shock divisions crossed the swampy Ailette River in front of the defensive position on previously emplaced assault bridging. The attackers rapidly overran the supposedly strong emplacements, quickly advancing to seize the bridges over the Aisne River. By evening, the leading elements of the German Seventh Army had gained the Vesle River, which was the planned limit of advance.[49]

Apparently having learned nothing from their previous operations, however, the Germans once again were enticed into continuing the attack, thereby disrupting their strategic plans. By the evening of the second day, the attack had created a salient 40 miles wide and 15 miles deep. This time, the large stocks of French supplies captured by the attackers helped them to maintain the momentum of the attack. The advance continued, ever deepening the salient. By June 3, the nose of the advance had reached the Marne River east of Château Thierry, but efforts to correspond-

A British Bomber Is Prepared for an Interdiction Mission

ingly widen the shoulders of the gap met with increasing resistance. Pétain had reacted to the destruction of his Sixth Army with a piecemeal deployment of his reserves, which now included American divisions. However, he was unable to mount a concentrated counterattack, and could only succeed in slowing the assault by local counterstrokes. But this offensive's surprisingly easy success and the ambitious extension of its scope merely meant that Ludendorff did not have the resources necessary to continue or exploit it. Even the Germans now realized that the third offensive had been carried too far.[50] The only result could be an eventual grinding halt to the advance and a third dangerously exposed salient. The operation closed on June 3, and the fourth drive, another diversion on both sides of Noyon, began.

Disregarding the unsettled public reaction in France to the Aisne drive toward Paris, Foch accurately foresaw the new diversionary effort. French aerial and ground observation detected the more open preparations for this attack, and several German deserters confirmed the intelligence reports. This time, the French acted first. On June 8 at 11:50 p.m., ten minutes prior to the commencement of the German artillery bombardment, the French artillery began a counterbattery fire program.[51] The soldiers of Hutier's now famous Eighteenth Army began their assault knowing that they no longer had the great advantage of surprise. Nevertheless, the German infantry teams were still able to breach the first two defensive positions on the first day, and they continued to make limited gains on the tenth. But when they halted on the eleventh, they were hit with a tank-supported Franco-American counterattack that stopped the drive.[52] Although the coordinated action of the French and American divisions made only slight inroads into the territory captured by the Germans, it signaled the

stalling of yet another German offensive. On June 12, the adjoining German army attempted to revive the attack from the eastern face of the Aisne salient, but achieved little. A month would now pass before the next major military operation commenced.

Ludendorff still clung to a fading hope that one more diversion could pave the way for the final HAGEN offensive in Flanders. Now, however, the depleted ranks of his armies had to be refilled, reorganized, and trained. The brave young soldiers who had died in the recent series of frustrating offensives were being replaced by older men from the rear area and former prisoners of war from the Eastern Front who were now reluctantly being returned to battle.[53] The general staff had decided that it could not further reduce the size of its forces in the East because the situation there was extremely unsettled. A military presence was required in the Russian provinces and Rumania to insure the efficient collection and distribution of foodstuffs and raw materials vital to the war effort.[54] To add to Ludendorff's problems, a great epidemic of Spanish influenza broke out on the Western Front and spread throughout the world.[55] This epidemic victimized large numbers of the poorly fed and disheartened German soldiers, cutting deeply into the lists of effectives that the combat units could muster.

While he awaited the final spasm of the German Peace Offensive, General Foch was already planning the counterattacks that would reduce the German-held salients. Throughout the period of the German offensives, there had been numerous minor actions by both British and Franco-American units in areas not undergoing major attack. These had stressed economy of manpower, limited objectives, and close cooperation between tanks, infantry, and artillery. The confidence and experience gained during these operations were to be put to good use in the closing months of the war.[56] Another bright and much publicized phenomenon during this period of anticipation was the appearance and resolute performance of the first massive American divisions.* The 1st Division had successfully seized Cantigny, near Montdidier, on May 28. Elements of the 3rd Division had bravely withstood the German advance on June 1 at Château Thierry on the Marne. And the Marine Brigade of the 2nd Division had attacked and seized a part of Belleau Wood in June.[57] These actions, while decidedly minor in the great maelstrom of German offensives, were encouraging reminders that Allied strength was being renewed and that the new American troops were worthy adversaries when properly trained and led. Contemplating his last drive, Ludendorff could

*The strength of an American division was more than three times that of a French, British, or German division.

not have been heartened by the prospect of an increasing American presence.

The Fifth German Drive

The fifth German drive, or the Champagne-Marne offensive, might properly be called the Second Battle of the Marne. The tragic irony of Kaiser Wilhelm's armies fighting their last offensive action on virtually the same ground upon which they had been stopped during the initial campaign of 1914 was merely heightened by the realization that nearly four long and bloody years separated these two actions. Attacking on both sides of Rheims, the mass of 52 German divisions was to crash against a forewarned Allied line. The French army group commanders had once more divined the coming attack, principally because of the less subtle methods of concealment used by the enemy. However, they had also benefited from a growing stream of German deserters who were more than willing to trade information to the enemy rather than die in another futile attack.[58]

The attacking infantry east of Rheims struck the well prepared zonal defenses of the French Fourth Army under General Henri J.E. Gouraud and were shattered in the battle zone.[59] The western attack achieved initial success and was able to establish a bridgehead across the Marne; infiltration tactics and surprise allowed the German Seventh Army to expand this bridgehead to a depth of four miles. Although this new thrust greatly alarmed Premier Clemenceau and the public, it fit nicely into Foch's planned counterattack. The combined reaction to the new thrust toward Paris completely contained the small pocket of six German divisions that stood with their backs to an unfordable river. Using both artillery and aircraft, Foch commenced a heavy bombardment of these troops and the bridges behind them. The Germans were now in a trap. Unable to advance and cut off from supplies and reinforcement from the other side of the river, they could now only await the inevitable French counterattack.[60] Although the German High Command would continue to hope and plan for a return to the offensive, this fifth drive would prove to be the final time in the war that such an action would be possible. Henceforth, until their final defeat, the Germans would be responding to the initiatives of the Allied armies.

The War at Sea—Another German Defeat

Although the antisubmarine war had largely been won before Ludendorff unleashed his land offensives, his decision to attack in the West was closely linked to the campaign of unrestricted submarine warfare against all shipping en route to Great Britain. This naval policy was adopted because the experts promised that it would help Germany's strategic position. Presumably, any adverse results would be manifest only after the war had been won.[61]

In fact, the unrestricted submarine warfare campaign was another aspect of the western Allies' struggle to survive and, ultimately, turn the balance of power in their favor. In historical treatments, the entire subject of the conflict between the German undersea raiders and the Allied naval and mercantile fleets has usually been relegated to a position of secondary importance to the gigantic clash of arms between the land armies.* Yet some authorities credit this methodical and nerve-racking struggle between the German and British Navies as being the ultimate decisive factor in the outcome of the war.[62] It was an unceasing struggle—from first to last, a modern war of materiel. Measures such as stockpiling, the strict allocation of scarce raw materials, the use of substitutes, and, in the case of the Central Powers, the exploitation of conquered territories could alleviate the problems created by blockade and commerce raiding. But these measures could never fully compensate for the trade lost by the heavily industrialized societies.

Late in 1916, Admiral Henning von Holtzendorff, the Chief of the German Naval Staff, convinced Hindenburg and Ludendorff that Great Britain could be driven from the war within six months by an unrestricted campaign of submarine warfare. His argument rested upon the fact that of the nearly 11 million tons of cargo vessels serving the British Isles, about two-thirds were of British registry. He estimated that his expanded fleet of U-boats could sink approximately 600,000 tons per month. In addition to this devastation, his program would have the effect of frightening away all neutral ships serving England. The result, as Holtzendorff saw it, would be famine in England before the summer.[63]

When questions arose about the side effects of a renewed campaign—such as Allied naval reaction and the diplomatic reaction of neutrals, especially the United States—they were minimized. Holtzendorff claimed that the British would not employ convoys, since these would increase the size of the targets for the undersea raiders. Although technology was vastly superior to that of the prewar period, the countermeasures used against the U-boats were still relatively ineffective. As for the almost certain declaration of

---

*This stems, in part, from the attitude of the continental powers toward naval operations. Since the Royal Navy maintained unquestioned supremacy at sea throughout the war, it was only natural that the generals made light of the problems of the navies. General Sir Henry Wilson, Chief of the Imperial General Staff, was quoted as correcting a naval colleague who complained that the French did not regard Great Britain's command of the sea as important as one hundred bayonets. Wilson told him that they regarded it as less important than one bayonet.

An Undersea Raider Cruises on the Surface

war by the United States, both the German Navy and Army viewed this as a necessary risk; at any rate, its effect would come too late to assist the Entente because the Army would defeat the Franco-British forces in the field before the Americans could raise and train their armies. Also, once the Royal Navy and the merchant marine had been swept from the seas, the great resources of the New World would not be able to reach the beleaguered Europeans.

The renewed submarine patrols began in February 1917, concentrating on the Straits of Dover and the western approaches to the British Isles. By keeping heavier concentrations of raiders at sea along the normal routes to the commercial ports, the Germans increased the number of sinkings dramatically. Each month brought ever larger lists of tonnage sunk and seamen lost. Although German estimates of the damage were inflated, the predictions of the German Naval Staff appeared to be coming true.

In no other sphere of operations was the phrase "business as usual" more apt than in that of British commercial shipping. Even in the midst of war, the spirit of laissez faire characterized the attitude of the shippers, the Government, and the Navy on the subject of world trade. Submarines were accepted as inevitable; but as the German Navy developed improved boats and torpedoes and evolved better methods of attack, the loss rate increased steadily. With the introduction of unrestricted submarine warfare, the British and their allies began to lose ships faster than replacements could be built.

While the practice of convoying merchant ships had been used very successfully by the British during the Napoleonic wars, it was thought to be an outmoded and awkward approach in the age of steam. In the early nineteenth century, this system of grouping large numbers of commercial carriers together under the guardianship of naval escorts had reduced by five times the losses to enemy raiders. At that time,

however, the guiding force behind the convoy system had been the marine insurance underwriters, who charged exorbitant rates to ships that insisted upon sailing independently.[64] In 1917, the advent of larger capacity ships using regular routes and schedules convinced both naval and commercial leaders that this lesson of the past was no longer applicable. Those in charge of directing the antisubmarine effort pointed out that the introduction of steam propulsion to commercial vessels had allowed them to run on exact timetables and to conduct the vast overseas trade of the British Empire in a more efficient manner. If a system of convoying were adopted, the ships would lose valuable time awaiting others in order to form the protective groups.

Also, because of a misinterpretation of the great naval theorist, Alfred T. Mahan, many of the world's admiralties concentrated the efforts of naval defenses on protecting the regularly used sea routes, or "sea lines of communication." Those charged with the protection of seagoing commerce patrolled and swept routes in the vast ocean, rather than paying attention only to those ships that carried the goods. A final perversion of the role of the Navy in protecting commerce was the prevailing attitude that only offensive methods of search and destroy would result in adequate U-boat kills.[65]

A group of younger officers in the Royal Navy were unimpressed with the prevailing doctrine—especially since it was not working. Experimenting with the convoy method in the spring of 1917, they quickly discovered, for example, that when convoys were used in trade with Norway, the loss rate was 120 times smaller. But when presented with these statistics, Admiralty officials persisted in their objections to the convoy system. The Sea Lords viewed it as unworkable and refused to authorize a test. They pointed out that the speed of convoys is determined by the slowest vessels, and the resultant increase in time at sea would reduce overall shipping availability. Another argument raised was that the untrained merchantmen could not stay in formation and would actually increase damage through accidents. Finally, they claimed that sufficient naval resources could not be spared from offensive patrolling duties to guard the convoys.

The most fallacious argument against convoys was that their very size made them more vulnerable to enemy attack. The difference in size between one ship and a 30-ship convoy is insignificant when compared with the vast reaches of the oceans upon which they sail. If one ship can evade detection by a commerce raider, a group of them has virtually the same chance. Once safely through the danger area, moreover, the yield in goods is multiplied by 30. As experience would soon show, the naval experts were also wrong in their evaluation of the ability of ships' masters to learn and follow the techniques of convoying.

**United States Naval Escorts (Destroyers) Lay Down
a Smokescreen to Protect a Convoy**

The fear that the group would be slow moving and that their simultaneous arrival in port would overtax the unloading facilities also proved groundless. By grouping ships of similar characteristics in a convoy, a uniform speed could be maintained. The benefits derived from knowing the exact arrival dates and efficiently allocating docking and unloading facilities more than compensated for the peak periods of arrivals in port.[66]

The convoy system was finally authorized by the British Admiralty on April 30, 1917. As is often the case in a radical departure from accepted doctrine, the impetus had to come from outside the established bureaucracy. Admiral William S. Sims, United States Navy, was impressed by the statistics compiled by Commander Reginald Henderson, one of the junior naval officers who had experimented with the convoy system. Sims, in turn, ignored usual channels and explained the situation and the possible solution to the British Prime Minister, David Lloyd George. The fiery Welshman would brook no impediment to the institution of the system. He strode into the Admiralty and, from the chair of the First Lord, issued a direct order for convoy operations to be tested in the North Atlantic.[67] The immediate success gained made the initial intransigence of the

Royal Navy almost inexplicable. Convoying was shortly extended to all of the other endangered shipping routes, and losses due to U-boat attacks diminished as sharply as they had risen at the beginning of the campaign. The rate of loss to ships sailing independently of a convoy was 12 times greater than that of ships sailing together. The U-boat threat had been conquered. Yet another German gamble to win the war had come to naught, but not until after many anxious months had passed.

Thus, the first half of 1918 ended with the dashing of several German hopes. After effectively ending the war on the Eastern Front, Ludendorff had recklessly authorized the employment of unrestricted submarine warfare. Because he was confident that his armies would quickly end the war, he had disregarded the certain entry of the United States into the war on the side of the Allies. His offensive land operations, begun with promising victories, had been allowed to bog down as the Allies persevered until the American Army could be formed and transported to Europe. The Allied military and naval forces had been able to thwart the designs of their principal enemy, but it had been a "near run thing."

**A Destroyer on Convoy Escort Duty Tows a Kite Balloon
to Observe U-Boats**

Notes

[1]Wolfgang Foerster, *Count Schlieffin and the World War*, trans. by William J. Berry (Berlin, 1921), pp. 107–108.

[2]Hermann von Kuhl, *Genesis, Execution and Collapse of the German Offensive in 1918*, trans. by Army War College (2 vols.; Washington, D.C. 1934), II, 1.

[3]Erich Ludendorff, *Ludendorff's Own Story* (2 vols.; New York, 1919), II, 158–163.

[4]Basil H. Liddell Hart, *The Real War, 1914–1918* (Boston, 1930), pp. 372–373.

[5]C.R.M.F. Cruttwell, *A History of the Great War, 1914–1918* (Oxford, 1936), pp. 486–489.

[6]Kuhl, *German Offensive*, II, 6.

[7]James E. Edmonds (ed.), *History of the Great War: Military Operations, France and Belgium, 1918* (5 vols.; London, 1935–1947), I, 143. Hereinafter referred to as *BOH, 1918*.

[8]Foerster, *Schlieffen and the World War*, p. 112.

[9]Wetzell's study is contained in Annex B, Appendix 6 in this text.

[10]Georg Wetzell, "The Offensive Against the British," quoted in Kuhl, *German Offensive*, II, 17.

[11]See p. 71.

[12]Barrie Pitt, *1918: The Lost Act* (New York, 1963), p. 43.

[13]Extract of German training literature quoted in Edmonds, *BOH, 1918*, I, 156–157.

[14]Ludendorff, *Own Story*, II, 202–204.

[15]Edmonds, *BOH, 1918*, I, 154.

[16]Frederick B. Maurice, *Lessons of Allied Cooperation: Naval, Military and Air, 1914–1918* (London, 1942), pp. 173–174.

[17]"Decisions of a Conference of Representatives of the British, French and Italian Governments Assembled at RAPALLO on November 7, 1917," *The Diaries and Papers of Field-Marshal Sir Douglas Haig*, National Library of Scotland, H. 134.

[18]"General Tasker Bliss to Newton Baker and General Peyton March, July 13, 1918." *Supreme War Council Records*, quoted in David F. Trask, *The United States in the Supreme War Council* (Middletown, Conn., 1961), p. 39.

[19]John Terraine, "Lloyd George's Expedients," in *The Western Front, 1914–1918* (Philadelphia, 1965), pp. 96–113.

[20]Trask, *Supreme War Council*, pp. 20–37.

[21]"Executive War Board Note No. 1," *Diaries and Papers of Haig*, H. 124.

[22]Hubert Gough. *The Fifth Army* (London, 1931), pp. 222–223.

[23]"G.H.Q. Memorandum On Defensive Measures, 14th December, 1917" in Edmonds, *BOH, 1918*. I, App., pp. 22–29.

[24]Cyril Falls, *The Great War* (New York, 1959), pp. 331–332.

[25]Gough, *Fifth Army*, p. 241.

[26]"D. Haig to Henry Wilson, March 2, 1918," O.A.D. 770, *Diaries and Papers of Haig*, H. 124.

[27]Llewellyn Woodward, *Great Britain and the War of 1914–1918* (London, 1967), p. 331.

[28]Georges Clemenceau, *The Grandeur and Misery of Victory* (New York, 1930), p. 37.

[29]William R. Griffiths, "Alliance At Armageddon: Franco-British Military Cooperation, 1914–1918" (unpublished thesis, Fort Leavenworth, Kans.; 1971), pp. 78–79.

[30]Pitt, *Last Act*, pp. 75–76.

[31]Gough, *Fifth Army*, p. 238.

[32]Kuhl, *German Offensive*, II, 36–38.

[33]Robert Blake (ed.), *The Private Papers of Douglas Haig, 1914–1919* (London, 1952), pp. 296–297.

[34]*Ibid.*, p. 297.

[35]"Telegram from C-in-C British Armies in France to C.I.G.S. [Henry Wilson]," *Diaries and Papers of Haig*, H. 124.

[36]Cruttwell, *Great War*, p. 513.

[37]Ludendorff, *Own Story*, II, 233.

[38]*Ibid.*, II, 221; opposing view is in Foerster, *Schlieffen and the World War*, p. 125.

[39]Liddell Hart, *Real War*, pp. 404–405.

[40]Hubert Essame, *The Battle for Europe, 1918* (New York, 1972), p. 48.

[41]General Plumer's Second Army had voluntarily retired from the Passchendaele ridge earlier. Edmonds, *BOH, 1918*, II, 330–339.

[42]"General Order of the Day, April 11, 1918." Handwritten facsimile in Winston S. Churchill, *The World Crisis, 1916–1918* (2 vols.; New York, 1927), II, 156.

[43]James E. Edmonds, *A Short History of World War I* (New York, 1951), pp. 312–314; Falls, *The Great War*, p. 340.

[44]Ludendorff, *Own Story*, II, p. 245; Kuhl, *German Offensive*, II, pp. 57–58; Cruttwell, *Great War*, p. 513.

[45]Essame, *Battle for Europe*, p. 32.

[46]Edmonds, *Short History of World War I*, p. 316. In this instance, the German casualty figures are believed to be accurate.

[47]Kuhl, *German Offensive*, II, 59.

[48]Jere Clemens King, *Generals and Politicians: Conflict Between France's High Command, Parliament and Government, 1914–1918* (Berkeley, Calif., 1951), pp. 224–225; Liddell Hart, *Real War*, pp. 412–414.

[49]Cruttwell, *Great War*, pp. 526–527.

[50]Falls, *The Great War*, p. 345.

[51]Vincent J. Esposito, "Western Front, 1918: The Year of Decision," in Vincent J. Esposito (ed.), *A Concise History of World War One* (New York, 1964), p. 114.

[52]Essame, *Battle for Europe*, pp. 73–75.

[53]*Ibid.*, p. 80.

[54]Ludendorff, *Own Story*, II, 183–185.

[55]Ralph H. Major, *Fatal Partners: War and Disease* (Garden City, N.Y., 1941), pp. 268–273; H.H. Hockling, *The Great Epidemic* (Boston, 1961), p. 3.

[56]Edmonds, *Short History of World War I*, pp. 328–330.

[57]Edward M. Coffman, *The War To End All Wars, The American Military Experience in World War I* (New York, 1968), pp. 156–157, 213–221.

[58]Cruttwell, *Great War*, p. 534.

[59]Falls, *The Great War*, p. 348.

[60]*Ibid.*, pp. 348–350.

[61]John D. Hoyes, "The War at Sea," in Esposito, *Concise History*, p. 253.

[62]Liddell Hart, *Real War*, pp. 309–310.

[63]E.B. Potter (ed.), *Sea Power, A Naval History* (Englewood Cliffs, N.J., 1960), p. 460.

[64]*Ibid.*, p. 461.

[65]*Ibid.*

[66]Churchill, *World Crisis, 1916–1918*, II, 80.

[67]Lord Beaverbrook [William Maxwell Aitken] *Men and Power, 1917–1918* (London, 1956), pp. 152–155.

Counteroffensive to Victory

9

The counterattack is, perhaps, the most delicate of military maneuvers. It requires precise timing, adequate preparation and stability. Stability is achieved by slowing and halting the enemy drive in order for the counterattack to push off from a firm base. Preparation requires, no matter how tenuous the situation, reconnaissance, fire planning and detailed instructions, supply and communications. Above all the counterstroke must achieve surprise and come at the earliest practical moment. Despite conflicting requirements, the general must choose his time and place.

C.R.M.F. Cruttwell

As Ludendorff's battered and morally shaken soldiers recoiled from their final frustration in the attack, the Allied forces, inexorably gaining in strength, exhibited a rekindled will to conclude the war. Perhaps the greatest error that the German High Command had made in the preceding six months was to promise too much from the 1918 offensives. As in other battles and other armies, the effect of defeat or repulse had been magnified by the promise of certain victory.* The best and the bravest of the German troops had inevitably fallen during Ludendorff's series of offensives. These troops were being replaced by former prisoners of war returned from Russia and rear area soldiers with less stomach for fighting. The rapid change in fortune of the German forces was also due to the strangling effects of the British naval blockade. Shortages of

*These armies include the French after the Nivelle offensive, the Italians after Caporetto, and the Russians following the Kerensky offensive.

all supplies, including food and equipment, were now apparent, and the thought that those on the homefront were receiving much less merely added to the depression of morale.

The Allies now realized that the initiative was finally returning to them. The realization that this might be the last opportunity to achieve victory, however, imposed a serious restraint on any premature or reckless plans to return to the attack. Most military and political leaders were reluctant to advance proposals that promised final victory before the spring or summer of 1919. Since their superiority in all areas could only increase with the addition of a growing flood of American troops and the freedom of commerce gained in the antisubmarine victory, it appeared logical to await the accumulation of huge stocks of ammunition, tanks, and men to assure that when the final stroke came, it would end the war. Therefore, Marshal Foch's plans for the remainder of the year called only for the mounting of limited assaults to control railroad centers in preparation for the final onslaught in 1919. The rallying cry of the battlewise French and British forces was "wait for the Americans and the tanks." Tanks were being produced in unheard of numbers, and the American Expeditionary Force was growing in strength and experience daily. Therefore, the mood of the Allied ranks was marked by cautious confidence, rather than the brash optimism that had resulted in dejection so many times in the past.

To the south, in Italy, the Allies were also content to bide their time until a final victory was assured. Although the morale of the Italian forces had been revived, there seemed little reason to attempt grand offensive schemes while Germany might still reinforce the degenerating Austro-Hungarian forces. This was General Diaz' plan, and he would not be dissuaded from believing that his course was to defend until the war had been won on the Western Front.

The End of the War in Italy

With the coming of 1918, the armies of King Victor Emmanuel remained in defensive positions behind the Piave River line, exactly where the disastrous Battle of Caporetto had left them in November 1917. Sizable contingents of French and British units still bolstered the Italian Army, but these were the only reminders of the "Miracle of Caporetto" that had thrust the Italian Theater into prominence for a brief time.[1] General Armando Diaz concentrated his efforts on rebuilding his shattered forces while taking advantage of the national rejuvenation that had been spurred by invasion and defeat.[2] The Allied situation in the Italian Theater had also been aided by the rapid redeployment of the German strategic reserve divisions to the Western Front.* Now that the Russian threat had been eliminated, Ludendorff and his staff felt that the Austro-Hungarian Army, even in its present condition, could bring about the final defeat of the enemy in this minor theater.[3]

Emperor Charles and his Chief of Staff, General Roberto Arz, were more acutely aware of the declining condition of both their nation and their Army. Separatist movements among the numerous national minority groups that composed the ramshackle Hapsburg Empire had been encouraged by the pronouncement of President Wilson's Fourteen Points[‡]; these groups seemed more interested in guaranteeing their own postwar autonomy than in prosecuting the war effort. Such social and political divisions, when combined with the staggering military losses sustained by the Army and the deplorable living conditions on the homefront, easily nullified the brief elation that had been caused by the victory at Caporetto. Thus, when the German General Staff requested the temporary transfer of Austrian combat units to support the Western Front operations, they had received a few poorly equipped units, fit only for quiet sectors. Ludendorff also asked that the Austrian High Command conduct an offensive in Italy, timed to coincide with his planned spring offensives; the response was delayed and ineffective.[4] The coordinated offensive drive that the

Germans had desired was postponed until its effect was minimal. Arz, who was never in full charge of the Empire's army, allowed the Emperor and two of his own subordinates, Conrad and Baron Svetozar Boroević von Bojna, to compromise the meager resources of the Dual Monarchy.[5] The resulting offensive, known as the Battle of the Piave, would initiate a series of events that were a miniature replica of those on the Western Front.

Boroević and Conrad each insisted on conducting the major offensive against the Italian line in his own sector. The resulting dispersion of forces denied both of the attacks the combat power necessary for decisive results.[6] On the tactical level, the operations were designed to follow the successful infiltration assault tactics of the German Army. However, they were of inferior quality, suffering from poor coordination, lack of surprise, and the selection of unrealistic objectives. The Austrian version of breakthrough tactics also lacked the highly trained storm troopers and the strong reserves that had insured German success in the spring.

The battle began on June 15, during the death throes of the Ludendorff offensives on the Western Front, and long after it could have drawn Allied resources away from the Western Front. Conrad's army group attacked from the mountainous area with 27 divisions, while Boroević moved with 23 divisions across the Piave. This ambitious twin advance was to be supported by a two-division attack on the Tonale Pass near the Swiss border. However, this diversionary operation was stopped without gain two days before the main assault. The Italian intelligence service, smarting from its poor showing prior to the Caporetto disaster, had ample evidence of the exact date and locations of

---

*In addition to the seven German divisions recalled to the Western Front, four of the six French divisions and two of the five British divisions had also left to participate in the coming clash of arms in the spring offensives. In token repayment, the Italians sent two divisions to fight with their allies. The Austrians also moved some second-class units to quiet sectors of the Western Front. However, on balance, the Italian Theater of Operations was a drain on the resources of the major belligerents and cost both the Allies and the Germans more in terms of combat power than could reasonably have been expected in terms of ultimate victory. As an interesting sidelight, a Czechoslovak division was now fighting alongside the Italian Army, a sign of the rapid disintegration of the multinational Austro-Hungarian Empire.

‡In an address to Congress on January 8, 1918, Wilson outlined a peace program that consisted of Fourteen Points. Eventually, Germany sought terms on the basis of this program, which, however, was not enthusiastically endorsed by France or Great Britain.

**Operating in Mountainous Terrain, an Austrian
Machinegun Crew Adjusts Fire from a Precipice**

the attacks. Therefore, the defenders were able to brace themselves and counteract the surprise artillery preparation with counterbattery fire.[7]

Conrad's Eleventh Army at once ran into French and British units on the line. Consequently, it made only minor gains, all of which were retrieved by counterattacks within 24 hours. Facing the Italian Third Army, however, Boroević was initially much more successful. On the Piave, the Austrians showed their final spark of offensive vigor, advancing along a 15-mile front to a maximum depth of five miles. For a brief period, it seemed as though another Italian rout was in the making. But units on the shoulders of the bridgehead remained firm in the defense and prevented its enlargement. The next day, Boroević's weakness in reserves became evident as his forward movement slowed. Also, the inter-Allied air support provided to the Italians was effective. The air units concentrated on the 20 bridges that the Austrians had thrown across the Piave to carry the flow of supplies and reinforcements. The effect of these interdictive actions was compounded during the night of June 17, when the river rose to flood stage, washing away several of the bridges and making many others unusable. Stymied in his assault, lacking adequate reserves, and unable to solve the problems of sustaining his troops on the far bank of the river, Boroević ordered a withdrawal on June 22.[8]

The final result of Austria-Hungary's offensive was virtually the same as the German attempts to end the war victoriously. For negligible gain, the offensive flower of the Army had been lost. The 150,000 casualties sustained by the attackers left them open to eventual counterattack and defeat. Unjustified hopes for a victorious conclusion to the war were now dashed, causing a final decline in troop morale.

Foch now urged his philosophy of attack everywhere upon General Diaz, but the Italian commander chose to continue rebuilding his forces until final victory was assured. Diaz waited until the tide of battle on the Western Front had definitely turned, and the Central Powers were less than a month from capitulation.[9] In the interim, he reorganized his forces so that two armies were commanded by the British and French contingent commanders. His plan envisioned a two-pronged thrust across the formidable Piave River obstacle, one against Feltre and the other to penetrate as far as the town of Vittorio Veneto, which gave its name to the battle. (*See Atlas Map No. 20.*) Since the Italians did not have numerical superiority, such an ambitious operation might be criticized as repeating the error that had brought the Austrians to ruin four months earlier. Diaz, however, realized that defeat had lowered the combat effectiveness of the Austrian defenders, largely negating their numerical advantage. The Allies could also count on the logistical means necessary for a river crossing and the superior quality of their supporting arms. The attack was thus a militarily calculated risk. It was conceived after the collapse of Bulgaria, and its main motivation appears to have been Italian political fears that if the war did not end in a victorious campaign, their postwar territorial claims would be denied.[10]

The battle began on the night of October 23 when the British, under General Lord Cavan, seized a large island in the middle of the Piave River. The main attack commenced the next day, on the first anniversary of the Battle of Caporetto. The execution of the first stage did not meet the expectations of the military planners, with the Italian Fourth Army on Mount Grappa being repulsed by a surprisingly stout Austrian defense. Moreover, on the Piave, the waters rose once again to flood stage and temporarily prevented a lodgment on the far shore. On the night of October 26, however, a French division managed to gain a bridgehead, and the units of the Twelfth Army began crossing the next day. To the southeast, Lord Cavan's Anglo-Italian Tenth Army simultaneously smashed the defensive line and secured a larger bridgehead. Debouching from this crossing area, the Allies cleared the entire river front, forcing the Austrians to withdraw to the next obstacle. The advance was halted at the Livenza River for two days, at which time the Allies forced a crossing at Sacile. This move coincided with the complete collapse of Austrian resistance.[11]

On October 27, Emperor Charles had resolved to seek a separate armistice and had informed the German Government of his hopes to save his throne. But his decision came too late. In a desperate gesture on October 16, Charles had granted autonomy to the nationalities within the Empire, albeit as continuing members of a federal state. As news of this political move reached the front, Magyar, Czech, Croat, and Slav units began to mutiny, and troops began to drift back to their homes.[12] "The body politic was thus writhing in the last throes,"[13] and it did not take long for the disintegration at home to spread to the Army and turn it into a rabble. Allied units pursued the fleeing remnants of the Austro-Hungarian Empire's Army until November 4, when the Empire's fumbling leadership was able to arrange a cessation of hostilities. By the date of the armistice (November 11), more than 500,000 prisoners and 7,000 guns had been captured, and Allied land forces had retaken almost all the territory lost the previous year. A naval expedition secured the port of Trieste the day before the fighting ended.[14]

The armistice terms forced the Austrians to withdraw behind a demarcation line that gave the Italian Government control of all of the territory promised by the Treaty of London upon its entry into the war. The Allied forces were also granted passage into Germany's southern state of Bavaria. This development encouraged revolution in southern Germany against the Imperial Government.[15] Concurrent with

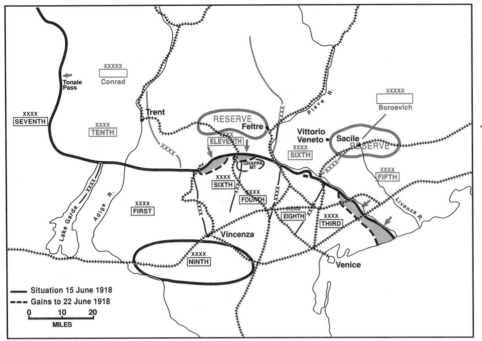

The Battle of Piave, June 15–24, 1918

these operations on the Italian Front, the principal belligerents were conducting the final battles of the war on the Western Front.

Victory in the West

By the middle of July 1918, General Ferdinand Foch had been in charge of all Allied operations on the Western Front for four months. In the eyes of both the public and the political leaders, his tenure had been marked by a continuation of the series of defeats that they had hoped would halt upon his elevation to the Supreme Command.[16] The Allies had been reacting to German initiatives all along the front, and the fact that the enemy's efforts had in all cases been checked provided small comfort. The latest German drive into the heart of France was widely believed to have been aimed at the final capture of Paris, rather than being just another diversion intended to draw attention from the planned HAGEN offensive in the north.* Still, there was no guarantee that the enemy would not continue to march south; and in scenes reminiscent of September 1914, government officials nervously began to prepare for an evacuation of the city. As it turned out, these were unnecessary, for by July 17 Ludendorff had issued orders to break off the offensive on the Marne and to transfer combat units north to the group of armies commanded by Crown Prince Rupprecht of Bavaria.[18]

The Second Battle of the Marne

Foch had foreseen Ludendorff's move, and, after a long period of planning, was now ready to seize the initiative and strike a counterblow before the German offensive could be launched. (*See Atlas Map No. 18.*) With the cool calculation of a professional gambler, Foch concentrated his precious

**Italian Infantry Attacks the Faltering
Austro-Hungarian Army**

*Even military analysts immediately following the war incorrectly assumed that this was the German objective.[17]

French Rifle Grenadiers Prepare to Support a Local Attack With Volley Fire

forces around the Marne salient, allowing Haig's armies in the north to remain dangerously weak in the face of Rupprecht's growing strength.[†] Foch, to use his own metaphor, was about to conduct a performance by a "great military orchestra" composed of varied elements working toward a common goal.[20]

The two ranking French generals, Pétain and Foch, disagreed on the proper method to be employed to reduce the Marne salient.[21] The more cautious and systematic Pétain wished to mount a single strong thrust across the chord of the salient. This plan, if carried out rapidly, would entrap the sizable German forces still in the pocket. Foch, however, was unwilling to wait for the transfer and massing of the necessary combat power on the western face of the salient. He ordered that convergent pressure be applied all along the front in order to push the defenders back to the base of the salient along their natural avenues of retreat.[22] This tactical disagreement highlights the basic differences between the two men. Foch, despite numerous reverses as a commander throughout the war, was still an apostle of the "Spirit of the Offensive," whereas Pétain had learned the value of judicious maneuver and the advantage of substituting the weight of materiel for that of manpower. In this particular dispute, Foch insisted that his plan be carried out. As the war progressed, however, the Generalissimo adjusted his demands to the more reasonable tactical views of his subordinate national commanders. It appears that he was willing to moderate his desire for attacks everywhere as long as operations continued to be successful.

The second phase of the Second Battle of the Marne began at 4:35 a.m. on July 18. (*See Atlas Map No. 21a.*) Using the method of artillery support evolved since the Battle of Cambrai—a brief preparation followed by a violent rolling barrage—the French forces moved forward, heavily dependent upon a mass of 346 tanks to provide direct fire support and crush the defensive wire. The tanks used were mainly of the light "Renault" type that could achieve speeds of six miles per hour. Another feature of this first counterstroke was the integration of eight American divisions into the operation. Their stalwart actions heralded the American Army's assumption of a major share of the fighting.[23]

General Jean M.J. Degoutte's French Sixth Army moved forward at Zero Hour, followed, after a 25-minute wait for artillery preparation, by the main attack conducted by the fiery General Charles Mangin's Tenth Army. Surprise was achieved all along the 25-mile front on the western face of the Marne salient. The German commanders and staff had been too intent upon shifting combat power north for their final offensive in Flanders. The secondline, or trench, divisions, which remained to defend the salient, were neither properly alerted nor adequately supported. As the Franco-American troops advanced, they noted further evidence of the decline of the German Army's fighting ability. Proper defensive trenches and wire obstacles—previously the hallmark of the German soldier—were not encountered. The enemy's usually strict measures of field sanitation were equally lax; the dead remained unburied, and latrines had not been constructed. The French *poilu* and the American doughboy, encouraged by their initial success, moved forward with enthusiasm.[24]

General Charles Mangin, Commander of the French Tenth Army

[†] While Haig was well aware of Ludendorff's plan to strike the decisive blow against his armies, he loyally supported Foch's authority in this matter. However, the British Government, fearing another overwhelming defeat, became extremely agitated. Lloyd George and his advisers were now forced to realize what their acceptance of Foch's authority in command entailed in terms of sacrificing their national goals to those of the coalition.[19]

A Mammoth French Trench Mortar is Readied for an Attack of the Enemy Defenses

The Franco-American advance into the Marne salient found Ludendorff at Rupprecht's headquarters in Mons, preparing to issue final orders and coordinate final instructions for the long-awaited HAGEN offensive. As the first reports of the Allied counterattack came in, Ludendorff ordered two, and then four, reserve divisions to react. Finally, as reports of penetrations of up to three miles were confirmed, he ordered the final postponement of his HAGEN offensive. It was now obvious that the Marne salient was untenable and had to be evacuated. The rail lines and roads supporting the units in the salient were under Allied fire, and the only alternative to leaving large numbers of prisoners and equipment trapped in the areas was a methodical retirement. Although not apparent at the time, Ludendorff's decisions marked the beginning of the end of the war in the West.

The six German divisions that were in an extended position on the south bank of the Marne hurriedly began their recrossing on the night of July 18.[25] Fortunately for the retreating force, the French units on the eastern face of the salient found the terrain more difficult, and therefore moved at a slower pace than their comrades on the western side. Additionally, the great tactical and moral advantage provided by the tank force was rapidly diminishing as German gunners and mechanical breakdowns reduced their numbers with each mile of advance. By August 2, the major elements of the two German armies that had been in the salient were safely in position behind the Vesle River. These groups were fatigued, but after their initial collapse, they had fought stubbornly in retreat. Nearly 30,000 prisoners and 800 guns had been lost to the Allies, but the two German armies remained intact. On August 6, Pétain decided to halt the Allied counteroffensive. This decision was oc-

casioned by the casualties his own forces had sustained as well as his aversion to fruitless frontal attack against prepared positions.

General Ludendorff mistook the Allies' reluctance to continue as a sign that this counteroffensive had been an isolated incident and that no further attacks were to be expected in the near future.[26] Holding to this belief, he made the tragic error of basing his plans upon what he expected the enemy to do, rather than what the enemy was capable of doing. He clung to this assessment because he still wanted to end the war with a final German offensive victory—despite the fact that the original plan had now been scrapped. Other German leaders, however, now demanded a more realistic appraisal of the situation. The German Crown Prince, "Little Willie" to his enemies, showed a flash of good judgment when he warned his father in a strongly worded letter that the war was lost and that peace terms must be accepted no matter how stiff they might be. Field Marshal von Hindenburg, the titular head of the command team, appeared more frequently at Ludendorff's field headquarters in order to provide perspective and a calming influence for his mercurial subordinate, who was given more and more to fits of depression.

The Battle of Amiens

Six days prior to the French counterattack on the Marne, Foch had proposed to Field Marshal Haig that the British armies initiate offensive operations on the southern flank of the Lys River salient. During the previous year, however, Haig and his staff had learned about the difficulties of attacking in Flanders during the month of August.[27] As a counterproposal, the British commander stated that he was preparing for a highly secret offensive east of Amiens to free the rail network in that area. He requested a combined attack with the French forces immediately to the south of the British Fourth Army.[28] Showing a reasonable and adaptable attitude toward the proposals of his theoretical subordinate, Foch not only accepted the plan, but placed the French First Army under Haig's command to carry it out. This exchange of ideas was the genesis of the actions around Amiens and Montdidier. If the Second Battle of the Marne was the beginning of the end of trench warfare on the Western Front, then surely the Battle of Amiens was the final turning point in that struggle. (*See Atlas Map No. 21b.*)

Haig designated General Henry Rawlinson's Fourth Army to conduct the battle in conjunction with General Marie Eugène Debeney's French First Army. In the northern portion of the attack sector, Rawlinson secretly concentrated 15 infantry and 3 cavalry divisions along a 14-mile front held by 6 skeleton German divisions.* To support the limited objectives of the attack, 2,000 guns and 17 air squadrons were assembled. In keeping with procedures used in recent successful operations, there was no artillery preparation in order to gain surprise. Ten heavy and two light battalions of tanks provided shock action and fire support with their 414 vehicles.† One unfortunate aspect of this support, however, was that the two battalions of light Mark A (Whippet) tanks were ordered to remain with and under the control of the cavalry divisions. This unhappy arrangement meant that the horse cavalry sped ahead of the tanks when there was light resistance, while the tanks moved forward alone when the chatter of automatic weapons from a strongpoint held up the cavalry. Thus, the tanks were not able to exploit their armored protection, speed, and maneuverability.[31] The French First Army began its attack with its leftmost corps 45 minutes after the British Zero Hour. They had required this time for an artillery preparation. Thereafter, the French army advanced in an echeloned formation, functioning as a flank guard to the main attack.‡ Although this supporting attack was assigned only 72 light tanks for direct ground support, it had more than 1,000 French aircraft at its disposal.

The British attack was spearheaded by the Canadian Corps, led by Lieutenant General Arthur Currie, and the Australian Corps, led by Lieutenant General John Monash. These troops, generally regarded as the finest infantry fighters on the Allied side, provided the punch for the tremendous initial success of the offensive battle. Because these soldiers were greatly respected by the German defenders, a deliberate deception program was undertaken to make the enemy believe that the Canadians were preparing for an attack in Flanders and that the Australians were assuming defensive duties from the French. In the meantime, the mass concentration of combat power continued in the Fourth Army area. Artillery pieces were infiltrated in and carefully registered without breaking the normal firing patterns in the zone of attack. Once again, the air service, using fighter aircraft and a heavy barrage of kite balloons, blocked direct observation by enemy reconnaissance flights. Friendly air-

planes also flew over the areas of concentration to detect and report on any unusual activity that might give the enemy a clue to the operation. Perhaps the most telling indication of the security measures taken to shroud the great offensive, however, was the fact that the War Cabinet in London was kept completely in the dark regarding the planned operations. Even the units that would participate in the assault were not briefed until 36 hours before the battle began.[32]

The artillery barrage and the forward movement of the tanks and infantry began simultaneously at 4:20 a.m. on August 8. Once again, as in so many other successful attacks in 1918, a thick ground fog allowed the infantry to approach the first defensive positions without being observed or fired upon. Using an innovation first employed by the Germans in their successful attack of March 21, the British began the forward movement of their reserve formations at Zero Hour in order to assure the maintenance of the momentum of the assault.*

The overall results of this meticulously planned operation were most encouraging. By 10:30 a.m., the first day's objective line was rapidly secured, except for portions on the extreme flanks. Advances of six to eight miles ruptured the enemy defensive positions and in many cases caused his supporting artillery to be captured. By evening, more than 16,000 prisoners of the eventual total of nearly 30,000 were being marched back to the prisoner of war (POW) cages. An indication of the German Army's low morale was noted by a famous former POW—Winston Churchill—who commented on the fact that the many captured enlisted men appeared jovial in comparison to the grim countenances upon the faces of the few captured officers.[33] The columns of prisoners were guarded only by the wounded Dominion troops returning to the rear for medical attention. Staff officers and commanders were riding about the field of battle on horseback—a sure sign of confident and rapid advance.[34]

The subsequent progress of the offensive was never as great, but the effect of that first day's success colored the remaining days of the war. As the attackers attempted to continue their progress, it soon became evident that the old problems of tactical mobility had not been completely solved. After advancing more than eight miles, the leading elements encountered the ruins of the old Somme battlefield. The maze of rusted barbed wire, old trenches, and shell holes made movement extremely difficult. The German headquarters also contributed to the slowdown. In panic, it had rapidly assembled and transferred a reserve

---

*A striking sign of the declining state of the German forces was that these divisions could muster only 3,000 men each—one-third of their authorized strength.[29]

†The 342 Mark V heavy and 72 light (Whippet) fighting tanks were supplemented with 120 tanks designed specifically to transport supplies for the tank and infantry units over the open country. In addition, a machinegun battalion of 16 wheeled carriers proved most effective against the retreating German formations.[30]

‡This method of attack was ordered by Debeney in direct disobedience of Foch's instructions to advance frontally with the main attack. It was also in contravention of Haig's request that his army advance at the same time as the British army. In light of Debeney's weakness in armor, however, it was probably a wise decision.

*The lessons learned by the Allies from the tactics of their enemies were employed against General Georg von der Marwitz' Second Army and Oskar von Hutier's Eighteenth Army. These were the very organizations that had achieved such smashing successes during the first German offensive in this same locale.

of 16 divisions—10 more than had been foreseen by the Allied intelligence sections—to stem the tide of battle.

But an even greater factor in the slowing of what seemed an irresistible offensive was the deliberate limitation of resources allocated to it by the British High Command.[35] Haig did not concentrate all of his available divisions to continue the attack, but instead ordered the Third Army to prepare a second offensive to the north of the Fourth Army area. When Foch encouraged the British Fourth Army to continue the frontal pressure on the enemy, Haig refused. He stated that a continuation in this area would be costly and difficult, and that only limited results could be expected; his detractors would say that he was a renowned expert on this subject. In a memorandum sent on August 14, Haig informed Foch of his preparations in the Third Army area. Thus, a strategic concept that depended upon a series of related but geographically separated offensives evolved from this battle.

The total German losses in the Battle of Amiens were close to 70,000, as compared with 42,000 for the Allies. Yet, great as the results of these actions were in terms of inflicting physical damage on the enemy and buoying the morale of the Allies, these results only begin to mark it as a turning point in the long conflict. The really decisive aspect of the battle was its chilling effect upon the German Army and the will of the German High Command. The divisions that were hurried to counter the British initiative represented the last of the effective German reserves on the front; thenceforth, the ability of the defenders to react would decline dramatically. Behind the lines, newly captured German soldiers appeared both relieved to be out of the fighting and convinced that the war had been lost. The mental shock of the unexpected British victory finally shredded German hopes for an eventual victory. In a state of nervous exhaustion, Ludendorff notified his political superiors "that the war would have to be ended." At a joint political and military conference held at OHL on August 14, a distraught Ludendorff tendered his resignation, which was refused. He stated that Haig's completely unexpected victory had convinced him that there was no longer any hope of a German victory.[36] Hindenburg was more optimistic, realistically pointing out that much conquered territory still remained under German control. The pessimistic Ludendorff countered with the judgment that the future German strategy must try to affect the enemy's war will with a strategic defensive. Such a radical change in the military outlook dismayed the statesmen, who understood how politically difficult it would be to disabuse the German people of their ideas of imminent victory. Although the First Quartermaster General would regain his composure and revise his estimate of the ability of the Army to resist, the damage done to the morale of the German leadership was irreparable. Thus,

The Growing Capabilities of Airpower . . .

August 8 emerges as the "Black Day of the German Army" in Ludendorff's postwar memoirs.[37]

Throughout the period of Allied victories, the importance and usefulness of combat and service support of ground troops by the air forces became more apparent. Before mounting an offensive, commanders would plan to achieve complete air superiority in their area of operations. The airplane was now regarded as a vital component of combat power.

While 1918 proved to be the year of fruition for the ground tactical doctrines of both sides, to an even greater extent it provided successful demonstrations of the value of airpower in modern total war. With the onset of each new campaign on the Western Front, the tactical missions of the air forces of all belligerents were expanded and refined. The aircraft themselves were constantly improved, and new types of machines with specialized roles were conceived. New doctrines also evolved for the integration of airpower and land forces. High flying daylight bombers, carrying high explosive bombs, were used to soften enemy defenses before a battle and to isolate the battlefield from the flow of enemy reserves. Direct machinegun fire from low flying strafing runs provided the infantry with welcome support against enemy strongpoints. Of course, as the earlier roles of artillery spotting and reconnaissance were continuously refined, they became almost routine aids to the ground commander.[38]

From the beginning of 1915, the German air forces had bombed England and, to a lesser extent, French cities behind the front. At first, high flying dirigibles were used, but these vulnerable, fragile, and clumsy craft were gradually replaced by specially designed bombers. Although these strategic bombing raids actually inflicted little real damage on the civilians on the homefront, they seriously affected the morale of workers, who now realized that they were not safe from the ravages of total war. The doctrine of strategic bombing was eagerly developed by the young officers of the air services, who saw in this mission an independent role for themselves.

By their very nature, the air services were more adaptable to inter-Allied cooperation and support than were their land-bound comrades. For example, the British bomber wing, which was established late in 1917 in retaliation for the bombing of England, was stationed near Nancy, France. Far from the British sector, the base had as its mission the destruction of industrial targets within Germany. Initially, this force evolved into the Independent Air Force; later, on April 1, 1918, it became the basis for the amalgamation of British naval and military air units known as the Royal Air Force.[39] While no other national air force developed into an independent arm or service during the war, the unique missions and equipment of all aviators encouraged innovative solutions to specific problems in an atmosphere of intellectual flexibility. All of the currently accepted missions of air forces had their beginnings in the First World War. Additionally, nearly all of the weapons and equipment used by the air armadas of the Second World War were conceived during the Great War. Strategic bombing, the air arm's single separate mission, was only marginally effective during the war, and served more as a terror weapon. While the air forces were growing in importance, as was indicated by the insistence of the Allied commanders on the maintenance of overwhelming air superiority, they remained only a supporting arm to the advance of the ground forces.

With the buildup of Allied forces, the wary German High Command had to face the threat of offensive action along its entire front. Preparations for the entry of the American Expeditionary Force into the line, British threats in the Third and Fourth Army sectors, and French reinforcement behind the Tenth and Fourth Armies, all portended battles that would require defensive actions by Germany's dwindling combat power. August 20 marked the continuation of the Allied effort to force the Germans back onto the first of their prepared defensive positions, the *Siegfried* and *Wotan Stellung*. On that day, General Mangin's Tenth Army struck north of the Aisne River in a continuation of the victorious counterattack of the Second Battle of the Marne. In one day, his forces drove to the Oise River valley. The British Third Army then conducted an offensive north of Albert on August 21, as planned by Haig and reluctantly agreed to by Foch. These offensives now required less combat superiority, and the masses of tanks and aircraft previously employed by the Allied forces could be safely reduced; in fact, in some cases numerically inferior forces went over to the attack.[40] One reason for this change was that potential threats all along the line required the Germans to scatter

An American Antiaircraft Battery on Alert

their reserves. Ludendorff had also decided to defend on successive lines, reacting to the Allied pressure, rather than making voluntary retirements to the established, heavily fortified positions that lay to the rear.

On August 23, the British Fourth Army renewed its movement forward in Picardy, thus straightening the line between the two British-held salients. Three days later, the British First Army of General Henry Horne moved to outflank the withdrawing enemy. After Horne's army had advanced four miles, Ludendorff realized the danger his forces would be exposed to if they remained in the area that had been captured by the Germans in the Somme offensive in March. He therefore ordered a retirement of 10 miles along the 55-mile front from Noyon to Ham. Then, on the twenty-eighth, Ludendorff gave orders to evacuate the Lys River salient in Flanders at the mere hint of an outbreak in that sector.[41]

As this withdrawal was in progress, constant pressure was applied by the British and French. Numerous small but bloody engagements were fought, and the new form of relatively open warfare began to strain the logistical systems of the Allied armies. Foch was constantly prodding his commanders to advance everywhere, but Haig and Pétain, striving to conserve manpower and lessen the number of casualties, translated these instructions into a succession of coordinated thrusts that were halted as soon as they met sig-

A.D. Nineteen Fifty.
"I see the War Babies' Battalion is a coming out."

**The End of Trench Warfare Appeared Possible
by the Conclusion of 1918**

nificant resistance.[42] While this pressure never approached the level of an exploitation, many of the characteristics of such an operation were present. The Allies were not seeking deep objectives; however, they were advancing on a wide front in an attempt to unhinge the German command and control facilities while retaining only minimum essential reserves to insure that the momentum of the advance would be maintained.

The Germans, striving to gain time, reluctantly traded space during their withdrawal into the imposing defenses of the *Siegfried Line.* If only they could delay the advancing Allied forces until the wet and cold months of late autumn, the eventual battle on the prepared defensive lines would be much more to their advantage. Their devoted machine-gun crews, in particular, were thrown into almost hopeless last-ditch situations in order to halt or at least disrupt the enemy. The answer to the German machinegun, however, was found in the tank. Although the Allies were expending the limited number of these new weapons rapidly, enough of them were available to prevent stalemate whenever a German strongpoint held up the advance.

Perhaps the crowning achievement of the Allied advance occurred on September 2, when the Canadian Corps

breached the *Wotan* position. By that time, the corps had been transferred to the First British Army's control and had advanced to a point where the fluid battles of the past month were impossible. The forward portion of this zone lacked the numerous concrete fortifications, deep dugouts, and tunnels evident in the southern section of the line (the Hindenburg Line). However, it was still a well planned and thoroughly organized trench system. When the Canadians hit the defensive lines, the period of rapid maneuver and outflanking temporarily ended. During the next phase, the attackers had to revert to the older method of frontal attacks against prepared positions until the line was breached.[43]

For two days, the concentrated artillery preparatory fires cut lanes through the webs of barbed wire—20 meters deep—that served as the first barrier to the advance of the infantry. At dawn of the day of the assault, 59 tanks (almost the entire combat-ready force of the Tank Corps) moved forward, leading the way for the two Canadian divisions, which spread out on a front of five miles. Almost miraculously, the attack succeeded all along the front. Apparently, the rot of defeatism had affected the defenders so greatly that they could not even hold the efficient and strong works designed by the defensive expert, Colonel Lossberg. The Drocourt-Quéant Switch Line (as this portion of the defenses was known to the Allied soldiers) had been breached, and the sister fortification, the Hindenburg Line, had been outflanked from the north.[44]

By September 9, all of Germany's gains from her spring and summer offensives had been lost.[45] In the month since the Battle of Amiens, when the counteroffensive had begun, the Germans had lost heavily in scarce war mate-

German Prisoners of War

riel and their most critical commodity, manpower. The compelling fact about these losses, however, was that the 100,000 prisoners who now filled the Allied POW cages exceeded the combined totals of all other types of casualties.[46] This was a sure sign of an army in the final stages of disintegration. To add to the worries of the harried German High Command, the American Expeditionary Force, of unknown but legendary size and strength, was about to initiate its first independent operation at the southern end of the line.

The Great American Army

General John Pershing had conducted a vigorous and, at times, acrimonious campaign against the French and British generals who desired to incorporate American battalions and divisions into their own armies. There was never a serious recommendation to use the American soldiers as individual replacements, but French and British political and military leaders felt that the relative inexperience of the American formations made their integration under the overall direction of the existing command structures the wisest course of action. It must also be remembered that when the American forces were becoming available, both the British and French were reeling under the offensive blows of the Germans, and it was only natural for them to wish to retain those spirited troops who were being trained under their guidance. It is also sometimes overlooked that in spite of Pershing's remonstrances, American divisions did remain with and fight under the command of Allied generals in several instances. This was particularly true of black regiments that were transferred to and equipped by the French. French social mores appeared to allow these fine black troops to fight more efficiently than they could under the conditions engendered by American segregation policies.

Pershing's letter of instructions from his government specifically stated that his army would be a distinct and independent force.[47] American leaders had to cope with the reality that their troops would never function effectively under foreign control; their spirit of national pride and individual independence prohibited such a system. The American public had belatedly but enthusiastically embraced the war against Germany, and expected Americans to be commanded by American generals and to achieve American victories.[48] During the initial period of training, which had coincided with the crisis of the German spring offensives, Pershing had allowed regiments and divisions to serve within British and French armies. But once his force was prepared to take the field as an independent army, he would not be coerced into allowing his men to remain under foreign command.[49] Finally, on July 27, during an inter-Allied conference at Bombon, Foch granted Pershing his own sector of the line and issued instructions to reduce the St. Mihiel salient.

The St. Mihiel sector of the line had lain quiet since the French had unsuccessfully tried to reduce the salient in 1915. The Germans remained entrenched on sacred French soil in this reminder of yet another offensive that had failed to achieve a breakthrough. Because it was viewed as a safe or "quiet" portion of the line, both sides had garrisoned it lightly and used it to rest and train their troops.[50] Therefore, it seemed the most logical area in which to establish the independent zone of the American force, which was about to come of age.

There were other considerations in the placement of this new army—an army that, it was hoped, would eventually tip the scales of battle in favor of an Allied victory. From the standpoint of preparation, the American units now streaming into France could complete their training and organize and equip themselves in relative safety while the major offensive blows were being struck in the north. Once prepared for battle, the American Expeditionary Force (AEF) could consolidate these new divisions with those that had been tested in battle and then conduct its first independent offensive operations. A new army, full of youthful enthusiasm and dedication, was to be christened in battle. Perhaps the most important consideration was the need for the soldiers and the American people to be rewarded with tangible success.[51] This requirement could be fulfilled in the sector around the St. Mihiel salient. Although the German defenses there fully incorporated the rugged terrain into their complex of fortifications, the line was manned by nine understrength divisions whose commanders realized their vulnerable position. In fact, the threat of an Allied offensive in this area caused Ludendorff to order an evacuation of the exposed salient as early as September 8.[52] The American divisions, which were two to three times the size of those of any other army, would be pushing against an enemy who was conducting a withdrawal; tactical success was assured.

The administrative and logistical requirements of warfare had now grown to the point where they nearly overshadowed all tactical or strategic considerations. The needs of an army of more than a million men was still another factor that dictated the selection of the southern portion of the trench line. The larger northern and western ports were fully committed to the support of the British and French forces. Therefore, food, clothing, ammunition, and the replacements for the AEF had to come through the southwestern and southern ports. These were serviced by railway lines that terminated in the new American portion of the line, thus avoiding the congestion around the Paris area.[53]

While strategic requirements were of relatively minor importance in the debut of the AEF, there were significant strategic advantages to an offensive in this area. First and foremost, it lay in the sensitive provinces of Alsace and Lorraine; renewed military activity in these lost areas could only revive the lagging spirits of the French nation. From a purely military standpoint, the salient held by the Germans was a constant threat to the fortress of Verdun. Any substantial Allied offensive from the Verdun or Nancy areas would be threatened by German retaliation from the rear. Beyond the rearward defenses of the *Michel Stellung* lay the ancient fortress complex of the Metz-Thionville. If these defenses could be breached, the Moselle River valley led directly to Coblenz and the Rhine River, the most formidable obstacle confronting any move into the German heartland. Additionally, this axis of advance would sever the main Metz-Lille lateral railroad line and seriously impair the usefulness of the Saar industrial area.* Such grand strategic plans, however, would have to await the solution of tactical and logistical problems that were deemed to be beyond the capacity of the fledgling American force to solve.

By August 30, Pershing's capable staff had prepared plans for the reduction of the salient and an advance of 10 miles beyond the base of the rearward German defenses on the *Michel Stellung*. The Americans had initially envisioned this initial advance as a prelude to their assault upon the formidable defenses of the fortified Metz area and the continuation of an independent American drive down the Moselle River valley into Germany.[55] In furtherance of this American concept, Foch and Pershing had viewed the operations on the American front as a part of the total program of reducing German-held salients to free the vital rail and road networks for the planned continuation of the offensive in 1919. (*See Atlas Map No. 23.*) By this time, however, British successes in the north had changed the entire strategic picture. Field Marshal Haig now sensed that the German Army was falling apart and could be defeated before the end of the year if the Allies continued to apply pressure on the retreating enemy. He therefore wished the Americans to abandon their independent operation around St. Mihiel and the offensive toward Metz, which would diverge from, or at least not support, the British drive planned against the rail junction of Aulnoye. The British commander requested that Pershing transfer his forces to the area of the Argonne

Forest and conduct an offensive toward the second vital rail junction at Mézières.[56]

This proposal for a combined advance of British and American armies, directed toward the isolation and destruction of the German armies in their fortified areas, was received enthusiastically by Foch. One reason for his enthusiasm was that Haig had couched his proposal in terms that promised an end to the war a year earlier than was predicted by even the most optimistic political or military leaders. Additionally, this course of action would place the French armies, under the economical Pétain, in the enviable position of simply holding on their front while the Americans and British defeated the main enemy forces. From his position on the left flank of the powerful AEF, Pétain and his countrymen could also exert a far greater influence upon the Americans than if they were advancing against Metz. The exuberant Foch, now armed with his new vision of offensive victory, went to Pershing's First Army headquarters at Ligny-en-Barrois to exert his authority and order a change of plans.[57] But he had not counted upon Pershing's singleness of purpose nor upon the AEF commander's spirit of independence.

As had Haig and Pétain before him, Pershing flatly refused to obey an order from Marshal Foch that he felt was not in the best interests of his national army. Pershing was willing to listen to the change of plans only so far as they concerned the continuation of the advance *after* the reduction of the St. Mihiel salient; this first step in the independent operation of the AEF, however, was not subject to discussion. He reluctantly agreed to shift his forces north to the area between the Argonne Forest and the Meuse River after the salient had been dealt with, but he would do so only on his own terms and as an independent army commander. To his credit, Foch realized that the momentum of the grand assault would be seriously impaired by an inter-Allied squabble over his authority, and so gave way gracefully on this point. What proved to be the final offensive of the Great War, therefore, was a product of several military minds forced into compromise by the press of events and the realities of command authority.

As mentioned previously, Ludendorff had ordered the evacuation of the St. Mihiel salient as soon as it became obvious that an attack on the German positions was imminent. By September 11, the garrison forces had begun to move heavy equipment and artillery pieces to the rear.[58] The long-awaited American attack came at 5:00 a.m. the next day, following a four-hour bombardment by more than 3,000 Allied artillery pieces. The assault of the Americans from both flanks of the salient was supported almost entirely by Allied equipment. In compliance with the wishes of his Allied comrades, Pershing had emphasized the shipment of infantry and machinegun units to France during the

---

*This point has been the subject of profound controversy. Pershing, Major General Joseph Dickman, and Brigadier General Douglas MacArthur felt that the tremendous strategic potential here warranted continuing the offensive and that the problems involved were not insurmountable. However, Lieutenant General Hunter Liggett, generally conceded to have been the AEF's best field commander, stated: ". . . the possibility of taking Metz . . . existed only on the supposition that our Army was a well coordinated machine which it was not as yet." Remembering this frustrating situation, Generals Omar Bradley and George Patton would not pass up the same strategic opportunity in the same area during the Second World War.[54]

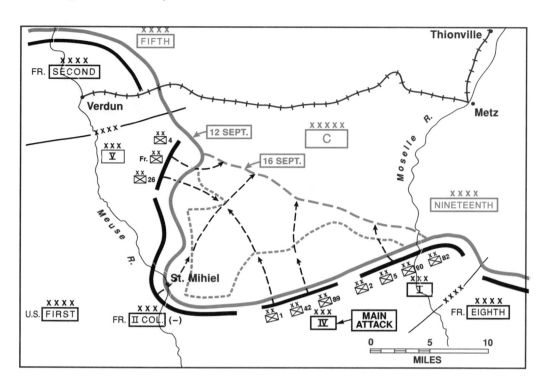

**The St. Mihiel Offensive,
September 12–15, 1918**

dark days of spring, and therefore was heavily dependent upon British and French units and weapons for his combat support.[59] Most striking was the air support provided for the advancing infantry. Colonel William Mitchell, the tactical commander of the American air forces, led a mixed organization of 1,400 planes flown by American, British, French, and Italian pilots.[60]

Acting in the dual capacity of commander of the AEF and commander of the newly formed American First Army, Pershing ordered the I and IV Corps on the southeastern

French 320-mm Railroad Artillery Supports the American Offensive in St. Mihiel

face of the salient to launch the main attack. The Franco-American V Corps was to conduct the supporting attack from the west, while the French Colonial II Corps conducted holding operations on the nose of the salient. The advancing infantry encountered only scattered resistance, and by the evening of the twelfth they had effectively trapped the remaining German defenders in the pocket. Within 36 hours, more than 15,000 German prisoners and 450 guns became the military fruit of the AEF's first independent victory.[61] This baptismal battle gave the American force practical experience, confidence in its leadership, and momentum. It also stripped yet another area from the hard-pressed Germans, and freed the Allied communications around the southern portion of the trench line. As agreed in the compromise between Foch and Pershing, however, the scope of the operation had been limited. The Americans now began shifting combat and support units north to the area of the Meuse River and the Argonne Forest, where they relieved the French of a new 90-mile sector in preparation for the final concentric drive of the war.

The Final Moves

The strategic plan for the offensive with which Foch hoped to end the war was simple and straightforward. Based upon the denial of the lateral railway system to the enemy, the plan highlighted the importance placed upon logistical considerations. (*See Atlas Map No. 23.*) The southern, or American, portion of the operation between the Meuse and Aisne

Rivers was aimed at the seizure of the Mézières-Sedan junction of this line. If the 25 miles between the American front and the Meuse could be traversed rapidly, more than three-quarters of the German frontline forces would be cut off from their southern alternatives to retreat and forced to rely on the constricted axis of Namur to Liège. The northern arm of the pincers was the responsibility of the British, who were given the objective of securing the rail junction at Aulnoye. If the two arms converged before the defenders could react, there was little doubt that the war would end before the rains of late autumn forced a halt to active field operations. Unfortunately, the tactical implementation of this strategy would be anything but simple. Despite the decreased efficiency of the German defenders, the British would have to overcome the most strongly prepared portions of the Hindenburg Line with forces that had been involved in constant fighting for the past month and a half.[62]

On the new American front, the task assumed by General Pershing was monumental. The transfer of the American forces to the Meuse-Argonne area required the movement of more than 600,000 troops and 93,000 horses, plus supporting equipment, over a 60-mile distance.[63] This task was accomplished within 14 days over three farm roads, which also had to support the withdrawal of the French units being relieved. Such an operation would have severely challenged the capabilities of even the most experienced army with a highly efficient staff. That the new American army was able to carry it out was truly remarkable and a credit to its small core of experienced staff officers. Due to the pressure of time, it was not possible to move the most seasoned American units from the St. Mihiel area. But Pershing stood ready to carry out his mission on September 26.[64] (*See Atlas Map No. 22.*)

Naturally, the enemy was fully aware of the vital nature of this area to his continued existence on the Western Front. During the past four years, the defensive arrangements had been worked out in this relatively untroubled zone. The meticulous care expended upon the defensive zone, combined with the hilly and broken terrain, boded ill for the attackers. There were other avenues of approach to the final objective much more conducive to the conduct of an offensive, but the pressure of time as well as America's desire for independence from French tactical direction demanded the selection of this zone, which bristled with defenses to a depth of 14 miles.[65]

Although expecting an attack, the Germans were dumbfounded when Pershing commenced his offensive so quickly after the major effort at St. Mihiel.[66] As a result, the five weak trench divisions manning the forward defensives were overwhelmed on the first day by the Americans, whose numbers were four to eight times greater than their enemy's. This advance of the Yanks greatly exceeded that of the French on their left. On the morning of September 27, stagnation of the advance, so familiar to other armies, became evident on the American front. The operation suffered from the very haste in which it had been mounted, and the inadequate logistical preparation that produced congestion and confusion.[67] The Americans' most valuable combat asset, superior numbers, soon became a serious problem, as units piled up against the methodical defenses in the heavily wooded terrain. By the first week in October, it was evident that the advance was not achieving the necessary forward movement, despite the frightful casualties suffered by the valiant American soldiers. Foch was dismayed as the tactical problems his American forces encountered endangered his dream of early victory.[68]

The northern pincer was greatly assisted by a detailed plan of the Hindenburg Line that had been captured during the Battle of Amiens.[69] Profiting from an exact knowledge of the location of all German defensive positions on the Fourth Army front, artillerymen were able to pinpoint their targets in the preparation that began on the evening of September 26. German command facilities, artillery positions, and troop shelters were soaked with thousands of tons of a new form of mustard gas.[70] On September 27, the British First and Third Armies moved out and captured the area around Cambrai, finally securing the elusive Bourlon Woods, which had foiled their actions a year earlier.[71] The next day, a combined force of Belgian, British, and French units moved forward in Flanders, capturing the pockmarked battlefield in front of Ypres. On the twenty-ninth, the British Fourth Army, supported by the French, managed at last to breach the legendary Hindenburg system.[72] However, the great hopes of forcing the enemy out into the open were not fully realized; the attackers paused as they marshaled support for a continuation of the advance.

The Allied advance along the most heavily fortified front ever constructed had begun with encouraging results, but by the first week in October it had stalled all along the line. The secondary attack in Flanders had bogged down in the all too familiar conditions of autumn rain and mud. The brilliant British assault on the Hindenburg Line had succeeded, but at such a heavy cost that Haig's armies required a regrouping of their resources before resuming the advance. On the Meuse-Argonne front, the Americans were only beginning to sort out their organizational and logistical problems before they could continue their move against the grimly efficient defenders of the *Kriemhilde* position in the Meuse Valley and the Argonne Forest.[73]

Events on the battlefield, however, were now waning in importance as diplomatic and political moves within the German nation overshadowed them. On September 29, as a result of the collapse of Bulgaria and the breach of the Hindenburg Line, Ludendorff had again reacted emotionally and advised the Kaiser to seek an immediate armistice. This time, Wilhelm had accepted the advice and appointed the liberal Prince Max of Baden as chancellor, hoping that his reputation for moderation and honor would enable him to negotiate a peace. Although Prince Max wanted a breathing space to enable him to bargain more effectively, on October 4 he finally acceded to the wishes of the OHL and telegraphed President Wilson an offer to end hostilities on the basis of the Fourteen Points.[74] Throughout the following weeks, the Allied armies continued to grind forward at a slow pace as the exchange of diplomatic notes continued. The final message from Wilson was received in Berlin on October 23. The terms offered were barely discernable from unconditional surrender.[75] On October 26, Ludendorff, now showing signs of reversing his views about wanting an armistice, was asked to resign. By this time, Germany's social and political condition at home was playing an increasingly more important role in the decisions of the Kaiser and his advisers. Revolution and riot now plagued the embittered homefront. In an attempt to preserve what remained of internal stability, Prince Max authorized the dispatch of a peace delegation on November 6.[76]

On November 8, in a railway station in the Compiègne Forest, the civilian delegates of the Imperial German Government met with Marshal Foch. The delegates humbly accepted Foch's armistice conditions, which were designed to insure Germany's complete inability to resume hostilities. The armistice commenced at the eleventh hour of the eleventh day of November, 1918. The Great War was over.

The final series of Allied offensives had redeemed the military policies of attrition on the Western Front. Given the strategic realities of an impregnable front that rested both flanks on impassable obstacles, only two strategic alternatives were open to secure victory by offensive means. One was to defend on the Western Front while attempting to defeat the enemy in other theaters, such as the Eastern Front or Salonika. The other—and the course chosen by a long list of commanders on both sides—was to continuously wear down the enemy's combat forces, consuming his strength in materiel and manpower reserves. Then, when the propitious moment arrived, the Allies would conduct a series of coordinated attacks, either to break through the enemy defenses or to collapse them. The decision as to which was the correct strategy determined if a strategist was an Easterner or a Westerner.

The first course of action was attempted by supporting the operations of the Russian Army and by opening theaters of war in Italy, Salonika, and the Middle East. But these moves ultimately had little real effect upon the outcome of the war. Until Germany, the driving force of the Central Powers, could be defeated, the war would drag on.

On the other hand, the strategy of attrition that has so repulsed generations of students of the Great War was a prodigal one for both defender and attacker. The key for the Allied generals was to determine when the time had come to mount the final series of attacks. On numerous occasions prior to 1918, the generals had optimistically assumed that the enemy was on his last legs and had ordered their million-man armies into the jaws of a still powerful defense. In many ways, Ludendorff's 1918 offensives achieved what the initiative of the Allies could not. These attacks eroded German combat power beyond the point of effective defense. Once the German forces had been weakened to this extent, the time was ripe for the coordinated counteroffensive. The widely dispersed offensives conducted by the Allies from July 18 until the end of the war achieved success because they were sprung at exactly the right time and were able to maintain the proper momentum. Momentum was achieved by suspending one phase after it had encountered stiff resistance and immediately opening a new one before the defenders could react. That this strategy was not necessarily dictated by Marshal Foch, as has often been suggested, in no way detracts from its effectiveness.

While these military operations were the immediate catalysts of the final collapse of Germany, their seeming inconclusiveness at the time has tended to obscure their value. The mental and physical collapse of the Second Reich occurred off the battlefield. The German troops marched back to their homes in an orderly fashion to be hailed as heroes. The war will of the nation had been broken by a combination of military operations, economic blockade, and exhaustion. Certainly, the end came more quickly than it would have if it had depended solely upon the advance of the Allied armies, but there seems to be little reason to believe that the German armed forces could have prevented eventual defeat. Total war had brought a new concept of battle. It had also brought an unfamiliar form of peace.

The First American Horse Drinks from the Rhine River

Notes

[1]Luigi Villari, *The War on the Italian Front* (London, 1932), pp. 168–174.

[2]John Buchan, *A History of the Great War* (4 vols.; Boston, 1922), IV, 395.

[3]Erich Ludendorff, *Ludendorff's Own Story* (2 vols.; New York, 1919), II, 117–118.

[4]Piero Pieri, "Italian Front," in Vincent J. Esposito (ed.), *A Concise History of World War I* (New York, 1964), pp. 172–173.

[5]Cyril Falls, *The Great War* (New York, 1959), pp. 383–384.

[6]C.R.M.F. Cruttwell, *A History of the Great War, 1914–1918* (Oxford, 1936), p. 599.

[7]Villari, *War on the Italian Front*, p. 201.

[8]Cruttwell, *Great War*, p. 600.

[9]James E. Edmonds, *A Short History of World War I* (New York, 1951), p. 363.

[10]Arno J. Mayer, *Politics and Diplomacy of Peacemaking* (New York, 1967), pp. 88, 197–198.

[11]Vincent J. Esposito, *The West Point Atlas of American Wars* (2 vols.; New York, 1967), II, Section 1, p. 45.

[12]Falls, *The Great War*, pp. 386–387.

[13]Cruttwell, *Great War*, p. 601.

[14]Pieri, "Italian Front," p. 176.

[15]"Terms of Armistice With Austria-Hungary," November 3, 1918 in Buchan, *History of the Great War*, IV, Appendix III.

[16]Richard Thoumin, *The First World War* (New York, 1963), p. 481.

[17]Frederick Maurice, *The Last Four Months* (Boston, 1919), pp. 90–91.

[18]Barrie Pitt, *1918, The Last Act* (New York, 1963), pp. 183–184.

[19]*Ibid.*, pp. 184–185. Accordingly. Lord Milner had revised Haig's orders in June. Letter, Lord Milner to Douglas Haig, June 21, 1918, in *The Diaries and Papers of Field-Marshal Sir Douglas Haig*, National Library of Scotland, H. 128.

[20]Cruttwell, *History of the Great War*, p. 543.

[21]James E. Edmonds (ed.), *History of the Great War: Military Operations, France and Belgium, 1918* (5 vols.; London, 1935–1947), III, 233–239. Hereinafter referred to as *BOH, 1918*: Basil H. Liddell Hart, *The Real War, 1914–1918* (Boston, 1930), pp. 424–427.

[22]Cruttwell, *Great War*, p. 544.

[23]Hubert Essame, *The Battle For Europe, 1918* (New York, 1972), pp. 86–92.

[24]Pitt, *Last Act*, pp. 185–192.

[25]Edmonds, *BOH, 1918*, III, 241–242.

[26]OHL memorandum, August 2, 1918, quoted in Edmonds, *Short History of World War I*, p. 339.

[27]Letter, General Foch to F.M. Haig, July 12, 1918, quoted in Edmonds, *BOH, 1918*, III, pp. 223–224.

[28]Letter, Field-Marshal Sir Douglas Haig to General Foch, O.A.D., 895, July 17, 1918, in Edmonds, *BOH, 1918*, III, p. 365, Appendix XVIII.

[29]Liddell Hart, *Real War*, p. 435.

[30]Edmonds, *Short History of World War I*, p. 341.

[31]Pitt, *Last Act*, pp. 201–202.

[32]Edmonds, *BOH, 1918*, IV, 9, 16–18; Pitt, *Last Act*, pp. 195–197.

[33]Winston S. Churchill, *The World Crisis, 1916–1918* (2 vols.; New York, 1927), II, 235. Churchill, who had written about his experiences as a POW during the Boer War, made these observations after visiting General Rawlinson's headquarters.

[34]Essame, *Battle For Europe*, p. 128.

[35]John Terraine, *The Western Front, 1914–1918* (Philadelphia, 1965), p. 174.

[36]Pitt, *Last Act*, p. 240.

[37]Ludendorff, *Own Story*, II, 326.

[38]Philip M. Flammer, "The Airplane in the Great War," in *Development of Airpower* (West Point, N.Y., 1973), pp. 1–11.

[39]Llewellyn Woodward, *Great Britain and the War of 1914–1918* (London, 1967), pp. 370–376.

[40]Pitt, *Last Act*, pp. 215–216.

[41]Ludendorff, *Own Story*, II, 347.

[42]C.R.M.F. Cruttwell, *The Role of British Strategy in the Great War* (Cambridge, 1936), pp. 87–90.

[43]Falls, *The Great War*, p. 380.

[44]Esposito, *West Point Atlas*, I, Section, p. 67.

[45]Buchan, *History of the Great War*, IV, 331.

[46]Edmonds, *BOH, 1918*, IV, 518.

[47]John J. Pershing, *My Experiences in the War* (2 vols.; New York, 1931), II, 243–246.

[48]Falls, *The Great War*, p. 356; Essame, *Battle For Europe*, p. 154.

[49]"Memorandum On Instruction of American Infantry Units Attached to Large French Units," *Grand Quartiers Général des Armées du Nord et des Nord-Est*, May 1, 1918. Translation with covering memorandum by AEF A.C. of Staff, G-5, Colonel H.B. Fisk, *United Stares National Archives*, Record Group 120, Folder 695–B.

[50]*American Battle Fields in Europe* (Washington, 1927), pp. 68–69.

[51]Cruttwell, *Great War*, p. 559.

[52]Ludendorff, *Own Story*, II, 361.

[53]Harvey A. DeWeerd, *President Wilson Fights His War: World War I and The American Intervention* (New York, 1968), pp. 211–212.

[54]Liddell Hart, *Real War*, pp. 458–459.

[55]Pershing, *Experiences in the War*, II, 262–263.

[56]Robert Blake (ed.), *The Private Papers of Douglas Haig, 1914–1919* (London, 1952), p. 325. Diary entry, August 27, 1918.

[57]Edward M. Coffman, *The War to End All Wars: The American Military Experience in World War I* (New York, 1968), pp. 270–271.

[58]*Ibid.*, p. 283.

[59]James G. Harbord, *The American Army in France, 1917–1919* (Boston, 1936), p. 417.

[60]William Mitchell, *Memoirs of World War I.* (New York, 1960), pp. 238–239.

[61]Edmonds, *Short History of World War I*, p. 359.

[62]Edmonds, *BOH, 1918*, V, 12–13.

[63]Coffman, *War to End All Wars*, pp. 303–310; Harbord, *American Army*, pp. 429–430.

[64]Pershing, *Experiences in the War*, II, 289–294.

[65]*American Battle Fields in Europe*, pp. 115–120.

[66]Buchan, *History of the Great War*, IV, 364–365.

[67]Pitt, *Last Act,* pp. 235–239.

[68]Churchill, *World Crisis,* II, 265.

[69]Cruttwell, *Great War,* pp. 568–569.

[70]*Ibid.,* p. 569.

[71]Edmonds, *Short History of World War I,* pp. 412–415. In the Battle of Cambrai, the British foundered at the Bourlon Woods.

[72]Essame, *Battle For Europe,* pp. 190–191. This occurred on October 5.

[73]DeWeerd, *President Wilson Fights His War,* pp. 354–360.

[74]Churchill, *World Crisis,* II, 269–271; Maurice, *Last Four Months,* pp. 173–176.

[75]"Terms of Armistice With Germany" signed 5:00 a.m., November 11, 1918 in Buchan, *History of the Great War,* IV, Appendix IV.

[76]Charles Seymour, *American Diplomacy During the World War* (Hamden, Conn., 1964), p. 362.

Aftermath: The Unfinished War

10

Dick turned the corner of the traverse and continued along the trench walking on the duckboard. He came to a periscope, looked through it a moment, then he got up on the step and peered over the parapet. In front of him beneath a dingy sky was Beaumont Hamel; to his left the tragic hill of Thiepval. Dick stared at them through his field glasses, his throat straining with sadness. . . . "This land here cost twenty lives a foot that summer. . . . See that little stream—we could walk to it in two minutes. It took the British a month to walk to it—a whole empire walking very slowly, dying in front and pushing forward behind. And another empire walked very slowly backward a few inches a day, leaving the dead like a million bloody bugs. No Europeans will ever do that again in this generation."

F. Scott Fitzgerald, *Tender is the Night*

On November 9, 1923, the fifth anniversary of the proclamation of the Weimar Republic, General Erich Ludendorff provided a tragicomic footnote to his brilliant military career. At the head of a column of 3,000 Nazi storm troopers, shoulder-to-shoulder with Adolf Hitler and the leadership of the Nazi Party, the befuddled former supreme war lord of the German Army was attempting to overthrow the new state and establish an anti-Communist dictatorship. Bitter over the loss of the war and the harsh peace terms imposed by the victorious Allies, Ludendorff was willing to assist the motley collection of thugs and murderers composing the Nazi Party because they called for a return to the greatness of the German Empire and a renunciation of the Treaty of Versailles.[1]

The night before, in the so-called Beer Hall Putsch,

Hitler had intimidated the three leaders of the Bavarian State into supporting his movement. In order to lend credence to the rebellion with his famous name, Ludendorff had been hurriedly recalled from an unfamiliar existence as a writer and publisher of rightwing tracts and apologies for the lost war. The agreements of the Bavarian triumvirate, forced from them at gunpoint, however, were repudiated the next morning. By then, the Government and the Army, under General Hans von Seeckt, were attempting to restore order. In a last-ditch attempt to save the revolution, Ludendorff gambled all on the charisma of his name and the respect that German soldiers would have for his general's uniform. Accordingly, he ordered that the Nazi column march to the relief of Ernst Roehm and his small detachment, which was surrounded by the local police in the War Ministry building.[2]

After pushing through several small police roadblocks, the column wended its way along Berlin's narrow *Residenzstrasse*. At the end of this gully-like street, however, 100 armed policemen blocked the way; these would not yield. When Hitler's personal bodyguard invoked the name of "His Excellency Ludendorff" and called on the police to surrender and join the revolt, a shot rang out. This signaled the firing of volleys from both sides. Hitler, his arm entwined with that of a mortally wounded comrade, fell to the ground and quickly stole from the scene. The revolution had been crushed. Only Ludendorff and his military aide remained standing in the face of the police rifles; the rest of the leaders were dead or wounded, or had fled. This lonely and pitiful remnant of the great Imperial German Army calmly strode up to the police line and was promptly arrested.

The symbolic collaboration of the man who had been the *de facto* commander of the German Army in 1918 with Adolf Hitler, a lowly lance corporal in that same organization, attests to the confusion and unrest that plagued Germany in the postwar era. The political and economic instability of the German Federal Republic was

**General Erich Ludendorff, the Former German War
Lord, with Members of the Nazi Party on the Day
of Their March on the War Ministry Building**

only one of the legacies of the Great War. Within two decades, the complex problems either caused or compounded by the four years of world war would lead to a continuation of the hostilities. This first stirring of the fascist Nazi movement in Germany, however, was largely ignored as a seeming aberration on the road back to a peaceful and prosperous state. As one of the early events in the regrettable series of miscalculations that would lead to another war among the nations of Europe, it does not concern us at this writing. Rather, we shall turn our attention backward to the period immediately following the war and attempt to assess the effect of the Great War upon the societies and armies of 1919.

An Assessment

The final armistice agreement of the Great War* was signed by the civilian representatives of the German Republic at 5:10 a.m. on November 11 in Marshal Foch's drawing room railway carriage.[3] In order to keep the stain of surren-

---

*The persistent use of the term Great War by the author is influenced by the most common name used by the participants. Because it was known as the European War in a neutral United States, this inaccuracy continues in many libraries today. It was also called the World War by societies never expecting a recurrence of such a widespread conflict. From the standpoint of geographical scope, it was less extensive than the Seven Years' War between the French and British Empires. The term First World War was, perhaps, coined by Colonel Charles A'Court Repington in his memoirs published in 1920. The fact that this term was accepted long before another worldwide conflict appeared certain may attest to the insensibility of the postwar generation, which could deal with such a horrible concept without serious thought or reservation.

der from the Army,[4] Field Marshal von Hindenburg had specifically refused to allow a military man to head the German delegation. Matthias Erzberger, representing the Chancellor, headed the delegation, which was escorted across the line to Rethondes in the Forest of Compiègne. The Allies were represented by Marshal Foch and Admiral Rosslyn Wemyss, the British First Sea Lord. In this august company, Erzberger was told what was expected of his country.

None of the Allied field commanders was present at the armistice meeting, but they all had been consulted regarding the terms that should be imposed on Germany. Reflecting the youthful buoyancy of his army and the fact that less than half of his forces had arrived in the line, Pershing wanted to continue the advance into Germany and impose an unconditional surrender. Pétain, while demanding the imposition of harsh terms on the Germans, reiterated that the French offensive capability was extremely limited and that peace must come soon. In assessing the situation, Haig was the most realistic. Although his armies had achieved the significant victories that had caused the Germans to ask for an armistice, Haig saw that his forces were tired and in need of time for recuperation and resupply. In his view, the Americans were undergoing extreme growing pains, and because of inexperience, lacked sophistication in battle. As for the French, he noted that Pétain's forces had not acted aggressively in recent months, being content to follow the advance of the Americans and British. Therefore, Haig stated that only moderate demands should be made upon the Germans—ones sufficient to insure peace. He concluded his recommendations with an expression of Great Britain's traditional view of a balance of power on the Continent and the need to promptly assimilate Germany into the family of nations.[5] After considering the views of his field commanders, Foch concurred with the majority, favoring the imposition of harsh and humiliating terms.[6]

The terms imposed by the Allies assured that Germany could not resume hostilities, even if she had the desire to do so.[7] The Germans were forced to agree to the evacuation of all invaded territories and the provinces of Alsace and Lorraine. They had to surrender to the victors a huge stock of modern weapons, including all of their submarines and most of the High Seas Fleet. Under the agreement, the Treaties of Brest-Litovsk and Bucharest—which the German Empire had imposed upon Russia and Rumania, respectively—were abrogated. Moreover, the Allies demanded the right to occupy all German territory west of the Rhine River and three bridgeheads over that obstacle. Barely three weeks later, their armies marched into the German homeland, establishing enclaves of 30 kilometers' radius each at Mainz, Coblenz, and Cologne in order

Marshal Ferdinand Foch Imposed Harsh Terms of Armistice On Germany. In 1940, This Same Railway Carriage Would Serve as the Site for French Capitulation.

to enforce the terms of the armistice and, later, the peace settlement.[8]*

The conclusion of hostilities at the eleventh hour of the eleventh day of the eleventh month of 1918 provided an orderly conclusion to a most confusing war. Nearly all of the units on both sides of the line complied with their instructions to cease firing and assume a defensive posture. The exuberant artillerymen of the United States Army, however, vied for the honor of firing the last round of the war,[10] and it took orders from increasingly higher authorities before the gunners would cease firing. In some locations, the truce came as a blessing, and the men rose from their subterranean trench homes, for the first time able to stand erect in what had been No Man's Land. Small groups from opposing sides made contact and joined in spontaneous celebration. However, these isolated scenes of fraternization were quickly suppressed by the military chain of command; after all, this was only an armistice, and the men might soon have to return to the work of a soldier.[11]

As might be expected, the reaction to the news of the armistice varied on the different homefronts. In London, the pent-up emotions of the British exploded into a gay and carefree celebration upon the eleventh stroke of the chimes of Big Ben. Happy crowds surged toward Buckingham Palace, where they sang "God Save the King" as their monarch appeared to address them. On this occasion, it probably mattered little that he could not be heard through

the din of the crowd and had to retire to his chambers after numerous appearances. In New York City, the festivities were delayed by the time zone differential. But in Times Square, a celebration, equally as emotional and joyous as that in Trafalgar Square, was held after breakfast. The people of Paris greeted the news in a more somber and reserved manner. France had suffered much more heavily, and her people responded to the occasion with dignified, if weary, resignation.

The scenes in the capitals of the Central Powers were decidedly morose. The news of defeat piling onto the already difficult living conditions in Germany and Austria-Hungary was more than many could bear. Winter was approaching, and food and fuel stocks were inadequate. Because the Royal Navy would not lift the economic blockade for another six months, there was little reason to believe that the situation would improve.[12] In both countries, the Spanish influenza was claiming thousands of victims each day in populations now worn to the point of exhaustion. Even the spiritual underpinnings of the people had been destroyed. To those who had been brought up with a great respect for authority and the rigid class system, the departure of their monarchs* and the establishment of participatory democracy was a psychological blow that jarred their sense of order. Revolution by Communists in Berlin and by separatists in Bavaria added to the confusion of the transfer of power to the Republic,[13] even though the return of the German Army

*Wilhelm's abdication was announced by Prince Max of Baden on November 9, the same day on which the Weimar Republic was proclaimed. Fearing for his safety, the Kaiser fled to Holland the next day. In Vienna, Charles abdicated on November 12. The Austrian and Hungarian Republics were proclaimed respectively on November 13 and November 16.

The Allies Celebrate Their Victory at the Arch of Triumph in Paris

---

*The American army of occupation remained at Coblenz until January 1923 when it was withdrawn over the strong protests of Marshal Foch. The British contingent departed in December 1929, but the French and Belgian troops remained to enforce the peace treaty until June 1930.[9]

from the front in formation would bring a semblance of order to the chaos of the homefront. Although the soldiers were used to suppress the revolution, many eventually joined what were called the *Freikorps,* and drifted eastward in an attempt to hold German gains from the Treaty of Brest-Litovsk.[14] In the former domains of Austria-Hungary, separatist revolts had already split the country into its component parts. A mood of uncertainty prevailed throughout Central Europe, but it was plain that the rule of the Hapsburgs was over. While Russia had officially been out of the war for more than a year, on November 11 bitter fighting continued throughout the country as supporters of the new Communist regime battled with reactionary armies and the contingents of Allied troops sent to support them. The defeat of Germany had negated the territorial provisions of the Treaty of Brest-Litovsk, and the question of boundaries on the Soviet Union's western frontiers would not be settled for many years.

The guns lay silent on all fronts. Europe—indeed the world—now had the painful job of counting the costs of total war. Through more than 50 months of prodigal conflict, people on both sides of the line had been sustained by the vision of a peace that would in some way justify the privation and death with which it was being purchased. With the conclusion of hostilities, the hopes of one side lay in ruins; it would be only a matter of time before the victors realized that their hopes were also to remain unfulfilled. From the beginning, World War I had been a war of frustrated dreams.

The first groundless hopes had been for a quick and economical victory. During the early months of war, phrases such as "the troops will return before the leaves fall from the trees" and "we shall return before Christmas" indicated the almost universal belief that modern war in 1914 would be a bloody but quick and decisive affair.[15] This idea was soon dashed against the hastily improvised defenses in the West, and invalidated by the open spaces and poor communications of the East. Although signaled by earlier experiences in America and Asia, technological advances in weaponry, combined with the large conscript armies of the major belligerents, gave a decided but unexpected advantage to the defensive form of warfare. This, in turn, stood in the way of achieving victory through a series of decisive battles.

When it became obvious that the war would be a prolonged affair, the nations set about mobilizing their total resources to support a war of attrition. Each month, the war grew remorselessly in scope and intensity, consuming ever greater quantities of material resources and precious human lives. In an attempt to bypass the stalemate and achieve victory through maneuver, leaders desperately sought ways to outflank the direct confrontation and cut costs. While these moves by the western Allies, including the opening of new

Harnessed to Support the War of Attrition, Industry Produced Great Weapons

theaters of war, never seriously threatened the Central Powers, they did serve to *increase* the costs of the war.

Shortly after its outbreak, the civilian populations of Belgium, northern France, and Eastern Europe felt the vise-like grip of war in a very personal way. Total war demanded the complete subjugation and tacit cooperation of all those living in occupied territories.[16] Soon, even those civil populations far from the areas of combat began to feel the physical effects of the fighting. Strategic bombing, long-range artillery, and the commerce-raiding tactics of the submarine, brought death and privation to noncombatants who had never anticipated playing a role in war.

As the demands of the war grew, new and ever more stringent methods of controlling and mobilizing the economic and human resources of the nation states were introduced. Great Britain's shift from applying a traditionally liberal approach to the war in 1914 to exercising a high degree of control over society in 1918 provides the most striking example of the pervasiveness of the war's influence.

In 1914, Winston Churchill coined the phrase "business as usual" to express England's hope that the war would affect her to a very limited degree.[17] Many thought that the Royal Navy would provide the only significant British contribution to the war. In this scenario, the British Expeditionary Force would serve merely as a token to stress the solidarity of the Anglo-French effort. Besides, most leaders thought that the war would be over before a more

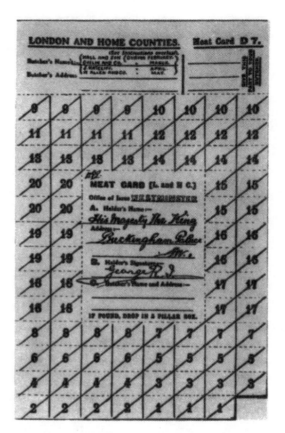

The War Brought with It New Forms of Governmental Control, Such as Meat Ration Cards

thorough mobilization could be accomplished. When the "wastage" at the front began to drain the French Army of its lifeblood, the BEF was forced to assume an ever greater role. The British nation had to turn first to large volunteer armies and then to conscription and rationing in order to prosecute the war. These measures tended to blur the social class distinctions that had endured for centuries.[18] Gradually but inexorably, the entire structure of Great Britain was modified by the war experience, as was its own relative position of power and leadership in the British Empire and the world. By 1918, during the vociferous "Coupon Election," Sir Eric Geddes coined another phrase—"Squeeze the Germans until the pips squeak"—in a reference to the British public's desire to impose the most stringent terms upon the defeated Central Powers.[19] The war demonstrated that four years of bloody fighting sufficed to transform benevolent democratic states into thoroughly vindictive belligerents who demanded the utmost in retribution from the enemy who had caused them to suffer.[20]

Naturally, patriotism and xenophobia were two emotional responses to war that were vital to the success of the political leaders as they strove to maintain the full support of their people. These emotions were manipulated with great skill by a new breed of propagandist, who came to the fore during the war. Using motion pictures, along with more traditional mass circulation newspapers and vivid posters, these dedicated men enthralled the imagination of the great mass mind.[21] Unexpectedly, the democratic societies of the West proved much more skillful in this new field than did the autocratic Central Powers. Compared to the imaginative and demonic propaganda campaigns of the French, British, and Americans, attempts by the Germans to justify the morality and legality of their position were often clumsy and inappropriate.

The goading of the American people into almost unanimous support for the war was a truly remarkable achievement. After more than three years of strict neutrality, the American public clamored for an unconditional surrender of the enemy. Among the great powers, the United States was the nation that most strongly favored continuing the war into German territory. This rapid reversal of public opinion was due in large measure to the machinations of the United States Committee of Public Information, headed by George Creel.[22] Americans who had marched in pacifist parades only months before enthusiastically participated in loyalty rallies and huge Liberty War Bond Drives. The nation's heroes—soldiers, movie stars, and athletes—led the patriotic movement to support the war. The writers of Tin Pan Alley were called upon to provide a musical expression of the changed attitude toward the war. The American public's hopes for total victory and a peace based upon idealistic virtues would eventually lead to great disappointment and bitterness. When peace came, it neither followed a total victory nor took the form that political leaders had promised.

At war's start, the people had eagerly sent their men off to fight the "perfidious Hun," to assist God in punishing England, or "to make the world safe for democracy." However, when the end finally came and millions of these young men did not return, these same people were equally violent in their denunciation of the futile conflict. In any event, the new methods of influencing public opinion had served their purpose by maintaining support on the homefronts almost up to the bitter end. These methods and the successes of the various propaganda ministries would not go unnoticed in the postwar years. They would serve as models for such diverse efforts as Franklin D. Roosevelt's New Deal and Joseph Goebbels' vast program of mind control in Nazi Germany.[23]

The families of the soldiers at the front early on became accustomed to the endless stream of casualty lists and the formal notifications that a loved one was either dead or wounded. The enormity of the conflict, however, often prevented accurate tallies, and it would be years before even realistic approximations of the cost of the war could be made. A total of 67,438,810 troops were mobilized to fight the war. Of these, the Allies lost a total of 5,152,115 killed in action as compared to 3,386,200* for the Central Powers.[25] These figures do not take into account civilian deaths.† Casualty figures, however, are an extremely poor method of weighing the suffering caused by the fighting, the disruption of families, and the traumatic shock that left the world numb and beyond caring for the endless stream of official statistics. When the wounded, prisoners of war, and missing are added to the roster, the total number of direct military casualties known or surmised by the governments stands at some 37.5 million. When casualties are viewed as a percentage of mobilized strength, Austria-Hungary suffered proportionally the heaviest toll at 90 percent, while the British Empire suffered the smallest number of casualties at under 36 percent. The United States, whose troops were only engaged in the last four months of fighting, had more than 8 percent of its 4,335,000 mobilized soldiers killed, wounded, or lost.[27] While loved ones mourned the human toll, statisticians and economists attempted to place a dollar value on the physical destruction caused either directly or indirectly by the fighting.

The economic costs of the war were truly staggering. While they were not of the magnitude of the subsequent war, they far exceeded the cost of any previous war. The most significant fact about the costs of this war is that they were extracted from societies that were in the habit of balancing national budgets and strictly accounting for international debts in hard currencies.[28] The debts of the First World War were never really settled, a situation that introduced an era of instability on the world financial scene. The Allies spent nearly $126 billion as opposed to more than $60 billion for the Central Powers.‡ Even the neutral states were forced to spend nearly $2 billion to protect their borders and interests.[29]

These figures are only a cold and misleading summation of the economic costs of the war. By disrupting the world's work and commerce, by siphoning off the manufacturing capabilities of nearly all of the industrialized nations, and

America's Unknown Soldier Comes Home from the War

by killing or maiming millions of the world's most productive and imaginative young men, the war proved to be truly cataclysmic in its effect on economic development. Perhaps most tragically, the experiences of the First World War inured the sensibilities of man to total war. Twenty years later, the costs of the Second World War, greater in virtually all aspects, were accepted without question.[30]

The war was financed by increased taxation, deficit financing, extensive war loans either from other nations or from the people in the form of war bonds, and voluntary contributions. When the war ended, all of these, except the last, were expected to be repaid. For example, the United States had lent $4,316 million to Great Britain during the war, but Great Britain had made loans to her allies in the amount of $8,695 million. Thus the interdependence of the world's economies demanded that either all pay their debts or all forgive them.[31] The war debts remained, however, and became a great incentive for those seeking reparations from the defeated powers in the peace settlement. Public officials, earlier so expert at rallying their people to the cause of war and financing the mammoth enterprise, now had the awesome task of putting the world back together. In this they would find themselves unequal to the task.

One of the greatest stumbling blocks to a realistic peace settlement was the existence and propagation of dangerous myths about the nature of the postwar world. Each of the powers that imposed the settlement had dreams of the world in 1914 to which it could not return, or hopes of increased national power and wealth that were illusory. This situation was fueled by a belief that the defeated nations could somehow bear all of the costs of the war and repair

---

*Some sources assume that approximately one half of the number listed as missing and prisoners actually died. If this perfectly reasonable calculation is accepted, the military dead totaled 9,265,279 for the Allies and 3,725,291 for the Central Powers. These same sources also assume that civilian deaths equaled those of the military at 12,990,570. This figure still does not fully account for civilian deaths caused indirectly by the war.[24]

† The great Spanish Influenza Epidemic, which was indirectly caused by the war, alone claimed between 10 and 27 million lives.[26]

‡The Carnegie Endowment for International Peace calculated that the indirect costs of the war constituted an additional $151,646,942,560, for a grand total or nearly $338 billion. These costs included such valid items as lost production, value of property destroyed, and war relief. There is one inane entry that placed a dollar value upon the war dead. Based upon a sliding scale for each nation, values ranged from $4,720 for each American to $2,020 for each Russian. This exercise illustrates the fascination of the people of the time with the precise costs of the war in order to present their bills to the reparations committees.

all of the damage done. In truth, however, these nations could hardly keep their own people fed and clothed.

Throughout the war, many national leaders played upon the growing spirit of nationalism, which had been a dominant movement throughout the last half of the nineteenth century. With little regard for the political realities of the postwar era, they expressed strong support for the concepts of national self-determination, democracy, liberalism, and—above all—perpetual peace. In their quest to restore the international balance, order, and prosperity of the prewar period, however, these leaders could not count upon a perfectible and resurgent world; new concepts of warfare, morality, and centralization had made it impossible to return to the conditions of 1914. New forces, such as socialism, communism, and the growing awareness of the lower economic classes and women, prevented forever a return to the halcyon days of the nineteenth century.

President Woodrow Wilson, perhaps the most idealistic of the world leaders, addressed the American nation regarding the task that lay ahead:

> The Armistice was signed this morning. Everything for which America fought has been accomplished. It will now be our fortunate duty to assist by example, by sober friendly counsel and by material aid in the establishment of a just democracy throughout the world.[32]

Wilson's promises could never be fulfilled, and his rhetoric merely encouraged aspirations that would end in bitter disappointment. The President would become the tragic symbol of the death of idealism and its replacement by cynicism.

In fact, however, the end results of the war did seem to vindicate democracy and the Western conception of liberalism. Autocratic regimes had been toppled everywhere by the conflict. (*See Atlas Map No. 51.*) The great democratic states had led the way to final victory. Czarist Russia, an embarrassing anomaly in the Entente alliance, had fallen under the double blows of defeat on the battlefield and revolution at home.[33] Even though a more ruthless and autocratic Bolshevik form of government had replaced the old one, it was generally assumed that this was a passing phase that would soon give way to democracy and self-determination. The Allies were even willing to assist this process by allowing military expeditions to land in northern Russia and Siberia to fight the Red armies alongside the reactionary White forces.

The 503-year reign of the envied and hated house of Hohenzollern had come to an end with the abdication of Kaiser Wilhelm II. Even before his departure, the German *Reichstag* had changed its constitution in order to make the Government responsible to the people's elected representatives.[34] Later, the Weimar Republic would attempt to rule the shaky remnants of the Second Reich.

In central Europe, numerous successor states emerged spontaneously from the ruins of the ancient Hapsburg Empire. Austria, Hungary, Czechoslovakia, Yugoslavia, and parts of a new Polish state were carved from the Austro-Hungarian Empire.[35] From the crumbling domains of the perennial "sick man" of Europe—the Ottoman Empire—emerged the Republic of Turkey, reduced considerably in size and influence. The demise of this relic of the past left the entire Middle East open to nationalist bickering and the competition of the European powers for new colonial mandates.[36]

It is from the First World War that the enmity between Arab and Jew dates. The Arabs had been led to believe that their active support of British military operations against the Turks would be rewarded by the establishment of independent nations following the war. In November 1917, however, in direct contradiction to this policy, British Foreign Secretary Arthur Balfour issued his government's invitation to the Jewish people to re-establish their national home in Palestine. Neither of these promises were kept after the war. T.E. Lawrence, who had so ably led the Arab irregular forces in support of Allenby's conventional forces, was so disgusted by his government's lack of integrity that he discarded his military decorations and refused to accept his nation's gratitude for his exploits.

This brief account of the political and diplomatic problems that lingered after the war should indicate that there was much truth in Marshal Foch's dismissal of the peace settlement as being merely the beginning of a 20-year armistice.

The Military Perspective

The military developments of the First World War have often been cavalierly dismissed as insignificant. While most observers grant that great technological advances were made during the conflict, little attention has been given to the concomitant advances in military theory and doctrine. The following assessment of the effects of the war, excerpted from a respected military text, is typical of most evaluations:

> Therefore, it is a war remembered chiefly for the mass employment of new weapons. . . . Innovations in strategy and tactics were rare. The few that appeared were usually ignored or misunderstood, especially by the victorious Allies.[37]

To the contrary, the conduct of the war had brought about a dizzying transformation in military tactical doctrine. Early in the war, the machinegun and rapid-firing artillery relegated the formerly pivotal massed infantry formations to a position of secondary importance. As attrition became

**French Cavalrymen Look to Their Replacement,
the Airplane**

decentralization of control. Of course, this method also depended heavily upon the revolutionary technology of gas warfare to pave the way for the advance.

Coincidentally, all of these methods of breaking the tactical stalemate required massive logistical support in order to succeed. As a result, by the end of the war, all of the belligerents possessed logistical systems that would have boggled the minds of the prewar military planners.

In condemning the dearth of tactical innovation in the First World War, many students conveniently forget that the stalemate was broken in the final year. This in no way excuses the tremendous losses that were incurred in the process of finding the solution, but it does emphasize the fact that several answers were eventually found. Virtually all of the weapons and tactical concepts with which the Second World War was fought were in existence and had been proved in 1918.*

Postwar revulsion with warfare, coupled with the inertia of military institutions, tended to obscure the military lessons of the war experience. The American, French, and

---

*The one notable exception to this statement is the introduction of atomic weapons during the Second World War. However, these devices were used in the very last months of World War II, and therefore really mark the beginning of postwar military doctrine.

the generally accepted method of wearing down enemy defenses before attempting a breakthrough, unfamiliar concepts had to be dealt with by the military leadership of both sides. The first reaction to the seeming impregnability of the defensive lines was to pour more firepower onto the defenders. Even today, the brutal offensives at Verdun and the Somme mark the zenith of this approach.

Another answer to the problems posed by trench stalemate was provided by the internal combustion engine. The development of the tank and the refinement of the airplane were made possible by great advances in technology. As with all such revolutionary technological advances, these had to be fitted into the overall scheme of tactical employment. The halting steps taken to integrate these weapons into battle doctrine throughout 1916 and 1917 bore fruit in 1918. This is an undeniable fact, despite the valid criticism that the military leaders were often too inflexible to appreciate new concepts.

The German Army pointed the way to achieving decisive victory without complete dependence upon technology. It must be remembered that Germany, alone among the major belligerents, gained experience on both the Eastern and Western Fronts, and therefore could evaluate theories in light of the vastly different conditions on the two fronts. The efficient German General Staff analyzed the problems of trench warfare and decided that these could be solved by relying on the traditional techniques of surprise, training, and military professionalism. They developed infiltration assault tactics and returned the infantryman to his position of central importance in battle. This concept called for specialized training, indoctrination, complete surprise, and the

There are times when Private Lightfoot feels absolutely convinced
that it's going to be a War of Exhaustion

**Despite the Period of Open Warfare That Ended
the War, Most Would Remember the Misery
and Comradery of the Trenches**

British military and naval establishments soon tried to return to many of their prewar doctrines. Once their large conscript armies had been demobilized and the Regular officers had returned to the more comfortable surroundings of peacetime, the military men seemed to forget the glaring realities of warfare in the twentieth century. The victorious Allied armies appeared to be echoing the ludicrous comment of one regimental officer: "Thank Heavens the war is over, now we can get back to real soldiering."

Among the Allies, only in France were the professional military planners forced into a completely transformed concept of warfare. Since France had suffered such grievous losses in the fighting, she could no longer tolerate a return to the prewar doctrine of offensive warfare. Instead, the French Army developed a pessimistic defensive approach to warfare that relied upon the continuous front, permanent fortifications, and reaction to enemy initiative. This development, however, sprang more from the necessities of her postwar shortage of manpower than from any perceptive deductions drawn from wartime experiences.

In Germany and Russia, the two significant powers that had experienced defeat, a different postwar attitude prevailed in military circles following the war. The Weimar Republic, restricted to a professional army of 100,000 men, was able to prune off the wartime leadership and search for new theories and methods, unencumbered by the vested interests of the old military bureaucracy. General Hans von Seeckt, the guiding spirit behind the interwar military developments in Germany, was able to enforce a rigid adherence to traditional precepts of professionalism in the Army, making it the finest and most forward-looking military service in the world. It would only require a strong political leader to free it from the military restrictions of the Versailles Treaty, thereby permitting its transformation into the most powerful military force. In the Soviet Union, changing internal power relationships caused the Red Army to remain in a state of flux throughout the interwar period. Nevertheless, the Army continued to play a vital role in the life of the nation, and never suffered from the neglect common to the armed forces of the Western democracies. In fact, during the early part of the interwar period, Germany and the Soviet Union cooperated closely in developing new equipment and doctrine for warfare.

The Victor's Peace

In 1918, the great democracies of the world—the United States of America, Great Britain, and France—bestrode the world as unquestioned victors. Having endured the debilitation of the World War, they would dictate the peace terms. Because the large number of nations in the alliance* at the conclusion of hostilities precluded any attempt to decide upon peace terms in general session, the work was assigned to a committee of 10 of the larger nations.[38] This committee was further reduced to a nucleus of the three great powers and the second ranking power of Italy. In fact, Italy's representative, Premier Vittorio Orlando, was often absent from the consultations and was included only when his nation's territorial settlements were being discussed.[39]

World leaders knew the initial costs of the war—nearly 10 million dead soldiers and uncounted numbers of dead civilians, billions of dollars lost, and the resources of nature scattered on the battlefields. But the deeper changes in the political and economic structure of the world could only be guessed by the time the delegates convened in Paris in January 1919. Although deep feelings of hatred and revenge existed in most of the Allied delegations to the conference, these emotions were most evident in French Premier Georges Clemenceau. He had witnessed the humiliation of France in 1871 and the invasion of the nation again in 1914. It was France's fervent desire to protect herself from any future threat from a resurgent German state that would enable Clemenceau to dominate the formulation of the final peace terms.[40]

Great Britain's Prime Minister, David Lloyd George, represented the more pragmatic and less emotional desire of his nation and his King's Empire to secure a balance of power on the Continent. Unfortunately, he had chosen to conduct a national election immediately prior to the peace conference in order to strengthen his bargaining position. This "Coupon Election" soon degenerated into an emotional outpouring against the hated enemy. Slogans such as "Hang the Kaiser" and "Make Germany pay every last penny," vividly expressed the rabid demands of the British electorate. Although Lloyd George's coalition government was returned with a large majority, the emotions provoked by the election severely hampered the British delegation's ability to moderate the more extreme views of the French.[41]

As emphasized throughout America's participation in the war, she sought a "peace without victors." This was the official policy of Woodrow Wilson, who led his Democratic Party into the congressional elections of November 1918.[42] The American voters, however, had apparently had enough of idealism, because they returned Republican majorities in both houses. The business-dominated Republican Party, in favor of advancing American commercial interests in the peace settlement, played upon the aroused emotions of the people for a return upon their investment of blood and money.[43] Therefore, Wilson, while immensely popular with the people of Europe, was representing a minority party at

---

*The Allied nations numbered 32.

The "Big Four": Orlando, Lloyd George, Clemenceau, and Wilson

the convention. Yet the peace treaty that he signed would eventually have to be ratified by a hostile Congress. Wilson deluded himself into thinking that the tumultuous welcome he received from the people of Europe signaled the support of the people of the world for his idealistic peace proposals. In fact, these demonstrations were merely an expression of gratitude for the American assistance that had saved the Allies from defeat. The power of public opinion, a force recently emphasized by the war, would dominate the politicians who sat down to chart a new course for the civilized world.

The world of 1919 was particularly changed from the standpoints of ideology and power. (*See Atlas Map No. 52.*) Although most leaders either refused or were unable to recognize the fact, the center of world power had inexorably shifted away from Europe. The old power had been replaced by two new powers—the United States of America and the Union of Soviet Socialist Republics. To differing degrees, both were isolated from the diplomatic, social, and economic flow of events in the postwar world; this unfortunate situation compounded the instability of international relations. These growing superpowers were imbued with new political doctrines that would have a momentous impact on the twentieth century. Both states represented radical shifts from the old world's traditional ideologies. The United States championed the egalitarian philosophy of national self-determination, which was based upon a vague belief in the righteousness of democracy and capitalism; the Soviet Union espoused the secular theology of Marx and Lenin, which called for the overthrow of capitalism and the

establishment of a dictatorship of the proletariat. Neither of these concepts was in accordance with the practical power politics of European leaders. But Europe was no longer the seat of world power, and the traditional goal of its diplomats—a balanced power structure on the Continent, coupled with dictation of policy throughout the world—was no longer valid. It would, however, take the trauma of a worldwide economic depression and a second devastating war to enforce the acceptance of these realities.

It would be presumptuous to attempt to convey in any single work the numerous and far-reaching effects of the Great War. Aside from being a physically impossible task,

President Woodrow Wilson, the Symbol of Idealism, Is Greeted Throughout Europe as a Hero

it should be evident that the consequences of this conflict are still being felt today and may never be fully appreciated. The changes wrought during the 52 months of world war affected every aspect of man's endeavors—from military operations to the manner in which he records the hours of the day.* The physical toll of the fighting was appalling.

*Daylight-saving time was introduced by the English in 1916 in order to conserve energy and increase productivity in manufacturing facilities.

But an even greater result was the damage done to the psychological underpinnings of society. No longer could men view the future with complacency and optimism. An era of international mistrust, insecurity, and irrationality had been ushered in. The doleful prediction of a British statesman that the war would extinguish the lamps all over Europe had been all too accurate. They were, in fact, extinguished throughout the world and have yet to be rekindled.

Notes

[1]The description of the Beer Hall Putsch and the march on the War Ministry building is taken from William L. Shirer, *The Rise and Fall of the Third Reich* (New York, 1960), pp. 52–75.

[2]D.J. Goodspeed, *Ludendorff, Genius of World War I* (Boston, 1966), pp. 301–302.

[3]Ferdinand Foch, *The Memoirs of Marshal Foch,* trans. by T. Bentley Mott (Garden City, N.Y., 1931), pp. 476–486.

[4]James E. Edmonds, *A Short History of World War I* (London, 1951), p. 425; Paul von Hindenburg, *Out of My Life* (2 vols.; New York, 1921), II, 272–278; Erich Ludendorff, *Ludendorff's Own Story* (2 vols.; New York, 1919), II, 429.

[5]Robert Blake (ed.), *The Private Papers of Douglas Haig, 1914–1919* (London, 1952), pp. 330–336; Foch, *Memoirs,* pp. 459–461.

[6]Hubert Essame, *The Battle for Europe, 1918* (New York, 1972), pp. 199–200.

[7]John Buchan, *A History of the Great War* (4 vols.; London, 1922), IV, App. IV.

[8]Edmonds, *Short History of World War I,* p. 427.

[9]Vincent J. Esposito, "Western Front, 1918: The Year of Decision," in Vincent J. Esposito (ed.), *A Concise History of World War I* (New York, 1964), p. 135.

[10]Buchan, *History of the Great War,* IV, 417–418.

[11]Barrie Pitt, *1918, The Last Act* (New York, 1963), p. 271.

[12]The Naval Blockade was rigorously enforced through March 1919 and was not completely lifted until mid-July. Winston S. Churchill, *The Aftermath, 1918–1928* (New York, 1929), pp. 56–57.

[13]Cecil F. Lavell, *Reconstruction and National Life* (New York, 1919), pp. 56–73.

[14]H.W. Kock, "The Freikorps," in Peter Young (ed.), *History of the First World War* (8 vols.; London, 1969–1971), VIII, 3181–3189.

[15]Cyril Falls, *The Great War* (New York, 1959), pp. 32–40.

[16]C.R.M.F. Cruttwell, *A History of the Great War, 1914–1918* (Oxford, 1936), p. 624.

[17]Winston S. Churchill, "Speech at Guildhall," November 9, 1914, in John Bartlett (ed.), *Familiar Quotations,* 13th ed. (Boston, 1955), p. 868.

[18]Arthur Marwick, *The Deluge: British Society and the First World War* (Boston, 1965), pp. 299–310.

[19]Eric Geddes, "Address to the Cambridge Conservative Association," November 1918, in Philip Burnett, *Reparation at the Peace Conference* (2 vols.; New York, 1940), I, 12. This phrase was a slogan derived from Geddes' exact words: ". . . the Germans, if this Government is returned, are going to pay every penny; they are going to be squeezed as a lemon is squeezed—until the pips squeak."

[20]Paul Birdsall, *Versailles, Twenty Years After* (Hamden, Conn., 1962), p. 4.

[21]Arthur Ponsonby, *Falsehood in Wartime* (New York, 1971), pp. 13–29.

[22]Frederic L. Paxson, *American Democracy and the World War* (3 vols.; Boston, 1939), II, 283–285.

[23]Harvey A. DeWeerd, *President Wilson Fights His War: World War I and the American Intervention* (New York, 1968), pp. 243–244.

[24]Ernest L. Bogart, *Direct and Indirect Costs of the Great War* (New York, 1920), passim; Esposito, *Concise History,* pp. 363–369.

[25]As noted in the text, the exact casualty figures for the war will never be fully resolved. The author has consulted the official statistics of the major belligerents as well as the following works: Cruttwell, *Great War;* Young, *History of the First World War;* Esposito, *Concise History;* and Irving Werstein, *1914–1918, World War I* (New York, 1966), which reproduces the statistics of the United States War Department.

[26]Cruttwell, *Great War,* p. 624; Young, *First World War,* VII, 2973–2978; Adolf A. Hoehling, *The Great Epidemic* (Boston, 1961), passim.

[27]Charles F. Horne (ed.), *Source Records of the Great War* (7 vols.; Washington, 1923), VII, 135; Esposito, *Concise History,* p. 372.

[28]Ernest L. Bogart, *War Costs and Their Financing* (New York, 1921), pp. 1–6, 82–86.

[29]Esposito, *Concise History,* pp. 363–369.

[30]John M. Clark, *The Costs of the World War to the American People* (New Haven, Conn., 1931), pp. 215–217.

[31]Harold G. Moulton and Leo Pasvolsky, *World War Debt Settlements* (New York, 1929), pp. 130–133; David Lloyd George, *The Truth About Reparations and War Debts* (New York, 1932), pp. 122–129.

[32]Woodrow Wilson, "Proclamation of the Armistice with Germany," November 11, 1918 in James B. Scott (ed.), *Official Statements of War Aims and Peace Proposals* (Washington, 1921), p. 474.

[33]Edmonds, *Short History of World War I,* pp. 261–266.

[34]Gerhard Schulz, *Revolutions and Peace Treaties, 1917–1920,* trans. by Marian Jackson (London, 1972), pp. 105–123.

[35]Victor H. Rothwell, *British War Aims and Peace Diplomacy, 1914–1918,* (Oxford, 1971), pp. 245–249; Birdsall, *Versailles,* p. 7.

[36]James T. Shotwell, *At the Paris Peace Conference* (New York, 1937), pp. 93, 201.

[37]Vincent J. Esposito, (ed.), *The West Point Atlas of American Wars* (2 vols.; New York, 1959), II, 71.

[38]Churchill, *The Aftermath,* pp. 194–197.

[39]Harold Nicolson, *Peacemaking, 1919* (New York, 1939), pp. 163–171.

[40]Georges Clemenceau, *Grandeur and Misery of Victory,* trans. by F.M. Atkinson (New York, 1930), pp. 145–165.

[41]Lloyd George's reasonableness was indicated in a speech that he made the day following the armistice: ". . . the conditions of peace . . . must lead to a settlement which will be fundamentally just. No settlement which contravenes the principles of eternal justice will be a permanent one. . . . Let us be warned by [the example of the peace of 1871]. We must not allow any sense of revenge, any spirit of greed, any grasping desire to override the fundamental principles of righteousness." "Address to Liberal Party Leaders," November 12, 1918 in Scott (ed.), *War Aims and Peace Proposals,* p. 473.

[42]Because of his party's defeat in these elections, President Wilson was unable to obtain the Senate's approval of the peace treaties or the entry of the United States into the League of Nations. The United States negotiated bilateral peace treaties with Germany and Austria in November 1921, three years after the armistice. Thomas A. Bailey, *Woodrow Wilson and the Great Betrayal* (New York, 1945), pp. 352–353.

[43]Bailey, *Woodrow Wilson,* pp. 118–120.

EPILOGUE

The Great War differed from all ancient wars in the immense power of the combatants and their fearful agencies of destruction, and from all modern wars in the utter ruthlessness with which it was fought. All the horrors of all the ages were brought together. . . . Every outrage against humanity or international law was repaid by reprisals often on a greater scale and of longer duration. . . . When all was over, Torture and Cannibalism were the only two expedients that the civilized, scientific, Christian States had been able to deny themselves: and these were of doubtful utility.

Winston S. Churchill, *The World Crisis*

Selected Bibliography

General

Baldwin, Hanson. *World War I, An Outline History.* New York, 1962. Brief but perceptive study of the entire war.

Cruttwell, C.R.M.F. *A History of the Great War, 1914–1918.* Oxford, 1936. Perhaps the finest single-volume history of the war. Contains provocative opinion as well as a narrative description of the flow of war.

Edmonds, James E. *A Short History of World War I.* London, 1951. Despite its title, this work provides very useful detail on many military aspects of the war. Compiled by the editor of the British official history of the war.

Esposito, Vincent J. (ed.). *The West Point Atlas of American Wars.* 2 vols. New York, 1959. Volume II, pages v-71, provides an excellent outline of the military operations of the war.

Falls, Cyril. *The Great War.* New York, 1959. A complete view of the conflict. Slightly biased toward the British outlook.

Liddell Hart, Basil H. *The Real War, 1914–1918.* Boston, 1930. While omitting certain vital portions of the war, this volume provides a personal account that dares to lay blame for the tremendous frustration that existed on World War I battlefields.

Marshall, S.L.A. *The American Heritage History of World War I.* New York, 1964. The narrative highlights most important issues of the war. The photographic coverage is superb.

Woodward, E. Llewellyn. *Great Britain and the War of 1914–1918.* London, 1967. Provides an excellent view of the diplomatic pressures that influenced the conduct of military operations. Also gives a useful summary of the war in the air and at sea.

Battles and Campaigns

Allen, William E.D. and Paul Muratoff. *Caucasian Battlefields.* Cambridge, 1953. Long and detailed, but the only good account of the Russian-Turkish theater available in English.

Barker, A.J. *The Bastard War.* New York, 1967. A thorough account of the Mesopotamian Campaign up to 1918. Very pro-British.

Bradley, John. *Allied Intervention in Russia.* New York, 1968. Traces the development of the combined expeditions of the western Allies into Russia. Beginning with the attempt to reinvigorate the Eastern Front, the narrative extends to the Allies' active intervention on behalf of the reactionary White Russian elements.

Churchill, Winston S. *The Unknown War.* New York, 1931. Pro-Allied view of the operations on the Eastern Front.

Coffman, Edward M. *The War to End All Wars: The American Military Experience in World War I.* New York, 1968. This work is useful in understanding the tremendous organizational and logistical problems involved in fielding the American Expeditionary Force.

Essame, H. *The Battle for Europe, 1918.* New York, 1972. A brief, thoughtful account of the battles in the last year of the war.

Falls, Cyril. *Armageddon: 1918.* New York, 1963. A complete, accurate, and reasonably short account of the Battle of Megiddo.

Golovin, N.N. *The Russian Army in World War I.* New Haven, 1931. Excellent account of the Russian military system.

Horn, Daniel. *The German Naval Mutinies of World War I.* New Brunswick, N.J., 1969. Excellent treatment of the rebellion of the admirals and the mutiny of the navy that culminated in the Revolution in Berlin in November 1918.

Horne, Alistair. *The Price of Glory, Verdun 1916.* New York, 1963. Part of a trilogy on French military campaigns. This is a lucid and stirring account of the bloodiest campaign of the war.

Legg, Stuart. *Jutland.* New York, 1967. The best short treatment of the battle.

Marder, Arthur J. *From Dreadnought to Scapa Flow: The Royal Navy in the Fisher Era, 1904–1919.* 5 vols. London, 1970. An objective analysis of the war at sea, this exhaustive study gives due recognition to the exploits of other nations and frequently highlights misconceptions of naval warfare on both sides.

Moorehead, Alan. *Gallipoli.* New York, 1956. The best single book on the Gallipoli Campaign. Although it contains no documentation, it is accurate.

Palmer, Alan. *The Gardeners of Salonika.* New York, 1965. The author feels that the object of the Salonikan Campaign was worthwhile, but that tactical and strategic blunders negated its potential.

Pitt, Barrie. *1918, The Last Act.* New York, 1963. With the skill of a journalist, the author makes the events of the fateful final year of the war realistic and understandable.

Ritter, Gerhard. *The Schlieffen Plan: Critique of a Myth.* New York, 1958. A definitive critique of the fabled German mobilization plan that was implemented in 1914.

Rommel, Erwin. *Infantry Attacks.* Trans. by G.E. Kidde. Washington, 1944. Most useful for its description of the application of small-unit tactics to overcome stalemate.

Siney, Marion. *Allied Blockade of Germany, 1914–1916.* Ann Arbor, 1957. Excellent treatment of a most important but often unrecognized aspect of the great struggle.

Spears, E.L. *Prelude to Victory.* London, 1939. Personal account of a British liaison officer on the preparation and conduct of the Nivelle Offensive of 1917.

Terraine, John. *The Western Front, 1914–1918.* London, 1964. A collection of essays about several critical issues on the Western Front. The central theme is the costly stalemated nature of warfare in this theater.

Tuchman, Barbara W. *The Guns of August.* New York, 1962. An engrossing account of the events during August 1914 and the opening campaigns of the war.

Tyng, Sewell. *The Campaign of the Marne, 1914.* New York, 1955. An excellent, detailed account of the background and execution of the first campaign on the Western Front. Contains useful appendices of orders and tables of organization.

Watt, Richard M. *Dare Call It Treason.* New York, 1963. Fascinating account of one of the least known episodes of the war, the French Army mutinies of 1917.

Wavell, Archibald P. *The Palestine Campaigns.* London, 1928. A good account of the entire campaign.

Wolff, Leon. *In Flanders Field: The 1917 Campaign.* New York, 1958. This work vividly portrays the "blood and mud" of the Third Ypres Campaign, which, to many, has come to represent the frustrations of the entire war.

Political, Social, Economic, and Technological Issues

Albrecht-Carrié, René. *The Meaning of the First World War.* Englewood Cliffs, N.J., 1965. Summarizes the cataclysmic nature of the changes wrought in European society by the experiences of the war.

Brodie, Bernard and M. Fawn. *From Crossbow to H-Bomb.* Bloomington, Ind., 1962. Chapter 7 provides a nontechnical discussion of the development and refinement of the weapons used in the war.

Dooly, William G., Jr. *Great Weapons of World War I.* New York, 1969. Simple but extensive discussion of weapons development during the Great War.

Guinn, Paul. *British Strategy and Politics, 1914–1918.* London, 1965. Superb treatment of the growing problems of coordinating national aims with military resources.

King, Jere Clemens. *Generals and Politicians: Conflict Between France's High Command, Parliament and Government, 1914–1918.* Los Angeles, 1951. One of the few works in English that deals with the problems existing between France's military strategy and civilian political reality.

Maurice, Frederick B. *Lessons of Allied Cooperation, Naval, Military and Air: 1914–1918.* London, 1942. Study prepared for leaders of World War II on the practical problems of coalition war.

Millis, Walter. *Road to War: America 1914–1917.* Boston, 1935. Author accurately conveys the spirit of the American shift from neutrality to rabid support for the war.

Panichas, George A. (ed.). *Promise of Greatness: The War of 1914–1918.* London, 1968. A remarkable view of the Great War composed upon the fiftieth anniversary of the armistice. It places emphasis upon social and literary commentary.

Remak, Joachim. *The Origins of World War I, 1871–1914.* New York, 1967. An excellent interpretive essay on the numerous long-range causes of the war.

Trask, David F. *The United States in the Supreme War Council.* Middleton, Conn., 1961. One of the few works dealing with the vital Supreme War Council. Although written from the American perspective, it does explain the operation and effect of this unique body.

Personalities

Barnett, Correlli. *The Swordbearers: Supreme Commanders in the First World War.* New York, 1963. Vivid accounts of four pivotal leaders: Moltke, Jellicoe, Pétain, and Ludendorff.

Callwell, C.E. *Field-Marshal Sir Henry Wilson: His Life and Diaries.* London, 1927. Insights into the career of a political general without peer.

Coffman, Edward M. *The Hilt of the Sword: The Career of Peyton C. March.* Milwaukee, 1966. Biography of United States Army Chief of Staff during a period of critical military change in the American Army.

Goodspeed. D.J. *Ludendorff: Genius of World War I.* Boston, 1966. As the title indicates, a biased account of the man who became Germany's virtual dictator in the last two years of the war. Useful on interrelationships in the General Staff.

Hoffman, Max von. *The War of Lost Opportunities.* New York, 1925. The architect of the Central Powers' victory on the Eastern Front describes his conflicts with the enemy and his superiors.

Liddell Hart, Sir Basil H. *Colonel Lawrence, The Man Behind the Legend.* New York, 1934. The most objective book available on Lawrence of Arabia.

_____. *Foch, The Man of Orleans.* Boston, 1932. A fine picture of the man who directed the final Allied victory.

Ludendorff, Erich. *Ludendorff's Own Story, August 1914–November 1918.* 2 vols. New York, 1919. Naturally, the general attempts to cover his errors, but his breadth of knowledge and position make his perspective most interesting.

Pershing, John J. *My Experiences in the World War.* 2 vols. New York, 1931. A dry but detailed account of the formation, deployment, and combat actions of America's great army in the war.

Terraine, John. *Ordeal of Victory.* New York, 1963. Balanced, well-written biography of Field Marshal Sir Douglas Haig, perhaps the most misunderstood of the principal commanders.

Vandiver, Frank. *Black Jack: The Life and Times of John J. Pershing.* 2 vols. College Station, Tex., 1977. A recent biography with interesting new insights.

Wavell, Archibald. *Allenby: A Study In Greatness.* New York, 1941. Well-written and informative study of the career of one of the most popular heroes of the war.

Annexes

Annex A

Chronology of Events of World War I*

1914	WESTERN FRONT	EASTERN FRONT	BALKAN FRONT	ITALIAN FRONT
August	4—Germany Invades Belgium. Battles of the Frontiers and Great Retreat.	7—Russia Invades East Prussia. Battle of Tannenberg. 23—Hindenburg, Commander of Eastern Front.	1st Invasion of Serbia.	
September	Battle of the Marne. 1st Battle of the Aisne.	Galician Battles. 1st Battle of Masurian Lakes. German Operations in S.W. Poland.	2nd Invasion of Serbia.	
October	Outflanking to the Sea. 9—Antwerp Falls. Battle of Yser. 1st Battle of Ypres.	Russian Counteroffensive Against Silesia.		
November		Battle of Lodz.	3rd Invasion of Serbia.	
December	Battle of Givenchy.			
1915 January	Battle of Soissons. 19—German Zeppelin Raid on London.			
February	German Attacks in Champagne.	Winter Battle of Masuria.		
March	Battle of Neuve Chapelle.			
April	2nd Battle of Ypres (Poison Gas)			
May	2nd Battle of Artois. Battle of Festubert.			23—Italy Declares War on Austria-Hungary.
June	Battle of Argonne.			1st Battle of the Isonzo.
July		Gorlice-Tarnow Breakthrough and General Central Powers Advance.		2nd Battle of the Isonzo.
August				
September	Battles of Loos and Champagne.	5—Czar Nicholas, Commander of Russian Army.		
October			Final Invasion.	3rd Battle of the Isonzo.
November			Serbia Eliminated. Salonikan Front Established.	4th Battle of the Isonzo.
December	15—Gen. Haig, Commander of BEF.			

*1. Numbers denote day of month.   2. Battles designated on first day.

184

1916	WESTERN FRONT	EASTERN FRONT	BALKAN FRONT	ITALIAN FRONT
January			Austria-Hungary Overruns Montenegro. 16—General Sarrail, Allied Commander in Salonika.	
February				
March		Lake Narotch Operations.		5th Battle of the Isonzo.
April				
May				
June				Asiago Offensive.
July	Battle of Verdun.	Brusilov Offensive.	25—Serbian Army in Line.	
August		27—Rumania Joins Allies.		6th Battle of the Isonzo.
September	Battle of the Somme (Tanks Introduced).	Rumanian Offensive.		7th Battle of the Isonzo.
October		Rumania Eliminated.	Allied Offensive in Salonika.	8th Battle of the Isonzo.
November			19—Fall of Monastir.	9th Battle of the Isonzo.
December	12—Gen. Nivelle, Commander of French Army.			
1917 January				
February				
March	German Withdrawal to the Hindenburg Line.	1st Russian Revolution.		
April	Battles of Arras and 2nd Aisne (Nivelle Offensive).		Limited Operations and Advance to the Greek Frontier.	
May	15—Gen. Pétain, Commander of French Army.			10th Battle of the Isonzo.
June	Battle of Messines. 25—U.S. Troops Land in Europe.	4—Gen. Brusilov, Commander of Russian Army.		
July		Kerensky (2nd Brusilov) Offensive.		
August				
September	Third Ypres Campaign (Passchendaele).	Operations at Riga.		11th Battle of the Isonzo.
October		Bolshevik Revolution.		
November				Battle of Caporetto. 9—Gen. Diaz, Commander of Italian Army.
December	Battle of Cambrai.	5—Russian Armistice (Brest-Litovsk). 12—Rumanian Armistice.		

1916	WESTERN FRONT	EASTERN FRONT	BALKAN FRONT	ITALIAN FRONT
January			Austria-Hungary Overruns Montenegro. 16—General Sarrail, Allied Commander in Salonika.	
February				
March		Lake Narotch Operations.		5th Battle of the Isonzo.
April				
May				
June				Asiago Offensive.
July	Battle of Verdun.	Brusilov Offensive.	25—Serbian Army in Line.	
August		27—Rumania Joins Allies.		6th Battle of the Isonzo.
September	Battle of the Somme (Tanks Introduced).	Rumanian Offensive.		7th Battle of the Isonzo.
October		Rumania Eliminated.	Allied Offensive in Salonika.	8th Battle of the Isonzo.
November			19—Fall of Monastir.	9th Battle of the Isonzo.
December	12—Gen. Nivelle, Commander of French Army.			
1917 January				
February				
March	German Withdrawal to the Hindenburg Line.	1st Russian Revolution.		
April	Battles of Arras and 2nd Aisne (Nivelle Offensive).		Limited Operations and Advance to the Greek Frontier.	
May	15—Gen. Pétain, Commander of French Army.			10th Battle of the Isonzo.
June	Battle of Messines. 25—U.S. Troops Land in Europe.	4—Gen. Brusilov, Commander of Russian Army.		
July		Kerensky (2nd Brusilov) Offensive.		
August				
September	Third Ypres Campaign (Passchendaele).	Operations at Riga.		11th Battle of the Isonzo.
October		Bolshevik Revolution.		
November				Battle of Caporetto. 9—Gen. Diaz, Commander of Italian Army.
December	Battle of Cambrai.	5—Russian Armistice (Brest-Litovsk). 12—Rumanian Armistice.		

MIDDLE EASTERN FRONTS			POLITICAL AND DIPLOMATIC ACTIVITY	THE WAR AT SEA	1916
DARDANELLES	MESOPOTAMIA	PALESTINE			
Evacuation Completed.					January
					February
	Siege of Kut.		9—Germany Declares War on Portugal.	1—"Unlimited" German Submarine Campaign. 24—*Sussex* Torpedoed.	March
	Fall of Kut.		20—Germans Land Irish Rebels. 24—Irish "Easter Rebellion."	18—U.S. Note to Germany on *Sussex* Incident.	April
		British Advance and Clearing of the Sinai Desert.		Battle of Jutland	May
			8—Conscription Begins in Great Britain.	5—Earl Kitchener Drowned.	June
					July
			29—Field Marshal Hindenburg, German Chief of General Staff.		August
					September
			5—Central Powers Declare Poland Independent.		October
			7—President Wilson Reelected.	29—Admiral Jellicoe, 1st Sea Lord.	November
	Second British Advance.		5—Lloyd George, British Prime Minister. 12—German "Peace Note." 30—Allies Reject "Peace Note."		December
		British Arrive at at Turkish Border.		31—"Unrestricted" German Submarine Campaign.	1917 January
	2nd Battle of Kut.		3—U.S. Severs Ties With Germany. 17—Ribot, French Premier.		February
	Capture of Baghdad.	1st Battle of Gaza.	6—U.S. Declares War on Germany. 28—U.S. Conscription Law.		March
		2nd Battle of Gaza.			April
			11—King Constantine of Greece Abdicates.	15—U.S. Destroyer Flotilla Arrives in Europe.	May
			6—*Reichstag* Peace Vote. 17—Dr. Michaelis, German Chancellor.		June
			14—Papal Peace Proposal.		July
					August
					September
		3rd Battle of Gaza.			October
		Battles of Junction Station and Jerusalem.	1—Hertling, German Chancellor. 8—Bolsheviks Seize Power. 9—Allied Supreme War Council. 15—Clemenceau, French Premier.		November
				17—Admiral Wemyss, 1st Sea Lord.	December

1918	WESTERN FRONT	BALKAN FRONT	ITALIAN FRONT	MIDDLE EASTERN FRONTS		POLITICAL AND DIPLOMATIC ACTIVITY	THE WAR AT SEA
				MESOPOTAMIA	PALESTINE		
January						8—Wilson's "14 Points" Speech. 28—Labor and Food Strikes Begin in Germany and Austria-Hungary.	20—*Breslau* Sunk Near Dardanelles.
February						16—Gen. Wilson, Chief of Imperial General Staff.	1—Austrian Navy Mutinies.
March	THE GERMAN OFFENSIVES Somme Offensive.					3—Treaty of Brest-Litovsk. 5—Rumanian-Central Powers Peace Treaty Signed. 26—Allied Conference at Doullens on on Unity of Command.	
April	1—RAF Established. 14—Gen. Foch, Commander-in-Chief of Allied Armies. Lys Offensive.						22—British Naval Raids on Zeebrugge and Ostend.
May	Aisne Offensive.	Defensive Operations.					
June	Noyon-Montdidier Offensive.		Battle of the Piave.				
July	Champagne-Marne Offensive. THE REDUCTION OF THE SALIENTS.		15—Field Marshal Conrad Retires.			16—Ex-Czar Nicholas Executed.	
August	Aisne-Marne Offensive. 8—"Black Day" of German Army. Battle of Amiens. Lys Salient Evacuated.					1—Allied Expedition Lands at Archangel. 3—Allied Expedition Lands at Vladivostok.	
September	St. Mihiel Offensive.	Allied Offensive. Bulgarian Armistice.			Battle of Megiddo. Pursuit.	14—German Peace Offer to Belgium. 15—Austria-Hungary Suggests Peace Moves. 18—Allies Reject Peace Attempts. 29—Bulgaria Surrenders.	
October	Final Allied Offensives. 26—Gen. Ludendorff Resigns.		Battle of Vittorio-Veneto.		30—Turkish Armistice.	4—Germany and Austria-Hungary Request Peace on "14 Points." 16—Peace Demonstrations in Berlin.	
November	11—German Armistice. Allied Troops Enter Germany.		3—Italians Occupy Trieste.	Advance on Mosul.		3—Allied-Austria-Hungary Armistice. 9—Kaiser Wilhelm Abdicates. Revolution in Berlin. 13—Emperor Karl Abdicates.	3—German Navy Mutinies. 21—German Navy Surrenders.

Annex B
Selected Orders and Directives

This section consists of extracts and translations of several of the critical instructions issued during the war. They were selected because they are representative of the types of orders issued by the various headquarters.

When examining these instructions, the reader should observe the wide variation in style, format, and clarity. Appendices 1 through 6 cover the critical first months of the war on both the Eastern and Western Fronts. Appendices 7 through 12 constitute a group of orders issued by the western Allies in an effort to achieve unity of command. The final Appendix, 14, is an official order instructing Russian spldiers to democratize their units. This order destroyed the discipline and cohesiveness of the Russian Army.

Appendix 1

Austro-Hungarian Declaration of War on Serbia*

No. 3523. Handed in at Vienna July 28, 11:10 a.m., received at Kraguevitz 12:50 p.m.

The Royal Government of Serbia not having replied in a satisfactory manner to the note which was sent to them by the Minister of Austria-Hungary at Belgrade under date July 23, 1914, the Imperial and Royal Government finds itself obliged to provide for the safeguarding of its rights and interests, and for this purpose to have recourse to force of arms. Austria-Hungary therefore regards herself from this moment as in a state of war with Serbia.

The Minister for Foreign Affairs
of Austria-Hungary
COUNT BERCHTOLD

*James B. Scott (ed.), *Diplomatic Documents Relating to the Outbreak of the European War* (2 vols.; Oxford, 1916), I, 99.

Appendix 2

Grand Duke Nicholas' Orders to General Jilinsky (Commander of Northern Army Group) to Commence Invasion of East Prussia*

August 10, 1914

Germany has directed her main forces against France. Against us there may be assumed to be Four German Corps—Ist, XXth, XVIIth, and Vth, together with some Reserve Divisions and Landwehr Brigades. On our side, by the evening of the 12th day of Mobilisation (11th August), there will be concentrated in the First Army—All the Cavalry ($5\frac{1}{2}$ Divisions), IIIrd and IVth Corps, 5th Rifle Brigade, 28th Division (XXth Corps), and possibly Two Regiments of the 29th Division (XXth Corps)—in all, 96 Battalions and 132 Squadrons. The Guard and Ist Corps will not be included in the First Army, and it may be taken that this Army will have completed its concentration by the evening of the twelfth day (11th August).

The Second Army, except the XIIIth Corps, will complete its concentration earlier than the First Army. This Army will, by the evening of 12th day (11th August), be composed as follows—Four Cavalry Divisions, the IInd, VIth, XVth, XXIIIrd Corps, and the 1st Rifle Brigade—in all, 136 Battalions and 96 Squadrons. If Two Divisions and the 1st Rifle Brigade are excluded for the defence of Novo Georgievsk, the Second Army will contain 112 Battalions and 96 Squadrons.

Thus the total of the Armies of the North-West Front, by the evening of the 12th day (11th August), will be 208 Battalions and 228 Squadrons of field troops to oppose 100 Battalions of German field troops disposed in Four Corps.

Taking into consideration that war was first declared against us, France as our Ally has considered it her duty to advance against Germany immediately, in order to support us. Naturally, it is our duty to support France in view of the great stroke prepared by Germany against her. This support must take the form of the quickest possible advance against Germany, by attacking those forces left behind in East Prussia.

The First Army should commence its advance with the object of drawing upon itself the greatest possible enemy strength. The advance must be carried out North of the Masurian Lakes, turning the enemy's left flank.

The Second Army should advance round the South of the Masurian Lakes, with the object of destroying those German Corps concentrating between the Vistula and the Lakes, and of preventing the Germans from withdrawing to that river.

The closest liaison must be maintained between the First and Second Armies, a sufficient screen being placed in front of the Lake position.

The Advance of the Armies of the North-West Front should be in a position to commence on the 14th day of Mobilisation (13th August).

JANUSCHKEVITCH, Chief of Staff

*N.N. Golovin, *The Russian Campaign of 1914* (Fort Leavenworth, Kansas, 1933), pp. 42–43.

Appendix 3

General von Prittwitz' Order to the German Eighth Army to Establish Defense of East Prussia*

August 14, 1914
4 p.m.

1. It appears not unlikely that the enemy may advance South of the Forest of Rominten against the line of the Lakes. His advanced troops—Infantry and Artillery—are advancing from the line Gr. Czymachen-Mierunsken.

2. The Army will concentrate on its left flank to take the offensive against the enemy's advance.

3. The XXth Corps will advance to the neighbourhood of Ortelsburg. To this Corps falls the task of protecting the Army against any enemy advance South of Lake Spirding. An offensive against Johannisburg is to be kept in view, and the detachment at Bialla will therefore remain there for the moment. The 3rd Reserve Division, with the 6th Landwehr Brigade, will hold the line Nikolaiken-Lotzen. The Ist Reserve Corps will hold the line of the R. Angerapp, with its right wing on Lake Mauer. The XVIIth Corps will entrain via Allenstein and Konigsberg for Insterburg-Norkitten, and thence by road to Darkehmen.

The Ist Corps will remain for the moment at Gumbinnen-Insterburg.

The 2nd Landwehr Brigade will hold the line of the Memel.

The covering of the right flank of the Army against the, in any case, very unlikely event of a Russian advance from the Narew is placed in the hands of General von Unger with the following detachments:

   (a) Garrison of Thorn at Strasburg.
   (b) Garrison of Graudenz at Lautenburg.
   (c) 70th Landwehr Brigade at Mlawa-Soldau.
   (d) Garrison of Danzig at Neidenburg.

4. Reconnaissances will be carried out as follows:—

XXth Corps—Makow—Lomja—Osowiec.
3rd Reserve Division—Osowiec—Augustow.
1st Reserve Corps—Augustow—Suwalki—Wizanjny.
1st Corps—Przerosl—Kalwarja.
1st Cavalry Division—Wylkowyszki.

Air Reconnaissances:—

XXth Corps—towards and beyond the Narew.
Ist Corps—R. Niemen to Tilsit.

General Unger will issue his own instructions for reconnaissance of the line Ciechanow-Przasnysz.

5. Aviation Detachment 8 will be moved to Nordenburg, and will be placed at the disposal of the Ist Reserve Corps.

6. Rear Communications:—

XXth Corps—Allenstein—Osterode.
3rd Reserve Division—Lotzen—Rastenburg—Sensburg.
Ist Reserve Corps—Angerburg—Bartenstein—Bischofstein—Heilsberg.
XVIIth Corps—Darkehmen—Nordenburg—Gerdauen—Schippenbeil—Bartenstein.
Ist Corps—Insterburg—Jodlauken—Muldzen—Allenburg—Friedland—Pr. Eylau.
Konigsberg Garrison—Roads on each side of the R. Pregel to Konigsberg.

7. Headquarters will remain till the evening of the 15th in Marienburg, after that Bartenstein, opening at 12 noon on the 16th.

V. PRITTWITZ
Commander-in-Chief

*Sir Edmund Ironside, *Tannenburg: The First Thirty Days in East Prussia* (Edinburgh, 1925), pp. 88–90.

Appendix 4

General Joffre's Order to Abandon Plan XVII and Meet German Offensive In Northern France*

August 25, 1914

General Instructions No. 2 The Commander-in-Chief to the Army Commanders.

I. Having been unable to carry out the offensive manoeuvre originally planned, future operations will be conducted in such a way as to reconstruct on our left a force capable of resuming the offensive by a combination of the Fourth and Fifth Armies, the British Army and new forces drawn from the east, while the other armies hold the enemy in check for such time as may be necessary.

II. Each of the Third, Fourth and Fifth Armies, during its retreat, will take account of the movements of the neighbouring armies, with which they must remain in liaison. The movement will be covered by rear-guards left at favourable points in such fashion as to utilize all obstacles to halt the enemy's march, or at any rate to delay it, by short and violent counter-attacks in which artillery will be the principal element employed.

III. Limits of zones of action among the different armies:

Army W. (British):[†] Northwest of the line Le Cateau, Vermand and Nesle inclusive.

Fifth Army: Between the latter line (exclusive) to the west and the line: Rocroi, Liart, Rozoy-sur-Serre, Craonne (inclusive) to the east.

Fourth Army: Between the latter line (exclusive) to the west and the line: Stenay, Grand-Pré, Suippes, Condé-sur-Marne (inclusive) to the east.

Third Army (including the Army of Lorraine): Between the line Sassey, Fléville, Ville-sur-Tourbe, Vitry-le-François (inclusive) to the west and the line: Vigneulles, Void, Gondrecourt (inclusive) to the east.

IV. On the extreme left, between Picquigny and the sea, a defensive line will be held along the Somme by the Territorial divisions of the north (i.e. d'Amade's Group), having as reserve the 61st or the 62nd Reserve Divisions.

V. The Cavalry Corps is on the Authie, ready to follow the forward movement on the extreme left.

VI. Before Amiens, between Domart-en-Ponthieu and Corbie, or behind the Somme between Picquigny and Villers-Bretonneux a new group of forces will be constituted by elements transported by rail (7th Corps, four Reserve divisions, and perhaps another Active army corps) between August 27th and September 2nd.

This group will be ready to take the offensive in the general direction of St. Pol-Arras or of Arras-Bapaume.

VII. The Army W. (British), behind the Somme from Bray-sur-Somme to Ham, will be ready to move either towards the north on Bertincourt or towards the east on Le Catelet.

VIII. The Fifth Army will have its main body in the region Vermand, St. Quentin, Moy (offensive front) to debouch in the direction of the railway station of Bohain. Its right holding the line La Fère, Laon, Craonne, St. Erme (defensive front).

IX. Fourth Army: Behind the Aisne on the front Guignecourt, Vouziers, or in case this is impossible on the front Berry-au-Bac, Rheims, mountain of Rheims, always reserving means to take the offensive towards the north.

X. Third Army: Supporting its right on the fortress of Verdun and its left on the defile of Grand-Pré, or at Varennes, Ste. Menehould.

XI. All the positions indicated should be organized with the greatest care, so as to offer the maximum resistance to the enemy. We shall start from these positions on the offensive movement.

XII. The First and Second Armies will continue to contain the enemy forces which are opposed to them. In case of retirement they will have as zones of action:

Second Army: Between the road: Frouard, Toul, Vaucouleurs (inclusive) and the road: Bayon, Charmes, Mirécourt, Vittel, Clefmont.

First Army: South of the road: Châtel, Dompain, Lampain, Montigny-le-Roi (inclusive).

J. JOFFRE

*Sewell Tyng, *The Campaign of the Marne, 1914* (New York, 1935), pp. 369–371.

† For some unknown reason, the French referred to the British Expeditionary Force as L'Armée "W" throughout this war and into the Second World War. This may be a reference to General Henry Wilson, the prewar British planning officer, or it may refer to the Army of the West.

Appendix 5

General von Moltke's Directive Abandoning the Schlieffen Plan*

September 5, 1914

The enemy has eluded the enveloping attack of the I and II Armies and has succeeded, with a part of his forces, in gaining contact with Paris. Reports from the front and information from reliable agents lead furthermore to the conclusion that he is transporting towards the west forces drawn from the line Toul-Belfort and that he is also proceeding to withdraw forces from before our Armies III to V. It is therefore no longer possible to roll up the whole French army towards the Swiss frontier in a southeasterly direction. We must rather expect to see the enemy transfer numerous forces into the region of Paris and to bring up new forces in order to protect his capital and to threaten the right flank of the German armies.

The I and II Armies must therefore remain before the eastern front of Paris. It will be their mission to oppose offensively any enemy effort coming from the region of Paris and to lend each other mutual support in these operations.

The IV and V Armies are in contact with important enemy forces. They must endeavour to drive these forces back without respite in a southeasterly direction, which will have the effect of opening the passage of the Moselle to the VI Army between Epinal and Toul. One cannot as yet predict whether this operation, conducted in concert with the VI and VII Armies, will have the result of throwing important enemy forces against the Swiss frontier.

The VI and VII Armies will initially conserve their present mission of holding the enemy forces which are before their front. They will advance as soon as possible to the attack of the line of the Moselle between Toul and Epinal, covering themselves towards these fortresses.

The III Army will march on Troyes-Vendoeuvre; as circumstances dictate, it will be employed either to support the I and II Armies beyond the Seine in a westerly direction or to participate in a southerly and southeasterly direction in the operations of our left wing.

Accordingly, His Majesty orders:

I. The I and II Armies will remain facing the eastern front of Paris to oppose offensively all enemy attempts starting from Paris: the I Army between the Oise and the Marne; the crossings of the Marne below Château Thierry will be held to permit of passage from one bank to the other. The II Army between the Marne and the Seine; the possession of the crossings of the Seine between Nogent and Méry is very important. It is recommended to the two armies to keep the main bodies of their forces far enough away from Paris to be able to retain sufficient liberty of action for their operations. The 2nd Cavalry Corps will remain under the orders of the I Army and will transfer one division to the 1st Cavalry Corps. The 1st Cavalry Corps will remain under the orders of the II Army and will transfer one division to the III Army.

The mission of the 2nd Cavalry Corps will be to observe the northern front of Paris between the Marne and the Lower Seine and to reconnoitre between the Somme and the Lower Seine as far as the coast. Distant reconnaissance beyond the Lille-Amiens railroad line will be undertaken by the aviation of the I Army.

The 1st Cavalry Corps will observe the southern front of Paris between the Marne and the Seine below Paris; it will reconnoitre in the directions of Caen, Alençon, Le Mans, Tours and Bourges and should receive the aviation necessary for this purpose.

The two cavalry corps will destroy the railroad lines leading to Paris as near to the capital as possible.

II. The III Army will march on Troyes-Vendoeuvre. A division of cavalry will be transferred to it by the 2nd Cavalry Corps. Reconnaissance towards the line Nevers-Le Creusot, aviation necessary for this mission should be attached to it.

III. The IV and V Armies advancing resolutely towards the southeast will open the passage of the Moselle to the VI and VII Armies. Right wing of the IV Army by Vitry-le-François and Montierender, right wing of the V Army by Revigny-Stainville-Morlaix. With its left wing the V Army will cover the fortifications of the Meuse and will capture the Forts of Troyon, Les Paroches and the Roman Camp. The 4th Cavalry Corps will remain under the orders of the V Army. It will reconnoitre before the front of the IV and V Armies in the direction of the line Dijon-Besancon-Belfort. It will transmit information also to the IV Army.

IV. The mission of the VI and VII Armies remains unchanged.

VON MOLTKE

*Sewell Tyng, *The Campaign of the Marne, 1914* (New York, 1935), pp. 381–383.

Appendix 6

Instructions from Secretary of State for War, Earl Kitchener, to Field Marshal Sir John French, Commander BEF*

August 1914

Owing to the infringement of the neutrality of Belgium by Germany, and in furtherance of the Entente which exists between this country and France, His Majesty's Government has decided . . . to send an Expeditionary Force to France and to entrust the command of the troops to yourself.

The special motive of the Force under your control is to support and co-operate with the French Army against our common enemies. The peculiar task laid upon you is to assist the French Government in preventing or repelling the invasion by Germany of French and Belgian territory and eventually to restore the neutrality of Belgium, on behalf of which, as guaranteed by treaty, Belgium has appealed to the French and to ourselves.

. . . you will have every opportunity for discussing with the Commander-in-Chief of the French Army, the military position in general and the special part which your Force is able and adapted to play. It must be recognized from the outset that the numerical strength of the British Force and its contingent reinforcement is strictly limited . . . it will be obvious that the greatest care must be exercised towards a minimum of losses and wastage.

Therefore, while every effort must be made to coincide most sympathetically with the plans and wishes of our Ally, the gravest consideration will devolve upon you as to participation in forward movements where large bodies of French troops are not engaged and where your Force may be unduly exposed to attack. . . . In this connection I wish you distinctly to understand that your command is an entirely independent one, and that you will in no case come in any sense under the orders of any Allied General.

In minor operations you should be careful that your subordinates understand that risk of serious losses should only be taken where such risk is authoritatively considered to be commensurate with the object in view.

The high courage and discipline of your troops should, and certainly will have fair and full opportunity of display during the campaign, but officers may well be reminded that in this their first experience of European warfare, a greater measure of caution must be employed than under former conditions of hostilities against an untrained adversary.

You will kindly keep up constant communications with the War Office, and you will be good enough to inform me as to all movement of the enemy reported to you as well as to those of the French Army.

I am sure you fully realize that you can rely with the utmost confidence on the whole-hearted and unswerving support of the Government, of myself, and of your compatriots, in carrying out the high duty which the King has entrusted to you and in maintaining the great tradition of His Majesty's Army.

KITCHENER

*James Edmonds (ed.), *History of the Great War: Military Operations, France and Belgium, 1914* (2 vols.; London, 1937), I, 499.

Appendix 7

Instructions from Secretary of State for War, Earl Kitchener, to General Sir Douglas Haig, Commander BEF*

December 28, 1915

1. His Majesty's Government considers that the mission of the British Expeditionary Force in France, to the chief command of which you have recently been appointed, is to support and cooperate with the French and Belgian Armies against our common enemies. The special task laid upon you is to assist the French and Belgian Governments in driving the German Armies from French and Belgian territory, and eventually to restore the neutrality of Belgium, on behalf of which, as guaranteed by Treaty, Belgium appealed to the French and to ourselves at the commencement of hostilities.

2. You will be informed from time to time of the numbers of troops which will be placed at your disposal in order to carry out your mission, and in this connection you will understand that, owing to the number of different theatres in which we are employed, it may not always be possible to give the information definitely a long time in advance.

3. The defeat of the enemy by the combined Allied Armies must always be regarded as the primary object for which the British troops were originally sent to France, and to achieve that end the closest co-operation of French and British as a united Army must be the governing policy; but I wish you distinctly to understand that your command is an independent one, and that you will in no case come under the orders of any Allied General further than the necessary co-operation with our Allies above referred to.

4. If unforseen circumstances should arise such as to compel our Expeditionary Force to retire, such a retirement should never be contemplated as an independent move to secure the defence of the ports facing the Straights of Dover. . . . The safety of the Channel will be decided by the overthrow of the German Armies rather than by the occupation by our troops of some defensive position with their backs to the sea. . . .

KITCHENER

*James Edmonds (ed.), *History of the Great War: Military Operations, France and Belgium, 1914–1916* (6 vols.; London, 1932), V, App. I, 40–41.

Appendix 8

French Proposal for Organization of Unified Command on the Western Front, February 26, 1917*

1. By delegation of the British War Committee, with the assent of the French War Committee, and in order to ensure unity of command on the Western Front, the French General-in-Chief will, from the 1st March 1917, have authority over the British forces operating on this front, in all that concerns the conduct of operations, and especially:

—the planning and execution of offensive and defensive actions;
—the dispositions of the forces by Armies and Groups of Armies;
—the boundaries between these higher formations;
—the allotment of material and resources of all nature to the Armies.

2. The French Commander-in-Chief will have at his disposal a British Chief of the General Staff who will reside at the French GQG.

This Chief of the General Staff will have under his orders:

(a) A General Staff entrusted with the study of the questions concerning operations and the relations with the British War Committee;
(b) The Quarter-Master General . . .

3. Questions of personnel and general discipline in the British Armies will be dealt with by the British Commander-in-Chief . . . in accordance with the powers which are allotted to him by the War Office. . . .

M. BRIAND

[Editor's Note: This proposal was withdrawn in favor of the following Agreement.]

*James Edmonds, Cyril Falls, and Wilfred Miles, *History of the Great War: Military Operations, France and Belgium, 1917* (3 vols.; London, 1947), I, App. I, 62–63.

Appendix 9

Agreement Signed at Anglo-French Conference Held at Calais, February 27, 1917*

1. The French War Committee and the British War Cabinet approve of the plan of operations on the Western Front as explained to them by General Nivelle and Field-Marshal Sir Douglas Haig on February 26, 1917.

2. With the object of ensuring complete unity of command, during the forthcoming military operations . . . :

(i) Whereas the primary object of the forthcoming military operations referred to . . . is to drive the enemy from French soil, and whereas the French Army disposes of larger effectives than the British, the British War Cabinet recognizes that the general direction of the campaign should be in the hands of the French Commander-in-Chief:

(ii) With this object in view the British War Cabinet engages itself to direct the Field-Marshal Commanding the British Expeditionary Force to conform his plans of operation to the general strategical plans of the Commander-in-Chief of the French Army:

(iii) . . . during the period intervening between . . . this agreement and the date of the commencement of the operation . . . [F.M. Haig] shall conform his preparations to the views of [General Nivelle] except insofar as he considers that this would endanger the safety of his army . . . in any case where F.M. Haig may feel bound on these grounds to depart from General Nivelle's instructions, he shall report the action taken together with the reasons for such action, to the CIGS. . . .

(iv) . . . after the date of the commencement of the forthcoming operations . . . up to their termination [F.M. Haig] shall conform to the orders of [General Nivelle] in all matters relating to the conduct of the operations, it being understood that the British Commander will be left free to choose the means he will employ and the methods of utilizing his troops in that sector of operations allotted to him . . . in the original plan.

(v) . . . When [the operations] are ended the arrangements in force before the commencement of the operations will be re-established.

BRIAND	D. LLOYD GEORGE
LYAUTEY	W.R. ROBERTSON, CIGS
R. NIVELLE	D. HAIG, F.M.

*James Edmonds, Cyril Falls, and Wilfred Miles, *History of the Great War: Military Operations, France and Belgium, 1917* (3 vols.; London, 1947), I, App. I, 64–65.

Appendix 10

Orders of the Secretary of War Newton Baker to Major General John J. Pershing, Commander AEF*

May 26, 1917

The President directs me to communicate to you the following:

1. The President designates you to command all the land forcees of the United States operating in Continental Europe and the United Kingdom of Great Britain and Ireland, including any part of the Marine Corps which may be detached for service there with the Army. . . .

2. You are invested with the authority and duties devolved by the laws, regulations, orders and customs of the United States upon the commander of an army in the field in time of war and with the authority and duties in like manner devolved upon department commanders in peace and war, including the special authorities and duties assigned to the commander of the Philippine Department insofar as the same are applicable to the particular circumstances of your command.

3. In military operations against the Imperial German Government you are directed to cooperate with the forces of the other countries employed against that enemy; but in so doing the underlying idea must be kept in view that the forces of the United States are a separate and distinct component of the combined forces, the identity of which must be preserved. This fundamental rule is subject to such minor exceptions in particular circumstances as your judgment may approve . . . you will exercise full discretion in determining the manner of cooperation. But, until the forces of the United States are in your judgment sufficiently strong to warrant operations as an independent command, it is understood that you will cooperate as a component of whatever army you may be assigned to by the French Government. . . .

NEWTON D. BAKER

[Editor's Note: On the same day, Major General Pershing received a second set of orders from the Acting Chief of Staff of the Army, Major General Tasker Bliss. While these instructions ordered Pershing to "effectively . . . plan and conduct active operations in France against Germany and her allies," they mentioned nothing about cooperation with the French or about the independence of his command.]

*John J. Pershing, *My Experiences in the World War* (2 vols.; New York, 1931), I, 38–39.

Appendix 11

Protocol Between British, French, and American Representatives Concerning General Foch's Authority*

Beauvais, France   April 3, 1918

[It is agreed] to entrust to General Foch the strategic direction of military operations. The Commanders-in-Chief of the British, French and American Armies will have full control of the tactical action of their respective Armies. Each Commander-in-Chief will have the right to appeal to his Government if, in his opinion, his Army is endangered by reason of any order received from General Foch.

Sir Douglas Haig then requested that the meeting should come to a decision that a French offensive should be started as soon as possible in order to attract the enemy's reserves and withdraw pressure from the British. Generals Foch and Pétain stated that it was their firm intention to launch an attack as early as possible in a few days.

P.M. LLOYD GEORGE	PREM. CLEMENCEAU	GEN. PERSHING[†]
F.M. HAIG	GEN. FOCH	GEN. BLISS
GEN. WILSON	GEN. PÉTAIN	
B.G. SPEARS		

[Editor's Note: The title selected for General Foch was *Général en chef des Armées alliées en France*. Foch's authority did not extend outside the Western Front, nor did it include control of Belgian, Italian, or other forces on that front.]

*James Edmonds (ed.), *History of the Great War: Military Operations in France and Belgium, 1918* (5 vols.; London, 1935–1947), II, 115.

† American approval was subject to the concurrence of the U.S. Government, which was subsequently given.

Appendix 12

Instructions of the Secretary of State for War [Lord Milner] to Field Marshal Sir Douglas Haig, Commander British Armies in France*

June 21, 1918

In consequence of the concurrence of His Majesty's Government in the appointment of General Foch as Commander-in-Chief of the Allied Forces on the Western Front, it has become necessary to modify in some respects the instructions given to you in War Office Letter dated 28th December 1915.

(1) The general objects to be pursued by the British Armies in France remain the same as those set forth in the first and second paragraphs of that letter.

(2) In pursuit of those objects you will carry out loyally any instructions issued to you by the Commander-in-Chief of the Allied Forces. At the same time, if any order given by him appears to you to imperil the British Army, it is agreed between the Allied Governments that you should be at liberty to appeal to the British Government before executing such order. While it is hoped that the necessity for such an appeal may seldom, if ever, arise, you will not hesitate in cases of grave emergency to avail yourself of your right to make it.

(3) It is the desire of His Majesty's Government to keep the British forces under your command as far as possible together. If at any time the Allied Commander-in-Chief finds it necessary to transfer any portion of the British troops to the French area in order to release French troops for the purposes of roulement, it should be distinctly understood that this is only a temporary arrangement. . . .

(4) You will afford to the American troops forming part of the Allied Armies in France such assistance in training, equipment, or administrative matters as may from time to time be required of you by the Commander-in-Chief of the Allied Forces. . . .

MILNER

[Editor's Note: The remaining portions of Haig's instructions of December 28, 1915 were confirmed as remaining in effect.]

*James Edmonds (ed.), *History of the Great War: Military Operations, France and Belgium, 1918* (5 vols.; London, 1935–1947), III, 351–352.

Appendix 13

Estimate of the Situation by Lieutenant Colonel Wetzell,* December 12, 1917†

The Offensive in the West and its Prospects of Success

General

Any prospect of success in the West depends upon other principles than those which hold good for the East or against Italy. We must be quite clear what these principles are before estimating what is attainable and taking into account in the light of our previous experience in the West human probabilities; otherwise we shall be led astray and select objectives which, in view of the character of our opponents, we are not likely to reach.

We must bear in mind that in 1918 France will have a rested and strategically free Army, reinforced by Americans, and determined leaders, political (Clemenceau), as well as military.

The British will probably renew their attempts to obtain a decision in Flanders.

Enemy

The British Army has certainly suffered very severely in the Flanders battle, but it has available so many trained re-inforcements that it will be able to undertake the same tasks next year as it has this year. The artillery, like the British tactics as a whole, is rigid and stiff "(*Reichlich starr*)."

The British infantry is very fully equipped with machine guns, etc.

We have a strategically clumsy, tactically rigid, but tough enemy in front of us.

The French have shown us what they can do. They are just as skillful in the tactical use of their artillery as of their infantry. Their use of ground in the attack is just as good as in the defence. The French are better in the attack and more skillful in the defence, but are not such good stayers as the British.

The British are tied strategically to Flanders; the French are free.

Our Army

If our opponents on the Western Front leave us the winter months for training, our Army in the West, most of which has suffered severely but has now been reinforced by troops brought from elsewhere, will by the spring of 1918 be thoroughly fit for an offensive and will be able to show that it is superior to all enemies in such an operation.

Relative Strengths and Position of Reserves

At the present moment on the Western Front there are 106 British and French divisions opposed to 118.5 German. In reserve, 62 British and French divisions as against 42 German. The troops which we can bring from the East to the West in the course of the winter will to a small degree be balanced by American troops. We can now with

---

*Wetzell was the Chief of the Operations Branch of the German General Staff. This document was prepared prior to the German offensive of 1918.

†James Edmonds (ed.), *History of the Great War: Military Operations, France and Belgium, 1918* (5 vols.; London, 1935–1947), III, App. I, 130–135.

certainty count on a numerical superiority in divisions, although it is not a very big one. We can count less on superiority in artillery and air forces.

Since the dying down of the Flanders battle, and since the fighting at Cambrai, the British reserves on those two fronts are fairly evenly distributed. Behind the French front the reserves are more suitably distributed, and are strongest on the left flank (in front of the Seventh Army).

Possibility of the Transfer of Enemy Forces

We are in a position very quickly to transfer extraordinarily large forces by rail, but our enemy on the Western Front can do so to a still higher degree, thanks to the excellent railway communications behind his front. Besides, both hostile armies possess a very large number of motor vehicles, which have already often contributed decisive services (Verdun) by the rapid bringing up of reinforcements.

Surprise

One cannot count on the complete surprise of an attack on any front in the West, and least of all on one which has hitherto been quiet. Actually, the Champagne, the Somme, the Arras, the Aisne, the Aisne-Champagne, the Flanders and, last of all, the Verdun and the Laffaux offensives, were all known to us beforehand. Surprise only succeeded at Cambrai, and there only with small forces.

The most various means, patrols, aircraft, photography, wireless, and observations by the survey companies, offer all sorts of possibilities by which one or other of the preparations for attack may be recognized. Artillery registration can easily betray an offensive.

Without doubt, the attacker, even on the Western Front, will always be able to reckon on a considerable start, but also on the enemy taking the most rapid and most powerful counter-measures; for example, as we did at Cambrai.

Rapidity of the Break-Through Attack

Further, it must not be forgotten that in a successful offensive, the attacker will be forced to cross a difficult and shot-to-pieces battle area and will get gradually further away from his railheads and depots, and that, having to bring forward his masses of artillery and ammunition columns, he will be compelled to make pauses which will give time to the defender to organize resistance.

Too optimistic hopes should not be conceived, therefore, as regards the rapidity of the break-through attack on the Western Front. If our foes act only in a more or less planned and rapid manner, as we have done so far in spite of the most desperate situations, they also will succeed in bringing our offensive to a stop after a certain time.

We can only achieve a great and decisive success by a skillful combination of a series of attacks carried out in close connection with each other.

Prospects of Success of the Different Attacks

I hold that the double attack to pinch out Verdun from the Argonne and the west front of Army Detachment C is the most decisive, because, if it succeeds, it will strike a deadly blow against the French, who in this year are the most dangerous enemy because they are strategically free.

The French Army would never recover from the loss of Verdun and the mass of artillery material there, and, in spite of American help, would be compelled to adopt the absolute defensive. Besides, it would close once and for all the most probable sortie gate the French have available for 1918. The complete military political collapse is not excluded. [Editor's Note: This statement mirrors Falkenhayn's assessment in 1916.]

I also hold that a great attack in the general direction of Hazebrouck against the obstinate British would be both strategically and tactically favourable: but I consider this attack will not be specially advantageous, as I shall explain later, except as the last link in a combined attack against the British front. It is very often accepted that our attack against one of our two enemies on the Western Front will automatically bring on a great attack of the other against our front. This seems to me only to be justified in the case of an attack on the British wing in Flanders. It might at once provoke a French relieving attack against the Group of Armies Crown Prince and the Group of Armies Albrecht.

It is even very probable that, independent of our intentions, a French attack may be launched very early in 1918. This must be carefully taken into account in our measures, as our situation in the West would then become extraordinarily strained. The more so because the French would have the choice of the place of attack. [Editor's Note: This indicates the German General Staff's ignorance of the condition of the French Army and General Pétain's intentions.]

In any case if we decide to take the offensive against the British, we must leave very considerable reserves opposite the French front.

If we attack the French front, whether or not the British make a relieving attack depends on the time of year. In February-March such an attack is improbable in Flanders. If another attack in grand style on another sector of the front were to be made, the British would have to undertake a tiresome regrouping of their artillery and infantry forces.

Whether one of our opponents would support the other directly on the front attacked depends, in my opinion, entirely on the success of our attack. If it is great, we must reckon with certainty on immediate mutual support. . . .

. . . we should carry out the break-through in grand style from the front of the Second Army in the neighbourhood of St. Quentin.

Against this it must be noted that this sector of the Second Army is a quiet one; the attack preparations can scarcely remain hidden, and the necessary surprise will be difficult to obtain.

In view of the favourable and numerous railway communications, the possibility of very rapid counter-measures from the north by the British and from the south by the French must be regarded as on [sic] the cards. We must reckon with certainty that, should we have a striking initial success, we shall soon be involved in a wearisome struggle with the main forces of both our opponents.

We shall send our forces into a battleground which we voluntarily evacuated and devastated according to plan, and which has many lines of trenches in it constructed by ourselves and our opponents in the years 1914, 1915, 1916, 1917, right back to behind the Somme. Certainly some of these trenches have not been kept up, yet they will give considerable advantages to the defender, and hinder the advance of the attack.

The probability that the impulse of the break-through will gradually be brought to a standstill is very great in this particular attack.

If we decide to attack the British—which promises success on account of their lack of strategical flexibility—in my opinion, we must set the whole British front tottering by a skillful combination of successive attacks definitely mutually connected with each other, on different sectors of the front and finally in the direction of Hazebrouck, making full use of railways for the rapid transfer of forces.

In my opinion, we shall not achieve this purpose by a single attack at one spot, however carefully it is prepared. For this the British front is too narrow in relation to the available British forces, and the favourable possibilities of shifting these forces. . . .

WETZELL

Appendix 14

Order Number One of the Petrograd Soviet*

March 14, 1917

To the garrison of the Petrograd District. To all the soldiers of the Guard, army, artillery and fleet for immediate and precise execution, and to the workers of Petrograd for information.

The Soviet of Workers' and Soldiers' Deputies has decided:

1. In all companies, battalions, regiments, depots, batteries, squadrons and separate branches of military service of every kind and on warships immediately choose committees from the elected representatives of the soldiers and sailors of the above mentioned military units.

2. In all military units which have still not elected their representatives in the Soviet of Workers' Deputies elect one representative to a company, who should appear with written credentials in the building of the State Duma at ten o'clock on the morning of March 2.

3. In all its political demonstrations a military unit is subordinated to the Soviet Workers' and Soldiers' Deputies and its committees.

4. The orders of the military commission of the State Duma are to be fulfilled only in those cases which do not contradict the orders and decisions of the Soviet of Workers' and Soldiers' Deputies.

5. Arms of all kinds, as rifles, machine-guns, armored automobiles and others must be at the disposition and under the control of the company and battalion committees and are not in any case to be given out to officers, even upon their demand.

6. In the ranks and in fulfilling service duties soldiers must observe the strictest military discipline; but outside of service, in their political, civil and private life soldiers cannot be discriminated against as regards those rights which all citizens enjoy.

7. In the same way the addressing of officers with titles: Your Excellency, Your Honor, etc., is abolished and is replaced by the forms of address: Mr. General, Mr. Colonel, etc.

Rude treatment of soldiers of all ranks, and especially addressing them as "thou," is forbidden; and soldiers are bound to bring to the attention of the company committees any violation of this rule and any misunderstandings between officers and soldiers.

This order is to be read in all companies, battalions, regiments, marine units, batteries and other front and rear military units.

Petrograd Soviet of Workers' and Soldiers' Deputies

Chronicle of Events, The Revolution of 1917 (3 vols.; London, 1920), I, 186–187.

Annex C
Prewar Plans

FACTORS INFLUENCING THE DISREGARD FOR THE BELGIAN FRONTIER

1. Desire to be seen internationally as not provoking German military action.

2. Internal political distaste for integrating the reserve and active military forces.

3. Excessive expense for military expansion.

4. Conviction pervading the Army leaders that an attack into Alsace and Lorraine would be decisive.

FIFTH ARMY (5 Corps; 1 Cavalry Division)

The northern boundary of the zone of operations of the Fifth Army will vary according to circumstances and cannot be laid down beforehand.

General Idea. — This Army is to operate against the right wing of the enemy forces. The theatre of operations may be limited, to begin with, to the territories of two belligerents; or it may extend at once into neutral territory (Luxembourg and in particular Belgium). In the first case it will operate northward at once. It should hold a part of its force in reserve behind its left wing to protect itself against any enveloping movement the enemy may attempt by violating Belgium territory in the immediate proximity of the frontier. It will also be prepared for a strong offensive against Thionville with its active corps or for the investment of that place with the Reserve Divisions at its disposal.

FOURTH ARMY (3 Corps; 1 Cavalry Division)

General Idea. — This Army will at first be, temporarily, in second line and ready to move on the . . . day of mobilization, with the objective either to advance into the southern Wöevre between the Second and Third Armies to co-operate ultimately in the operations of the Second Army, or to move northward west of the Meuse to the left of the Third Army, in the direction of Arlon.

THIRD ARMY (3 Corps; 1 Cavalry Division)

General Idea. — The Third Army forming the connecting link between the main operations to be carried out on the right bank of the Moselle, to the south, and north of a line Verdun — Metz [*Line 2*], to the north, will be ready either to force back on to Metz and Thionville any enemy forces which may have advanced from that direction, or to prepare the preliminary investment of Metz.

SECOND ARMY (5 Corps; 2 Cavalry Divisions)

General Idea. — This Army is to be ready to attack in the general direction Château Salins — Sarrebruck. For this purpose, it will make use of the Nancy bridgehead, for the protection of which it will be responsible.

FIRST ARMY (5 Corps; 2 Cavalry Divisions)

General Idea. — This Army will attack in the general direction Baccarat — Sarrebourg — Saarguemines — the right of the main body following the crest of the Vosges, and the extreme right advancing into the plains of Alsace so that the right of whole battle front may rest on the Rhine.

Appendix 1
French Plan XVII

Each Army Commander received on 7 February 1914 a copy of the section of this document that referred to his command.

DIRECTIONS FOR THE CONCENTRATION

General Situation. — From a careful study of information obtained it is probable that a great part of the German forces will be concentrated on the common frontier. They may cross this frontier in places before our general operations can be developed.

Intentions of the Commander-in-Chief. — Whatever the circumstances, it is the C.-in-C.'s intention to advance, all forces united, to the attack of the German Armies.

The action of the French Armies will be developed in two main operations: one, on the right, in the country between the wooded district of the Vosges and the Moselle below Toul [*Line 1*]; the other, on the left, north of a line Verdun — Metz [*Line 2*].

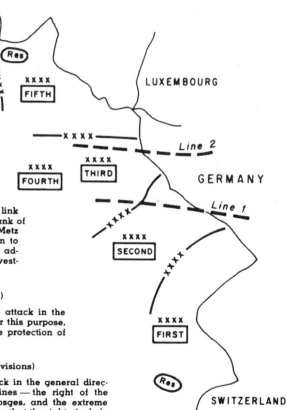

Appendix 2

Modified Schlieffen Plan

**FACTORS INFLUENCING VON MOLTKE TO
MODIFY THE 1905 SCHLIEFFEN PLAN**

1. **Changing international balance of power.**

   a. Rapid Russian recovery from the Russo–Japanese war 1904-1905.

SCHLIEFFEN PLAN—1905				
NORTHERN GROUP	**CENTER GROUP**	**SOUTHERN GROUP**	**FLANK GD**	**TOTAL**

OFFENSIVE GROUP

	NORTHERN GROUP	CENTER GROUP	SOUTHERN GROUP	FLANK GD	TOTAL
Armies	First & Second	Third	Fourth & Fifth		5
Active Army Corps	9	6	8		23
Reserve Corps	7			5	12 1/2
Cavalry Divisions	5	1	2		7/8
Reserve Divisions		1			1
Landwehr Brigs.					16
MISSION	Cross Holland, Belgium, the Meuse; turn south between Namur & Brussels, then into France outside left of French line. 5 Res Corps invest Antwerp.	Cross Belgium & the Meuse, then into France between Namur & Mezieres, turning south west.	Cross Luxembourg and the Meuse between Mezieres and Verdun.	Cover left flank of Offensive Group.	
ZONE OF CONCENTRATION	Vic Aix-la-Chapelle along Dutch border	German-Belgian border north of Luxembourg	Vic Trier and fortified zone Thionville-Metz	Vic Metz	

REINFORCEMENTS FOR OFFENSIVE GROUP

a.) Two Army Corps withdrawn from Defensive (Left Wing) Group as soon as possible.

b.) Six Ersatz Corps follow extreme right wing and relieve it of diversions for secondary missions (siege opns, for example).

DEFENSIVE GROUP

	Sixth & Seventh
Armies	Sixth & Seventh
Army Corps	3 1/2
Reserve Corps	1 1/2
Cavalry Divisions	3
Ersatz Divisions	
Landwehr Brigs.	9 1/2

Mission: Attack toward Nancy to induce major commitment of French forces in unfavorable terrain of Alsace-Lorraine and to draw them away from advancing right wing. If French do not attack, release two corps to reinforce extreme right wing.

ZONE OF CONCENTRATION

Along frontier between Metz and Swiss border

EASTERN FRONT

Initially: Small force of Landwehr and fortress troops.

If Russians move sooner than expected: Ten Inf. Divs. and from two to four Cav. Divs. to be moved from Western Front.

b. Russia's expansion and improvement of her armed forces.
c. Weakening of the Triple Alliance. (Italy's participation no longer assured).
d. Modernization of the British Army.
e. Increased emphasis on compulsory military training in France.

2. **Increased importance of the Saar coal mines and the Rhineland industrial area to the German railroads and the armaments industry. Therefore these areas had to be defended.**

3. **The German Army was denied increased funds and could only train 52% of available conscripts.**

MODIFIED PLAN — 1914

OFFENSIVE GROUP	NORTHERN GROUP	CENTER GROUP	SOUTHERN GROUP	FLANK GD	TOTAL
Armies	First & Second	Third	Fourth & Fifth		5
Active Army Corps	7	3	6		16
Reserve Corps	6	1	4	E L I M I N A T E D	11 ½
Cavalry Divisions	5		2		7
Reserve Divisions					
Landwehr Brigs.					
MISSION	Same except that Holland not to be invaded. Thus axis of advance moved s o u t h, necessitating reduction of Liege.	Substantially t h e same	Substantially t h e same		

ZONE OF CONCENTRATION

REINFORCEMENTS FOR OFFENSIVE GROUP	NONE

DEFENSIVE GROUP	Sixth & Seventh	
Armies		**Mission:** Essentially the same but evidence of apparent intent to meet expected French attack with greater strength. Unwilling to give up as much territory as envisaged in Schlieffen Plan.
Army Corps	6	
Reserve Corps	2 ½	
Cavalry Divisions	3	
Ersatz Divisions	6	
Landwehr Brigs.	2	

ZONE OF CONCENTRATION	Same

EASTERN FRONT	**Eighth Army activated:** Army smaller than planned by Schlieffen but units came from troops planned for use on Western Front (nine Inf. Divs. and one Cav. Div.).

Glossary

This glossary provides definitions for words and phrases that were commonly used during the First World War and that now often appear in World War I texts. It should assist the reader in understanding those terms that are unique and those terms whose meanings have changed over the years. Also included are some foreign terms that were adopted and adapted by American and British soldiers. The author intends this section to be a useful source of definitions and to provide an interesting and informative illustration of the way language is transformed by warfare.

ace. (Fr. *as*) Originally, a gallant cavalryman. Later applied to airmen who downed five enemy airplanes.

AEF. American Expeditionary Force.

ambulance. First applied to a medical section, the term was later applied to the wheeled evacuation vehicles used by these sections.

ammonal. A type of high explosive chemical used in shells and saps, ammonal is a mixture of ammonium nitrate, TNT, and flaked or powdered aluminum.

Angel of Mons, the. The legendary force that supposedly intervened during the British retreat after the Battle of Mons and saved them from annihilation.

ANZAC. The Australian-New Zealand Army Corps, or a member of the Australian-New Zealand unit. *See also* digger.

archies. Antiaircraft batteries or guns. Also called AA guns.

arrival. An incoming enemy shell.

askaris. Native colonial troops from Africa.

attaque à l'outrance. (Fr.) The pre-1914 military doctrine of the French Army; attack to the utmost. At the heart of this doctrine was the belief that offensive spirit and moral supremacy are everything, and that supporting or defensive operations cannot be decisive, and are therefore unimportant. This phrase is a possible source of the English term "all out."

Bangalore torpedo. A tube of sheet iron, with a conical wooden head, filled with high explosives; used to destroy wire and other obstacles to advance. Named after the Engineer Depot in Bangalore, India where the British developed the weapon.

barrage. (Fr.) A barrier formed by artillery fire (Army). An antisubmarine net and mine barrier (Navy).

battle-bowler. The soldier's steel helmet. Also called a tin hat.

bayonet strength. The number of effective combat infantry soldiers in a unit. *See also* saber strength.

BEF. British Expeditionary Force.

Big Bertha. German 420-mm siege howitzer. Mounted on either railroad or road carriages, it fired a one-ton shell to a range of nine miles. "Big Bertha" was the Allied name for this gun. It was called the "Wipers Express" by the British soldiers, who first encountered it during the Second Battle of Ypres. Nicknamed *Die Dicke Berta* after the granddaughter of Alfred Krupp, it is not to be confused with the long-range Paris gun.

blighty. A word used by the British to refer to the British Isles. Derived from the Hindi word for "over the seas," it was used in such terms as "blighty wound"—a wound that was sufficiently serious to return a soldier to his home.

Boche. (Fr.) The German enemy. Literally, "hard-headed ones." Also called Fritz, the Hun, Heine, or Jerry.

body snatcher. A stretcher bearer. Occasionally used to describe a sniper.

bois. (Fr.) Forest or woods.

bomb. Hand grenade, whether offensive (concussion) or defensive (shrapnel). Grenadiers were known as bombers.

bombproof. A covered emplacement or shelter that was supposedly secure from enemy artillery shelling.

booby trap. A device left behind by retreating troops to injure the enemy; usually explosive in nature.

brass hat. A high ranking officer. The term is derived from the gold embroidery on the peak of the officers' hats.

Camel. Nickname of a type of Sopwith scout airplane. This single-seat, single-engine biplane was armed with both Vickers and Lewis machineguns. The Camel's name was derived from its shape.

Camion. (Fr.) A sturdy truck with a low silhouette.

camouflage. (Fr.) The disguising of personnel or materiel in an attempt to conceal identity and location.

canister. Used on a gas mask, the canister contained chemicals for filtering or neutralizing toxic agents.

Catalan, the. This affectionate nickname for Marshal Joffre refers to his birthplace in southern France near the Spanish border.

Central Powers. Germany and her allies: Austria-Hungary, Turkey, and Bulgaria. The name was derived from the countries' central location.

char d'assaut. (Fr.) An armored car or tank. Literally, an "assault carriage."

charnel house. A term applied to Verdun during the heavy fighting that took place there during 1916; an allusion to a burial vault.

Chauchat. (Fr.) The French light machinegun, Model 1915, an awkward weapon that often misfired. Literally meaning "hot cat," it was the first automatic weapon light enough to accompany assaulting infantry.

Cheveaux 8, Hommes 40. (Fr.) Railroad boxcars used to transport men and materiel behind the lines. From the French inscription on the side: "8 horses or 40 men." Also called Forty and Eights, Hommes-Forty, and Sidedoor Pullmans.

Chinese attack. A false infantry assault. After the artillery preparation, the frontline troops would simulate an assault, but the artillery fire would be shifted back onto the enemy trenches. The defenders would often suffer heavily after leaving their shelters to counter the assault.

CIGS. British Chief of the Imperial General Staff.

coal boxes. Shells from the German 5.9-inch howitzer. The name was derived from the black high explosive clouds the shells made upon impact. The Germans used a similar term, *Kohlenhasten.*

communication trench. A trench system connecting frontline trenches with the rear. Usually dug in a zig-zag pattern. Where possible, they were sloped to allow drainage from the front. The French equivalent was "Boyaux."

Cossacks. Russian cavalrymen from the Steppes and Don River basin. These fierce but skilled fighters were feared greatly by the average German soldier.

Daisy Cutters. Artillery shells fitted with an instantaneous or impact fuse. These shells burst before entering the ground, thus providing a large area of lethality.

digger. An Australian or New Zealand soldier. *See also* ANZAC.

DMC. Desert Mounted Corps; a largely Australian Force used for horse-mounted envelopments during the campaign in Palestine of 1917–1918.

doughboys. American soldiers. The nickname was probably derived from the 1862 term for the large brass buttons on Union soldiers' uniforms that resembled dumplings or "dough boys." Also called Yanks and Sammies.

drum fire. Artillery preparation prior to an infantry assault; especially unexpected, concentrated fire on enemy trenches designed to immobilize defenders. Also called hurricane barrage or typhoon barrage.

Dual Monarchy. The Austro-Hungarian Empire.

Establishment. (Br.) Table of Organization and Equipment.

fascines. Bundles of brushwood sticks bound together and carried on tanks. When the leading tank came upon a trench obstacle, the crew would fill it with fascines and pass over the obstacle.

flak. From the German *Flugabwehrkanone;* an antiaircraft cannon. The term was later applied by pilots of both sides to the shells fired from antiaircraft guns.

Flamenwerfer. (Gr.) Flamethrower.

Flying Circus. Nickname of Baron Manfred von Richthofen's elite aerial pursuit squadron.

F.M. Field Marshal. The French equivalent is *Maréchal de France,* while the German is *Feld-Marschal.* It is the highest military rank in European armies.

franc-tireur. (Fr.) Literally, a free shooter; a sniper or irregular rifleman whom the Germans considered subject to execution without trial.

frog. Derogatory term for Frenchmen in general, and French soldiers in particular.

front. Russian term for an army group, which usually contained four armies. More commonly used to designate a theater of operations (e.g., the Western Front).

gas. After its introduction by the Germans in 1915, war gas was developed and used by all participants of the Great War. The use of this weapon was prohibited by the Hague Convention, but once one side employed it, the other felt no restraint in its use. The variety of war gasses developed stemmed from the effects that the user desired and the countermeasures employed by the victims. The weapon was used to incapacitate, irritate, maim, or kill the enemy's troops, or to deny the use of specific areas to them. The markings placed upon the artillery shells by the German Army became, to some extent, standardized by both sides, and were often used as a convenient method of referring to the type of gas contained in the shell.

Effect of Gas	Chemicals Used	Shell Marking
Asphyxiant (affects respiratory system).	Phosgene, diphosgene, chlorine, lewisite, and chloropicrin.	Green cross.
Irritant (causes sneezing, itching, etc.).	Arsine, xylyl bromide, and diphenychlorodysine.	Blue cross.
Vesicant (causes persistent blistering). Usually used in liquid form.	Mustard gas (also called Yperite).	Yellow cross.
Lachrymatory (causes watering of eyes).	Tear gas.	White cross.

GHQ. Abbreviation for American and British General Headquarters.

gone west. Trench slang for "killed in action." Also called "hanging on the wire" and "bought the farm."

Gotha. Generic term for all large German bombing aircraft.

GQG. Abbreviation for *Grande Quartiers Général,* the French General Headquarters.

grand blessés. (Fr.) Seriously wounded men.

Hans Wurst. Popular Allied nickname for a German infantryman.

H-L. Winston Churchill's literary abbreviation for the German High Command team of Hindenburg and Ludendorff. The abbreviation indicates Hindenburg and Ludendorff's close command and general staff relationship.

Holy Joe. A chaplain, or a man affecting piety.

in the clear. Term for the transmission of a message in an unencrypted form over either wireless radio or telephone communications.

Inter-Allied Supreme War Council. War policy coordinating body established by the western Allies at Rapallo on November 7, 1917.

iron ration. Canned emergency rations. Also called the "last hope."

Ivan. Allied term for the Russian Army or an individual Russian soldier.

Jack Johnsons. German 15-inch guns. The name, which was derived from the black high explosive cloud made by the shells upon impact, is an allusion to the black world heavyweight boxing champion.

Johnny. Allied name for a Turk; the term dates from the Crimean War.

Kamerad. (Gr.) Comrade; usually used by surrendering German soldiers in phrase "*Kamerad—Pardon!*"

Ladies from Hell. Kilted Scottish Regiments. The name was coined by a German newspaper.

Landwehr. (Gr.) German Territorial Reserve units.

Lebel mam'se-le. (Fr.) Colloquial French Army term for the French Lebel rifle, a magazine rifle used in both World War I and World War II.

Levens projector. Permanently installed mortar-like weapon set up in No Man's Land or directly in front of the friendly trench line. Fired in volley by an electrical charge, the projector hurled a 200-pound projectile, usually of poisonous gas or smoke, up to 1,806 meters.

Lewis Gun. English drum-fed light machinegun.

Limogé. (Fr.) Being relieved of command. The term alludes to the town of Limoges, where discredited French generals were sent to await reassignment. English terms were "Stellenbosched," a Boer War term, or "degommered," from the French word meaning "to become unstuck."

Long Tom. Originally, a nickname for the British 60-pounder gun; later applied to any long-barreled gun.

lorry. British term for a truck.

Magyars. The Hungarian element of the Austro-Hungarian population and army.

Mills bomb. English hand grenade. Named for its inventor, Sir William Mills, it weighed about one and a half pounds.

Minenwerfer. (Gr.) A trench mortar.

Miracle of the Marne. The victory of the Franco-British forces during the First Battle of the Marne in 1914. The Allies felt that their success had been divinely inspired.

mitrailleuse. (Fr.) General French term for a machinegun.

mopping up. The mission assigned to special parties of infantrymen following the assault waves. Its purpose was to explore and clear captured enemy trenches and dugouts. By dealing with "stay behind" troops, this protected the advance force from attack in the rear.

Nissen hut. Corrugated iron and wood structures, semicylindrical in shape, used for shelters and hospitals behind the lines.

OHL. Abbreviation for *Oberste Heeresleitung,* the German Army General Headquarters.

Opolchenie. (Rus.) Russian national militia; equivalent to the German *Landwehr,* the American National Guard, and the British Territorials.

over the top. Infantry slang for the initiation of an assault over the top of the trenches.

parabellum machinegun. A German airplane machinegun.

parados. A mound of earth constructed at the rear of a trench to provide protection from shell fragments.

Paris gun. Extremely long-range gun used by the Germans to hurl a 250-pound shell up to 75 miles. Used in 1918, it caused more psychological than physical damage.

P.C. (Fr.) Abbreviation of *poste de command.* The English equivalent is C.P., command post. The *P.C.* or C.P. is the headquarters of a battalion or smaller sized unit.

permission. (Fr.) A leave of absence or a pass that allows such a leave.

Plattsburg Movement, the. Officer candidate schools established in the United States prior to her entry into the war. This system was a part of the preparatory movement that was a voluntary expression of public concern over America's military weakness. The name referred to the pilot installation established at Plattsburg, New York.

pneumatic cavalry. Cyclist battalions.

poilu. (Fr.) Allied term for the common French soldier. Literally, "a hairy one."

Polish Quadrilateral. Russian fortified area in the Polish Salient, Warsaw-Novo Georgievsk-Ivangorod-Brest-Litovsk.

pom-pom gun. The Vickers-Maxim one-pounder automatic machine cannon. Used as an antiaircraft weapon, the gun derived its name from the distinctive sound it made when fired.

potato masher. A type of German hand grenade, so nicknamed because of its resemblance to the kitchen tool.

Pound Wonder. The 37-mm direct fire cannon that accompanied infantry troops. Its maximum range was one and a half miles.

Pour le Mérite. (Fr.) Germany's highest award for valor. Established by Frederick the Great, it was nicknamed the "Blue Max" during the war.

pusher. An airplane with the propeller in the rear.

Q.F. or **quick firing.** Guns that fired shells with brass casings and had hydraulic buffer systems, thus allowing the firing of rounds in rapid succession without re-laying the piece.

Q-ships. Fighting ships disguised as cargo vessels or trawlers and designed to lure German submarines into a surface attack. The Q-ship would gain surprise and, hopefully, sink the submarine with her gun. Also called trap ships or decoy ships.

Race to the Sea, the. The imprecise term applied to the series of outflanking maneuvers conducted by both sides on the Western Front between the First Battle of the Aisne and the stabilization of the Western Front.

regulating station. An intermediate supply distribution point between the depots and the frontline dumps.

revanche. (Fr.) Literally, revenge. The term applies to the burning desire of the French to recover the provinces of Alsace and Lorraine, which had been lost to Germany during the Franco-Prussian War of 1870–1871.

revitaillment. (Fr.) Supplies of any kind, but usually food.

roulement. (Fr.) The rotation of frontline troops for rest and retraining.

Russian sap. A trench excavated by the explosion of a subterranean tube of explosives.

saber strength. The number of combat-ready soldiers in a cavalry unit.

sap. A narrow trench or tunnel.

sausage. So called because of its shape, this was a slang term for a kite balloon or a tethered artillery observation balloon. The French equivalent was *saucisse.*

Schwarze Maria. (Gr.) Nickname for Allied heavy artillery shells. The name, which translates into "Black Mary," refers to the shells' characteristic black explosion.

Senegalese. French territorial troops from Africa. Applied generically to all black French troops regardless of their origin.

shell shock. Psychoneurotic disorders, such as hysteria or depression, caused by exposure to prolonged or intense artillery fire. The name indicates the mistaken notion that the illness was a brain concussion caused by the exploding shells.

short arm inspection. Inspections conducted periodically by the unit medical officer to detect symptoms of venereal disease. The men were inspected as a unit, without privacy. By obvious analogy, the term is a reference to the inspection of rifles.

soixante-quinze. (Fr.) The French 75-mm rapid-fire field gun. French troops also called it the Josephine, a reference to Napoleon's wife. American artillerists equipped with this piece called it the French 75.

SOS. Service of Supply, the United States Army logistical organization in Europe.

SPAD. An abbreviation of *Société Pour Aviation et ses Dérivés,* the SPAD was a single-seat biplane.

stand-to. The danger period shortly before dawn when an enemy attack was most likely. The term was derived from the order "Stand to your arms." All men manned the parapet until daylight and "stand-down," when only part of the unit remained in its prepared firing positions.

Stavka. (Rus.) The Russian military general staff; the equivalent of the GHQ, OHL, and GQG of other armies.

Stokes mortar. The English trench mortar.

storm troops. Special German formations of picked troops used to lead attacks, these troops were parcelled out in assault companies of 100 men with attached squads of bombers, machinegunners, and flamethrowers. They were composed of bachelors and childless husbands. Also called shock troops or, in German, *sturm truppens* and *stoss truppens.*

strafe. To rake with artillery or aircraft fire.

sturmpanzerkraftwagen. (Gr.) German term for tank. Later in the war, a shortened form of the term, *panzer,* was adopted for common usage.

Système D. (Fr.) A French army expression derived from the verb *se débrouiller* (to manage). The British soldier's equivalent was "muddling through." The German equivalent was "*notbehelfe,*" which translates into "makeshift." All of these terms were coined by frontline troops to voice their contempt for the poorly coordinated staff work of higher headquarters, which led, at best, to minor inconvenience and, at worst, to unnecessary slaughter.

tank. A fully tracked, armored fighting vehicle. The name was derived from the code name originally used to conceal its purpose. The male version mounted six-pounder quick-firing guns and two Lewis machineguns, while the female version was armed with four heavy machineguns. These designations derived from the fact that the two types were meant to support each other. A later modification, the hermaphrodite, mounted guns on one side and machine-guns on the other, completing the sexual analogy. Lighter tanks such as the Whippet and Renault were developed to move more rapidly in order to support cavalry formations.

Tannenberg maneuver. A double envelopment. This term was used to describe the encirclement and annihilation of the Russian Second Army by the Germans during the Battle of Tannenberg in 1914. It is often compared to Hannibal's maneuver during the Battle of Cannae in 216 B.C.

taxicab army. A reference to those elements of the French Sixth Army that in 1914 were transported to fight in the First Battle of the Marne in civilian taxicabs and trucks.

Tommy. A nickname for the common British soldier; named after Kipling's Tommy Atkins.

traverse. Sandbags or other obstructions placed across a trench to block enemy enfilading fire.

trench foot. A medical ailment caused by a prolonged immersion of the feet in the damp and freezing conditions of the trenches. The physical manifestations were either frost-bite or soft, rotting skin that would not heal. In either case, the victim was immobilized and had to be evacuated.

Triple Entente. The understanding between Russia, France, and Great Britain that led to their alliance against the Central Powers during the Great War. The term is usually used to refer to the alliance itself.

Uhlans. German elite light cavalry.

Voivode. (Serbian) Literally, "leader." This was the highest military rank in the Serbian Army. It was often used exclusively to refer to Radomir Putnik, commander of the Serbian Army.

wastage. Daily casualties from trench warfare, as opposed to those from a planned offensive operation.

Whiz Bangs. British soldier's term for the German 88-mm flat trajectory gun and the shells it fired. The name was derived from the short interval between the sound of approach and the explosion.

Wipers. British slang for the town of Ypres, Belgium. Also called Eeps or Weeps.

Woyrsch Corps. An unnumbered German Reserve Corps referred to by its commander's name. It often stiffened the Austro-Hungarian sectors of the Eastern Front or provided a link between units of the two allies.

Index